Creating Colorado

WILLIAM WYCKOFF

Creating Colorado

The Making of a

Western American

Landscape

1860 – 1940

Yale University Press   New Haven and London

Designed by
James J. Johnson and set
in Fairfield Medium type
by The Composing Room
of Michigan, Inc.

Printed in the United
States of America by
Edwards Brothers, Inc.,
Ann Arbor, Michigan.

A catalogue record for
this book is available from
the British Library.

The paper in this book
meets the guidelines for
permanence and durabil-
ity of the Committee on
Production Guidelines for
Book Longevity of the
Council on Library
Resources.

10 9 8 7 6 5 4 3 2 1

*Library of Congress
Cataloging-in-Publication
Data*

Wyckoff, William.
   Creating Colorado :
the making of a western
American landscape,
1860–1940 / William
Wyckoff.
      p.   cm.
   Includes bibliograph-
ical references and index.
ISBN 0-300-07118-3 (alk.
paper)

   1. Colorado—Histor-
ical geography.   2. Colorado—History—To 1876.
3. Colorado—History—
1876–1950.   4. Land-
scape—Colorado—His-
tory.   5. Human
geography—Colorado.
I. Title.
F781.W98   1999
978.8—dc21   98-35056

for Linda, Thomas, and Kathleen

We primeval forests felling,
We the rivers stemming, vexing we and piercing
deep the mines within,
We the surface broad surveying, we the virgin
soil upheaving, Pioneers! O pioneers!

Colorado men are we,
From the peaks gigantic, from the great sierras
and the high plateaus,
From the mine and from the gully, from the hunting trail we come,
Pioneers! O pioneers!

—WALT WHITMAN, "Birds of Passage"

Contents

Preface

Colorado. Imagine the journey. It was more than six hundred miles from Kansas City to the Rocky Mountain gold mines in 1859. Water and feed were scarce, bison roamed the prairie, and the weather was savagely un-predictable. Yet tens of thousands came, drawn by an elusive dream that gave Colorado a special place in western American history. They poured into the mountains, rushing through the narrow canyons of the Front Range, fanning out across the high country, all in search of an El Dorado that only a few were able to claim. Still, it was an epic migration and a fa-bled beginning that continues to capture the popular imagination. Today the allures of gold and silver have been replaced by the attractions of high country scenery, world-class ski slopes, and amenity-oriented western ways of life. The Colorado mystique remains, however, a powerful and per-sistent identity in the geography of the American West.

My first boyhood encounter with Colorado came on a family vacation, and it paralleled the path of the early goldseekers. The July day was hot and hazy and my young eyes searched in vain for the state's famed moun-tains as we left Nebraska and rapidly ascended the South Platte Valley northeast of Denver. Finally, low on the western horizon, the tops of moun-tain thunderheads hinted at the changing terrain ahead. Soon the Front Range appeared in the distance, shimmering across fifty miles of high and mostly empty plains. Another hour—more than two days' travel for those earlier adventurers—and we were threading our way through Big Thomp-son Canyon west of Loveland. The temperature dropped, the land greened up, we rolled the windows down, and I drank in the magical air of the Col-orado Rockies. Thus began a love affair that has endured and deepened over a quarter-century of travel, research, and appreciation for Colorado's people and its landscapes.

It was a love affair that took me to horse pastures on the edge of La Veta, a place in southern Colorado that marks a cultural and physical meeting ground between the Hispano Southwest, the sweeping openness of the southern Great Plains, and the idyllic attractions of the Rockies. It

reminded me that Colorado was home to many Wests and superbly representative of that larger American region, both physically and culturally. My
love affair also took me to Crested Butte, where an old coal mining town
has been reinvented as a fashionable ski and mountain biking resort. A
winsome waitress with a New Age smile served me a macrobiotic lunch in
a former miner's saloon as I pondered the growing crowd of condos
muscling their way up nearby slopes. Here, past and present mingle in a
new amalgam as high country landscapes are redefined in an era of easy
affluence, baby-boom amenities, and all-too-conspicuous consumption.
And my love affair took me to Colorado's most dramatic modern frontier,
to a hill on the southern edge of Littleton that separates Denver's sprawling suburbs from the open spaces beyond. Upscale subdivisions, shopping
malls, and commercial strips boldly reveal a new settlement geography
against a backdrop of rolling plains and nearby mountainslopes. Even
among the hayfields, real estate banners flutter everywhere, suggesting the
complex interminglings of urban and rural worlds in the modern West.

Within this book I explore the origins of that Colorado landscape that
is still very much in the making today. Given the variety I encountered
along the way, I also ponder the unity of the larger American West. What,
in fact, does define the West if it is as diverse as the multiple geographies
I discovered? I conclude that there *is* a common western consonance that
resonates within the state and across the larger region. It is a working definition of the West that took shape as I drew together the three major
themes for this book. First, the West is defined by the rapidity and the timing of its Euro-American occupance, a process that put in place a settlement system and an areal organization that reflected a set of dominant
technologies and institutions present in America between 1860 and 1920.
Second, the West is defined by the unique juxtaposition of peoples who
came to live there. These newly proximate and often uneasy neighbors created different communities that represented fresh mixings of Native
Americans, Hispanos, blacks, Asians, midwesterners, Yankee bluebloods,
Slavs, Cornish, Germans, and a bewildering variety of other groups, both
large and small. Third, the West's landscape defines and separates it from
other settings. The persisting presence of wild nature, the space between
areas of settlement, the clarity of the sky, and the dryness in the air combine with the characteristic cultural signatures to produce a multiform yet
palpable regional identity superbly revealed in Colorado's varied geographies.

Finally, my journey through Colorado was an invitation to examine how
its story is a part of much larger historical and geographical processes. How
were Coloradans connected to the outside world? Who were the cultural

progenitors of its communities and landscapes? How did local economic developments reflect global economic imperatives? What national political and technological impulses were expressed upon the Colorado scene? All of these questions fed my curiosity as I ventured into the Centennial State. I found it was a journey well worth taking and the pages that follow are a reminder that Colorado's modern scene is inextricably wed to its past geographies and to the men and women who labored to create them.

Acknowledgments

Many people have guided and informed my explorations of the Colorado landscape and I thank them for their assistance and inspiration along the way. In particular, the staff that oversees the Western History Collection at the Denver Public Library proved indispensable, always more than willing to help me, no matter how esoteric the request! I especially acknowledge the support of Eleanor M. Gehres, Kathey Swan, Augie Mastrogiuseppi, and Philip Panum. Across the street, the always generous assistance at the Research Library of the Colorado Historical Society proved equally essential, and I gratefully acknowledge the guidance given me by Jim Lavender-Teliha, Pat Fraker, Rebecca Lintz, Jennifer Bosley, and Barbara Foley. Elsewhere, I would also like to single out the Pueblo Public Library, the Starsmore Center for Local History, the Colorado College Tutt Library, and the Penrose Library in Colorado Springs and the staffs of many other local public and university libraries around the state who helped me dig through innumerable treasure troves of material that were simply unavailable elsewhere.

I also am grateful for the generous financial assistance provided by the American Philosophical Society. Their research and travel grant allowed me to explore every county of the Centennial State and to seek out the riches of both the archive and the landscape. In addition I wish to thank the Department of Earth Sciences at Montana State University, particularly department heads Steve Custer, Dave Lageson, and Andrew Marcus, for their unfailing support of this project. The original maps in this book owe their production to the generosity of the Department of Earth Sciences (Carto Projects Fund) and to the many hours of technical and creative assistance given me by Juliet Lauber and Lee Murray. The uncountable challenges of word processing were also made surmountable with the cheerful assistance of Ann Parker.

I wish also to thank Don Meinig, not only for perusing portions of the volume, but also for his more general encouragement and inspiration along the way. My intellectual debts to Don's work and the perspective he brings to historical geography are evident on every page of this book. In addition, I benefited from the advice and good counsel of anonymous reviewers of the manuscript as it made its way through the publication process at Yale University Press. At the Press, the persistent but gentle push of Senior Editor Judy Metro helped sustain my enthusiasm for the project over several years and I appreciate her willingness to encourage me amid my busy life of teaching and child-raising! As my manuscript editor, Laura Jones Dooley also deserves my sincere thanks for her assistance in guiding the book to publication.

Essential to my understanding of the Colorado scene was the earlier work of dozens of scholars, mostly geographers and historians, who provided detailed insight into varied portions of the state and the larger American West. Particularly valuable—and abundantly evident in the endnotes—were the thoughtful and meticulous contributions of Carl Abbott, Gunther Barth, Bill Cronon, James Fell, Stephen Leonard, Patricia Limerick, Thomas Noel, Richard Nostrand, John Reps, Duane Smith, Tom Vale, Richard White, and Don Worster. I hope that some small part of their creative imagination is reflected in the perspective I take.

Most important, I wish to thank my family for their unfailing encouragement. My parents instilled within me a love of the West and its many geographies. My wife, Linda, and my children, Tom and Katie, shared thousands of miles of Colorado highways with me as well as many a no-name motel and small town café! For their patience and sense of adventure, I am eternally grateful.

Colorado
The Geographer's View

Nature, capitalism, and the impress of American culture produced a new human geography across Colorado between
1860 and 1940. It was a geography created as a varied western
environment was transformed by an expanding American
economy, an ever more dominant American political presence, and an increasingly diverse American culture. The resulting pattern of settlements,
the new social geographies that accompanied them, and the fresh assemblages of cultural landscapes that marked their impact upon the visual
scene are all central concerns of this book.

As a historical geographer, I explore Colorado localities and how they
have evolved. Mine is a selective view of the past, one that concentrates
on Colorado as place. I view the state as a dynamic area that has changed
over time, and I recognize both the uniqueness of Colorado localities and
the importance of broader forces that intersected with place to shape people's lives and the land they lived on. More generally, this book is also a regional study because Colorado sits squarely in the midst of the Transmississippi West. As such, its boundaries capture a diverse and representative
assortment of western American peoples and landscapes. Most broadly, I
examine the creation of new geographies when global forces of natural resource-based capitalism combined with powerful national impulses encouraging continental expansion. By the early twentieth century, Colorado's human geography was the product of those generative forces as
they played themselves out upon a varied array of mountains, prairies, and
plateaus.

Our search for the geographer's view begins with a photograph, a look
into the past that is an appropriate visual parable through which to enter
the complex tale of Colorado's settlement patterns, social communities,
and cultural landscapes (fig. 1). In a state famous for its spectacular
scenery, L. C. McClure became one of its best-known photographers in
the early years of the twentieth century.[1] His views preserved a slice of the
American West caught up in sweeping changes as new populations and
novel technologies rapidly refashioned the Colorado scene. One of Mc-
Clure's most characteristically Coloradan views captured the upper South

1

FIGURE 1. Colorado landscape: L. C. McClure's photo of South Park (Courtesy Denver Public Library, Western History Collection)

Platte River as it meandered through South Park. Elegant in its simplicity and grandeur, the photograph reveals a great deal about the diverse and changing human geographies that are the focus of this book.

As one gazes into the scene, mountains, clouds, and the river dominate, acknowledging a bold physical framework that has long molded the pattern of human occupance and still characterizes popular American perceptions of the state today. But within this vast sweep of country, set amid the bold fundament of nature, are signatures of people within our view. Most obviously, we can follow the rulerlike geometry of the rail line with the road and utility poles paralleling it nearby. These are human connections, rapidly forged into an unfamiliar land. They remind us of the relatedness of this place to other places, the impact of new technologies, and the reach of distant economic, political, and cultural powers into the resource-rich recesses of the still-developing West. On even closer inspection, the land itself has already undergone dramatic change: a corral along the railroad reveals the arrival of exotic animals, distant acres upon second glance become hayfields, and a farmhouse beyond suggests the arrival of new communities. Finally, the river itself is reworked, its waters redirected to serve the needs of local residents.

   The changes gleaned through McClure's lens are ubiquitous across the
Centennial State by the early twentieth century. Some views would show
even greater transformations while others would reveal simpler, yet still
profound shifts. Overall, our task in the pages that follow is to become
keener observers of these changes, to see with a clearer eye how a diverse
area of western North America was reorganized and its landscape refashioned over the past 150 years. Indeed, an entirely new visible scene took
shape across Colorado between 1860 and 1940, one that has shifted with
extraordinary rapidity from the modest adaptations of Native Americans
to the more recent impress of gold miners, sodbusters, city builders, and
steelworkers.

   The timing of Colorado's extraordinary development between 1860 and
1940 is crucial, and it is no accident that the bulk of this volume focuses
on how the state's varied regions evolved through that pivotal period. Converging historical events suddenly brought large and diverse numbers of
people together in the region after 1860. In a broader sense, the rush of
settlers marked the arrival of an expanding natural resource-based North
American frontier that began centuries earlier in such disparate places as
the Atlantic Coast and southern Mexico. That frontiering impulse represented a form of capitalism closely tied to the successful development of
natural resources. In late nineteenth-century America, rapidly growing
populations and the meteoric rise of the industrial economy added momentum to that impulse, dramatically shaping settlements and landscapes
in its path.

   Concomitant with and complementary to the era's economic expansion was the parallel story of both a vibrant and destructive American im-
perialism that fundamentally transformed the geographies of all of western North America, particularly after 1840. The nation was rapidly in the
process of assuming its continental dimensions and the political events of
the time quickly brought Colorado into the reach of the expanding national domain. A growing federal largesse continued shaping Colorado
into the twentieth century as the national government grew and became
more directly involved with developing and managing the resources of the
western United States.

   By 1920, however, new settlement across the state was mostly over.
Thereafter, the stamp of industrial-era capitalism peaked in the West as
the region, indeed the nation, moved toward various postindustrial economic adjustments. By then, much of Colorado's fundamental human geography was in place, a lasting legacy of the resource frontier. More prone
to change than the basic locations of settlements and cities, other elements of the cultural landscape evolved considerably after 1920, reflecting
many postindustrial economic shifts as well as a continually evolving cultural mosaic.

Complicating our story is the fact that this onrush of new people, economic impulses, and political imperatives did not take place upon a blank tableau: within Colorado, diverse environmental settings were present. The state's center was filled with complex mountain ranges that confounded early cartographers but rewarded later argonauts. To the east, Piedmont and plain presented a seemingly uniform landscape, but one that proved unpredictable. On the western slope, a mix of forested mountains, wind- and water-sculpted plateaus, and sand-and rock-bound river valleys offered other settings for human adaptations. Not surprisingly, even as common economic and political processes unfolded in such diverse ecological settings, distinctive regional settlement patterns, societies, and landscapes resulted. They are a reminder that no easy generalizations unify the disparate geographies of the state or of the larger American West. Indeed, many American Wests took shape within the Centennial State between 1860 and 1940.[2]

Posing Geographical Questions

Reconstructions of the past are selective, shaped by the predispositions of various disciplines. Historical geographers ask questions of the past that emphasize *location, place,* and *landscape* as central concerns.

An interest in *location* involves investigating how areas are organized spatially, how settlements are connected to form systems of circulation that shape flows of people, goods, money, and information.[3] This perspective focuses on Colorado's settlement nuclei as well as the links that tie them together and to the world beyond. It examines how and why such settlement systems originate and how they organize flows and movements within and between regions. Different cultural groups and economic institutions organize these systems in distinctive ways, and they create disparate patterns across the Colorado scene. The distributions of population, towns, and transportation facilities on the placer mining frontier are fundamentally different from those of an Anglo ranching area or those of a Hispanic farming district. Mapping the evolution of centers and linkages in such spatial systems is an integral part of such an approach. How can one understand mining in the San Juan Mountains, for example, without seeing how an entirely new geography of towns, wagon roads, rail lines, and freight flows reorganized the region's human geography, binding it more coherently together and linking it with the national and global economy (fig. 2)?

The rapid changes in Colorado's settlement geography between 1860 and 1920 were fueled largely by the forces of natural resource–based capitalism, and thus this locational perspective is concerned not only with reconstructing spatial systems within the state but also with analyzing how

FIGURE 2. An evolving settlement system: E. Fischer's map of the San Juan mining districts, 1883 (Courtesy Denver Public Library, Western History Collection)

these new human geographies were transformed by and linked with more distant forces.[4] Colorado's dramatically expanding dry farming frontier in the 1880s, for instance, was but a western extension of similar activities in Kansas and Nebraska, and the associated speculative bubble in real estate and grain prices reflected larger-scale national excesses that could not be sustained. Similarly, industrial Pueblo's economic health became tied to decisions made by distant investment trusts and holding companies. How does capitalism reshape the geographies of Colorado's settlement systems over time? The state's rich regional mosaic offers varied responses to that key question and suggests how geographers can contribute to such discussions generally.

Place refers to the process by which people give meaning to location, particularly to how they create social geographies that are rooted in community.[5] Increasingly, American historians and social scientists focus not on the "Great Men" of the past but rather on how communities are established—by both men and women—and what institutions play key roles in holding them together or in changing them over time. This emphasis on "common people" has a corollary within geography, an emphasis centered upon how distinctive social and cultural groups invest meaning in places, into their local neighborhoods and communities. Colorado offers an ideal setting within which to examine many new social geographies that became rooted within the American West. Indeed, the West is a meeting ground of many cultures and classes. How did these communities define themselves, both spatially and socially? What elements of their traditional ways were retained and what was modified in new settings? How did groups interact? This perspective—the study of people in place—traces the creation of these new social geographies in varied Colorado locales. Indeed, late nineteenth-century Colorado offers diverse social settings: the formative influences of middle-class midwesterners, Hispanos, southern Europeans, and others contributed to the creation of a new cultural mosaic that continues to evolve today.

Landscape is another central concern to the historical geographer.[6] This third set of questions refers to the signatures people leave upon the visible scene and what those imprints can tell us about a culture and its relation to the environment. Reading the cultural landscape, as we saw in McClure's view of South Park, requires a sensitivity to seeing, a penchant for observing the everyday scene in fresh ways. Geographers believe that the landscape can tell us important things about the people who created it. Their ways of life and values are revealed in the artifacts that surround them. In this sense, landscape is material culture, a concrete expression of habits, technology, and the distributions of power and authority within society. Ponder, for example, the economic significance of a large, smoking smelter on the edge of a Colorado mining town or the quieter signature of an adobe Catholic church positioned at the center of a Hispano *placita*. As we traverse Colorado, we shall find that every place has a unique cultural landscape and yet that common cultural, economic, and political threads combine to weave predictable patterns onto the visible scene that remind us of the larger significance of the localities within our purview. Tracing those threads from their origins to their new settings helps us to understand how a place acquires a particular personality and how it reflects diverse cultural, economic, and political roots.

The study of landscape also implies assessing relations between people and nature.[7] Colorado settlements are intimately wedded to their physical surroundings. What is the interplay among nature, capital, and culture? People modify environments, but physical settings also demand human adaptations. The result is a cultural landscape rooted in its natural environment. As environmental historians have argued, the western American setting was hardly a neutral stage. Nature, with all its vicissitudes, mattered a great deal when it came to shaping patterns of human settlement and livelihood. Altitude, slope, climate, geology, soils, vegetative cover, and many other natural variables shaped the course of human occupance within Colorado and the evolution of its cultural landscape. Just as surely, such human practices as hydraulic mining, irrigation, farming, ranching, and city-building dramatically altered the natural scene. Exotic plants and animals flowed into the region. Topography and drainage were altered to meet human needs. Metals and fossil fuels were unearthed. The resulting cultural landscape suggests the outcome of these complex interactions between people and the land. Even Colorado's urban settings owe their economic primacy to the development of the surrounding countryside. What would Denver or Pueblo be without the nearby resource bases that fueled their rise? Indeed, everywhere in Colorado, one scratches the surface of human occupance and finds the raw ingredients of nature beneath.

The complex interconnections between people and their environment suggest another set of geographical questions focused upon the landscape. Central to our inquiry is a concern for how people perceived, evaluated, and responded to the Colorado landscapes they encountered.[8] In particular, Colorado offered a novel mix of spaciousness, wildness, and physical features that challenged newcomers to find new ways to understand and articulate what they were seeing. That story begins with the simple mapping of Colorado's physical setting, a task that took Europeans and Americans centuries to complete. It also involves understanding how people evaluated the land as they settled the region. What was its economic potential and its limitations? No one knew for sure. At times, assessments transcended purely utilitarian concerns and our appreciation for how people encountered landscapes also involves how they imbued their surroundings with cultural and aesthetic significance. Indeed, artists and writers as well as settlers struggled with what they saw when they ventured west, and much of the visible scene they encountered—the region's vast plains, towering alpine topography, and steeply incised canyons—demanded a new aesthetic vocabulary that blended European Romanticism and American exceptionalism into a fresh response to the natural world.

After sketching Colorado's pre-1860 geographies, the book centers on a series of regional chapters that examine patterns of geographical change between 1860 and 1920. That formative period throughout the state is characterized by unparalleled population growth, the initial creation of enduring settlement systems and communities, and the dramatic impress of new cultural landscapes. We examine these patterns and processes first in mountain and Piedmont zones because they become initial destinations for most new migrants to the state before 1880. Later chapters concentrate on Colorado's diverse hinterlands: the varied stories of the eastern plains, southern periphery, and western slope are chronicled. Our areal encounters address the three geographical questions posed and suggest that although each of the state's major regions experienced similar economic and political changes after 1860, their distinctive environments and varied cultural milieus produced persisting geographical differences. A final chapter summarizes patterns of change within Colorado between 1920 and 1940 and places the state in larger regional and national contexts as it shifts from its traditional emphases on natural resource extraction and toward mass consumption, postindustrial economic growth, and the amenity-oriented lifestyles of the later twentieth century.

Colorado Geographies: Five Themes

Posing our three geographical questions regarding location, place, and landscape across the varied Colorado scene yields a diverse response to which this book will soon turn. Before doing so, however, it is useful to consider several themes that can inform and direct our inquiry. With these in hand, our explorations, whether they be into Hispano villages or Denver's suburbs, will gain coherence and context. Rather than predictive theorems, they are intended as general guides to understanding the patterns, places, and landscapes we encounter. Although they are place-specific— they seem to work well in Colorado—they also have wider relevance for much of the American West and for analogous settings elsewhere.

1. Colorado's historical geography reveals the importance of the *doctrine of first effective settlement*. As articulated by cultural geographer Wilbur Zelinsky, the argument states that "whenever an empty territory undergoes settlement, or an earlier population is dislodged by invaders, the specific characteristics of the first group able to effect a viable, self-perpetuating society are of crucial significance for the later social and cultural geography of the area, no matter how tiny the initial band of settlers

may have been."[9] In other words, timing matters. Persisting cultural and economic dominance often goes to those early on the scene. They have the opportunities to select premium locations for farming or business, to develop the richest concentrations of natural resources, and to create initial trade and financial contacts with the world beyond. Inevitably, early arrivals shape an area's settlement system, social geography, and cultural landscape. Consider the importance of arriving early in the development of a mining district in which a limited resource base is quickly parceled out among hopeful argonauts. In a related manner, ponder the pivotal advantages that accrue to irrigating farmers who have early established rights to water.

A corollary to the doctrine is that growth attracts more growth.[10] Once established, a vibrant settlement is apt to grow further as newly arriving populations and capital gravitate toward centers of developed infrastructure and proven opportunity. Thus Denver, once it is established as the territory's gateway city, increases its economic dominance in later decades. Social and cultural institutions such as churches and schools also bear the inordinately important stamp of first families who, once settled, form a sustaining core of local influentials who guide the community's future course.

2. Colorado became a *meeting ground of many cultures,* and the resulting patterns of cultural blending and conflict produced new social juxtapositions that shaped the region's human geography in lasting ways.[11] Long before the discovery of gold in the late 1850s, Colorado was a zone of cultural mixing, first for a variety of Native peoples and later for a similarly eclectic collection of Europeans. Once settlement accelerated after 1859, diverse Americans converged upon the region, supplemented by foreign-born populations. A new cultural amalgam was forged in the process.

Colorado's position within the larger West also contributed to its cultural diversity: eastern counties became outposts of essentially midwestern farmers, the southern periphery felt the impress of largely Hispano settlement, and the far northwest became an extension of southern Wyoming's Anglo ranching culture. Urban and industrial settings attracted their own diverse mix of ethnic populations. The state's cultural landscape became a rich repository of these varied signatures: both city and country reflected the stamp of earlier cultural identities as they were reconstituted in new settings. Beyond these particularities, there were also larger homogenizing influences at work as national values and converging habits of popular culture increasingly asserted themselves across America, especially after 1920.

3. *Capitalism and liberal individualism* became dominant ideological impulses in Colorado's history, and their related characteristics—an econ-

omy oriented around natural resource extraction, cyclical patterns of economic boom and bust, and the structural realities of core-periphery relations—strongly shaped the visible scene between 1860 and 1920.[12] Colorado, given the timing of its settlement in the context of an expanding global economy as well as the considerable resource base within its borders, vividly bore both the fruits and scars of laissez-faire capitalism. Indeed, capitalism transcended mere economic matters: it implied a set of social and political relations that suffused the fabric of daily life and set the context for the state's settlement and subsequent evolution. The state's residents, regardless of cultural background, typically shared a loose consensus when it came to the virtues of materialism and individualism. A booster mentality was also endemic, coloring the way people envisaged the landscape and the potential of its natural resource base (fig. 3).

Unfortunately, the region's real economic opportunities were more constrained. The structure of late nineteenth-century capitalism preordained dominant and dominated populations. Cyclical demands for many of the commodities Colorado produced resulted in unpredictable economic swings. The collapse of silver prices in 1893, for example, was a reminder that the West was still largely a colonized periphery that had little control over its resources. Later, as the state grew in size, power within the region concentrated in the Piedmont cities, leaving the eastern, southern, and western fringes of the state parts of an enduring economic and political hinterland.

Human geographies strikingly bore the signatures of the region's economic raison d'être. Networks of wagon roads and rail lines—certainly the densest in the Intermountain West—were powerful testimony to the impact of capital investment on the state's rapidly evolving settlement system. Furthermore, the intimate links among railroad capitalists, town and irrigation developers, real estate speculators, and mining and milling operators—all so formative in molding spatial patterns—pointed to the key financial players, both local and distant, that directed the construction of an economic geography clearly oriented around the efficient extraction of natural wealth wherever it could be harvested. Whether it was the ostentatious bric-a-brac adorning a Denver plutocrat's home, the coal camps near Trinidad, or the hopelessly ambitious town plats on the eastern plains, the impress of capitalism dominated the Colorado scene.

The more extractive dimensions of the capitalist economy peaked early in the twentieth century as shortages and disruptions created by World War I pushed prices and demand to new heights. Thereafter, the Colorado landscape bore the signs of important economic shifts as the nation moved toward an era of postindustrial consumption: although Colorado's service industries and tourist amenities thrived in the new century, longer-settled

REAPING—A PRAIRIE HOMESTEAD—THRESHING.

FIGURE 3. The frontier idealized: dreams of plenty on a prairie homestead (Courtesy Colorado State Historical Society)

regions built around mining and farming struggled as excess laborers left abandoned homes and dreams behind.

4. *Nature matters*—Colorado's resource base, though varied and abundant, proved more fickle and fragile than was initially advertised.[13] Landslides, earthquakes, blizzards, cyclical droughts, floods, firestorms, and insects made life in the West eternally tenuous. Nature's omnipresence and unpredictability became a regional leitmotiv that touched the lives of all its inhabitants, shaped its cultural landscapes, and stamped it with a character few would deny even today. When combined with the economic vagaries of natural resource-based capitalism, results were dramatic and unpredictable. The marriage of land and people was rocky and neither party was ever the same again. Colorado environments were sometimes damaged beyond repair and almost everywhere the hand of human agency altered ecological systems. Mining landscapes most dramatically revealed human impacts as deforestation, erosion, and water pollution took their toll (fig. 4). Repeated episodes of exploiting prairie and rangeland environments also yielded tragic environmental outcomes. By 1940, the message was clear: the West, for all its spaciousness and magnificence, was a delicate giant, prone to human-induced environmental degradation.

FIGURE 4. Modifying nature in the high country: placer mining near Central City
(Courtesy Denver Public Library, Western History Collection)

5. Colorado's human geography also bears the stamp of *political insti-tutions*.[14] An imperial European political geography provided an early framework for exploration and resource assessment. By 1720, Spanish, French, and English empires carved up much of the interior West. Gov-ernment-supported explorations and surveys continued during the early nineteenth century as American interest in the West grew. As Americans asserted control over the region by the mid-nineteenth century, an elabo-rate system of territorial governance, military activity, and supply lines tied varied western political units to Washington, D.C. Contrary to frontier myths, the federal government often led rather than followed the course of settlement, gathering important geographical knowledge and protect-ing fledgling communities from hostile Indians. The colonial nature of the relation between Washington, D.C., and the West was clear, however, and even after statehood, many western states were denied much power at the national level because of their low populations and lack of congressional seniority.

As settlement accelerated, federal land surveys quickly partitioned the West into rectangular 160- and 640-acre parcels and a variety of land laws guaranteed the rapid if not always democratic disposal and development of the public domain. Federal investments into forts, roads, railroad surveys, and mail routes spurred development in many locales, essentially subsidizing such private economic initiatives as mining, farming, and trade. Similarly, at the local level, town and county political bodies were often little more than booster agencies for business and landowning constituencies. Indeed, America's fundamental legal system, with its property laws and guarantees of corporate freedom, spurred freewheeling economic development within Colorado and elsewhere in the West.

Colorado Nexus: Place Through Time, Time Through Place

Historical geographies can have multiple aims, and this exploration of Colorado carries with it three complementary objectives. As a traditional assessment of "place through time," *Creating Colorado* demonstrates how the perspective of historical geography—with location, place, and landscape as its central principles—can enrich our understanding of particular localities and how and why they evolved in the ways they did. As a work of regional geography, such a task, successfully completed, raises our sensitivity to and appreciation for the everyday scene that surrounds and shapes us.[15]

Creating Colorado is also an example to those who study the past that one can profit greatly by assessing "time through place." Those interested in western American history, for example, cannot divorce their story from its setting, not just as a passive backdrop of aridity or mountains, but as a dynamic dimension in which new environments, peoples, and institutions converge in fresh ways.[16] To social scientists generally, historical geographies are reminders that an emphasis on place can offer a powerful interpretative framework through which to study the impacts of large-scale economic, political, and cultural influences on societies both past and present.

Finally, Colorado's story contributes to larger dialogues focused on the impacts of capitalism in varied regional settings. This perspective, though ably addressed by such scholars as Immanuel Wallerstein at the global level and by William Robbins within the context of the American West, nevertheless can benefit from geographers trained to assess how varied forces, both natural and human, shape the earth's surface and the lives of its inhabitants.[17] *Creating Colorado* suggests that geographers can offer useful conceptual frameworks in such assessments. Capitalism's impact upon settlement systems, communities, and the cultural landscape be-

FIGURE 5. Creating new geographies: canal-building in the desert near Montrose (Courtesy Colorado State Historical Society)

come concrete, location-specific phenomena that connect general processes to particular places. Clearly, historical geographers can play active, imaginative, and diverse roles in pursuing those insights and, in doing so, demonstrate their centrality in discussions that wed nature, capital, and culture to place (fig. 5).

Pre-1860 Geographies

Four pre-1860 geographies within Colorado set the context for the dramatic transformations that followed. The state's physical environment, its Native American legacy, its partitioning by varied European powers, and its early, still ephemeral occupance by Anglo Americans provide essential geographical elements for understanding subsequent patterns of settlement and development.

Nature's Colorado

Colorado's natural fundament is built upon three well-defined landform regions, each representative of different parts of the American West (fig. 6).[1] Running north to south through the center of the state is mountainous Colorado, home to dozens of glaciated peaks, thick montane and subalpine forests, and several large grass-covered valleys or parks. No single ridge defines this mountain zone; rather it is a series of broadly parallel ranges that extend from the Medicine Bow Mountains of southern Wyoming to the Sangre de Cristo and San Juan Mountains along the state's southern border. Eastward lie the Great Plains, a more homogeneous physical landscape but one still marked by local variations that shape the lay of the land. Western Colorado is plateau country, a complex mosaic of dissected mesas and buttes whose rich sedimentary beds are carved into fantastic shapes by a series of down-cutting, mostly westward-flowing rivers. The Colorado River and its tributaries dominate the drainage pattern in the west and provide the bulk of the state's surface water flow.

Colorado's midlatitude continental location ensures profound seasonal changes in weather, and the state's diverse topography exerts a powerful influence on both daily weather patterns and longer-term climatic averages. Contrasts within the state can be striking even on a single day: Denverites might be sweltering in 100°F heat while tourists atop nearby fourteen-thousand-foot Mount Evans are shivering in freezing temperatures. Longer-term patterns of rain and snowfall also are dramatically influenced by the terrain. A map of average annual precipitation bears a re-

15

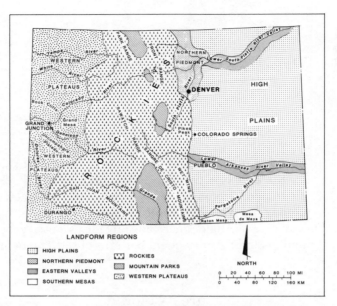

FIGURE 6. Landform regions of Colorado (Adapted from Kenneth Erickson and Albert Smith, *Atlas of Colorado* [Boulder: Colorado Associated University Press, 1985], 4–7; and Mel Griffiths and Lynnell Rubright, *Colorado: A Geography* [Boulder: Westview, 1983], 11–33)

markable resemblance to the state's landforms (fig. 7). The moist slopes of the San Juans and other uplifts along and west of the Continental Divide receive more than forty inches of precipitation annually, much of it in the form of winter and spring snow. Lesser peaks of moisture stand out along the more eastern reaches of the Front Range. By contrast, the lower western valleys of the state are much drier with precipitation along the Colorado River averaging fewer than ten inches per year. Other dry zones lie to the east: both the central mountain parks and the high plains are in the rain shadows of mountains that capture much of the incoming moisture.

Colorado Plains

A vast stretch of Colorado extends from the Front Range to the Kansas border. This is high plains, short-grass country averaging four thousand to six thousand feet in elevation. Thick accumulations of sediment repeatedly have been laid across the region. These gently rolling prairies are locally dissected by tributaries of the Arkansas and Platte Rivers. Younger volcanic extrusions in the south offer additional variety. Clothing eastern

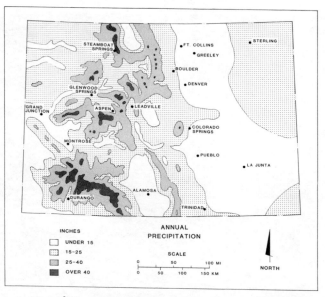

FIGURE 7. Average annual precipitation (Adapted from Erickson and Smith, *Atlas*, 14–19)

Colorado is a natural cover of buffalo and grama grass, although only vestiges of these wild species remain. These are short grasses, quick growing, well adapted to the vagaries of the plains environment. Woodlands are limited to riparian forests of cottonwood and willow along major streams and to colonies of straggly piñon pines and junipers dotting the rougher volcanic uplifts near the New Mexico and Oklahoma borders.[2]

The plains are carved and contoured into three distinctive regional landforms by circumstances of geology and drainage. Dominant are the true high plains that stretch between the Arkansas and Platte Valleys. These are lands of very slight relief, interrupted only occasionally by shallow and sparsely vegetated ephemeral streamcourses (fig. 8). Paralleling the Platte and Arkansas Rivers, the Colorado Piedmont offers a second distinctive plains landscape. Much of the overlaying cover has been removed in these actively eroding river valleys, and the result is a land surface distinctly lower than that of the high plains. The Piedmont, narrow along the length of the Arkansas River, broadens along the South Platte, particularly between Denver and Fort Morgan. A third plains landscape is increasingly apparent as one journeys south of the Arkansas Valley. The land's texture roughens. Hills and small buttes interrupt the relatively smooth topography of the high plains and Piedmont. This is a zone of volcanic uplands, and they form a surprisingly varied southeastern margin of

FIGURE 8. High plains north of Limon (Photo by the author)

the state. Here are highly dissected, often steeply sloped landscapes of lava flows and basalt-capped mesas that have been eroded by downcutting rivers, creating an intricate maze of piñon- and juniper-covered tablelands and canyons.

Colorado Mountains

Colorado's mountainous heartland straddles the roof of the continent. From the twisting Continental Divide flow the waters of a dozen major rivers, including the Platte and Arkansas on the east, the Rio Grande on the south, and the Colorado and its tributaries on the state's western slope. Further complicating this mountain zone is the fact that it is hardly an uninterrupted uplift, but rather a complex jumble of alternating ranges and valleys with tremendous local diversity in terrain, climate, and vegetation. Geologically, the mountain-building associated with the Laramide Orogeny about seventy million years ago accelerated the processes of uplift and landform change across the region. This structural arching and doming, combined with surface faulting and more recent vulcanism, fashioned much of the topographic superstructure that so dominates the scene today.[3] Concurrent with these mountain-building events, erosive agents, particularly water and ice, further shaped the landscape. Rivers have cut narrow, twisting canyons through the uplifts. Repeated cycles of alpine glaciation have produced even more dramatic results (fig. 9). Rocky cirques, angular ridges and peaks, and deeply carved U-shaped valleys sprinkled with meadows and lakes are the sharpened signatures left by multiple glacial advances.

The Front Range and Wet Mountains form a bold eastern bulwark to the Colorado Rockies (see fig. 6). Host to both Longs Peak and Pikes Peak, these eastern ranges dominate the skylines of Denver, Colorado Springs, and Pueblo and traditionally provide westbound travelers with their first glimpse of the mountains. Further west are additional groupings of major north-south–trending mountain ranges. Prominent among these are the Sangre de Cristo and Sawatch Mountains. The Sawatch feature some of the highest and most spectacularly glaciated landscapes in the state, while the Sangre de Cristo range is well-known for faults that border it and for large wind-deposited sand dunes that mark a portion of its western foothills. Finally, in the southwest corner of the state, the mostly linear arrangement of Colorado high country is broken by the sprawling domal uplift of the San Juan Mountains. This massif is the largest expression of Tertiary-era vulcanism in Colorado: portions of the range are carved from thick accumulations of volcanic ash extruded from a series of huge calderas between five and fifteen million years ago. Since then, alpine glaciation has also played a dramatic role in shaping the topography.

Separating these ranges are a series of large intermontane basins. Opening into northern New Mexico and lying between the San Juan and Sangre de Cristo Mountains is the San Luis Valley. Although averaging seventy-five hundred feet in elevation, much of the valley floor is almost flat, broken only occasionally by irregular volcanic hills and by the shallow course of the Rio Grande and its tributaries. North of the San Luis Valley, Colorado's mountain zone is again interrupted by three broad, mostly grass-covered structural basins. South, Middle, and North Parks punctuate the high country near the Continental Divide, sitting between spectacularly glaciated and densely forested ranges.

Colorado's mountains host an intricate mosaic of vegetation that can vary dramatically in only a few miles. Plants adapt to local differences in soil, slope, temperature, and availability of water. Beginning on the edge of the eastern plains, a transition zone of woodland vegetation offers a scattering of piñon pine, juniper, oak, and mountain mahogany. Above six thousand feet the forest thickens and foothill species are replaced by open stands of Douglas fir and ponderosa pine. Cottonwood, alder, and birch crowd streamcourses, while pockets of aspen dot the higher slopes. Dense and dark forests of subalpine fir and spruce replace these lower montane species above nine thousand feet. As timberline is approached between

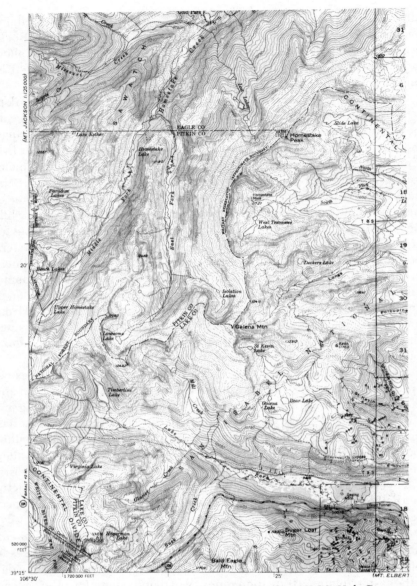

FIGURE 9. Alpine landforms northwest of Leadville (Source: USGS, Holy Cross quadrangle, 1949, 1:62,500 topographic map series)

eleven and twelve thousand feet, these subalpine trees, along with limber and bristlecone pines, shrink, dwarfed by the stress of coping with the harsh winds and low temperatures of such lofty elevations. Finally, forests are left behind, the sky opens, and the only plants remaining to colonize exposed alpine slopes and peaks are lichens, low-growing grasses, and herbs of the tundra zone. Such a journey, an easy morning's excursion in the Rockies is, in terms of vegetation change, the equivalent of a several-thousand-mile trek from the central United States to the arctic lowlands of northern Canada.

Colorado Plateaus

The westernmost quarter of the Centennial State is dominated by the Colorado Plateau. As one leaves the mountain fastnesses of the Colorado Rockies, the landscape assumes a new rectangularity and horizontality largely fashioned from gently dipping often brightly colored bands of sedimentary rock. This region is a diverse mix of variously sized tablelands, mesas, entrenched canyons, and floodplains. Drainage is to the west across much of the central and northern part of the region. The sinuous Yampa and White Rivers have carved canyons through the sage-covered plateaus in the northwest corner of the state as they flow toward the Green River in Utah. South of the Roan Plateau, the main stem of the Colorado and its major tributary, the Gunnison, dominate the drainage pattern. The picture shifts around the western and southern edges of the San Juan Mountains, where the Dolores and San Miguel Rivers flow northwestward and the varied branches of the San Juan River empty toward northern New Mexico.

Several characteristic kinds of country dominate the western slope. Mesas create blocklike islands that possess gentle relief, varying forest cover, and even examples of extensive alpine glaciation. Typically, these highlands are capped with resistant sedimentary rock, although the summit of Grand Mesa is made up of igneous basalts. Precipitous and highly dissected escarpments often mark the edge of the uplifts, and these steep slopes, actively eroding into the plateau, stand in sharp contrast to the flat or gently rolling summits (fig. 10). Downcutting streams entrenched across such uplifts produce another common western Colorado landform. The canyonlands are most dramatic along the Colorado River from just above Grand Junction to Glenwood Canyon near Glenwood Springs. Portions of the Yampa River, the Gunnison River near Black Mesa, and the Dolores and San Miguel Rivers west of the Uncompahgre Plateau are similarly incised and feature meandering tree-lined streams that lie between steeply walled and often highly colored rock formations. Where rivers

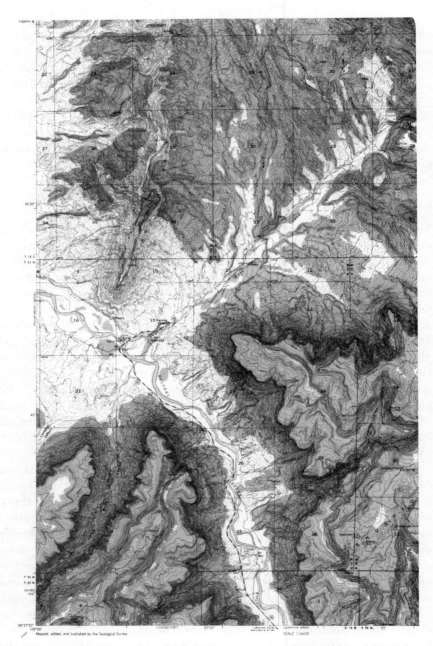

FIGURE 10. Plateau and canyon landforms in western Colorado near Gateway (Source: USGS, Gateway quadrangle, 1960, 1:24,000 topographic map series)

break out into the open, relatively flat, broad floodplains dominate the scene. The lower reaches of the Uncompahgre and Gunnison Rivers and the Colorado Valley near Grand Junction typify the floodplain landscape.

Native American Geographies

American Indians created their own Coloradan geographies centuries before the Pikes Peak Gold Rush. By 1860, the West was an already long-settled land, intricately shaped by many centuries of human occupance and subsistence. Colorado's plateaus and plains, even its isolated mountain heights, felt the impact of settlement for thousands of years. The resulting landscape was a complex cultural artifact expressing a varied set of changing human adaptations through time. Indeed, Native Americans discovered diverse ways to subsist across the West.[4] Borne of necessity, their knowledge of the landscape was often detailed and sophisticated. In addition, while Indian peoples did not dwell on a self-conscious and explicit "love of nature" in its modern preservationist contexts, their appreciation for the value of particular animals, plants, and places often extended to a religious reverence for the world that surrounded and sustained them.

Colorado's first residents arrived more than twelve thousand years ago. Paleo-Indian populations were well adapted to subsist on megafauna that roamed the cool and wet Colorado plains.[5] Prairie mastodons, mammoths, giant bison, and camels encouraged the development of a big-game harvesting technology. Such adaptations included the fashioning of stone-tipped spears, the identification of strategic kill sites, and a flexible social organization favoring small bands that traveled with the herds and with the seasonal appearances of other useful animals and plants. About ten thousand years ago, however, many of the large mammals became extinct. Whatever the cause, the shift prompted early peoples to concentrate on surviving bison herds and increasingly supplement their appetite for megafauna with smaller animals and a wider variety of collected plants.

West of the mountains, early Desert Culture peoples never depended so much on large mammals. For thousands of years scattered bands of hunters and gatherers survived by killing small game and effectively harvesting the limited local plant life. The western Colorado scene witnessed a rapid transformation, however, about two thousand years ago.[6] Change came with the arrival of agriculture and other Mesoamerican influences that diffused northward along the Colorado River. Early Basketmaker peoples, akin to their Desert Culture ancestors, were still hunters and gatherers, but increasingly they augmented their food supplies with the cultivation of maize, squash, and beans. The Basketmaker peoples who moved onto mesa top and river valley farming sites evolved into the Great Pueblo

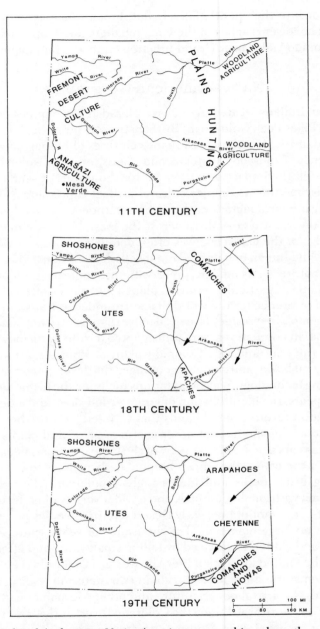

FIGURE 11. Colorado's changing Native American geographies: eleventh century, eighteenth century, nineteenth century (Adapted from J. Donald Hughes, *American Indians in Colorado* [Boulder: Pruett, 1977], 72–77)

or Classic Anasazi cultures of the twelfth and thirteenth centuries C.E. (fig. 11). During this period, population growth increased markedly, people became more sedentary, and clusters of population formed around larger villages and nearby farm fields.

The Anasazi cultural landscape reflected the impacts of these demographic and economic changes.[7] Especially after the ninth century C.E., accelerated population growth and cultural change led to more elaborate architectural traditions. The simple underground pithouses that served as Basketmaker-era accommodations were replaced by larger groupings of above-ground dwellings that often included hundreds of rooms, ceremonial kivas, and thick-walled watchtowers. Land-clearing also hastened the modification of the Anasazi visual scene. Stone axes felled piñon-juniper as well as riparian cottonwood forests for buildings and fuel. To increase yields, land being prepared for farming was often burned. Worked with stone hoes and simple digging sticks, Anasazi farm fields simplified the environment and accelerated patterns of runoff and erosion. Bighorn sheep that browsed on natural woodlands were gradually replaced with mule deer that subsisted well on Indian garden plots. Streams were dammed, creating silt-rich terraces that added fertile agricultural acreage to feed growing populations. The mysterious exodus of the Anasazi, hastily completed in the late thirteenth century, ended this chapter of Native American occupance, although its legacy remains today, particularly in the ruins preserved in southwest Colorado's Mesa Verde National Park.

Across northwestern Colorado, human impacts during this era focused upon the evolution of Fremont Culture between 1000 and 1200 C.E. (see fig. 11). Fremont Culture fused older Desert Archaic traditions from the Great Basin with Basketmaker-Pueblo influences from the south.[8] From Pueblo influences, Fremont peoples learned to concentrate their small settlements along streamcourses, live in pithouses, and cultivate fields of maize, beans, and squash. Supplementing these new exotics was their traditional diet of edible wild plants and game animals. Summertime forays into the mountains further augmented food supplies. Overall, Fremont peoples wrought even less change across the landscape than the Anasazi to the south. By the thirteenth century farming virtually ceased in the region and residents returned to older forms of hunting and gathering.

East of the mountains, the disappearance of much of the Plains megafauna forced later Archaic peoples into a more diverse diet which necessitated a greater knowledge of more limited foraging and gathering territories. This drift toward an increasingly sedentary settlement geography was reinforced two thousand years ago as agriculture crept westward into the high plains from Woodland Culture centers in the Mississippi Basin.[9] Along the Arkansas and Platte Rivers and their tributaries, populations cultivated maize, beans, and squash (see fig. 11). Larger clusters of earth lodges marked the village locales of these western outposts of Plains agriculture. These marginal farming operations continued to be supplemented by plains buffalo. In fact, after 1200 C.E., killing techniques improved as skilled Athapascan hunters migrated from Canada southward across the Colorado plains.[10] These people, ancestors of the Apache, also acquired the rudiments of agriculture and enjoyed the advantages of the mixed farming and foraging economy. After 1400, however, these plains peoples, dominated by Apache influences, began to lessen their dependence on farming. Cyclical drought or disruptions of village populations through disease may have contributed to a return to a more nomadic existence and a greater dependence upon buffalo hunting. Whatever the cause of the change, by the time Francisco Vásquez de Coronado explored the nearby southern Plains in 1540, there was an almost exclusive dependence on buffalo for food, tools, and clothing.

Although all of Colorado's native peoples felt the effects of European exploration and settlement, it was the human geography of the eastern plains that was most dramatically transformed (see fig. 11). Here, the horse, introduced by the Spanish in the seventeenth century, created opportunities for change.[11] Created in the process was a fusion of Native American and Euro-American traditions that produced a remarkably vigorous Plains Indian cultural adaptation between the early eighteenth and mid-nineteenth centuries. Most fundamentally the horse offered Native Americans increased mobility as they tracked the wanderings of the plains buffalo. The horse also changed plains political geography because it encouraged new forms of social organization and modified traditional patterns of warfare. Within Colorado, the Comanche profited most from the horse. Once receiving horses from the Utes after 1680, they expanded rapidly southward and eastward across the Colorado plains. Their main adversaries were the Apache. By the 1720s only a few scattered bands of Jicarilla Apache remained in southern Colorado. Meanwhile, Algonquian-speaking Cheyenne were gradually moving westward across the Great Plains during the eighteenth century. Although they were once upper midwestern agriculturalists, the Cheyenne transformed their economic geography by adopting the nomadic hunting life style of the mounted Plains Indian. Once in the region, they allied with the Arapaho, another Algonquian people, who were a recently arrived hunting tribe from Canada. Much of eastern Colorado fell under Arapaho and Cheyenne control after 1800 as these tribes shoved the Comanche mostly south of the Arkansas River, where they mingled with the Kiowa of the southern Plains (see fig. 11).

West of the Plains, Utes dominated Colorado's recent past (see fig. 11).[12] Ute subsistence patterns were altered by the horse, but less dra-

FIGURE 12. Late nineteenth-century Utes in the central Colorado mountains, photo by H. S. Poley (Courtesy: Colorado State Historical Society)

matically than was the case for tribes to the east. The Ute remained a hunting and gathering people strongly shaped by the annual cycle of seasons across the mountain and plateau country. Various Ute bands wintered in the San Juan, Uncompahgre, Gunnison, Colorado, and Yampa Valleys. They hunted small game that moved out of the mountains. With warmer weather, Ute mobility increased. Their detailed knowledge of western Colorado's edible plants enabled them to forage effectively across their semi-arid homelands, gathering yucca, yampa roots, grass seeds, piñon nuts, and berries. As upland snows melted, hunting parties ventured into the high country in search of deer, elk, and mountain sheep. Here the horse proved especially valuable, extending Ute inroads into the mountains (fig. 12). Some Ute bands, after acquiring the horse, also made autumnal forays eastward onto the plains to hunt buffalo.

As Euro-American explorations across Colorado increased in the seventeenth and eighteenth centuries, the newcomers gradually improved upon their scanty knowledge of the native inhabitants. They pieced together the still-changing geography of Indian settlement and appreciated the fact that the West, although still a wilderness in the context of European settlement, was nevertheless a peopled wilderness that had long been shaped by human occupance. As accidental and purposeful connections between these two vastly different cultures accelerated, the pace of change and conflict increased. Neither Euro-American or Indian remained the same thereafter and the native population barely survived the contact.

Europe's Colorado

Europeans only slowly rolled back the mists of uncertainty that shrouded their geographical understanding of western North America. Experience and enterprise gradually replaced fantasy and fortune in shaping their geographical knowledge of the continent's complex interior. Akin to the pieces of a jigsaw puzzle, drainage basins and mountain chains, once the fancy of the early mapmaker's imagination, gradually fell into place and the shadows of terra incognita faded before the light of a new European dawning. The process took several centuries and involved a number of often competing European powers as well as a new postcolonial American presence. The actual imprints of these new peoples upon the land were subtle and minute compared with the doings of the modern farmer or construction engineer. Yet once the process began, western North America as well as its native residents inexorably became more and more a part of the European world. Although Colorado remained in the shadows of this encroachment longer than most western American regions, even it succumbed ultimately to the glare of the new European order upon the land.

Ironically, though Colorado sat near the physical center of the Transmississippi West, it sat on the periphery of European and Anglo-American development while neighboring regions saw more rapid exploration and settlement. Several things explain Colorado's enduring remoteness. The region's relative location—distant from coastlines and far upriver from major settlements—precluded early or easy reconnaissance by water. As the West became better known during the late seventeenth century, New Mexico's Rio Grande and the great Missouri River corridor offered approaches from the south and east, but Colorado remained beyond the pale of permanent European settlement for more than a century longer.

Colorado's remoteness was enhanced by the complexity of its high mountain backbone. Its function as a headwaters region for the Platte, Arkansas, San Juan, and Colorado River systems and the Rio Grande proved an enduring headache for explorers and mapmakers. Even more confusing were the string of broad upland valleys or parks that extended from the San Luis Valley to the Wyoming border. Flanked by mountains east and west, these parks confounded cartographers for more than a century. Added to this were large and complex mountain blocks such as southwestern Colorado's San Juan range.

Native Americans also discouraged the peaceful passage of European travelers. In fact, Colorado correctly was perceived by the Spanish and French to be a source area of persistent Indian problems. In the west, the Ute alternately traded with and raided Spanish settlements in northern New Mexico. On the plains, especially after 1720, Europeans also felt the tough intransigence of the Comanche as they wreaked havoc on natives and newcomers alike. And the Arapaho and Cheyenne often cooled the ardor of early nineteenth century traders and trappers. As a result, Colorado's Indian populations were a very real threat to early travelers and deterred casual journeying across the region.

European political geography also conspired against the rapid settlement of Colorado. The area long remained a persistent political borderland between various European powers. The Spanish were first on the scene (fig. 13).[13] Santa Fe was founded in 1610 as the new administrative capital of their northern province, but settlement concentrated along the nearby Rio Grande Valley and did not extend into present-day Colorado. Punitive expeditions against the Indians did take the Spanish into the southeastern portions of the state. In the 1660s Juan de Archuleta probed the Arkansas Valley. Four decades later Juan de Ulibarri mounted a similar effort, taking him near modern-day Pueblo. Through such contacts Colorado effectively became part of Spain's North American frontier, but it remained a zone of dangerous Indians and little-known geography.

Making matters worse for the Spanish were French encroachments in the Great Plains.[14] French activity, beginning with Jacques Marquette and Louis Joliet's Mississippi journey in 1673, accelerated thereafter. By the close of the seventeenth century French trappers and traders were ascending the Missouri at least to the Platte, and those upcountry connections were reinforced in 1714 by Etienne Veniard de Bourgmont's plains expedition to visit and trade with local Indian populations. Although Colorado's upper Platte and Arkansas Valleys were probably not visited directly by the French early on, knowledge of the Europeans and their trade goods traveled upriver in a rapidly expanding sphere of French influence.

By 1720 Colorado's eastern plains clearly sat in the geopolitical balance between New Spain and French Louisiana (fig. 14). These two colonial empires envisioned the Colorado plains in distinctive ways. For Spain, the Colorado plains remained a defensive buffer zone that served as a haven for troublesome Indians and that distanced Santa Fe from French contacts. The French, in contrast, saw the region in less strategic and more utilitarian terms. The Plains Indians and resource base were readily incorporated into the expanding French trading network that had been steadily broadening across the North American interior for more than a century. Complicating these overlapping European spheres of influence were the Comanche, who were enjoying their own geopolitical ascen-

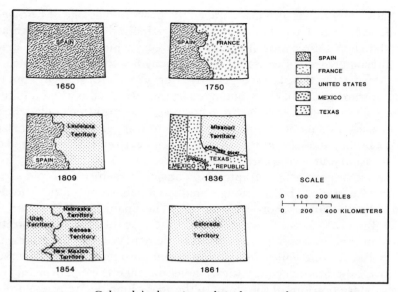

FIGURE 13. Colorado's changing political geographies, 1650–1861

dancy.[15] This new political force proved to be an ongoing and unpredictable Indian menace for New Spain's northern perimeter, and similarly, the Comanche mostly refused the friendly overtures of French traders, thus maintaining their independence from both European claimants to the region.

Colorado retained its peripheral status on the edge of the Spanish and French empires between 1720 and 1760 (see fig. 13).[16] An expedition of Spaniards led by Pedro de Villasur in 1720 reconnoitered eastern Colorado but was slaughtered by French-allied Pawnee in the Platte Valley. Villasur's defeat ended Spanish plans for extending their influence beyond Colorado's Arkansas Valley, but it also sent a signal to the French that encroachment to the south and west would be actively opposed by Santa Fe. Ironically, in the twenty years following the Villasur massacre, conflict between the two European powers was largely avoided, less from their own mutual efforts at peacekeeping than from the continued rise of the common Comanche threat. These Indians drove a broadening wedge between the two European nations that in effect encouraged their retreat from Colorado in the 1720s and 1730s. The relation between Spain and France, however, changed after 1739. In that year, brothers Pierre and Paul Mallet crossed the plains from the Mississippi Valley and initiated an era of irregular but significant trade with the Spanish at Santa Fe. In so doing, the French effectively redefined the role of eastern Colorado's plains. Now the

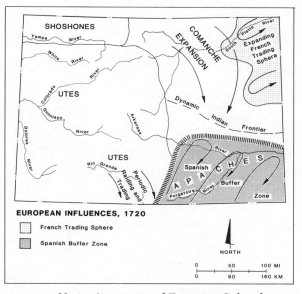

FIGURE 14. Native American and European Colorado, 1720

region became an active transit zone, a distance to be conquered between points east and west. The Mallets' pioneering efforts initiated a series of commercial contacts that lasted until 1752. Soon thereafter, the French exited the North American interior, leaving all of Colorado and much of the Great Plains under nominal Spanish control after 1760. But the Spanish did little to advance northward because the Comanche presence precluded any viable permanent settlement in the region.

One exception to this relative Spanish inactivity on its northern frontiers was the increasing frequency and importance of contacts between Santa Fe and the Ute settlements of southwestern Colorado.[17] Juan Maria de Rivera's 1765 expedition to Ute encampments along the Gunnison River was a key step in the effective incorporation of southwestern Colorado into the Spanish sphere of influence. Even more remarkable was the expedition of Francisco Atanasio Dominguez and Francisco Silvestre Vélez de Escalante in 1776. Their journey was designed to strengthen contacts with the Indians, spread Christianity, and establish an overland route to California. Their path took them into present-day Colorado south of Pagosa Springs in early August 1776 (fig. 15). For the next several weeks they toiled slowly northward to the Dolores River, then over the forested Uncompahgre Plateau to the Uncompahgre and Gunnison Valleys. From there they explored new ground, the first Europeans to record their impressions of Grand Mesa, the Colorado River, and the barren plateaus of northwestern

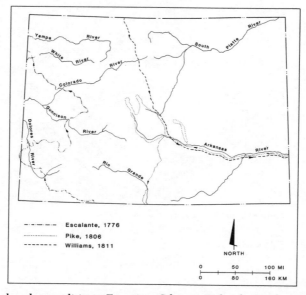

FIGURE 15. Colorado expeditions: Francisco Silvestre Vélez de Escalante (1776), Zebulon Pike (1806), and Ezekiel Williams (1811)

Colorado. Once they left the state, they circled west, then southwest through Utah and northern Arizona before returning to Santa Fe. Although the journey failed to establish a new road to California, the Spanish picture of western Colorado was greatly sharpened as a result of the journals, reports, and maps of the expedition.

Just as the Spanish were extending their influence across southwestern Colorado and throughout the Missouri Valley, the British and the Americans threw the Great Plains into a geopolitical quandary after 1780.[18] Initial problems for the Spanish centered largely on the British and their role in the upper Midwest. The British post at Prairie du Chien became the focus of an even more aggressive Anglo presence across the Plains. Spain responded with an increased number of exploratory and trading expeditions in the Missouri Valley in the 1780s and 1790s, successfully defending against any possible British commercial or military expansion.

Unfortunately for the Spanish, they were less successful in defending their northern flanks against the upstart Americans, who, by the turn of the century, were rapidly becoming a real and unpredictable threat in the West. European politics intervened further in 1800 when Napoleon obtained from Spain the retrocession of Louisiana in the Treaty of San Iledefonso. This had no immediate effect on Colorado, which remained effectively in Spanish hands, but when the French sold the entire Louisiana Purchase to the distrusted Americans in 1803, Spain's worst fears were realized: suddenly the Americans were knocking on the door of the interior West (see fig. 13).

Imposing American Control

The Louisiana Purchase ushered in a new era of expanding American influence across the western interior. Zebulon Pike's famous 1806 trek into the politically murky borderlands of the region was the initial American assertion of power within Colorado.[19] Although Pike was ostensibly seeking the headwaters of the Red River, the presumed Spanish-American border, it is widely believed that he was also instructed to find his way to Santa Fe, where he could reconnoiter the Spanish settlements at firsthand. Pike's approach followed the well-known path of the Arkansas River (see fig. 15). After failing to climb Pikes Peak, the party wandered west in the dead of winter, discovered they were in the upper reaches of the Rio Grande, and were subsequently captured by Spanish authorities and taken to Santa Fe before being later released. Pike's final report describing the adventure contained abundant information on the West, including Colorado. His well-known comparison of the Great Plains to the "sandy deserts of Africa" contradicted more optimistic images of the region.[20] Though Pike's reconstruction of Colorado's geography proved deeply flawed, the expedition effectively demonstrated American resolve to challenge Spanish claims along the edges of their newly acquired Louisiana Territory.

Other Americans made less-publicized inroads into Colorado, but the results of their efforts also contributed greatly to the ultimate imposition of American control.[21] Chiefly involved with fur trapping and wholesale trade, this early group of entrepreneurs saw new economic opportunities in the region that effectively though still informally linked Colorado with an expanding American economy. After 1804, an increasing number of American traders moved goods between St. Louis and Santa Fe, using both the Platte and Arkansas Valleys. Even more pathbreaking were the Colorado mountain men who searched the Rockies for furs. Trapper Ezekiel Williams journeyed deep into the mountains in 1811, his epic journey taking him through the heart of the little-known high country parks in the center of the state (see fig. 15). American activity in Colorado increased further after Mexican independence in 1821. The Mexicans actively promoted fur trapping in their northern interior and pushed for expanded trade with the United States along the famed Santa Fe Trail (fig. 16).[22]

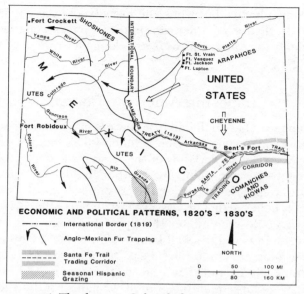

FIGURE 16. The dynamic Colorado frontier, 1820s and 1830s

More formal assertions of American control also increased by 1820. In 1819, Major Stephen H. Long became the head of a federally sponsored scientific and exploring expedition in the West (fig. 17).[23] But Long's trek deep into Colorado along the South Platte and Arkansas Rivers was also a powerful political statement of American presence deemed necessary by President James Monroe and his hawkish secretary of war John C. Calhoun. It was a message to both Native Americans and Hispanos that Anglo Americans were in the region to stay. Reinforcing this de facto extension of political control from the east was the Dodge expedition of 1835. Colonel Henry M. Dodge's dragoons followed Long's route by ascending the South Platte to the Colorado Piedmont, then cut south to the international boundary at the Arkansas River, and returned via the Santa Fe Trail to Fort Leavenworth. Dodge's expedition was an even more explicitly military maneuver designed to assert an American presence in the high plains Indian country.

American geopolitical interests in Colorado were again served by Colonel John Charles Frémont's remarkable journeys through the region between 1842 and 1845 (see fig. 17).[24] Frémont represented the increasing federal interest in the American West. In particular, Senator Thomas Hart Benton of Missouri felt that it was imperative to expand American influence to the Pacific, ultimately challenging Mexican claims in the South-

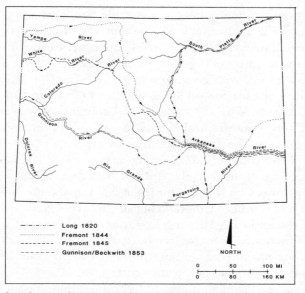

FIGURE 17. Colorado expeditions: Stephen H. Long (1820), John Charles Frémont (1844), Frémont (1845), and John W. Gunnison and Edward G. Beckwith (1853)

west as well as British interests in the Northwest. It was Benton that planned for Frémont's western expeditions to be carried out under the auspices of the recently organized Topographical Bureau of the War Department. The forays served both scientific and geopolitical purposes. Frémont's first expedition in 1842 reconnoitered a potential Oregon Trail in southern Wyoming. Two years later Frémont's expedition to California took him through Colorado both on the way west and on his return trip. In particular, Frémont's eastbound course led him across the little-known northwestern corner of Colorado and south through the heart of the mountain parks. The following year (1845), a second California trip, full of diplomatic intrigue, also took the "Pathfinder" through Colorado along a route that explored the Tennessee Pass country in the midst of the Rockies.

The significance of Frémont's expeditions for Colorado was threefold. Frémont's assertion of American presence portended trouble for Mexico. Indeed, Mexico was about to engage in and lose a war with the United States that succeeded in removing all Mexican claims to the region. Second, Frémont's broader goal of providing a reconnaissance to guide potential western settlement marked a distinct shift from the travels of Long or Dodge that defined the West in more purely scientific or military terms.

Third, Frémont's cartographers finally made public what a generation of fur trappers knew about much of Colorado's mountain geography. This vastly improved accuracy greatly aided subsequent expeditions and settlement in the region over the next twenty years.

The hasty exit of Mexico from much of the interior West in the late 1840s set the stage for several key geopolitical events in Colorado's pre–Gold Rush history. With the creation of Utah and New Mexico territories in 1850 and of Kansas and Nebraska territories four years later, Colorado became for the first time fully incorporated into the political geography of the United States (see fig. 13). As a result, a new mosaic of sprawling and mostly unsettled counties covered Colorado. The plains region suddenly was a far western hinterland of Kansas and Nebraska territories. Much of southern Colorado became a part of New Mexico, logical because of the enduring Hispano legacy across the area. Colorado's Pacific slope functioned as an eastern outpost of Mormon Utah, though local Ute Indians discouraged initial white settlement. Thus, by the middle 1850s, Colorado sat near the vacant center of the West, carved into four territorial pieces. Although it proved to be a peripheral region in all four of the western territories involved, the structure and mechanisms for settlement were in place.

As these geopolitical events unfolded, the federal government pushed for more formal economic development of the western interior. In a bold move, Congress in 1853 authorized a series of comprehensive Pacific Railroad surveys to identify the best transcontinental railroad route through the West.[25] The ambitious surveys were conducted roughly along the 47th, 38th, 35th, and 32d parallels to satisfy the variety of regional interests involved. The 38th Parallel Survey, led by Captain John W. Gunnison, crossed through the heart of Colorado via Cochetopa Pass and, while adding substantial amounts of valuable scientific and cartographic data on the region, found little to support Benton's argument for an easy passage across the interior West at that latitude (see fig. 17). The long-term impact of the surveys—to encourage the selection of an alternative 41st parallel route across southern Wyoming in the 1860s—actually reinforced Colorado's peripheral status in the West. Still, important new information was gleaned in the Gunnison survey to suggest that although Colorado's mountains were less than ideal for a railroad, they could be traversed, at least in an appropriate season.

The federal government also pushed for a changing relation between the United States and western Native Americans during the same period. Through the 1840s, Colorado's Indian populations and the slowly increasing trickle of traders and trappers coexisted across the region with relatively few difficulties. The Trade and Intercourse Act passed by Congress in 1834 controlled white and Indian contacts by requiring all white traders to obtain a license before venturing onto the Colorado plains.[26] Although some saw fit to ignore the act altogether, it did limit interaction between the two groups by designating American portions of Colorado as "Indian Country."

But such sweeping proclamations of western Indian freedoms changed for Colorado's native residents beginning in 1849.[27] In that year the government negotiated its first formal treaty with the Ute tribes in western Colorado. It was agreed that the Indians would stop their raiding and settle on assigned agricultural lands. Two years later, the Treaty of Fort Laramie redefined Indian relations on the east side of the Rockies. Most of the principal tribes were assembled by Indian agent Tom Fitzpatrick. In return for gifts and annuities, the tribes agreed for the first time to defined limitations in their plains domains and to acknowledge "the right of the United States Government to establish roads, military and other posts" within the region. In these two agreements, the status of Colorado's native peoples changed forever. No longer conceived of as equals to the whites and no longer free to roam as they pleased, the Indians inevitably resisted, especially after seeing treaty provisions repeatedly abrogated and their lands steadily chipped away by invading whites. Along with the territorial transformations of the 1850s, this new relationship with the Indians set the political geographical stage for the rapid American occupance of the region once gold was discovered.

Evolution of the Arkansas Valley Axis

Although Colorado remained on the periphery of western growth before the Pikes Peak Gold Rush, the region was not devoid of American settlement between 1820 and 1860. In fact, two zones of activity provided an important initial geographical infrastructure that was later greatly elaborated upon by the goldseekers. Not surprisingly, the Arkansas Valley evolved as one of these early centers of activity (see fig. 16). Ever since Archuleta's seventeenth-century reconnaissance of the Arkansas Valley east of Pueblo, the corridor functioned as a key entryway to both northern New Mexico and the southern Colorado Rockies. The commercial importance of the valley was enhanced greatly by the evolution of the Santa Fe Trail in the 1820s and by the growing fur trade tapping into the nearby mountains during the same decade. These economic factors and the valley's political role as an international boundary combined to promote the creation of a series of small trading and agricultural settlements during the 1830s and 1840s.

Forerunner to these more permanent Arkansas Valley settlements were seasonal hunting and trading camps established by Mexicans and Ameri-

cans.[28] In 1829, a small buffalo hunting party led by William Bent wintered
on the Arkansas River near Huerfano Creek. The group built a sizable
stockade from cottonwood logs and constructed a series of platforms to
cure strips of buffalo meat. Three years later John Gantt and Jefferson
Blackwell constructed another short-lived post nearby to take advantage
of the buffalo robe trade that was increasingly replacing the traditional emphasis on beaver. Taos-based deer hunters also ventured north into Colorado's Spanish Peaks and Sangre de Cristo Mountains. They spent several weeks gathering meat from temporary base camps before returning
home.

The construction of Bent's Fort, beginning in 1833, signaled a more permanent American presence in the Arkansas Valley.[29] Managed by William
Bent, his brothers, and the St. Vrain family, Bent's Fort represented the
spearhead of American commercial expansion in Colorado for more than
fifteen years. The fort's location on the banks of the Arkansas River near
modern-day La Junta revealed shrewd geographical reckoning on Bent's
part. The location was a common gathering point for central and southern Plains Indians, including Cheyenne and Arapaho from the north and
Kiowa and Comanche from the south and east. Its placement near Tim-
pas Creek also put it on the Raton Pass branch of the Santa Fe Trail, thus
ensuring ready commercial intercourse with Mexico while at the same
time benefiting from the security of being on American soil. Bent wisely
decided against a Colorado site closer to the mountains, correctly figur-
ing that the upland trade in beaver furs was being replaced by a plains-
based buffalo robe trade. Soon, a small collection of Mexican and American farmers were cultivating nearby garden plots to support the fort's
residents and to trade with passing travelers. After fifteen years, Bent destroyed the "Old Fort" at La Junta and relocated about forty miles downriver at the "New Fort" near Big Timbers. Bent continued at the New Fort
for another decade until the Indian trade declined in the late 1850s.

Upstream, the Arkansas Valley near Pueblo became a second and
slightly later focus of activity in southern Colorado.[30] By 1842 a small
group of ex-trappers and their mostly Mexican wives constructed a small
adobe settlement at the confluence of Fountain Creek and the Arkansas
River. Settlers grew a little corn and attempted to compete with Bent's
trade in buffalo robes, furs, whiskey, and tobacco. Soon, another settlement called Hardscrabble took shape even further upriver, near present-
day Florence. A third nucleus on the Mexican side of the border on Greenhorn Creek south of Pueblo also grew during the middle 1840s. Because
of their location in the foothills, these upriver settlements proved vulnerable to Ute raiding parties, which no doubt discouraged much growth. Another complicating factor in the region was the Mexican establishment of

the Nolan and the Vigil and St. Vrain land grants south of the Arkansas River in 1843. These huge grants attempted to extend more direct Mexican control over their Arkansas Valley hinterlands, thus limiting the lucrative but illegal trade that flowed through the area. Although no effort was made to develop these grants for over a decade, they precluded other individuals from seeking legal settlement in the region.

Beyond the Arkansas Valley axis, the same commercial forces encouraged the establishment of several other significant but temporary outposts.[31] One locus of interest centered in the South Platte Valley between modern-day Greeley and Denver (see fig. 16). Between 1836 and 1837, three small fur and robe trade forts were built near the South Platte River about twenty miles north of modern-day Denver. Each of these centers hoped to capitalize on the buffalo robe trade and represented overt challenges to the Bent and St. Vrain interests to the south. Not to be outdone, Bent's company established Fort St. Vrain in 1838. Managed by Marcellin St. Vrain, the post was constructed a few miles north of the other three forts and effectively extended the Bent interests directly into the Platte Valley. Within a few years, however, all the posts ceased operations and trading activities focused on Fort Laramie to the north or Bent's Fort on the Arkansas River.

Finally, to the west, the commercial fur trade encouraged the establishment of at least two additional trading posts during the 1830s (see fig. 16).[32] Fort Robidoux (or Uncompahgre) and Fort Crockett (or Misery) represented the first abortive attempts at permanent settlement west of the Continental Divide. Both were gathering points for mountain fur trappers. Antoine Robidoux built his post on the Gunnison River near Delta and by the early 1830s employed a sizable corps of trappers who dominated the western slope through the decade before seeing the trade decline in the 1840s. A second small trading post was built in Brown's Hole at Fort Crockett in the 1830s. Located along the Green River in northwestern Colorado, the site was a popular wintering ground for trappers and functioned for a time as a branch post for the Bent and St. Vrain interests. Little remained of the center, however, beyond the middle 1840s.

Developments in the San Luis Valley

A separate and quite different zone of pre-1860 settlement centered in the San Luis Valley. Less commercial and more agricultural, this nucleus represented a northward migration of Hispanic settlers up the Rio Grande Valley above Taos.[33] The process was uncertain and unsteady but produced by the 1850s a collection of small, enduring agricultural settlements that remain a part of the valley's cultural landscape. Hispano activity in the valley increased early in the nineteenth century. Sheep and cattle herds were driven seasonally into the region to take advantage of pastures along the upper Rio Grande and nearby creeks (see fig. 16). Early nineteenth-century travelers in the region reported that more than fifty thousand head of stock sometimes grazed in the valley. Attempts at more permanent settlement from the south increased in the 1830s when the Conejos land grant was issued to a group of Hispanos for a large portion of the valley west of the Rio Grande. Persistent Navajo and Ute raids, however, rebuffed their efforts to occupy the area. Even when a second land grant, the Sangre de Cristo, was awarded in the eastern valley in 1843, the real threat of Indian attack prevented stable settlements.

A second, more enduring settlement phase commenced in 1851. Political changes suggested increased levels of protection from the Indians. What had been an outlier of Mexico's little-protected northern flanks was now part of the United States and its new Territory of New Mexico. An 1849 treaty with the Ute provided some encouragement along with the 1852 establishment of Fort Massachusetts on the eastern edge of the valley. The fort was a stabilizing presence in the valley and was manned by one to two hundred American troops. Moved to nearby Fort Garland in 1858, the outpost protected south central and southwestern Colorado until the late 1870s.[34]

With the promise of an increased American presence and continued growth of Hispano settlements to the south, the San Luis Valley became a significant destination for migrating farmers and stockraisers.[35] Much of the valley became part of New Mexico Territory's Taos County in 1852. Ironically, it was not until Mexico lost political control of the region that permanent Hispano settlements were initiated on the former Mexican land grants. San Luis de Culebra, established in 1851 on the Sangre de Cristo tract, was soon settled by a group of Taos farmers. Charles Beaubien, principal owner of the tract, encouraged this move to develop his land. Soon, similar settlements sprouted at nearby San Pedro, San Acacio, Chama, and San Francisco. On the southwest side of the valley, the 1850s also saw the establishment of the towns of Conejos, Guadelupe, Ortiz, and Magote as the old Conejos grant was developed within the relative safety of Anglo military protection.

Typically, these small New Mexican–style settlements were established along better-watered side creeks near the mountains rather than in the center of the more arid valley. Early on, the Hispano pioneers established clusters of walled fortified plazas along such tributary watercourses. Settler homes, usually framed with cottonwood and pine logs and then covered by adobe mud plaster, were grouped contiguously around a central square where stock could be protected from Indians at night. The local church, school, and community storerooms were often found within the confines of the plaza or they made up part of the encircling protective perimeter. Less formally clustered placitas also appeared in some settings, operating as an informal hamlet containing a few families. Once a nucleus appeared, each male settler, based on his need or his ability to develop the land, was granted a narrow acreage that usually fronted the local creek and extended back to the nearby foothills. More intensive grain and garden crops were cultivated on the lower end of the long lot in the alluvial bottomlands and the hillier country upslope was used for livestock grazing and wood-gathering. Irrigation ditches distributed precious water through the settlement. Most farm holdings were small, under one hundred acres, and supported the immediate needs of the local population. Some settlers specialized in sheep grazing, making common use of larger acreage and extending a rural cultural tradition long associated with the Hispano occupance of northern New Mexico. By the late 1850s, between one and two thousand new migrants populated the valley, making it the most significant non-Native American nucleus in Colorado before the discovery of gold at the end of the decade. Ultimately, however, the Hispano expansion in the south was truncated by an unprecedented onrush of Anglo miners, merchants, and settlers who were destined in only a few years to produce a new economic and human geography across the region.

Mountain Geographies
1860–1920

The year 1858 began quietly enough across the Colorado Rockies. In May, the high country was still snowbound even as the eastern foothills blossomed with a new season of prairie wildflowers. A closer look, however, revealed events already set in motion that were to transform the human geography of the region. Prospectors were arriving on the Colorado Piedmont and probing canyons of the Front Range. Among them were three brothers from Georgia. William, Oliver, and Levi Russell were keen to test the rushing waters of the Rockies for color. Legends of precious metals in the region extended back to Spanish days and more recent rumors of discoveries sparked new enthusiasm. Initial failures convinced some in the party to return to the comforts of civilization, but the Russell brothers and their companions persevered and fell into a rich pocket of placers on Dry Creek near the site of modern Denver.

Although they quickly played out, these definitive finds ushered in a new era of geographical change for the Colorado mountains. Over the next forty years, a radically new network of connections reached deep into the mountains and linked a constellation of mining camps with the outside world. Created was a spatial system of roads, rail lines, telegraph poles, capital flows, and migration that organized the region's economic geography around the pursuit of precious metals, no matter how isolated the canyon or steeply sloped the mountainside. Concurrent with these changes was the establishment of a new social and cultural geography that gave mining centers such as Georgetown and Leadville a character quite unlike that of nearby lowland farming towns. Undoubtedly the most immediate and recognizable alterations in the region's geography were written across the cultural landscape. Miners did not engage in subtleties when a gulch proved productive or when a lode mine revealed telltale color. Mountain landforms, streambeds, and vegetation were dramatically transformed, literally overnight, in the name of harvesting gold and silver. More than a century later, the mountains still display the vivid reminders of how thousands of miners collectively altered the landscape in this tumultuous period of the late nineteenth century.

Creating a New System of Settlements

It is no accident that the economic geography of towns and transportation routes in the high country evolved quite differently than elsewhere in the state. The region's physical setting and the unpredictable nature of the mining economy produced a mountain settlement system that even today reveals its distinctive origins. The genesis of a mining settlement was related to the locations of the precious metals and the ability of miners to find them. Geology mattered: the configuration of Colorado's human geography in the mountains is in no small way related to the intricacies of mountain tectonics as well as to the erosional processes at work to redistribute some of the metals once they were created. The general arrangement of mining activities was thus inevitably wed to the geology of the state's mineral belt, which snakes from the Front Range south and west to the San Juans.

Mining in the Colorado mountains was inherently unpredictable, prone to repeated booms and busts. The imposition of an extractive and largely nonsustainable settlement system had fundamental consequences for the Colorado Rockies. As historian Patricia Limerick notes, rather than settling an area, mining ventures "picked up the American West and gave it a good shaking," and the resulting human geography reflects that fact.[1] The imposition of a new settlement system upon these mountain localities was unpredictably swift and almost always unplanned. As J. G. Pangborn reported in his *Rocky Mountain Tourist* in 1877, "The towns here are a good deal like asparagus, for, figuratively speaking, where you see naught but the bare ground at night, you the next morning behold a healthy and rapidly developing centre of business."[2]

The rush typically produced a haphazard network of muddy, half-finished roads, a social community with a daily, even hourly turnover in population, and a landscape that everywhere displayed the imprint of an impatient populace determined to unearth every golden fleck and nugget as quickly as possible. Argonauts became strung out for miles along a mountain stream. Incipient towns, often only a mile or two apart, quickly coalesced at several points in the district to serve the miner's basic needs.

Often, as boom turned to bust, the rush to get out was no less furious. Once a locale yielded its best color, population drained faster than spring runoff from an alpine snowfield. Most dramatic were the placer camps, which quickly exhausted the local alluvium, folded their tents, and moved on.[3] After a season or two, all that might remain on the landscape was a scattering of lean-tos and broken shovels. Sometimes the declines were slower, extending the painful process over a period of years, and there were examples, too, of placer boomtowns gone bust only to reemerge in later years in the glow of new mineral finds.

The reasons behind the cyclical life of the mining town were complex.[4] Large-scale structural influences in the mining economy certainly played a part. The overall tendency of the nineteenth-century American economy to be somewhere on the roller coaster between expansion and recession was magnified in the mining industry. But as important as the larger setting was in shaping the mining economy, local geography ultimately determined the success or failure of a settlement. If mineral discoveries were limited to surface placer deposits along and near the streams, these were exhausted in a season or two, spelling the end to a short-lived mining camp. Furthermore, the proximity of new booms over the next mountain range often accentuated the decline of an existing settlement already straining to satisfy the hunger of its residents for new color. One camp's success, therefore, hastened the demise of other nearby centers. Critical for more enduring urban survival was the sustained mining of underground lodes of gold or silver. These centers often matured into larger towns as they became foci of metals processing and offered an increasingly specialized array of economic and social services to the surrounding community. Over time, however, declining mineral grades and rising extraction costs often curtailed activity in these lode mining centers, too.

Given the hyperbolic life of the typical mining town, what were the keys for longer-term success? George Crofutt was undoubtedly on the right track as he pondered this question in his *Guide to Colorado* in 1885.[5] First and foremost, Crofutt recognized the importance of a continuing flow of capital into a mining settlement. Turn off the spigot of money for new mining ventures and a community shriveled on the vine. Success often depended upon a small network of local and nonlocal capitalists who became actively involved in controlling an interrelated set of investments in real estate, mines, and transportation infrastructure. Second, Crofutt cited the erection of accessible ore processing works as a key step toward greater permanence. Smelters increased the value of nearby ore by lowering refining costs. A growing cluster of smelters in a town guaranteed the center's increasing economic centrality for its tributary region. The smelters operated like magnets of activity, drawing ore from the surrounding high country. Last, Crofutt recognized the critical role of the railroad in furthering the fortunes of a Colorado mountain town. Without low-cost access to the outside world, how effectively could mountain ores flow to potential markets? Isolation was anathema to success in the mining business. The calculus of transport rates had clear and dramatic spatial implications for economic growth: where rail lines penetrated the high country and superseded expensive and less dependable stage lines and freight wagons, new corridors of potential economic activity were instantly created.

Suddenly, in a span of a few decades, the Colorado Rockies were engulfed by this new, highly unpredictable world of commodity capitalism,
of smelters and railroad investments, of boomtowns and sudden busts, of
landscape changes so fundamental that they dwarfed the modest human
impacts made over the prior ten centuries. In 1866 traveler Bayard Taylor,
recognizing the scope of change, wrote, "Colorado has been, alternately,
the scene of exorbitant hopes and equally extravagant disappoints. Out of
these violent reactions a new order of things is gradually being involved."[6]
Indeed, a new order—spatial, social, and visual—was forged in the Colorado mountains from these tumultuous beginnings. By the end of the
nineteenth century, the human geography of the high country little resembled the scene at the close of the 1850s.

Mountain Mining Centers, 1859–1900

Activity concentrated in the mountain region just west of Denver in the
first twelve months of Colorado's Gold Rush. Henry Villard's 1860 map of
the "Pikes Peak Gold Regions" provides an ideal early view of a western
American mining region still in its formative stages (fig. 18). The map accurately depicts early centers of development as well as the trails connecting these incipient nuclei with the Piedmont and the world beyond.
The title of the map notwithstanding, already evident is the emerging centrality of Denver, complete with its weblike road network stretching along
and east of the Piedmont as well as probing at several points deep into the
Front Range.

Several localities on the Villard map are worth a closer look to assess
the initial unfolding of the mining frontier. Travel almost due west from
Denver, as did reporters Henry Villard, Horace Greeley, and Albert
Richardson in the early summer of 1859. The rough road took the trio
quickly into the heart of the early excitement. One focus of frenzied activity was the Gregory Diggings at Nevada Gulch. Named after its discov-
erer, John Gregory, the Diggings lined the north fork of Clear Creek about
forty miles west of Denver. Gregory's original placer finds were soon followed by the discovery of quartz veins, which gave the camp potential staying power. The haphazard assortment of tents and mining claims became
the nucleus for the famed Gilpin County gold mining region and its emerging metropolis, Central City.[7] In 1859, however, all was in a state of flux.
Editor Greeley described the disheveled scene along Clear Creek: "As yet,
the entire population of the valley—which cannot number less than four
thousand—including five white women and seven squaws living with
white men—sleep in tents . . . cooking and eating in the open air. I doubt

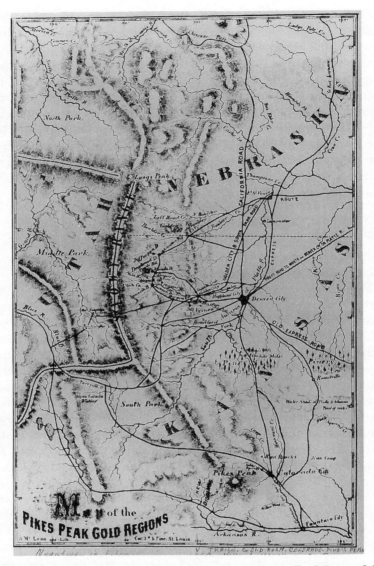

FIGURE 18. Colorado mining geography, 1860 (Source: Henry Villard, "Map of the Pikes Peak Gold Regions," St. Louis, 1860, Courtesy Denver Public Library, Western History Collection)

that there is as yet a table or chair in these diggings, eating being done around a cloth spread on the ground. . . . The influx cannot fall short of five hundred per day, balanced by an efflux of about one hundred."[8]

Nearby, Villard's map reveals other bursts of initial activity. Placer finds along the south fork of Clear Creek at Jackson Diggings and at Spanish Bar near present-day Idaho Springs spurred the successful discovery of quartz veins in 1859. Soon miners were spread along miles of the stream, marking the inception of the Clear Creek County mining region, which later became anchored around Georgetown, a dozen miles west of the original finds. To the north, up near the Kansas-Nebraska border, Boulder Creek sprouted yet another cluster of camps in the same year, and Boulder City and Golden Hill became a third nucleus of excitement as miners from Clear Creek and elsewhere swarmed over the accessible drainages of the Front Range. Particularly adventurous goldseekers found themselves in more isolated reaches of the Central Rockies even in that first brief season of 1859.[9] Villard's map reveals the initial probing into the headwaters of the Platte, Arkansas, and Colorado Rivers in a tangled knot of little-known high country west and southwest of Denver. Most of these interior strikes proved tentative and temporary because they were limited to placer finds, but they added to the rapidly growing base of geographical knowledge created in 1859 and demonstrated how swiftly a new spatial system could be forged in a rugged country previously beyond the pale of detailed exploration and permanent Anglo occupance.

Because of the frenzied mining in 1859 and the political fluidity of the Civil War era, Colorado quickly received formal territorial recognition in 1861 (see fig. 13). Ironically, however, many of the initial placer strikes played out in a year or two and contributed to a sudden depopulation of many of the camps even as the Territory was being established. Even in Gilpin County, where lode operations contributed to a steadier flow of gold, troubles mounted by 1863. In fact, that year marked a peak in gold shipments for the entire territory which was not matched for another decade.[10] Several problems contributed to the woes of the mining settlements. Much of the lode gold was locked in sulfur-rich rocks which resisted easy processing and many mining ventures ground to a halt until the technology could be found to process the stubborn ores. The flow of outside investment capital also slowed to a trickle in response to a speculative bust in Colorado mining stocks in 1864. Severe problems with the Plains Indians disrupted supply lines and further isolated the mining camps from the Missouri Valley. By 1868, however, hints of an economic turnaround appeared as chemical experiments yielded better results with the sulfur-rich ores, Native American resistance was crushed on the

Plains, and silver mining increased in importance, particularly in Clear
Creek County, near Georgetown.

A snapshot of mining production at the end of the decade reveals a
clear pattern (fig. 19). Tiny Gilpin County and the area around Central
City accounted for over 70 percent of the mineral production in the territory. Even with the challenges of the decade, Central City still claimed
more than two thousand residents, and over three thousand more lived
scattered in the nearby gulches and hills. The traditional focus on gold
mining in the county was already being supplemented by rising silver production. Neighboring Clear Creek County's silver ores also contributed
to its growing importance. Although gold placers petered out early in the
decade, silver ores discovered in the Argentine and Georgetown Districts
after 1865 attracted another rush of hopefuls into the area. By 1869, more
than fifteen hundred residents were evidence of the area's presumed
promise. Beyond these two centers of activity, placer gold still yielded uncertain returns in Summit and Lake Counties to the west and lode gold
and silver operations contributed to modest activity in nearby Boulder
County.

The years between 1869 and 1882 saw huge increases in mining activity. Older producing areas contributed to the gains. In the mining heartland of Gilpin, Clear Creek, and Boulder Counties, a maturing mining industry produced over four million dollars annually. The San Juan
Mountains in the state's southwest corner had their initial mining rushes
once native Ute Indians were removed and the area was opened to white
settlement in 1873. The lion's share of expanded activity, however, was focused in Lake County's Leadville area (fig. 20). Gold and silver production
in Colorado grew more than tenfold between 1868 and 1882, and Lake
County alone accounted for almost two-thirds of the output, principally
in rich carbonates of silver and lead.

Leadville's explosive growth in 1878 and 1879 is unequaled in the state's
raucous mining history.[11] Almost overnight, thousands of claims were
staked, hundreds of buildings were erected, and an abundance of fortunes
were made and lost as miners, merchants, and investors traded lies and
paper prospects. Underneath all the boosterism and hyperbole, however,
some of the state's richest carbonates gave sustained life and irregular
prosperity to a portion of the Colorado high country previously known only
for a brief placer gold strike in the early 1860s. By 1880 the population had
swelled to over 25,000 and more mail was flowing in and out of the new city
than either Saint Louis or San Francisco! And with this growth came
chaos, even in the basic business of supplying this mass of humanity with
food and daily supplies. Matters improved somewhat by 1881, when the
railroad's arrival in the two-mile-high metropolis increased the town's ac-

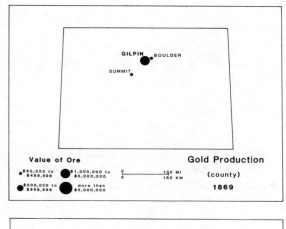

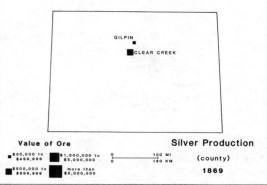

FIGURE 19. Colorado's major mining regions in 1869: *top*, gold; *bottom*, silver (Source: Charles W. Henderson, *Mining in Colorado* [Washington, D.C.: Government Printing Office, 1926])

cessibility to the rest of the world. The twelve smelters belching smoke and fumes symbolized Leadville's preeminence among Colorado's mining settlements. Some dreamers even proposed relocating the state capital to the carbonate camp high in the upper Arkansas Valley.

Leadville's success also affected adjacent counties. The flow of miners and investment capital washed beyond the borders of the upper Arkansas into the watersheds of nearby districts, both east and west of the Continental Divide.[12] Nearby Park and Chaffee Counties yielded steady flows of gold and silver. Most spectacular were the gains north and west of Leadville in Summit, Eagle, Pitkin, and Gunnison Counties. Here Leadville miners succeeded in expanding into dozens of new districts, among them Ohio City, Pitkin, and Tin Cup. By the late 1880s Aspen rose

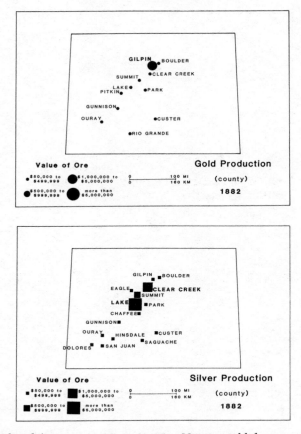

FIGURE 20. Colorado's major mining regions in 1882: *top*, gold; *bottom*, silver (Source: Henderson, *Mining in Colorado*)

to dominate mining production west of Leadville, the two cities forming a silver mining heartland across what had been one of Colorado's most iso-lated and inaccessible regions.

The San Juans in the southwest were the site of growth rates second only to the central Colorado experience. Taken together, these mountain counties annually produced another million dollars worth of gold and sil-ver by 1882. A lack of significant placer gold in the San Juans precluded the initial multiplication of mining camps. Instead, the general central-ization of retailing and smelting activities contributed to the consolidation of settlement into a few principal centers. Lake City and Silverton domi-nated activity in the upper Gunnison and Las Animas drainages, respec-tively, while nearby Ouray served the Uncompahgre country to the west.[13]

By the late 1880s newly opened regions in Dolores and San Miguel Counties also boosted such towns as Rico and Telluride into sudden, albeit temporary, prominence.

In the last decade of the nineteenth century Colorado's mining economy experienced tremendous local swings, a complex consequence of collapsing silver markets and the discovery of some of Colorado's last great mineral hoards (fig. 21).[14] An immediate cause of declining fortunes for many of Colorado's mining areas was undoubtedly the slump in silver prices and the associated national economic malaise that struck in 1893. Between 1890 and 1894, silver's price fell a third, crashing from one dollar per ounce to around sixty cents. Combined with the already declining output and quality of many of Colorado's silver mining districts, these larger economic factors spelled disaster for many mountain localities. Towns like Aspen, Leadville, Telluride, Rico, and Georgetown, all heavily dependent upon the flow of silver, were shaken to their foundations as mines closed, smelters shut down, businesses collapsed, and residents left to seek their fortunes elsewhere. Pitkin County is illustrative of the pattern: annual silver production in 1891 and 1892 averaged seven million dollars. During the following four years, production was barely half that, and silver output continued to spiral slowly downward thereafter. The county lost almost one quarter of its population between 1890 and 1900. Similar stories were played out in many other mountain localities in the tough years of the 1890s.

All was not bleak in Colorado's mining economy, however. Surprisingly, overall mineral production in the state rose over 20 percent between 1889 and 1896. One explanation was the latter-day boom at Creede in southwestern Colorado's Mineral County. The discovery of the Amethyst Mine in the summer of 1891 followed by the completion of rail connections just four months later propelled the Creede District into prominence. Given the timing of the silver price collapse, Creede's largest silver output came and went in 1892, but even with falling prices, continued lode finds made Creede a major silver producer through the balance of the decade.

Of even greater importance to Colorado's overall mineral output, however, was the resurgent gold mining industry. Annual production almost quadrupled from four million to fifteen million dollars between 1889 and 1896. Much of that increase came from another new bright spot on the map: Teller County and the Cripple Creek gold mines became the site of the state's last great mineral rush in the early 1890s. By 1896 this cluster of settlements accounted for half the state's output of gold bullion. Ironically, this final hurrah for the nineteenth-century mining industry was set almost in the shadows of Pikes Peak, the Colorado high point originally and incorrectly identified as the center of the mining excitement in the late

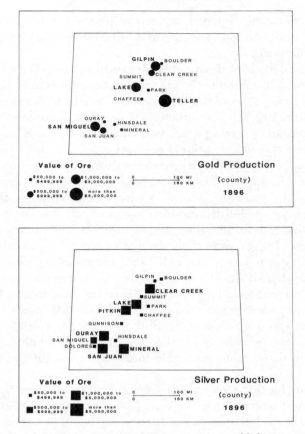

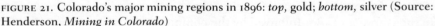

FIGURE 21. Colorado's major mining regions in 1896: *top,* gold; *bottom,* silver (Source: Henderson, *Mining in Colorado*)

1850s. By the end of the 1890s, tiny Teller County supported almost thirty thousand residents, almost twice the number remaining in any other mining county in the state.

New discoveries in other gold districts around the state brought life back into areas once in the shadows of surrounding silver mining activities. Significant gold output continued in Clear Creek, Gilpin, and Boulder Counties. San Juan and San Miguel Counties, their silver production tarnished, were revived with important lode gold finds in the early and middle 1890s. Similarly, Leadville, though suffering mightily amid the carnage of silver's lost glitter, managed to benefit from expanding gold production. The close of the nineteenth century thus brought complex spatial patterns of decline and renewal across Colorado's mountain regions. In particular, the shift from silver to gold mining produced a new geography of costs and benefits that brought pain and economic contraction to some districts and a new lease on life to others.

Mountain Mining Linkages, 1859–1900

In addition to dozens of new settlement nuclei in Colorado's high country, elaborate linkages connected these blossoming centers of activity with each other and with the outside world. Given the dynamic commercial nature of the mining economy, such spatial linkages were critical to the survival of any promising camp. Success was tied to the geographies of roads, rails, supply lines, telegraph and telephone poles, and flows of investment capital that wed even the most remote alpine locale to the affairs of the busy world below.

In the early years, roads, however poor and primitive, funneled people and supplies into new settlements and provided essential avenues for outbound bullion. But building wagon routes through and over the Colorado Rockies took time, money, expertise, and, in some cases, sheer imagination.[15] Narrow and rocky canyon walls plagued roadbuilders as they followed streamcourses into the mountains. Blasting, bridging, and boulder-clearing their way through rugged canyons, builders often ran up costs that exceeded forty thousand dollars for a few miles of crude roadway. A second constraint to mountain travel involved ascending the high passes between the stream valleys. Steep grades, unstable slopes, and mercurial climates complicated the chores of route construction. Once constructed, these lofty links were hardly superhighways. Stony Pass, connecting the early San Juaners to the San Luis Valley on the east, was infamous for its hazards. Wagons were lowered down gulches with ropes and guided across steep treeless slopes with logs and extra teams attached to prevent all from sliding seemingly off the face of the earth.

Financing these essential connections was an ongoing challenge. Federal and territorial monies did not contribute to road construction here as they did elsewhere on the frontier. Rather, local interests—communities and private entrepreneurs—largely shaped the geography of the mountain road system in Colorado.[16] To begin, members of a newly created mining district often pooled their labor and a bit of capital to survey, cut, and lay out critical local links. Once towns were platted and county seats selected, these government bodies hired unemployed miners to work on key routes. Taxes were levied and county bonds sold to pay surveyors, axmen, and laborers.

Private roads also played a key role, notably in the Clear Creek–Gilpin–Boulder County heartland during the 1860s and across central and southwestern Colorado in the 1870s and early 1880s.[17] Hundreds of toll road companies were incorporated, beginning in 1859 with the first routes into the Front Range. Particularly pivotal in the San Juans were the activities of an industrious Russian Jew named Otto Mears.[18] Mears constructed hundreds of miles of toll roads that became the key outside links for Telluride, Silverton, and Ouray (fig. 22). Although the rudiments of Colorado's mountain road network were largely in place by the 1880s, the resulting web of high country links was hardly the articulation of some grand design. Rather, it was the sum of innumerable local decisions made by miners, entrepreneurs, and toll road builders.

Initial geographies of commercial freighting into the Colorado high country linked these mountain roads with established trading networks on the Plains.[19] Stage and freight companies such as the Leavenworth and Pikes Peak line, the Overland Stage, and Wells Fargo were closely connected to the Missouri Valley, where existing trails, railheads, and urban centers served as natural jumping-off points for the mines. Kansas City, Independence, Leavenworth, Atchison, Saint Joseph, Nebraska City, and Omaha funneled food, dry goods, mining tools, and milling machinery along the well-known Platte River and Arkansas River routes to Denver and thence to the mountains. By the mid-1860s, twenty-seven firms were engaged in the Plains freighting business, employing five thousand wagons, seven thousand mules and horses, and more than twenty-five thousand oxen. Denver's role as a transshipment point in the freighting business was pivotal: wagons arrived at the Front Range and goods were stored there by wholesalers before being resold or forwarded to the mountains.

But even as new Colorado roads were probing the high mountains in the 1870s, railroads were appearing on the eastern Plains (fig. 23). As this new technology worked its way into the mountains, it reinforced major linkages between successful existing centers. Rarely did a railroad penetrate an area previously beyond the pale of a wagon road. Yet once constructed, a railroad fundamentally reconfigured costs and revenues for a mining settlement.[20] The result was a predictable stimulus to economic activity that, though certainly no guarantee for success, brought great advantages to adjacent settlements. Also not to be underestimated was the psychological boost provided to a community newly served by the railroad. Indeed, local boosters saved their greatest hyperbole for mining settlements targeted for railroad links to the outside world.

The economics of railroad geography also imposed chronic problems. Terrain sometimes imposed unscalable limitations, and even if the challenges of mountain canyons and passes could be navigated, the grim realities of financing and ongoing profitablilty often intervened to send even the boldest of western railroad entrepreneurs to their doom.[21] The startup

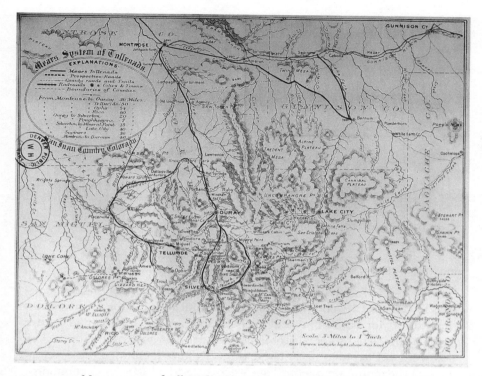

FIGURE 22. Mears system of toll roads, 1885 (Courtesy Denver Public Library, Western History Collection)

costs of a rail line were many times that of a simple wagon road. Financing involved elaborately marketed stock sales and debt offerings that often proved incompatible with the railroad's ability to make a profit. In addition, the cutthroat nature of railroad capitalism and the lack of coordination in the making of the state's rail links meant that many deserving communities went unserved by a single line while other towns reveled amid multiple and competing rail companies.

Before tracks were laid into the mountains, however, connections to the national rail system were established across Colorado's eastern plains. This critical development galvanized the commercial importance of the Piedmont and enhanced its regional status as an entrepôt between the American urban system on the east and the mountain mining settlements to the west. By the time Colorado became a state in 1876, three "great thoroughfares" linked Piedmont cities with the East.[22] Denver's primary role in the state's rail system was assured in June 1870 when the locally chartered Denver Pacific was completed to Cheyenne. Two months later, the

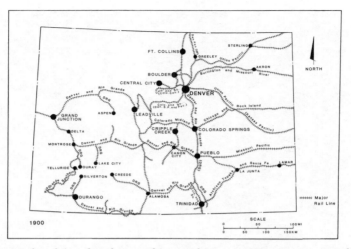

FIGURE 23. Colorado's railroad network: major lines, 1900 (Source: Los Angeles Saturday Post, *Unrivaled Atlas of the World* [Chicago: Rand McNally, 1901])

Kansas Pacific Railroad was completed from the east, providing direct access to Kansas City and Saint Louis. The southern Piedmont offered an opportunity for a third line, and the Atchison, Topeka, and Santa Fe, after being stranded by financial problems during the early 1870s, finally pushed westward to Pueblo in 1876. These three avenues facilitated the development of the mountain region. They were the critical arteries of commerce and capital necessary to enlarge the scope of activity in the mining districts, especially as major lode and smelting operations replaced the transient excitement of the frontier placer era.

Early railroad penetrations into the mountain regions first focused on the early mining areas west of Denver.[23] Completed in 1872, the Colorado Central followed Clear Creek Canyon and linked the Denver-Golden area with Black Hawk in Gilpin County. After switching to the narrow gauge line at Golden, passengers pierced the range front and ascended to the mining region. Within a few years, short extensions to the Black Hawk line reached nearby Central City and Georgetown. One other major penetration of the northern Front Range used the narrow defile of the South Platte Canyon southwest of Denver. The Denver, South Park, and Pacific Railroad, after initial financial woes, resumed construction in the late 1870s, reaching into South Park by the end of the decade.

To the south, other pre-1880 construction efforts offered new avenues into the mountains. The Atchison, Topeka, and Santa Fe line, after building up the Arkansas Valley, pushed southwest over Raton Pass into New Mexico in the late 1870s. Its chief competitor in the southern region was the Colorado-born Denver and Rio Grande Railroad, brainchild of Gen-

eral William J. Palmer. Palmer, always the enterprising entrepreneur, saw
the wisdom of constructing a north-south Piedmont line between Denver
and Pueblo. That route was completed in 1872 and was extended later in
the decade over spectacular La Veta Pass west of Walsenburg. By 1880
Palmer's narrow gauge line had reached the San Luis Valley and was
preparing to penetrate the San Juans to the west.

Colorado's impressive mountain rail system was extended and further
interconnected in the 1880s. By the middle of that decade, Colorado's high
country was better served by rail lines than any other mountain region of
the American West. Leadville's meteoric rise became quickly entwined
with the extension of key railroad lines into the upper Arkansas Valley. Railroad capitalists knew that tapping into the rich carbonate camp high in the
Rockies would yield handsome returns. Several lines successfully battled
their way to the prize by 1884. Beyond Leadville, the Denver and Rio
Grande Railroad dominated new connections across the Continental Divide (fig. 23).[24] A major line over Marshall Pass tapped into the growing
fortunes of the Gunnison region. The route then passed westward to
Grand Junction, another railroad-inspired settlement, ultimately linking
with other Denver and Rio Grande lines in the San Juan country. During
this same era, a second major thrust across the Continental Divide took
the Denver and Rio Grande directly north from Leadville, over Tennessee
Pass, and down the upper Colorado River Valley to Grand Junction, where
it linked up with the Gunnison Valley route. The Colorado River link also
had the advantage of accessing the rich opportunities of the Aspen silver
mining region during the boom times of the late 1880s. Although the line
faced competition in the central mountains from the Colorado Midland
Railroad and others, the overall network of transport linkages in that region still owes a great deal to the decisions and designs of General Palmer
and his creative high country engineers.

The rugged San Juan region in southwestern Colorado was another
setting for important post-1880 rail construction (fig. 23). Again the long
arm of the Denver and Rio Grande Railroad dominated the network, both
by laying key lines to major communities and by making investments in
major centers and important mining-related activities.[25] From the south,
the Denver and Rio Grande established a link to Durango, their company-
platted town along the Las Animas River. By 1882 the famed narrow-gauge
line to Silverton was completed, providing the first connection into the
heart of the San Juans. Other company links came from the north. The
railroad used their Gunnison Valley corridor to build into Ouray by 1887
and to Lake City by 1889. The colorful toll road builder Otto Mears provided temporary competition in the late 1880s and early 1890s. He raised
capital to build a rival line into the western San Juans that connected Du-

rango and Ouray via links with Rico and Telluride. But Mears's Rio Grande
Southern Railroad, completed in 1891, lasted only four years before it collapsed during the silver panic and was bought out by the larger Denver and
Rio Grande. Still, the Mears network reinforced Durango's role as the primary service and manufacturing center in the southwest.[26]

In addition to roads and rail lines, new flows of information, including
everything from personal letters and newspapers to business documents,
connected mining communities with the world beyond. Several variables
controlled the arrival of information in the mining camp.[27] The migrating
habits of the miners themselves shaped the news and rumors they took
from camp to camp. Rates of population turnover were high in the summer, but winter's isolation often meant fewer fresh arrivals and a dearth of
news. A similar seasonality frequently plagued mail delivery. And exorbitant rates precluded casual correspondence: a single letter might cost
twenty-five to fifty cents in the early years. Miners were hungry for general news, and the arrival of newspapers from Saint Louis, Chicago, New
York, and San Francisco was a much anticipated event. Once a camp became established, local papers provided information, though much of
what appeared on their pages was taken directly from the national press.

Technological changes also shaped flows of information.[28] The telegraph sped communications, especially for important business-related
transactions. Because it was much cheaper and easier to construct a network of telegraph poles than it was to engineer a narrow-gauge railroad,
telegraph lines often made it into a new mining camp within two or three
years of settlement. Transcontinental telegraph service began in 1861,
nearly a decade before the Union Pacific rail line was completed, and by
the 1880s, an integrated network connected most mining districts in the
state. Just as the Denver and Rio Grande Railroad dominated so much high
country travel, so Western Union shaped the geography of telegraph connections. Further technological marvels—namely, the telephone—offered even more remarkable communications improvements to the region
in the last twenty years of the century. The larger mining towns even
boasted their own telephone exchanges as an additional claim to the fruits
of modernity.

Also of critical importance were outflows of mining-related information, both factual and otherwise. The geography of these information flows
affected subsequent patterns of investment into the high country. Migrating miners and the correspondence they sent to friends and relatives
were important sources of news. For example, reports both confirming and
denying the riches of the region flooded the Missouri Valley in 1858 and
early 1859, adding to the general confusion and excitement as newspapers
and emigrant guide publishers picked up the stories.[29] The significance

of the early discoveries received added weight in the summer of 1859 when a collection of respected eastern newspaper editors traveled to the region and reported the level of activity with their own eyes. As the years passed, newspaper and popular magazine accounts continued as a major source of news for the American public as mining regions such as the San Juans, Leadville, and Cripple Creek aroused national curiosity.

Of growing importance were reports and guides published by Coloradans that contained more specialized information on the mines.[30] Several important books and pamphlets detailing the mining industry were published in the 1860s. Authors such as Ovando Hollister, Joel Whitney, and William Blackmore provided detailed descriptions of mining districts and technologies. An even greater outpouring of expertise appeared between 1870 and 1885 as observers such as George Crofutt, Frank Fossett, and Thomas Corbett published guides to the territory and state. Adding to the din were pamphlets, books, and maps published by Colorado towns, counties, mining companies, and railroad operations.

Flows of incoming capital were closely tied to these information networks and sources. Many early placer miners simply brought their grubstakes on their back, but even at the outset, larger-scale investments can be tracked into the gold camps. One measure, provided by an 1861 guide to Colorado's gold regions, identifies the geographical origins of quartz mill operations in Clear Creek County.[31] These small crushing mills were ubiquitous on the early mining frontier and represented an initial step in the ore refining process. Of the 105 mill operators reported in the county in 1861, 60 percent migrated from Illinois, Iowa, and Missouri. This strong Missouri Valley and Midwest source region for early Colorado migration and investment is also evident in the transportation network and freighting patterns of the period.[32]

The growing role of larger capital institutions and the increasing need for complex mining and milling machinery encouraged subsequent shifts in the geography of investment into the Colorado mountains.[33] After 1870 economic linkages with the Missouri Valley declined in relative importance. By the late 1870s the pace of mining company incorporations increased tremendously, spurred by external investment from major eastern cities. In Clear Creek County over 30 percent of the out-of-state corporations setting up business between 1864 and 1879 were based in the nation's financial capital, New York City. Philadelphia, Trenton, and Chicago also contributed significant capital to the county's mining economy. Even London investors were represented through several corporations, although most foreign investment into the state's mining economy came after 1880. Smaller towns, especially in the Midwest and Middle Atlantic regions, were also important sources for mining capital. The Graham Silver Mining Company, formed by investors from Sioux City, Iowa, for example, controlled fourteen mines in the San Juan country by the late 1870s.

The importance of in-state capital also needs to be appreciated in reconstructing the patterns of investment into Colorado's mining regions.[34] In 1880, 58 percent of the state's large, deep-mine operations were owned by Coloradans. Although some of this capital was probably funneled through a local Denver base from source areas beyond the state, the figure is still a reminder that, by the late 1870s, an in-state population of almost 200,000 (including 35,000 in Denver) served as a considerable base for investments in the mining districts. Local capitalists also had the advantage of proximity, suggesting that the quality of information they acted upon was often superior to that flowing out-of-state or overseas. Frequently these entrepreneurs made integrated business decisions that linked investments in mining, manufacturing, rail lines, and trade. Denver dominated this in-state investment geography with strong linkages in the mining sector to virtually every producing region in the mountains. Golden, Colorado Springs, and Pueblo established small, tributary spheres of investment, generally into regions directly west of each center. Finally, the larger mining towns themselves acted as sources of capital for newly expanding districts nearby. Leadville dominated such intraregional activities, especially into neighboring Gunnison, Park, and Summit Counties.

The Mining Townscape

The visible impress of thousands of new mountain residents dramatically altered the high country landscape after 1860. One focus of change was the mining town itself. Although every mining townscape expressed the unique aspirations of its residents, it also reflected many familiar economic needs and cultural values of the American Midwest, since that region served as the previous home for so many of the miners. Certainly some people experienced "a clean page to begin anew" as they arrived on the western scene, but collectively the communities and the cultural landscapes these immigrants created were cultural transfers from east of the Missouri.[35] Still, both the natural setting and the heightened social fluidity of the Colorado mining town provided a distinctive regional flavor. These towns were dominated overall by the straightforward goal of making quick money. But there were also additional impulses apparent to anyone who cared to look, signs on the landscape that more permanent communities were in the making.

The mining townscape included several defining elements. Town layouts generally differed depending on the natural setting, the degree of early planning, if any, and the extent and nature of the town's subsequent growth. The first miners on the scene simply pitched their tents and blankets in any available spot. Early descriptions of placer camps mention their strung-out pattern, paralleling a major streamcourse for a mile or more. Typically, however, the fruits of unplanned growth were reshaped and reorganized when local townspeople, often led by a group of investors and boosters, formally established a plat with designated lots and streets. In some cases the plat preceded significant settlement, while in others it came within a year or two of occupance.

Local topography exerted a strong influence on the layout of the mining center.[36] A stream often bisected the town, complicating the size and shape of lots and the configuration of streets. Terrain also shaped the overall layout. If presented with a choice, surveyors selected open, level sites upon which a simple grid could be established. This rectilinear bent was deeply ingrained in the American urban planning tradition, and the Colorado mountain town was no exception. J. G. Pangborn's description of Silverton captures the look and geometry of the mining town blessed with an open and expansive site: "The town is laid out as a parallelogram, a mile in length from north to south, and a half mile in width. The streets running north and south are 100 feet wide, lined with artificial courses, through which water from Cement Creek constantly flows. The cross streets are but 20 feet less in width, and the whole area is divided into 112 blocks of 24 lots each."[37]

Other sites were less amenable to manipulation. For example, the layouts for Cripple Creek, Telluride, and Breckenridge each had to cope with the realities of such natural impediments as steep slopes, narrow valleys, and disruptive streamcourses.[38] Undoubtedly one of Colorado's most convoluted layouts was the Black Hawk–Central City townscape in Gilpin County, where, according to one observer, there wasn't "enough level ground in these two cities to accommodate a circus tent."[39]

Georgetown's layout was more regular and spacious than Central City's but more constrained by its local setting than sprawling Silverton. The town survey included a little over 637 acres and averaged half a mile in width and one and a half miles in length.[40] Within a few years, the town grew to fill the upper Clear Creek valley, and houses and other mining structures began to creep up the sides of the adjacent hills (fig. 24). The overall layout focused on the familiar surveyor's grid, although the curving course of Clear Creek and the presence of steep slopes disrupted the rectangle in several places. Nonetheless, the Georgetown plat and the prevailing planning patterns that characterized many of the towns displayed strong links to urban traditions in the Midwest and East.

Even amid the mountainous terrain, town thoroughfares and buildings appeared familiar to most newcomers. The town was focused functionally

FIGURE 24. Georgetown, Colorado (Courtesy Denver Public Library, Western History Collection)

and visually around its commercial street or district. Again, local site constraints sometimes imposed themselves, giving downtown Central City, for example, a particularly cavernous look (fig. 25). More often, however, Main Street was wide, with sufficient space for wagons, horses, and pedestrians. Trees or urban parks were often missing initially because the available timber was quickly harvested and the mercantile mind-set considered such finery less than essential.[41] Streets were usually unpaved, often muddy, and almost always riddled with piles of trash. Once the center became an established town of a thousand or more settlers, there was an almost continuous line of varied commercial buildings on both sides of the street, their false fronts adding an air of permanence to the place and the blizzard of large and small signs advertising everything from billiards to books. Wooden sidewalks added further respectability to the townscape, with larger mining cities even adopting flagstone, brick, or concrete sidewalks and streets that were graveled, paved, or bricked.[42]

Construction materials in the town also reflected the evolution of the mining settlement from its initial status as a temporary camp designed to extract quick wealth to a more permanent community that could become an enduring home for a stable family-oriented population. Initial built landscapes featured tents, rough bough-covered log cabins, and crude unpainted frame board shanties. If the camp survived beyond this infant stage, hewn lumber and coats of paint began to make an appearance, especially in the commercial block. Within a few seasons, given sustained growth, truly dominant urban businesses, hotels, and public buildings featured brick and stone that superseded the older, often false-front frame construction.[43] Building size and height also increased over time. Whole blocks of integrated brick construction often characterized the principal commercial district, and the early one- and two-story frame businesses soon gave way to three- and four-story office buildings, banks, and hotels. These improvements were not acts of serendipity; they are best seen as conscious attempts on the part of their creators to fashion an urban landscape that declared its permanence and progress to all who happened upon it.

The commercial architecture of these mining towns suggests the propensity of builders to reproduce known styles from the East rather than be terribly innovative in the West.[44] The room layouts and V-notching patterns that held together early single-pen log structures resembled many examples of the time from the Midwest and Upland South, although the

FIGURE 25. Downtown Central City, 1864 (Courtesy Colorado State Historical Society)

western versions often had their principal entrance placed on the gable end, perhaps to shed heavy mountain snows. The larger false-front frame buildings also borrowed from older traditions, essentially replicating patterns from innumerable small towns in America. Although often simple and unadorned in the West, even these structures and their subsequent brick and stone counterparts often sported stylistically informed Greek Revival window detailing, Italianate door lintels and keystones, or a bit of Queen Anne flourish at the cornices. They added substance to the simple front-gable buildings that lined Main Street. All these features reinforced the stability and familiarity of the townscape to those arriving from more settled parts.

Several key community institutions were visually prominent in every mining town, and their presence symbolized the permanence and promise of the settlement. The public school was one essential initial commitment to community. As one historian of Clear Creek County suggested, "Probably the best criterion of the progress and permanence of a town is furnished by the reports of its public schools."[45] In Telluride, the building of the first wood-frame schoolhouse in 1881 was a richly symbolic act.[46] After a successful bond issue was voted on, three thousand dollars was put into the erection of the structure. By the mid-1890s, a larger population of young people and an expanded local investment of twenty-nine thousand dollars meant that an even more substantial brick schoolhouse could be built. Indeed, where a town's growth facilitated new investment, the shift from wood-frame construction to brick or stone increased the visual dominance of the school and announced to all that the community believed in the virtues of educating its youth.

Religion complemented education as a cornerstone of community in the mining town.[47] Itinerant preachers were a common initial solution for incipient centers. Early meetingplaces used by these interlopers varied from a saloon to the town hall or schoolhouse. In some cases, especially in smaller settlements, a modest wood-frame community church was built and used by a procession of ministers. More commonly, particularly in larger centers, each major denomination focused on the erection of its own church, which became the local symbol of its authority on the landscape. As with the schoolhouse, these structures offered key links to accepted and traditional forms of community. On Colorado's mining frontier, Methodists, Episcopalians, Congregationalists, Presbyterians, Baptists, and Catholics were frequent participants in community-making. Once built, churches housing these congregations became social centers for well-defined subgroups in the community who were bound by religion, ethnicity, and commitments to improvement projects. The structures themselves resembled the one-room schoolhouse in general layout.

Gothic embellishments such as decorative bell towers, lancet and rose windows, and scalloped shingles often distinguished these structures on the landscape.

The mining town hotel also communicated messages to both residents and travelers.[48] Early hotels were mere log boardinghouses, often constructed with funds pooled from several initial investors. Larger framed multistory examples followed, borrowing from the rambling tavern and roadhouse traditions of the East. Later brick and stone hotels reached three or more stories, occupied a central block or corner lot in the town, and mimicked in their urban finery the substantial hostelries of more settled lands. In the larger centers, the grand hotels often imported French chefs, invested in expensive wine cellars, and generally aspired to the gaudiest in European pretense. Once established, thousands of visitors passed through their doors, making them key meetingplaces where local capitalists and businessmen swapped stories and investments with outsiders.

Simpler in form but no less essential in function were the saloons of the mining town.[49] These ever-present landscape features lined blocks of the settlement, with such colorful names as Barney Harvey's Keg House in Georgetown and Telluride's notorious Pick and Gad, which combined a downstairs watering hole with upstairs pleasures of the flesh. The saloon served more generally as a male gathering place in the town where mining gossip was exchanged and where visitors could get a quick pulse on local affairs. Although exteriors were often nondescript two-story wood-frame or brick buildings, saloon interiors included a variety of elaborately carved bars, gambling tables, live music, waitresses offering the grog of the day, and food that varied from the indigestible to the less-than-sublime.

Communicating greater stability, at least on the surface, were mining town banks, which became expected additions to any settlement with a population of several hundred or more. Banks facilitated the economic maturation of the mining town by lending money, purchasing precious metals, and becoming involved with local stock and real estate transactions.[50] Usually occupying prominent sites in town, banks were early aspirants to brick and stone construction, eschewing the economies of simpler wood-frame design. As with other larger commercial structures, banks borrowed from the popular Romanesque and Victorian traditions of the late nineteenth century. They also participated in the construction of block-long building fronts, which added to the stability and appearance of many Colorado mining towns, especially after 1880.

Finally, the modest offices of the local newspaper must be recognized for their role in shaping a place-based community identity. Often combined with the services of the town printer, the newspaper was a window on the local scene as well as the larger world. It served many purposes: the newspaper informed the population about local events and news; reprinted stories from larger newspapers, which kept residents up-to-date on national and global affairs; and, more generally, operated as a booster for the settlement, reporting the latest tales, both factual and fanciful, from the surrounding high country.

Beyond these half-dozen townscape features, many other visual cues pronounced the success and maturation of the larger towns. Beginning in the boom years of the late 1870s and 1880s, centers such as Leadville, Aspen, and Central City further proclaimed their aerie sophistication with the construction of elegant brick or stone opera houses. At the very least, a theater or two brought culture to the town. In addition, although urban parks were always in short supply, larger centers made an effort to plant trees along main avenues and to bring a touch of greenery to a landscape that had often seen its native verdure stripped at the outset. Finally, the arteries of infrastructure marked progress in many mining towns, especially after 1880. Major centers supported municipal water supplies, an increasing maze of overhead electrical and telephone lines, and street car networks to connect suburbs to the central portions of the town.[51]

Beyond the commercial heart of the mining town sprawled the residential landscape. The gender gap typical of the early years was vividly revealed in the sizable number of miner's hotels and boardinghouses that were the mainstay of bachelor life in the town. Men could arrive, stay for a week or a month, and at least have a roof over their head and an evening meal. Initial canvas accommodations gave way to two-story frame buildings, often subdivided into eating, drinking, and living quarters. Longer-term residents built their own homes, but there was little interest in prettying up the landscape or in holding to a set of nonexistent building codes. Collections of cabins and shacks also crept up gullies and nearby slopes beyond the formally platted centers and served as simple one- or two-room homes for the early miners.

Later housing for the common folk was derived from eastern or midwestern roots—the ubiquitous rectangular frame cabin was often augmented after 1880 by more elaborate cottages boasting varied floor plans and with greater attention paid to external detailing.[52] Even more substantial residences were constructed on highly desirable town lots. Local leaders and growing numbers of families built Victorian frame homes, complete with the Gothic, Italianate, or Queen Anne add-ons of the time. Over the years, the elite increasingly distinguished themselves on the landscape, displaying in the size and layout of their residences the typically new-won wealth garnered in the mines or related investments.

The residential landscape was typically segregated by wealth and ethnicity.[53] Clearly defined neighborhoods distinguished the "good" and "bad" parts of town. Georgetown, for example, was bifurcated into a socially superior Upper Town of better, larger homes and a string of ramshackle cabins and shacks that defined Lower Town along the streambank. Railroad districts often became a similar home to a town's poorer residents in such larger centers as Telluride and Breckenridge. Social segregation frequently included nonresidential activities as well. Better parts of town played host to the school, churches, and better-quality stores and hotels while activities on the "other side of the tracks" featured a preponderance of saloons, dance halls, and bawdy houses.

Further complicating the mining townscape were clusters of distinctive ethnic groups that collected along particular residential blocks, especially in the poorer sections. Larger groups, often including German, Irish, and Cornish residents, also maintained their ethnic identity by establishing social clubs and meeting halls.[54] The greatest discrimination was usually reserved for blacks, Chinese, and Hispanic miners and businesspeople; these groups were compelled to cluster in neighborhoods well beyond the bounds of the town's "better" folk.

Another characteristic of the mining townscape was the development of true working-class neighborhoods, a phenomenon of the larger and later centers where most residents were no longer independent prospectors but instead labored in large numbers as industrial workers in mines and smelting operations.[55] Echoing the industrialization process in the East, these workers lived in simple mass-produced housing often supplied by the employer usually within walking distance of the mine or milling facility. A nearby lodge or union hall provided such neighborhoods with a locus of community. Aspen, for example, changed in the middle 1880s as large and well-capitalized mining ventures overwhelmed the opportunities for small-time claimseekers. Workers clustered in communities near the major mines, the rhythm of their lives set to the clock and shift schedules. Such routinization marked a dramatic shift from the wanderlust that often guided early-day prospecting, and it dramatically displayed the imposition of industrial-scale capitalism and the increasingly complex connections being forged between the area's resource base and those who came to claim it.

Further defining the character of these new labor communities were the unions that rose to represent the mineworkers in the last twenty years of the nineteenth century.[56] In fact, it was a rare town that avoided disruptions and strikes once the unions established themselves. Activist Michael Mooney, veteran of a variety of eastern labor conflicts, successfully organized a strike in Leadville in the spring of 1880. Mooney and the miners called for better wages, shorter hours, and healthier working conditions. Although the Leadville strike failed to win concessions, the Western Federation of Miners organized a more successful effort in Cripple Creek in 1894. Hardrock labor activity culminated over the following decade as the union's advocacy of a statewide standard of improved conditions for mineworkers met increasing resistance. Particularly bloody clashes between 1902 and 1904 failed to win lasting victories for labor as state militia, private police, and armed vigilantes combined to defeat union interests in both the mining and the smelting communities. The era, however, did redefine forever what it meant to be a Colorado miner, and the resulting labor communities within Colorado mining towns differed sharply from the more individualistic and entrepreneurial assemblages of argonauts that marked the beginning of mining within the state.

Mining's Impact upon the Land

In the last forty years of the century, mining wrought an unparalleled transformation on the mountains that still marks the scene today. Within the Colorado Rockies, both federal land surveys and the institution of the mining "district" facilitated the disposal of the public domain and the marking of claims. Claim-filing practices in the territory became fairly standardized, often using a model developed in Gilpin County's Gregory Mining District. Miners established boundaries of their district on the public domain and defined the type and dimensions of allowable claims. Placer claims along creeks usually extended for one hundred feet and ran from bank to bank, while mountain or lode claims were generally bounded by a rectangle that was often fifty feet wide and one hundred feet long. All claims had to be accurately recorded by a designated secretary within the district. Once the General Mining Law of 1872 established federal norms, even more standardized placer and lode claims were common across the territory. These included the potential consolidation of early placer claims into larger units, thus superseding prior developments, as well as a policy that allowed anyone to develop lode claims for fifteen hundred linear feet along the course of any mineral vein, including lateral extensions. In the tortuous geology of Colorado minerals, this provision produced a legacy of legal battles and challenges.[57]

Mining refashioned landforms and drainage patterns of the Colorado high country. By definition, placer mining involved landscape change: materials were dislocated, searched for metals, and redeposited elsewhere, literally turning the country upside down.[58] Simple placer mining produced modest alterations as stream gravels were sifted for color, creating a gulch landscape piled high with hummocks of discarded cobbles and sediment. More elaborate changes were wrought with the construction of boom dams, which released a flood of water on downstream placers in the hope of unearthing previously hidden treasures.

Even more telling was the impact of hydraulic mining, a process that applied water under high pressure to dislodge entire hillslopes of gravel deposits (fig. 26). Even the usually ebullient western promoter L. P. Brockett was left nonplussed by the scene when he wrote, "It is impossible to conceive of anything more desolate, more literally forbidding than a region which has been subjected to this hydraulic mining treatment; boulders of all sizes are scattered over the surface, and around them coarse gravel, incapable of sustaining vegetation; the streams are filled up with a fine clay . . . the whole vista is one of extreme desolation and ruin."[59]

Water was essential at every step of the way in placer mining.[60] From simple panning to hydraulicking, placer miners needed water to sift gravels. This meant that stream drainages were literally redrawn overnight. Everywhere on the landscape, water was manipulated and moved to suit miners' needs. One pioneering example was Gilpin County's Gregory Consolidated Ditch Company, which constructed a ten-mile ditch to guide precious water into the upper gulches of North Clear Creek. Even with donated labor of hundreds of placer miners, the ditch cost one hundred thousand dollars to build, complete with elaborate lateral extensions that served several areas being worked for gold. In nearby Summit County, observers reported hundreds of miles of ditches and flumes crisscrossing the high country by 1870, including the "Great Flume," which totaled twenty-one miles of twisting and branching water lines. Downstream, discarded gravels and sediments produced new streambanks, and soaring sediment levels in previously pristine mountain streams made a mockery of such appellations as Blue River and Clear Creek.

Underground lode mining operations produced less extensive landscape changes, but there was no mistaking the activity on a myriad of Colorado mountainsides.[61] Brown and yellow tailings piles marked entrances to innumerable shafts and tunnels of the underground mines, mute symbols of a livelihood that was literally turning the country inside out. For the vertical shaft mines, an additional feature was the gaunt headframe structure that held the hoisting and cables for the men and equipment bound for below. Shutes and storing bins facilitated the transport of ore via wagons or rail cars to nearby milling facilities that were usually located on the canyon floor or on lower slopes.

Vegetation was radically altered by mining activities. Every phase of nineteenth-century mining consumed wood in great quantities: placering stripped riparian sites within days; hydraulicking denuded slopes for decades; lode operations demanded wood for headframes, shaft houses,

FIGURE 26. Modifying the landscape: hydraulic mining in Summit County (Courtesy Colorado State Historical Society)

and tunnel supports; milling and smelting plants voraciously consumed whole hillslopes; and mining towns needed large amounts of sawtimber for building and waste wood for heating. In addition, frequent fires, the result of both accidental and purposeful burning, ravaged thousands of acres of high country forests in the last half of the nineteenth century. These changes did not go unnoticed. Although Horace Greeley remarked the slopes around Central City were still "densely wooded" in 1859, fellow traveler Albert Richardson commented that "through the whole day, the forests resound with the sound of the choppers' axe."[62] The results of such ambitious activity were soon apparent (fig. 27). By 1866 traveler Bayard Taylor scanned the same scene, noting, "The view of the intersecting ravines . . . and the steep, ponderous mountains which inclose them,

has a certain largeness and breadth of effect, but is by no means pic-
turesque. The timber has been wholly cut away, except upon some of the
more distant steeps, where its dark green is streaked with ghastly marks
of fire."[63]

The longer-term consequences of mountain deforestation were apparent by the end of the century.[64] Indeed, part of the impetus behind the
creation of federally managed forest reserves in 1891 can be traced to the
growing national perception that traditional users, particularly miners,
were laying waste a vast national resource. Many within the region felt direct effects of the destruction in later years as they saw the cost of wood
soar for building, milling, and smelting. Increased gullying and erosion on
surrounding mountain slopes were also vivid testimony to the complex impact of deforestation on the local ecosystem. Remarkably, many of the
same slopes fired and denuded of vegetation during the late nineteenth
century have recovered much of their tree cover today, dulling though not
erasing the mark of the mining era upon the Colorado landscape.

Mountain fauna also felt the brunt of the miners' presence. Native
American hunting grounds were decimated as big game and small found
their way into the gullets of hungry prospectors.[65] In particular, wildlife
populations around such major centers as Central City, Leadville, Aspen,

FIGURE 27. Modifying the vegetation: deforestation around Central City in 1866
(Courtesy Denver Public Library, Western History Collection)

BOSTON AND COLORADO SMELTING WORKS.

FIGURE 28. Modifying the atmosphere: the Boston and Colorado Smelting Works, Black Hawk (Courtesy Denver Public Library, Western History Collection)

and Silverton became major casualties. Undoubtedly, riparian environments were the most radically impacted when placer mining utterly reworked entire river valleys. Mammals dependent upon streamside vegetation had to browse elsewhere, and fish populations were dynamited when miners tired of the more traditional hook and line. In addition, the flood of sediments and pollutants poisoned many fisheries out of existence. Finally, widespread alterations of mountain forests altered thousands of acres of habitat for birds, mammals, and insects, compelling rapid redistributions of wildlife in the Colorado mountains.

The air itself bore the gritty impact of mining. Simply the thousands of fires and stoves used for heating and cooking created a hefty pall of smoke over many a mining town, particularly on cold winter days when local inversions held pollutants in. Most dramatic were milling and smelting centers, where vast quantities of black smoke filled the sky. Leadville, Durango, and Aspen all suffered, but the most infamous vapors lurked above the belching ore-processing facilities at Black Hawk, where travelers reported the atmosphere dank with fumes and smoke (fig. 28). Even with gasping lungs, however, Black Hawk's populace pointed with pride to the smoke-filled skies, arguing that it was a small price to pay for the industrial success enjoyed by the town.[66]

The Changing Mountain Economy, 1890–1920

The last decade of the nineteenth century marked a shift in the settlement geography of Colorado's mountainous heartland. Although the basic spatial structure of towns and transport linkages remained intact, three forces converged after 1890 to reshape the economic base, population geography, and cultural landscapes of the mountain zone. First, a longer-term structural decline in the metals mining and processing industries began in the 1890s. This reversal of fortunes had many consequences for both Colorado's mountain populations and its natural environment. Second, the growing importance of tourism between 1890 and 1920 reshaped many mountain localities in ways designed to attract and serve the needs of a growing array of visitors, including many from America's expanding middle class. Finally, the federal government's role in directly managing public lands within the mountain zone increased greatly after 1891 as a growing number of forest reserves were created in the state and as battle lines sharpened between prodevelopment interests versus those desiring to conserve and preserve the high country environment.

By 1920, even though mining's mark still dominated Colorado's mountain geography, these other impulses were widely displayed across the high country, and they marked a lasting evolution that persisted through the remainder of the twentieth century. Most broadly, the changes indicated a move away from the commodity-based industrial capitalism so dominant in transforming the region's human geography between 1860 and 1890. As the public sector grew more powerful and as amenity-driven demands for mountain resources replaced and in some cases displaced traditional mining operations, Colorado's mountain heartland was reflecting broader structural shifts at work in the American economy and political system after the turn of the century. The resulting cultural landscapes proved to be much more complex and diverse than those of the late nineteenth century. Indeed, the mosaic of land uses that evolved in the Colorado mountains displayed the increasingly divergent paths being taken by those who came to invest, manage, or live within the region.

The Decline of Mountain Mining, 1893–1920

Imagine a cloudless night high above the Colorado mountains in early 1893. Far below, twinkling lights reveal the size and location of dozens of Colorado mining communities. Leadville and Aspen glow brightly at the center of the mountain backbone while other clusters shimmer across the San Juans far to the southwest. Nearer Denver, the steady beacons of Gilpin, Boulder, and Clear Creek Counties continue to shine. To the south, a new constellation of gold camps is taking shape just west of Colorado Springs in the Cripple Creek region. As ubiquitous and promising as they appeared, however, the settlements within our gaze were soon jarred by the Silver Panic of 1893, and recovery thereafter for many mining centers was only partial. Global competition also increased as new mines were opened in Canada, Alaska, South America, and Africa.[67] Added to this was the reality that precious metals mining was not a sustainable activity and that many Colorado mines had already reached peak production.

Settlements specializing in silver were hit hardest after 1893 because of continued low prices until a brief uptick during World War I. The challenges of lower-grade deposits and rising labor costs also meant higher outlays for silver mining companies. Gold producers also saw mining costs rise, but production declines of the yellow metal were less dramatic than those for silver. Although the Cripple Creek stampede of the 1890s represented an important new gold strike, most of the older producing regions saw the quality of deposits decline as the easy color was removed from placer and lode operations. Technology mitigated the slump: by 1900, new processes of cyanide leaching made it viable to develop lower-grade deposits in some districts while in others huge dredges were constructed along watercourses to work the gravels. Although they were successful for a time, even these new leaching and dredging techniques could not reverse the nonrenewable nature of the resource or the fundamental shifts occurring in the global economy.

One global trend did benefit Colorado's mountain mining economy for a time. Rising demand and prices for a variety of base metals, including zinc and lead, accompanied the ongoing industrial expansions in Europe and North America. Many of Colorado's silver mining districts were rich in these two base metals. With zinc and lead output in the state increasing sevenfold between 1896 and 1917, many old silver mining towns received a new lease on life.[68] This expansion was highly cyclical, however, with production rising between 1900 and 1907 only to fall back with declining prices. Another uptrend lasted between 1910 and 1913, and a third expansion accelerated in 1916. Even with such volatility, this new demand for industrial metals slowed the decline of many mining communities. Growing demand for molybdenum, a metal used to strengthen steel, even gave birth to the new settlement of Climax during World War I. The end of the war, however, brought a severe contraction to all mining operations within the state. Declining output accelerated in 1920 as lower prices removed incentives for producers. Indeed, for many Colorado mining towns the Great Depression was already under way a decade before the stock market crash of October 1929.

Every mountain mining nucleus felt the unsettling effects of dramatic global metals price fluctuations between 1893 and 1920. The result was that many of the twinkling lights so apparent in 1893 were extinguished by the end of World War I. Smaller and more marginal centers with peak populations under one thousand people became the prime candidates for ghost-town status. Generally, the larger urban areas fared best, but even their lights burned more dimly by 1920 as mine closures and uncertain metals markets led to long-term population declines.

For some mountain localities, the story of tough times began before the turn of the century. The initial shock wave that arrived with the crash in silver prices early in the 1890s led to significant though selective declines in mountain populations by the turn of the century (fig. 29). Important silver mining districts in Pitkin, Clear Creek, and Custer Counties declined between 1890 and 1900, and such major mining centers as Ouray, Aspen, and Georgetown enjoyed their peak populations late in the nineteenth century.

The overall geography of metals production in the mountains fluctuated widely between 1893 and 1920, but the general trend indicated the ebbing import of mining in the state. A comparison of gold and silver production for the years 1896 and 1920 reveals basic shifts in both the level and location of production (fig. 30; see also fig. 21). Annual output stood at $15 million in 1896, peaked with the height of the Cripple Creek boom at nearly double that in 1900, and then declined to $7.5 million by 1920. Teller County's dominance remained unchallenged throughout: often it accounted for more than two-thirds of the state's output. Mine closings elsewhere reduced the number of significant gold-producing counties from thirteen to seven by 1920. Silver's story was even bleaker: the 1896 output, already hurt by the panic, remained around $15 million, with Lake and Pitkin Counties accounting for about half that total. By 1920, Colorado's silver mining industry produced less than $6 million annually, with the key Leadville region contributing less than a quarter of its former output.

Declining metals output led to a major urban exodus within the region. Consider the leading mining towns of Leadville, Aspen, Central City, Georgetown, and Cripple Creek. Those five mining metropolises boasted a combined total of more than thirty thousand residents in 1900. Twenty years later their collective populations shriveled to less than ten thousand stubborn survivors. Central City's story was typical.[69] The metals economy, mostly oriented around underground gold mining, began to suffer by the late 1880s as the costs of pumping water out of mine tunnels rose and as technical complexities associated with more mineralogically complex ores added to the headaches of mine owners and smelter operators. Many mines were bought out by larger corporate interests and consolidated under new ownership between 1890 and 1910. A similar process occurred in the smelting business, particularly with the organization of the huge American Smelting and Refining Company in 1899. Central City's Boston and

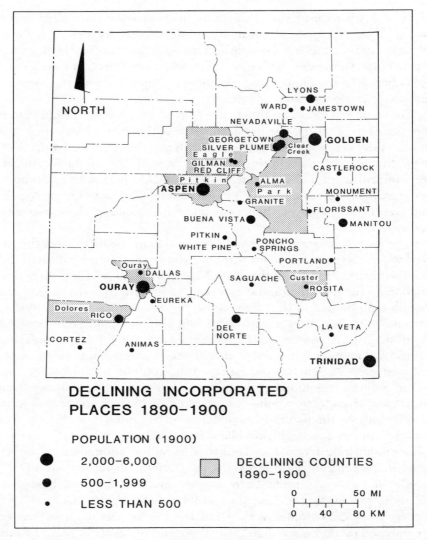

FIGURE 29. Colorado mountains: declining incorporated places between 1890 and 1900 (Source: United States, Bureau of the Census, *Eleventh and Twelfth Censuses of the United States*, 1890, 1900)

Colorado smelter complex burned in 1909 and closed a year later, accelerating production declines. Railroad service to the area was curtailed in 1917 and ceased entirely after 1925.

The cultural landscapes of these mining centers vividly revealed the strains of economic distress.[70] Shingles curled and peeled from structures. Abandoned buildings went unpainted, eventually burning, collapsing, or simply wasting away in the harsh mountain environment. Property values for both residential and commercial real estate inevitably headed lower as miners and townspeople drifted elsewhere. Cemeteries and schoolyards became overgrown with weeds, and communities scrambled to hold onto teachers, clergy, and physicians. Successful mining operations became fewer in number and larger in scale as the overall workforce declined and was increasingly replaced by new equipment and technology. Similar changes affected smelting operations as consolidation in the industry and as technological innovations eliminated marginal producers and concentrated activity in the hands of a few large corporations. Again,

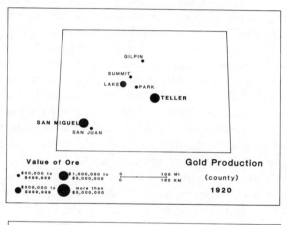

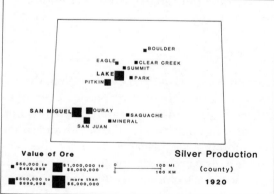

FIGURE 30. Colorado's major mining regions in 1920: *top*, gold; *bottom*, silver (Source: Henderson, *Mining in Colorado*)

the elimination of "excess" labor in the smelting business produced hardships in many industrial communities oriented around metals processing. Unemployed workers, half-empty neighborhoods, and idled equipment marked the success of a corporate strategy designed to maximize the efficiency of operations and the size of stock dividends.

Intriguingly, the same forces that led to significant population declines and community distress contributed to the beginnings of a selective environmental recovery for Colorado's mountain zone.[71] In the initial boom period, rapid deforestation denuded Colorado's mountain slopes. Recovering forests of aspen, spruce, fir, and pine began to change the look of the land as building and mine construction ceased in many areas after the turn of the century. At the national level, more productive forest lands in the Pacific Northwest and South made Colorado's marginal timberlands relatively less valuable for general building purposes. By the 1920s improved fire control on public lands also contributed to fewer forest fires. Turn-of-the-century dredging operations took longer to recover, but even dredge ponds filled with sediment and revegetated with time. Other topographic transformations related to mining also blurred after several decades: placer gravels partially resorted themselves along stream bottoms and tailings piles were gradually reworked downslope. Not all the impacts of mining were readily reversible, however, and some of the environmental consequences are being played out upon the modern landscape. One chronic problem that continues to haunt the region today involves the percolation of snowmelt and rainwater through closed and flooded mines, thereby leaching toxic heavy metals into the surrounding stream systems. One of the American West's largest environmental cleanup efforts in the late twentieth century related to such a problem in the upper Arkansas Valley near Leadville, a reminder of the persistence of mining's mark upon the Colorado scene.

The Switzerland of America

Colorado's mountain core was shaped by more than the miner's pick and shovel in the last half of the nineteenth century. Even in the 1860s an alternate vision of the high country appeared in the form of romanticized descriptions and paintings that extolled the health and sublimity of the territory's rarefied mountainous landscapes. Tourists who wandered the hills in search of mountain pleasures were not disappointed, and soon, with the aid of vigorous promotions, Colorado acquired a national, even global reputation for its alpine amenities.

This response to the Colorado mountains emphasized a different form of consumption from that of mining. Miners literally devoured the moun-

tain landscape, using the earth's very fiber to satisfy the needs of an expanding global economy based on industrial capitalism. Colorado's evolving tourist economy also consumed mountains, but in the form of scenery
appreciation and outdoor leisure activities. This variant represented
broader shifts in culture and economy that pointed to the emerging mass
consumer culture of the twentieth century. This shift produced new
mountain settlement patterns, distinctive landscape features oriented
around meeting the needs of the touring public, and an entire popular culture of enduring written and visual images that dominates the way Americans experience Colorado's mountainous environs today.

Several complementary impulses—some national, others local—fueled tourism's meteoric rise within the Colorado high country. Before 1890
only America's affluent could afford the time and expense of the extended
trip west necessary to indulge in Colorado's alpine attractions. The more
leisured class, born from the successes of mercantile and industrial capitalism and craving new delights beyond the yacht clubs of Newport, Rhode
Island, and the hotels of the Catskills, set the tone for Colorado's first quarter century of tourism. Their impact, particularly in such places as Colorado Springs, cannot be underestimated. After 1890, however, growing
numbers of ordinary Americans also came west for pleasure—first by train
and then in their automobiles—and this deluge fundamentally changed
the scope and impact of tourism within Colorado.[72]

An evolving cultural milieu in America set the stage for the nature-ori-
ented tourism that formed the core of Colorado's appeal. The aesthetics
of Romanticism, grounded in such writers as Samuel Taylor Coleridge and
William Wordsworth, included an enhanced appreciation for wild and
sublime landscapes. The Romantic movement in America, epitomized in
the mid-nineteenth century by the untamed landscape paintings of the
Hudson River School, appealed to Americans; in contrast with Europe,
much of the North American continent had an abundance of "wilderness"
that still overwhelmed and challenged. Experiencing such natural settings
firsthand became nothing less than a pilgrimage to a new array of sacred
places. Indeed, as such cultural historians as John Sears and Anne Hyde
have speculated, such a quest for sublime scenery and the associated
growth of early tourism were all part of a process through which Americans—always closely linked to the land—were developing a new cultural
identity through landscape images, images that acknowledged the providential character of the American encounter with the natural world.[73]

The West in its raw and unfinished state, full of natural wonders, was
an ideal setting to apprehend such landscape images. Colorado booster
William Byers aptly described the encounter in 1863 as he accompanied
landscape painter Albert Bierstadt into the Front Range west of Denver.

After an onerous mule trip into the alpine amphitheater below Chicago Lakes, Byers noted that the painter was unable to control himself any longer: "Patience vanished, and in nervous haste, canvass, paints and bushes were unpacked and a couple of hours saw, under his skillful hands, some miles of mountains, hills, forests, and valley reproduced with all its vivid coloring, and the cloud shadows that were sweeping over it."[74]

Without effective promotion, however, Colorado's mountain treasures might have remained more in the background. Bierstadt's early trips to the territory and the important paintings he produced, along with the constant boostering of Coloradans like Byers, formed a widely repeated imaginative response to the Colorado Rockies that emphasized the sublimity and beauty of the high country wilderness (fig. 31). Other early observers set the tone for the decades of ever-ebullient popular magazine pieces, railroad promotions, and resort advertisements that followed. One persisting theme in visual and verbal descriptions of the Colorado mountains centered on their favorable comparison to the European Alps.[75] Evident in Bierstadt's style was a landscape imagery shaped by European experience, and such parallels also guided commentator Bayard Taylor in 1867 as he observed that "no external picture of the Alps" could compete with the "breadth and grandeur" of the Front Range north of Colorado Springs. Similarly, the title of Samuel Bowles's description of his summer travels— *The Switzerland of America: A Summer Vacation in the Parks and Mountains of Colorado* (1869)—suggests the growing popularity of the alpine analogue.

Another essential component in cultivating Colorado's wildness was ironically its very accessibility. By the 1880s, the state offered Americans an ideal combination of spectacular natural wonders along with the benefits of convenient and comfortable access. As historical geographer Valerie Fifer has noted of tourists: "They favoured towering peaks, steep passes, and narrow gorges; they wanted their Rocky mountains high, all around them, and seemingly impenetrable—provided that in fact they were nothing of the sort, and that the way ahead had already been opened safely, comfortably, and with the minimum of delay."[76]

Both Denver and Colorado Springs became key tourist gateways to trips into the nearby mountains. Colorado tourism received a big boost in 1883 with the completion of the Denver and Rio Grande's line linking Denver directly with Salt Lake City and points west. Transcontinental travelers could see the state's Royal Gorge west of Pueblo, thrill at the prospects along the Continental Divide north of Leadville, and traverse western Colorado's canyon country, all on their way to the West Coast.[77] In addition, Colorado's extensive network of narrow gauge lines, constructed to serve the mining industry, became essential corridors of movement for moun-

FIGURE 31. The artist's view: Albert Bierstadt, *Estes Park* (Courtesy Denver Public Library, Western History Collection)

tain-bound tourists. Without the ease and convenience of these railroads, travelers would have halted their westward journeys in the urban hotels and perhaps limited their mountain experiences to day hikes and short stage trips. With the railroads, tourists could enjoy the pleasing mix of wild nature viewed from a safe prospect. They could also marvel at the genius of human developments in such spectacular environments as they gazed upon mountains conquered by mines, smelters, and railroad grades.

Before 1890 tourist experiences in mountainous Colorado were mainly the purview of the elite. With the completion of the transcontinental railroad by 1870, monied Americans increasingly came west to sample the richness and variety of scenery, new resorts, and novel experiences such a journey usually offered. No fundamental landscape changes accompanied this early tourist era within the Colorado mountains. The basic settlement pattern and visible scene remained dominated by mining. Wealthy travelers to Colorado limited their expectations of opulence and fine hotels to cities like Denver and Colorado Springs, and even there they were not always pleased with what they found.

Mountain excursions focused upon four types of activities. From early territorial days onward, a small group of mainly male travelers sought the more primitive stimulants of hunting, fishing, and climbing. A larger group, more family-oriented and inclined to remain along the rail corridors, simply wished for a view of Colorado's scenery and natural wonders, a touch of the sublime from the prospect of the Pullman car. Some of these sojourners did get out for a short camp "outing," and the railroads offered convenient lists of outfitters, small resorts, and ranches that catered to the needs of those hungry to "rough it," albeit briefly.[78] A third attraction, particularly for the more infirm or health-conscious, was the pilgrimage to the hot springs resort, already a well-established tradition in Europe and the eastern United States. Finally, many visitors simply enjoyed trips to the mining settlements, particularly if the route took them along some tortuous narrow gauge rail line that threaded its way through canyons and over mountaintops. The imposition of railroad technology upon the Colorado high country created a predictable set of aesthetic responses. An entirely new geography of "conquerable curiosities" was produced in this interplay of natural scenery and the feats of human engineering that lifted the visitor into formerly inaccessible territory.

What were the focal points of a turn-of-the-century itinerary into the Colorado mountains? For most visitors, Denver and Colorado Springs were comfortable Piedmont gateways, and each urban center supported an array of pleasures and attractions. Nearby slopes and canyons of the northern Front Range offered opportunities to reach the mountains. Many who came to Colorado for a taste of the sublime, including writers and artists, visited the most humanized and oft-visited part of the Rockies as they probed the mountains west of Denver and Colorado Springs. Immediately west of Denver, varied mountain canyons and prospects, the mining centers of Central City and Georgetown, the medicinal waters of Idaho Springs, the railway engineering eccentricities of the Georgetown Loop, and the alpine scenery of Chicago Lakes were immensely popular.[79]

West of Colorado Springs, people were encouraged to visit the therapeutic facilities at Manitou Springs and to ponder the sandstone outcrops at the Garden of the Gods.[80] Somewhat more vigorous were short rides and walks into North and South Cheyenne Canyons, where sublime waterfalls and towering canyon walls were sure to please. For the truly adventurous, a network of winding trails challenged Pikes Peak, although visitors were sure to find pleasant wayside stops and camps along the way. One "must-see" attraction by the mid-1890s became the Cripple Creek gold camps that boomed just west of Colorado Springs. The popular Short Line railroad counted more than fifty thousand tourists along its Colorado Springs to Cripple Creek route in the summer of 1902.

Beyond Denver and Colorado Springs, more adventurous travelers discovered other attractions.[81] Northwest of Denver, the Estes Park region gained an early blueblood fame for its comfortable guest ranches and an estate and resort promoted by the earl of Dunraven. Enchanted by the region during visits in the early 1870s, the earl later purchased over eight thousand acres of land in the area and opened the English Hotel there in 1877. By the 1880s Estes Park had become a popular summer resort, famed for its local hunting, fishing, horse trips, and mountain climbing.

Further west, another cluster of guest ranches, camping spots, and summer resorts took shape in the vicinity of Grand Lake and at nearby Hot Sulphur Springs in Colorado's Middle Park. Even in territorial days the area attracted the attention of outdoor enthusiasts, and Denverite William Byers was enamored with its resort potential. The area advertised its excellent hunting, fishing, and boating, and the hot springs appealed to healthseekers. Further west, Glenwood Springs emerged as a far larger hot springs resort. Stanley Wood's popular guidebook *Over the Range to the Golden Gate* (1912) called Glenwood Springs "the pleasure and health resort of Colorado," full of "scenic grandeur" and with hot springs that were "phenomenal, innumerable fountains" sure to cure one's ills. Begun by mine engineer Walter Devereaux in the late 1880s, the resort's elite reputation flowered in 1890 with the creation of the Glenwood Polo and Racing Association and was further enhanced three years later with the opening of the ostentatious Hotel Colorado (fig. 32).

Mountain attractions, not surprisingly, were concentrated along the narrow gauge rail corridors. Rail travelers thrilled at the altitudinal spectacles of climbing La Veta, Kenosha, or Marshall summits. True hyperbole, however, was reserved for the Royal and Toltec Gorges, where the rail lines penetrated particularly spectacular canyons. Royal Gorge, encountered along the Arkansas River west of Canon City, even challenged the verbal prowess of guidebook author George Crofutt, who simply told his readers, "Are you looking for a description? We cannot describe it! No pen ever has, and none ever can picture the wonders of this cañon. You can see and feel what no tongue can express or pen can portray."[82]

In southwestern Colorado, the Denver and Rio Grande Railroad passed through the rugged Toltec Gorge in the southern San Juans on its way to Durango. Ernest Ingersoll's description of the trip concentrates more on the triumphs of the railroad than on the natural scenery passing by the window: "Six miles ahead lay the cañon of which we had heard so much—the Toltec Gorge, whose praises could not be overdrawn. . . . How these passages of spongy rock resound as our engine drags the long train we have again mounted through their lofty portals! How narrow apparently are these curved and smooth embankments that carry us across the ravines, and how spidery look the firmly-braced bridges that span the torrents! . . . It hugs the wall like a chamois-stalker, creeping stealthily out to the end of and around each projecting spur; it explores every in-bending

FIGURE 32. Gilded Age tourism on the western slope: the Hotel Colorado, Glenwood Springs (Courtesy Denver Public Library, Western History Collection)

gulch, boldly strides across the water-channels, and walks undismayed upon the utmost verge . . . and lo! a gateway tunneled through,—the barrier is conquered!"[83]

After the 1890s, even as America's elite continued to delight in high country pleasures, a new middle-class invasion of the Colorado mountains far outnumbered the leisure set.[84] In the first twenty years of the new century, a flood of Americans of more modest means demanded their own assemblage of tourist experiences and accommodations that could meet their limited budgets and time. Several basic shifts in the interplay between tourists and the Colorado mountains became apparent between 1890 and 1920. Most fundamentally, a new scale of consumption, both in the number and variety of mountain attractions as well as in the sheer volume of visitors, exerted an ever greater impact upon mountain settlement patterns and landscapes. Colorado's mountain tourism was a clear sign of the fundamental cultural and economic shifts that were propelling westward increasing numbers of urban middle-class American families.

American culture embraced the virtues of outdoor life, both out of a nostalgia for frontier virtues and as an escape from an increasingly urban existence.[85] Popular periodicals like *Forest and Stream* and *Outing* flourished, Americans responded to such nature writers as John Muir and Enos Mills, and the western sagas of figures like Teddy Roosevelt became adventures of mythic proportions. By the 1890s, national rail lines also played major roles in extolling the virtues of western travel to the middle class. New tourist-class Pullman cars were offered as a budget alternative to Palace Car amenities. The Tourist Pullman Cars were less ostentatious than Palace Cars, but they were comfortable and often less than half the fare. The Denver and Rio Grande Railroad even offered free Pullman Tourist Car services along some of its Colorado lines during the 1890s to promote middle-class rail travel within the state. After 1910, the option of driving west in one's automobile also excited and challenged an increasing number of ordinary Americans. All of these cultural, technological, and economic tendencies shaped places in the Colorado mountains as dozens of new resorts, cabin colonies, tourist attractions, and campgrounds appeared. These features added further to an amenity-oriented landscape that grew amid the older industrial-era mining and smelting facilities that had created so much of the high country's early settlement geography.

Urban Denver and its nearby mountainous environs dramatically reflected the tourist revolution after 1900.[86] With middle-class tourism on the rise, city politicians agreed that they needed to market the scenic amenities of the nearby mountains. In 1912 a special "Parks Committee" observed, "a Mountain Park for Denver will be . . . perhaps the greatest step in the great movement of making our mountains available to the people. It is Denver's chance to open a gateway into the mountains, and to take the lead in making Colorado more attractive to tourists than Switzerland." Major municipal land acquisitions west of Denver soon followed, including Lookout Mountain, Genesee Mountain, Bergen Park, and the Echo Lake–Mount Evans areas (fig. 33). Landscape architect Frederick Law Olmstead, Jr., designed park details, including more than eighty-five miles of scenic automobile highways that linked the twenty nearby Mountain Park units with the Mile High City. Between 1915 and 1920, a Denver or Mount Evans National Park was proposed as part of a plan to lead Denver-based tourists into the nearby mountains. Although that idea ultimately failed, the Denver Mountain Parks system—completed in the 1930s—became a nationally famed example of marrying a major American urban area with its surrounding environment.

Other Denver-based initiatives contributed to Colorado's growing commitment to popular, automobile-based tourism.[87] Thousands of promotional pamphlets produced by the city's Tourist and Publicity Bureau extolled Denver's proximity to the mountains and its gateway status to all of the Mountain West's national parks. Denverites organized the Colorado Automobile Club in 1902, and six years later this evolved into the Rocky Mountain Highway Association. The association lobbied persuasively for a larger state and local commitment to road improvements to benefit the travel industry. The next year, in 1909, the Colorado Highway Commission was established, and its steadily rising annual budget contributed to the gradual betterment of Colorado roads. Denver was a leader in caring for the needs of the auto traveler, who often preferred the simple and inex-

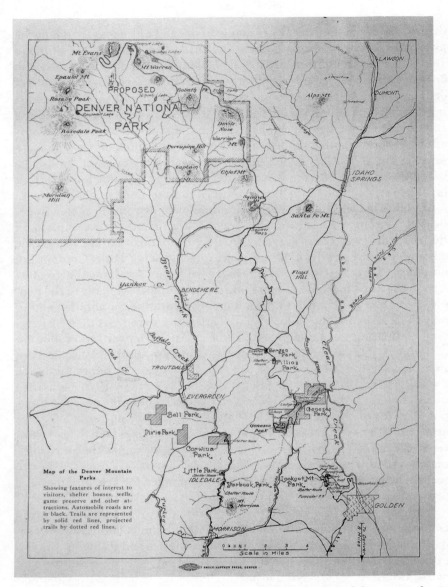

FIGURE 33. Denver's mountain hinterlands: the mountain parks and the proposed Denver National Park, 1919 (Courtesy Denver Public Library, Western History Collection)

pensive pleasures of camping to the pricier options of fine hotels. After 1915 Denver's City and Overland Parks offered free municipal camping with state maps, public baths, and evening entertainment at no cost. These campgrounds were closed during the Depression, but dozens of inexpensive motor courts, cabin camps, and trailer courts took their place along the city's main thoroughfares during the 1930s.

Colorado's mountain recreation lands thus acquired a new image after 1890: no longer simply watering holes for the elite, they now featured the simpler pleasures of fishing, climbing, and camping. Anyone with a car, a set of pots and pans, and a canvas tent was welcome to join in (fig. 34). In Estes Park and Grand Lake, both border towns for the new and very popular Rocky Mountain National Park (established in 1915), dozens of inexpensive cabin camps and rustic lodges sprouted to serve travelers of modest means.[88] After World War I, an expanding number of dude ranches also catered to middle-class American families. In addition, more than 600,000 campers annually visited some 250 Colorado campgrounds by the early 1920s. Most of these camps were in the Colorado mountains and many were constructed along lakes and streams by the U.S. Forest Service. Hundreds of miles of trails, many built on national forest lands, enhanced the tourist infrastructure in the high country landscape.

The upsurge in outdoor activity by both Coloradans and tourists led to a growing interest in the challenges of mountain climbing and skiing after 1900.[89] The Colorado Mountain Club was founded in Denver in 1912 and popularized the exhilaration of ascending many of the Front Range peaks. Frederick Chapin's popular *Mountaineering in Colorado* (1889) sang the praises of hearty outdoor life and detailed the virtues as well as techniques of climbing. Conquering Longs Peak southwest of Estes Park became one of the required rites of passage for enthusiasts. As outdoor recreation grew in appeal and daring, winter sports, particularly skiing and ski jumping, caught the imagination of many intent on enjoying the pleasures of the Colorado mountains year-round. Recreational skiing was locally popular as early as the 1880s around snow-rich mining towns like Gunnison and Crested Butte, but it was not until after 1910 that there was a sustained increase in winter sports clubs and carnivals in the Colorado mountains. Before 1920 skiers organized local clubs and competitions in Steamboat Springs, Silver Plume, Hot Sulphur Springs, Estes Park, Dillon, and Leadville. By 1919, the Colorado Mountain Club also helped construct a ski jump on Genesee Mountain in the Denver Mountain Park west of the city.

By the early twentieth century, Colorado's reputation as America's Switzerland complicated both the image and the reality of its mountain landscape. Although mining's impact certainly dominated many mountain

FIGURE 34. Recreating in the Colorado high country: the marriage of car and canvas near North Park (Courtesy Colorado Historical Society)

settings, a competing vision of the high country was created by and for tourists. This new form of resource consumption led to the creation of such settlement nuclei as Estes Park, Grand Lake, and Glenwood Springs, and it modified the function of many older mining settlements such as Georgetown, Ouray, and Aspen. This impulse reworked the cultural landscape to fulfill the needs and the imaginations of those who came to visit the Colorado mountains. Infrastructure was added, accommodations were provided, and attractions were invented to produce a new visual scene and tourist experience in the Rockies that resonated with evolving national predilections. By the late nineteenth century, Americans had clearly fallen in love with the scenic pleasures of the region, and this relationship, once established, proved to be a lasting romance that forever altered the human geography of the Colorado mountains.

The Imprint of the Federal Government

Mountain geographies were also molded by the impress of the federal government.[90] Early in the American period, the gathering of geographical information on the Colorado mountains involved the active participation of federally funded explorers. Even before the Colorado Gold Rush, federally sponsored explorations by Zebulon Pike, Stephen Long, John C. Frémont, and John Gunnison played important roles in assembling a clearer picture of the mountain region's complex drainage patterns and potential for development. Once mining began, land disposal and mining laws also involved the interplay of the federal government and the needs of local residents.

During the 1870s, a new round of scientific exploration by the federal government reassessed Colorado's mountain geography, producing much more detailed topographical and geological knowledge that directly shaped patterns of transportation and mining in the high country.[91] These later rendezvous spawned a federally created image of the Colorado mountain landscape quite different from the huge Romantic canvases of Albert Bierstadt. Although even trained geologists noted the beauty of what they saw, their mission was utilitarian: their high country transects aimed at an understanding and description of the diverse physical settings they encountered and thereby offered baseline information to spur economic development. This marriage of science and utility fueled a much more accurate and detailed understanding of Colorado's mountain landscapes and provided an invaluable set of federally financed reports, maps, and documents useful to a generation of mining prospectors, railroad engineers, and agriculturalists. The era of government reconnaissance also set the stage for later federal involvement that was dedicated to the direct scientific management of the mountain zone.

This scientific curiosity, combined with the potential for practical gain, reached its apex in the numerous geological surveys of Ferdinand V. Hayden and Lieutenant George Wheeler.[92] Beginning in 1869, Hayden's Colorado survey reports, as well as the visual documentation provided by photographers and artists William Henry Jackson, Henry Elliott, William Holmes, and Thomas Moran, produced a much more detailed and comprehensive picture of the Central Rocky Mountains. As Hayden correctly suggested for Colorado, "There is probably no portion of our continent, at the present time, which promises to yield more useful results, both of a practical and scientific character."[93] Particularly between 1873 and 1876, numerous Hayden survey crews, working for the U.S. Geological Survey of the Territories, crisscrossed the high mountains, pinning down the basic geography of peaks and parks and identifying potential sites for commercial mining. During the same period, Wheeler led army-funded expeditions across southern Colorado as part of the military's Geographical Surveys of the Territories of the United States West of the 100th Meridian. Indeed, so much scientific data-gathering went on between the Hayden and Wheeler parties that conflict and competition arose between the two operations.

In spite of the tensions, both federally funded expeditions revealed similar views of the mountains and the role of the government scientist in shaping a utilitarian and realist vision of the high country. As Wheeler wrote in 1873, "The time has come to change the system of examination, from that idea of exploration which seems to attach itself to a linear search for great and special wonders, to a thorough survey that shall build up . . . and fortify our knowledge of the structural relation of the whole."[94]

This effort to demystify the scenery and secrets of the Colorado mountains was nowhere better revealed than in the illustrations that accompanied the Wheeler and Hayden reports. A new kind of visual record was being created in these straightforward renderings of range fronts and geological formations (fig. 35), and it differed dramatically from the romanticized and idealized portraits provided by artists like Bierstadt (see fig. 31). These later images often retain an accuracy and real scientific utility to this day. The mountain panoramas of government artist William Holmes, for example, were "masterpieces of realism and draftsmanship."[95] Ultimately, the technology of photography improved vastly by the 1870s and brought remote western scenes even more directly to observers in the East without the interpretive filter of the painter or the sketch artist. Although photographs were obviously staged conceptions themselves, the work of William Henry Jackson and others provided a sense of realism and immediacy heretofore impossible to grasp.[96]

Following the creation of the U.S. Geological Survey in 1879, another round of even more meticulous and specialized studies was undertaken.[97] Often focused upon a particular mining district, these federal reports provided prospectors and investors with critical geological data on previous mining activity as well as potential ore veins. Virtually every major Colorado mining district was covered by such government reports over the next several decades. Notable examples include S. F. Emmons's *Geology and Mining Industry of Leadville* (1886) and W. Lundgren and F. L. Ransome's *Geology and Gold Deposits of the Cripple Creek District* (1906).

After 1891, however, yet another level of federal involvement unfolded in many mountain settings across the western United States. The creation of federally managed forest reserves set aside huge tracts of public land, mostly in the mountainous West, and fundamentally shaped their subsequent settlement and development. The U.S. Forest Service managed these lands with a complex mission that involved both using and conserving mountain resources. The stresses resulting from that often incompatible goal still reverberate in the region today, though their origins lie in the late nineteenth century.

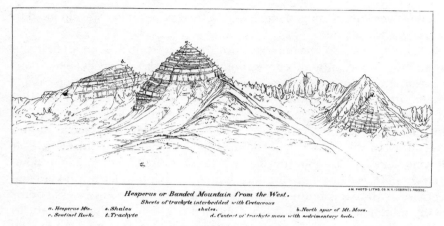

Hesperus or Banded Mountain from the West.
Sheets of trachyte interbedded with Cretaceous
a. Hesperus Mtn.   s. Shales   shales.
c. Sentinel Rock.   t. Trachyte   d. Contact of trachyte mass with sedimentary beds.   b. North spur of Mt. Moss.

Plate XLIV.

FIGURE 35. The scientist's view: Hesperus or Banded Mountain from the west
(Source: F. V. Hayden, *Ninth Annual Report of the United States Geological and Geographical Survey of the Territories* [Washington, D.C.: Government Printing Office, 1877], 271)

Much of Colorado's mountain region fell under the domain of the Forest Service between the 1890s and the 1930s. Federal control of public lands reached its apogee with the establishment of national parks, an initiative designed clearly to protect certain areas and features from excessive resource exploitation. Even here, the notion of preservation connoted a tension between a public anxious to enjoy the parks and critics who argued that such lands needed to be protected from too many users. In Colorado, these issues came to the fore with the creation of Rocky Mountain National Park in 1915, a park created precisely because it so well represented the scenic and recreational possibilities of Colorado's mountain zone.

This new level of federal intervention was related to the earlier impact of mining and its associated settlement. After 1859, mining settlements contributed to the widespread removal of timber within the mountains. Summer livestock grazing increased dramatically in the high country, with large herds of cattle ranging unchecked and uncounted across the upper reaches of almost every major watershed within the state.[98] By the 1880s widespread instances of environmental despoliation around the West convinced many observers that government intervention was necessary. Although ardent preservationists such as naturalist John Muir lobbied for government-imposed restraints primarily for aesthetic reasons, even more compelling arguments were based on the realities of resource economics: the mountains were being used to death, and if their forest and forage resources were not managed more wisely, the entire region was doomed to become a wasteland.

Within Colorado, the impulse toward conservation was apparent in the state's 1876 constitutional convention.[99] Frederick J. Ebert headed a convention subcommittee on forest culture and succeeded in inserting a statement into the constitution that pledged the assembly to "enact laws in order to prevent the destruction of, and to keep in good preservation, the forests upon the lands of the state." The Colorado Forestry Association and the Office of the State Forest Commissioner were formed during the following decade. Although they lacked state funding or enforcement powers, these forest advocates argued eloquently that lumbering and grazing activities within the mountains needed regulating to prevent excessive erosion and damaging runoff. They appealed to the federal government to provide the states with the power to impose such regulations. A growing number of Colorado irrigationists supported the call for conservation, arguing that adequate water supplies for farming depended upon the protection of nearby mountain watersheds.

Action from the federal government came swiftly in 1891 and 1892 as five forest reserves were set aside within Colorado.[100] Through a little-discussed provision in a congressional lands bill, President Benjamin Harrison was granted the power to proclaim forest reserves, which effectively withdrew these acreages from homesteading and unmanaged development. The impact of the Forest Reserves Act in Colorado first manifested itself in the fall of 1891 with the huge reservation of the White River Plateau Timber Reserve northwest of Glenwood Springs. Included in the reserve of approximately one million acres were valuable virgin timberlands atop the White River Plateau along with a number of west- and south-facing valleys that were being used as popular grazing pastures for cattle (fig. 36). Already the victim of large-scale lumbering depredations, the diversely forested region caught the attention of President Harrison through a series of letters and petitions signed by concerned local residents.

The White River Reserve was only the beginning. Soon the creation of the nearby Battlement Mesa Reserve withdrew a tract of similar country just to the southwest of the White River region. Three smaller reservations, the Pikes Peak, Plum Creek, and South Platte units, were also created in the early 1890s, ostensibly to protect essential urban and agricultural watersheds that lay just west of Colorado Springs and southwest of Denver. Suddenly, with a few strokes of the pen, more than three million acres of Colorado's mountainous public domain were legally removed from potential settlement, an action that was repeated in many other western states during that same decade.

In the five years following the creation of the initial Colorado forest reserves, both federal officials and local residents were unclear as to their

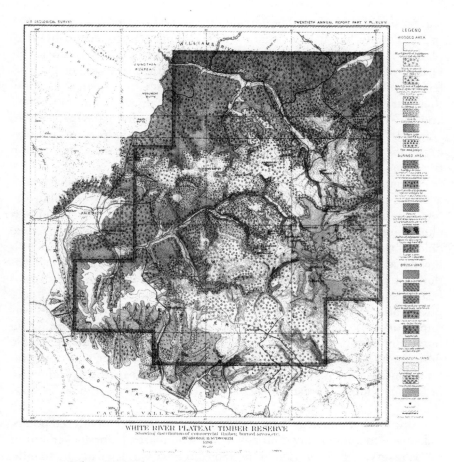

FIGURE 36. White River Plateau Timber Reserve, 1898 (Source: USGS, *Twentieth Annual Report*, 1898–99, pt. 5, pl. 48)

actual significance. Essentially, reserves went unmanaged and unfunded between 1891 and 1896.[101] Nearby residents were legally restricted from extracting anything from the reserves, although limits were almost universally ignored. If anything, irresponsible lumbering and grazing increased in the Colorado mountains during the mid-1890s as settlers and speculators feared the establishment of new reserves and more vigorous enforcement of restrictions on existing units.

Foes of the reserves saw them as a challenge to the basic rights of the pioneer and capitalist to develop the natural resources of the country around them. One Montrose newspaper editor decried limits on accessing timber within the reserves: "in one county in particular they do not leave a single stick of lumber outside the reservation line . . . every settler in the county has had to steal every stick that has gone into his fireplace. . . . These reservations ought to be knocked out of existence."[102] Other critics focused on their damage to the cattle business. The Denver-based *Field and Farm* lamented that "the system is the greatest calamity that ever befell the cattle interests of Colorado or any other mountain state and must have a damaging effect on the grazing industry for years to come."[103] At a minimum, there was a call to define the precise function of the reserves and to clarify what could and could not take place within their boundaries.

Federal reserve policies crystallized in 1897 around a more activist management philosophy articulated by Gifford Pinchot, a forester rapidly rising to national prominence. Pinchot headed a National Academy of Sciences inquiry into the nation's forest reserve policies in 1897 and became chief of the Agriculture Department's Division of Forestry during the following year. Pinchot's philosophy promoted a utilitarian-based conservation of forest resources that pushed for multiple but sustainable uses of reservation lands. Pinchot argued, much to the chagrin of such hard-core preservationists as Muir, that keeping all activity out of the reserves was impractical.[104] But Pinchot also forcefully stated that the unmanaged harvesting of forest resources would lead to their wanton and irreparable destruction. He advocated a middle course whereby timber, grass, and water resources were managed by scientifically trained experts to produce an orderly, productive forest landscape that could be used for many generations.

New federal policies in 1897 echoed this approach and offered potential solace to anticonservation advocates who feared being locked out of forest reserves.[105] Promised in the 1897 directive was legal access to mining claims, livestock grazing privileges (though permits were required and sheep were prohibited), local timber and water resources (permits also required), and rights-of-way for necessary private roads and stock trails. Ranger patrols would be scheduled to guarantee enforcement of local policies. Even with the new policies, timber and grazing resources on all five of the Colorado reservations were reportedly deteriorating rapidly in 1899.

In the first years of the new century Colorado conservationists renewed their calls for additional forest reserves. Although the directive of 1897 had been a move in the right direction, state advocates of conservation rightly noted that real management of existing reserves was inadequate and that other watersheds in the mountains remained unprotected. One step forward occurred in 1902 as President Theodore Roosevelt and Chief Forester Pinchot established the San Isabel Forest Reserve to protect the watersheds of the Wet Mountain and San Luis Valleys. The following year the

State Forestry Association came out with a new campaign to reserve all of the state's remaining unprotected lands above an elevation of 8,500 feet.[106] It was an ambitious wish that left anticonservation elements holding their breath over the next move of the Roosevelt administration.

National politics conspired to make the year 1905 particularly pivotal in the evolving relation between the federal government and the Colorado mountains. In that year the government created eleven new Colorado forest reserves, encompassing almost nine million acres of the mountain heartland.[107] Much of the state's modern geography of national forest lands was pieced together in a frantic period of several weeks in which Roosevelt and Pinchot almost daily demarcated new reserves (fig. 37). Many watersheds from the San Juans to the Front Range suddenly fell under the protection of the 1905 reservations. Although forest conservationists, many farmers, and even a few ranchers applauded the plethora of new federally managed units, others looked on in horror as they saw the long hand of the federal government imposing itself upon and forever locking away an invaluable mountain resource base.

Also in 1905 Chief Forester Pinchot galvanized his control over the newly enlarged system of reserves and made decisions destined to anger residents throughout the West. First, he managed to get direct control of the reservations—now renamed national forests—by having the lands transferred from the Department of the Interior to the Agriculture Department. He then cracked down on illegal timber cutting on forest lands by hiring more rangers and by backing them up with the threat of federal muscle. This closed down many small-scale illegal sawmilling and railroad tie-cutting enterprises, a result that actually pleased many larger corporate operators, who didn't much like the competition. And Pinchot imposed a new "grazing tax" on cattle and sheep (now allowed on certain national forest lands). Although the fees were reasonable—20 to 50 cents annually for cattle and 5 to 10 cents annually for sheep—the new system, which went into effect in 1906, provoked widespread protests, particularly in the important ranching counties of north-central and northwest Colorado.[108]

Roosevelt and Pinchot rose to the occasion, coming to the state to argue the merits of the controversial plan with vigor. Roosevelt was popular within the state, but many Coloradans did not rejoice in the impress of his federal policies upon the mountain landscape (fig. 38). Matters came to a head as anticonservation elements across the West organized the Denver Public Lands Convention in 1907. To his credit, Pinchot agreed to speak to the troubled delegates, and his strong advocacy of the merits of the national forest system probably helped to dilute the intensity of the group's final proclamations.

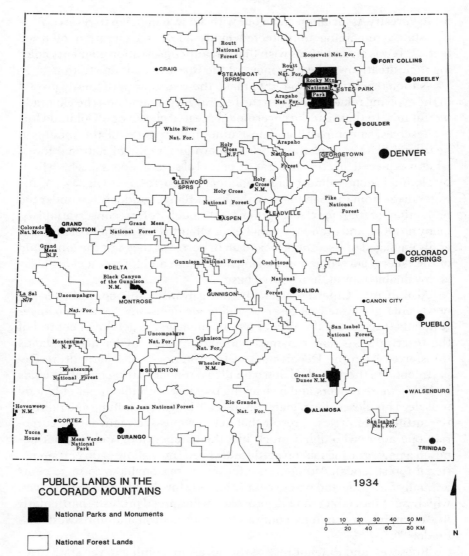

PUBLIC LANDS IN THE
COLORADO MOUNTAINS

1934

■ National Parks and Monuments

□ National Forest Lands

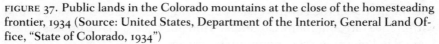

FIGURE 37. Public lands in the Colorado mountains at the close of the homesteading frontier, 1934 (Source: United States, Department of the Interior, General Land Office, "State of Colorado, 1934")

Following the anticlimactic convention in 1907, tempers within the state gradually cooled and Coloradans increasingly recognized the inevitability and even the value of working with the federal government in managing the forests.[109] A growing number of urban residents also recognized the benefits of the national forests in providing protection of

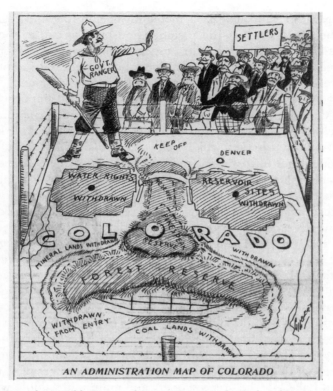

FIGURE 38. President Teddy Roosevelt's imprint upon the Colorado mountains: the anticonservationist's view, *Denver Times*, June 19, 1907 (Courtesy Colorado State Historical Society)

urban watersheds and offering a peaceful retreat from the chores of city life. In spite of the rhetoric, even some high country ranchers came around: as early as 1906 rangers on the Cochetopah National Forest co-operated with local livestock associations in developing coordinated plans for summer cattle grazing. Colorado cattle operators also appreciated the fact that the grazing permit system gave preference to them over itinerant sheep outfits that seasonally invaded the state from Wyoming, Utah, and New Mexico.

Colorado's mountain zone was forever altered by the imposition of the national forests. By 1934 more than thirteen million acres of the state's mountains and foothills constituted one of the West's outstanding con-centrations of federally controlled forest lands (see fig. 37). A new admin-istrative geography of supervisorial and field ranger offices dotted the mountains with local centers of control that everywhere proclaimed the federal presence. Timber continued to be harvested from public lands by private operators, but at least a modicum of controls and regulations shaped the process across the region. Thousands of cattle, sheep, and horses also grazed the high country, especially in summer, but forest officials increasingly regulated and monitored their numbers. In addition, national forest budgets included investments in livestock fencing, corrals, stock driveways, bridges, and spring development, all important infrastructure designed to improve and in many ways subsidize the activities of local ranching operations.[110] Other landscape changes included general road and trail construction, which helped control mountain wildfires and develop mountain tourism and recreation. Dozens of new federally financed campgrounds contributed to the amenity-oriented component of the national forest mission. More subtle ecological shifts also came with active forest management: newly planted seedlings changed forest composition, weed eradication programs altered the forest understory, millions of exotic fish were introduced into mountain lakes and streams, and "predator control" programs reduced prairie dog, coyote, and mountain lion populations while elk and deer numbers rapidly increased.

Colorado's preservationists, often frustrated at Pinchot's concepts of wise and multiple use, did have something to celebrate in 1915 with the creation of Rocky Mountain National Park, a federal designation that put much greater restrictions on development than was the case in the national forests. The 350-square-mile tract of remote alpine country sat astride the Continental Divide between the resort centers of Estes Park and Grand Lake.[111] The area's scenery and mountain wildlife were well known in the late nineteenth century. Tourists thrilled at climbing spectacular Longs Peak, and numerous nearby resorts and dude ranches catered to the camping and recreational needs of a growing number of visitors. By 1909 the mammoth and luxurious Stanley Hotel in Estes Park was open, and the region offered accommodations that ranged from the very rustic to the ultra-plush.

The movement to create the park gained momentum in the first decade of the twentieth century. Hotel owner F. O. Stanley, local national forest supervisor H. N. Wheeler, and naturalist and writer Enos Mills all reached similar conclusions about the region between 1905 and 1910, agreeing that ordinary national forest protection was insufficient to guarantee the preservation of its scenery and natural beauty. By 1906 many local residents and business leaders had formed the Estes Park Protective and Improvement Association and were soon calling for the creation of an Estes National Park. Other preservationists, such as forest ranger Wheeler, advocated a special game refuge status for the region, giving it extra protection but allowing it to remain within the national forest system. Opponents to the entire idea of preservation also surfaced, and by 1911 the Front Range

Settlers League were vocally opposing park plans. Park advocates won the day, however, after Robert Marshall of the U.S. Geological Survey visited the region in 1912 and concluded that a "Rocky Mountain National Park" be created, although its size was considerably reduced so as to eliminate controversial zones of mineral wealth. The purpose of the park was twofold: to preserve an area that was "representative of the noblest qualities of the whole" Rocky Mountain region and to create a park unit that was accessible to population centers in the Midwest and East.[112]

Over the next twenty years Rocky Mountain National Park fulfilled its promise to become one of the nation's most popular pleasuring grounds. By the late 1920s, more than 250,000 people entered the park annually, making it the most visited high mountain zone within Colorado. The park's glaciated peaks, rushing rivers, alpine tundra, and diverse wildlife epitomized the Colorado high country. Nearby Estes Park swelled in size, offering tourist camps, hotels, eateries, and souvenir shops. Park officials, though concerned about the rapid sprawl of Estes Park and sensitive to protecting the natural environment, actively promoted the development of park infrastructure. As was the case with the park system nationally, opening Rocky Mountain to auto travel became an early priority. Construction of the state-funded Fall River route was completed in 1920, sending a narrow and serpentine road over the Continental Divide to connect the east and west sides of the park. Twelve years later the much improved and federally funded Trail Ridge Auto Road was completed, and its twelve-thousand-foot summit and approaches achieved the same kind of fame and popularity accorded to well-engineered railroad routes from an earlier generation.[113] Park officials also constructed miles of recreational trails and opened new campgrounds. An active and interventionist approach to park animal life characterized the period as rangers attempted to control such "undesirable" predator species as mountain lion while stocking millions of fish that ended up in the frying pans of appreciative tourists.[114]

Colorado's new national forests and Rocky Mountain National Park exemplified the continuing hand of the federal government in shaping the settlement system and cultural landscape of the Colorado high country. It was a largely utilitarian vision of the region that saw the collection of accurate scientific knowledge and the rational use and management of mountain resources as priorities. Indeed, the complexity of the federal presence within the region aptly articulated the increasingly diverse national and local constituencies that were consuming mountain resources. In other words, as American capitalism evolved, so did the bonds between the private and the public sectors as well as the kinds of impacts that shaped regions like the Colorado mountains. Mining companies saw some of their activities curtailed by government, but they were largely free to continue developing mineral resources as market conditions warranted. Ranching and lumbering interests were also regulated, particularly where they operated on the public lands of the national forest system, but here government officials usually did little to discourage development, particularly by large-scale (and politically powerful) operators.

As the amenity value of select mountain environments and locations increased late in the nineteenth century, the federal government placated preservationists and resort operators, although in most cases the forces of recreational development won out over those of wilderness preservation. The result of these mingled influences, of ever more elaborate private economic interests combined with a continually increasing federal presence, could easily be seen on the Colorado mountain landscape by the 1920s. It was a mosaic that, though prone to some change, nevertheless bore the signatures of human geographies still dominant across the high country today.

Piedmont Heartland, 1860–1920

Any Colorado map makes apparent the state's bifurcated nature. Mountains and plains define these respective halves, each with their own historical geographies. Wedged between these two large regions, however, is a third distinctive landscape to which we now turn our attention. The Colorado Piedmont, a mix of open rolling country and well-watered stream valleys just east of the Front Range, commands a special place in the evolution of the Centennial State. Although its landforms resemble the high plains to the east, much of its human geography is intimately tied to the mountains on the west. As with the mountain zone, the Piedmont's modern urban and rural landscapes have their roots in an era of vastly accelerated change that shaped the region between the late 1850s and the early twentieth century.

As we have seen, the Piedmont attracted a scattering of settlements before the Gold Rush of the late 1850s. A succession of Native American peoples traveled through and used the region, culminating in the extensive nineteenth-century hunting activities of the Arapaho and Cheyenne. A sprinkling of trading posts and primitive farms also dotted the Arkansas and Platte Valleys by the 1850s, peopled with a polyglot population of Euro-American fur and buffalo robe trappers, Mexicans, and itinerant traders and soldiers. Overall, however, the Piedmont played no unique role in the geography of human settlement before the Gold Rush. Everything changed once color was struck in the mountains immediately west of the region. The ensuing intensification of settlement and accelerating pace of landscape change established distinctive Piedmont subregions that persist to this day (fig. 39).

At the heart of the Piedmont, the Denver–Golden–Boulder Urban Core established its economic centrality within a few years of the gold strikes in Gilpin, Clear Creek, and Boulder Counties. The Urban Core's intimate ties to mountain mining secured its gateway status. People, capital, and goods were funneled through the Piedmont, based on its nearness to the mineral regions and its relative accessibility to existing settlements. This early merchant- and transport-based economy broadened

101

FIGURE 39. The Colorado Piedmont

later in the nineteenth century to include widening roles for manufacturing and tourism.

Other Piedmont subregions derived their character from different
paths of economic and social evolution. A second distinctive settlement
landscape emerged in the Northern Agricultural Zone immediately north
of the Urban Core. Although this region supported such sizable towns as
Fort Collins, Loveland, and Greeley, it was the well-developed rural landscape that defined the area's character. This zone of intense cultivation,
still notable today, was initially made possible by the fertility of Piedmont
soils, the availability of water, and the proximity of local markets in the Urban Core and in the mining camps.

To the south, the Colorado Springs urban and resort complex defined
yet another Piedmont realm. This subregion's unique role as an early
tourist center, pleasure ground, and elite health spa stamped "the Springs"
with an enduring character. The brainchild of railroad and real estate developer General William Jackson Palmer and a handful of like-minded entrepreneurs, Colorado Springs had emerged by the 1870s as a required stop
on any grand tour of the continent.

The Arkansas Valley corridor, focused upon urban and industrial developments at Pueblo, defined a fourth Piedmont subregion. Pueblo's
modest beginnings predated the Gold Rush of the late 1850s, but this
sleepy farming and trading town did not come into its own until the rail-

road arrived in the 1870s, sparking an extended era of industrial growth. Pueblo's proximity to coal and iron ore combined with the region's improving transport infrastructure encouraged investors to develop the region. Pueblo was also far enough removed from other Piedmont cities that it became an important wholesaling and trade center for much of southern Colorado, including mining settlements of the upper Arkansas Valley and the San Juans.

Between 1860 and 1920 the Piedmont emerged as a key meeting ground within Colorado. It was a zone of complex cultural juxtapositions in which eastern bluebloods, midwestern farmers, and European laborers all contributed to an increasingly diverse regional society. Economically, the Piedmont was strategically positioned as the focus of the state's transportation network. The region that began as an ancillary appendage to the mountain mining districts in the late 1850s grew by the century's end to dominate the economic and human geography of the state as well as surrounding portions of the interior West.

The Urban Core: Patterns of Regional Spatial Organization

Just before World War I, Colorado booster and Denver resident Thomas Tonge could confidently write about his hometown: "The country tributary to Denver . . . extends far beyond the state of Colorado and practically embraces the whole of the territory West of the Missouri River. . . . In this vast region every new mine worked, every fresh acre cultivated, every new orchard planted, every new quarry opened, all increases in live stock and every manufacturing enterprise started, react beneficially on and send new life-blood to the heart—Denver."[1] These verities of economic geography notwithstanding, absolutely nothing in Denver's physical setting particularly destined the site for the greatness Tonge described after the turn of the century. Indeed, as the first flurry of mining excitement enthused prospectors in the autumn of 1858, it was entirely unclear how and where the Piedmont's emerging urban centers would take root. Available open ground, proximity to water, and nearness to the mining regions themselves were obvious locational concerns, but the actual urban geography that did take shape was only one outcome among many potential human geographies.

Consider the fluid circumstances in that fateful fall of 1858. By September dozens of hopeful miners roved the Piedmont and adjacent foothills. They came west after hearing of new gold finds, but so far most of their efforts were not being rewarded. A small placer camp convened around temporary color near the modern suburb of Englewood and another cluster of cabins sprouted a mile away at Montana City, but these centers proved as ephemeral as the pockets of placer gold in the nearby creeks. Just to the north, a pair of seasoned Indian traders, William Mc-Gaa and John Simpson Smith, combined with a group from Lawrence, Kansas, to establish the town of St. Charles where Cherry Creek flowed into the South Platte River. About the same time, a rival group of Georgia and Kansas miners established Auraria on the west side of Cherry Creek, opposite St. Charles. Within a couple of months, matters became more complicated. William Larimer, a Kansas town promoter, jumped the claims of the St. Charles group and established his own town of Denver, named for the Kansas governor. For good measure, Larimer soon crossed the nearby South Platte River to lay out yet another town, named Highland (fig. 40). Settlements also sprang up nearer to the mountains themselves: Arapahoe City and Golden Gate were platted along Clear Creek west of Denver late in 1858, and a group of Nebraska City goldseekers established their settlement at the mouth of nearby Boulder Canyon.[2]

This flurry of incipient urbanization produced inevitable rivalries, particularly by the spring of 1859, when it became apparent that the mountain country immediately west of the Piedmont did indeed hold great promise as a gold-producing region. The resolution of three key conflicts worked to Denver's ultimate advantage. First, there was the matter of the Indians, for this portion of the Piedmont was hardly unpeopled ground. Particularly around Denver and Auraria, encampments of Arapaho and seasonal use by bands of roving Cheyenne complicated the claims of the Anglo arrivals.[3] In the summer of 1859, almost three hundred Arapaho lodges dotted the Denver area. Both whites and Indians were uncertain as to legal claims in the South Platte Valley because the Treaty of Fort Laramie, signed in 1851, ambiguously gave the Indians the use of but not the outright ownership of the region. Negotiations with selected Arapaho and Cheyenne representatives led to the Treaty of Fort Wise early in 1861. This treaty, never agreed to by many of the Native Americans, gave the United States control over the Denver area as well as much of northeast Colorado. The Indians were given the option of relocating along the Arkansas River, where they could receive forty-acre land grants, an irrelevant acreage for a highly mobile buffalo-hunting society. Although the Indians never formally relocated to their appointed reserve, their retreat from the immediate vicinity of Denver in 1861 removed an important obstacle to white settlement.

A second conflict pitted boosters of the Denver town site against supporters of Auraria to the west.[4] Early in 1859, Auraria got off to a strong start, attracting many new residents and merchants. Even newspaper editor William Byers initially located in Auraria, although he soon moved his

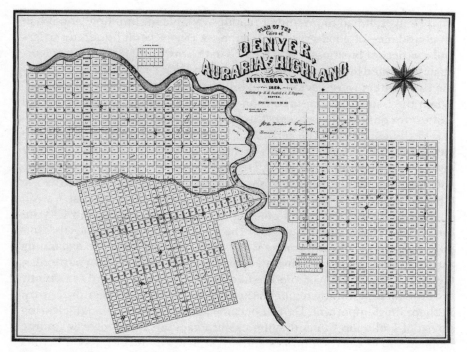

FIGURE 40. Plan of the cities of Denver, Auraria, and Highland, 1859 (Courtesy Denver Public Library, Western History Collection)

Rocky Mountain News office to more neutral ground in the middle of Cherry Creek's dry bed. National events fueled the rivalry: many in Auraria were natives of Georgia whereas the founders of Denver hailed from the unionist strongholds of northeastern Kansas. By mid-1859, the tide turned in favor of Denver with the help of its primary promoter, William Larimer. Larimer donated fifty-three town lots to the Russell, Majors and Waddell express company along with an additional half-dozen lots to company president William Russell. In return, the fledgling town on the east side of Cherry Creek found itself in sole possession of the stage connection to the Midwest. Within months Auraria citizens voted to merge with their Cherry Creek rival. As the rush was on into the western mountains, the Denver Town Company and its promoters were in clear command of the settlements along Cherry Creek.

The third challenge to Denver's regional hegemony was harder to defeat. Golden, established in 1859 by the Boston Company, sat at the mouth of Clear Creek Canyon about fifteen miles west of Denver and proved a worthy competitor to its sister city on the Piedmont.[5] Early visitors remarked on Golden's superior site characteristics: it was closer to the mines than Denver; it had more timber readily available for building; and it had an abundance of good grass and water. By 1860 several hundred settlers and a variety of businesses had located in the town and it was being vigorously promoted by boosters W. A. H. Loveland and E. L. Berthoud. By 1861 the two centers were backing rival toll roads into the nearby mountains. When the issue of a territorial capital arose the following year, a spirited contest for dominance ensued. No clear winner emerged. Golden was declared the capital but the territorial legislature met alternately in both cities until 1867, when Denver's greater clout wrested the political title away from its upstart competitor. Denver's dominance was secured in 1870 with the completion of the locally supported Denver Pacific Railroad to Cheyenne and the arrival of the Kansas Pacific line from the east.

Once Denver's emergent centrality was evident, the Queen City increased its relative dominance over the Piedmont economy. The city's importance was manifest in many ways. Most obvious were the expanding number of railways that converged upon Denver after 1870. In particular, General Palmer's Denver and Rio Grande line tied the capital to virtually every major new mining region in the state in the later nineteenth century. Perhaps most important, Denver became known as the financial "clearing house of Colorado," encouraging eastern capitalists and nearby mining magnates to locate their offices and investments in the city. Its numerous banks, merchants, transportation opportunities, and expanding cultural offerings made it the obvious business center in the state. Denver's financial and commercial reach went beyond the state's borders, and these linkages also added to its sustained growth.[6] In other words, accelerating growth after 1870 attracted more growth. Population figures tell the story: from a modest town of 4,000 in 1870, Denver grew in 1900 to 130,000 residents and by 1920 to well over 250,000. In 1920, Denver claimed no less than a fourth of the state's population. It was unchallenged in its urban dominance, not only in the Piedmont, but across the interior of the American West.

Denver, however, was not the only survivor in the Urban Core. Its early nemesis, Golden, carved its own niche in the evolving urban geography of the region.[7] The town established a viable economic base along two key fronts. The westward penetration of the Colorado Central Railroad to the mining centers of Central City and Georgetown created additional opportunities in ore milling and refining. In addition, by the late 1860s, the local business class invested heavily in a range of other manufacturing ventures. The town was located near many major population centers in the state and possessed a ready supply of cheap labor. Golden profited, too, from its proximity to coal mines, a collection of useful stone quarries, and Clear Creek, which rushed through the center of town. Golden became the "Lowell" of Colorado, widely recognized for its assortment of paper, flour, and sawmills, brick-making companies, ore smelting operations, and metal fabricating plants. It also became the home of the Colorado School of Mines, which enjoyed a growing professional reputation by the 1890s. Although Denver's larger boomtown experience and much broader economic base eluded Golden, the town prospered in its strategic foothill setting and supported a stable population of several thousand residents by the early twentieth century (fig. 41).

To the north, Boulder City also found its place within the Urban Core. Unlike Golden, Boulder never competed for outright dominance in the region, yet by 1920 it had emerged as a substantial city of more than eleven thousand with a diverse economic base second only to Denver's.[8] The center originated as a cluster of a dozen miner's cabins along Boulder Creek in the fall of 1858. Within a few months, the Boulder City Town Company formed, and though an elaborate plat of more than four thousand lots suggested the founders' grand plans for expansion, census takers in 1860 could find only 324 residents. The town's population had more than tripled a dozen years later, but the site still failed to impress traveler Isabella Bird, who described the place scathingly as "a hideous collection of frame

FIGURE 41. Golden and nearby Piedmont, early twentieth century (Courtesy Denver Public Library, Western History Collection)

FIGURE 42. Commercial Boulder: turn-of-the-century Pearl Street (Courtesy Denver Public Library, Western History Collection)

houses on the burning plain."[9] Boulder City's image improved after 1876 with the raising of Old Main, the first building on the site of the University of Colorado. By the early twentieth century, the economically diverse center counted over 6,100 residents, and its downtown district hosted thriving commercial enterprises (fig. 42). Still, Boulder's modest urban landscape paled in comparison with metropolitan Denver only thirty-five miles to the southeast. That larger center evolved as a distinctive urban place within Colorado and the American West between 1860 and 1920.

Surveying the Urban Scene:
Denver's Landscape, 1860–1920

Denver's economic growth shaped its cultural landscape in lasting ways. As the town matured from a ragged frontier outpost in the early 1860s to one of the nation's twenty-five largest cities just thirty years later, the character and changing rhythms of its enlarging economic base proved pivotal in bringing about four fundamental changes in urban geography. First, re-

markable elaborations in urban land use demonstrated the breadth of
Denver's economic activities. New industries, connections, and attractions colored the everyday scene. Each new page of the Local Business
Directory added sights, sounds, and smells to the growing metropolis. Second, what might be called a process of landscape intensification characterized the city's downtown and nearby neighborhoods as new wealth
flooded the visible scene with commercial and residential construction on
a new scale. This built landscape was rich in its display of Denver's enlarged self-image, one cast from the heady and recently acquired riches of
the plutocrat's wallet. Third, economic growth necessitated spatial expansion, and this horizontal sprawling was an ongoing theme, especially
after the middle 1870s. Denver's tentacular grasp was truly remarkable as
new streetcar lines reached blossoming suburbs to enlarge, both economically and politically, the reach of the central city. Finally, Denver's
new population imparted greater cultural complexity, which produced a
richly layered social geography quite unlike the initial collection of simple
pioneer miners and merchants who had huddled on the banks of Cherry
Creek in 1859.

An Expanding Economic Base, 1860–1920

In its first years Denver's grand aspirations were apparent only in the elaborate and ambitious survey grids laid out at the confluence of Cherry Creek
and the South Platte (fig. 40).[10] Once the the town merged with Auraria
in 1860, newly arrived settlers could buy hundreds of available lots from
members of the initial town companies. Aside from the size of the initial
plat, however, little suggested Denver's future successes on the landscape
in 1860. As newspaperman Albert Richardson reported, the place was "a
most forlorn and desolate-looking metropolis."[11]

    Things failed to improve immediately, even with the periodic mining
excitements of Denver's initial decade. Disasters, both natural and human, seemed to haunt the town.[12] Much of the eastern half of Denver
burned in April 1863. A year later a devastating flood washed away many
low-lying buildings along Cherry Creek and the South Platte. To make
matters worse, friction with the nearby Plains Indians increased in the
early 1860s, culminating in 1864 with the murder of several white settlers
as well as the massacre of two hundred or more Cheyenne sleeping under
a flag of truce at Sand Creek east of Denver.[13] Communications and transportation lines were disrupted in the conflict, and Denver's economy stagnated as its isolation from the "civilized" East increased. The local mining
economy faltered, too.

The Piedmont center, however, muddled through the mid-1860s, helped by its continuing role as a regional gateway. When Bayard Taylor arrived on the scene in 1866, he found a town that, though still small, had "an air of permanence" about it.[14] Indeed, the many brick buildings that had been erected over the preceding three or four years owed their rapid appearance to the disasters of flood and fire that had so damaged the town.[15] As new buildings replaced those destroyed, businessmen and wealthier residents made liberal use of handy local bricking clays and proceeded to give the town a rapid facelift from its frontier collection of canvas tents, log cabins, and crude frame-board buildings.

Events in the late 1860s presaged even greater economic changes in store for Denver. Work on the City Ditch brought dependable water from the South Platte River to gardens, lawns, and newly planted trees in 1867.[16] The economy was turning around, prompting new businesses to locate in town. New smelting operations in the mountains marked the successful technological response to the problem of processing sulfur-rich ores. New finds of gold and silver in the late 1860s also boded well for Denver. Finally, the ability of local leaders to galvanize the town around the Denver and Pacific Railroad provided a huge economic and psychological boost. The result was a pattern of accelerating population growth and construction in the town by 1870. Even though Denver's census figures recorded only a negligible change in total population between 1860 and 1870, its economic geography and cultural landscape were experiencing fundamental shifts. What had begun as a brawling frontier outpost was rapidly evolving into a dominant center of regional trade and, more important, into a community increasingly self-conscious of its own potential.

After 1870 Denver's broadening economic base diversified land uses in the city. The growing success of the state's mining economy was reflected on Denver's landscape, particularly between 1877 and 1892, when many new gold and silver mining districts opened. As booster H. W. B. Kantner reported in 1892, "The entire state depends upon Denver for its source of supplies."[17] With this continuing function as a gateway city, Denver's railyards and wholesaling houses assumed a more visible role on the western and northern edges of town.

The importance of mining was reflected in entirely new land use districts, as well. Mining machinery for use in the nearby mountains was manufactured in Denver by the late 1870s, offering low-cost in-state competition to machinery makers in the Midwest and East.[18] Even more important, Denver became a major site for the refining of gold and silver ores, not only for Colorado but for other western states, too.[19] The shift began with the arrival of the Boston and Colorado Smelting Company's operations from Black Hawk in early 1879. Mill owner Nathaniel Hill correctly figured that ores could cheaply be moved to Denver by rail and then processed there in large amounts with inexpensive sources of labor and energy. Others soon followed suit, and by the early 1880s the Omaha and Grant Smelter and the Globeville Smelter had been built. The resulting smelting district located a few miles north of downtown Denver created its own nearby working-class neighborhoods as well as predictably darkening the skies above the city.

Denverites realized that mining alone could not support the city, particularly when the industry contracted in the early twentieth century. Denver's diversity presaged its continuing success and non-mining manufacturing grew tremendously. By the 1890s the annual value of manufactured goods produced in Denver reached $50 million, and by 1912 that total grew to $80 million, the output coming from more than 750 factories.[20] Some production related to local needs: the town supported a large brick-making industry, a number of breweries, and several textile operations. Other factories had larger markets: the Denver Paper Mills, for example, sold their newsprint to many cities, and the town's livestock and agricultural processing industries were tied into eastern as well as statewide demand for foodstuffs.[21]

By the turn of the century, Denver's emergence as a regional manufacturing center elaborated upon the city's earlier role as a trade entrepôt and guaranteed that a truly industrial landscape would thereafter be an important part of the local scene. With the establishment of the Gates Tire Plant in 1914, Denver entrepreneurs successfully captured national markets, although the city's distance from the industrial heartland limited the magnitude of its expansion.[22]

Broader economic shifts also shaped the city landscape. An expanding base of regional agriculture produced land use change within Denver itself. As *Harper's Monthly* correspondent Edwards Roberts noted in 1888, "Seed is purchased at the Denver markets, agricultural implements are made and sold there, and the cereals are returned to the flouring mills that have been built."[23] Denver's many agricultural processing activities owed their presence to the tremendous post-1870 growth of both irrigated and dryland operations across the northern Piedmont and eastern plains. The continuing importance of livestock was also revealed by the construction of the expanded Union Stockyards on the city's north side in the late 1880s. At more than one hundred acres, the facility was a vivid, often fragrant reminder of the ongoing interplay between city and nearby countryside.

Tourism left its mark on the Denver scene. Although the capital city was often not the primary Colorado destination for travelers, most passed through Denver on their way to Colorado Springs, the mountain mining towns, or other scenic attractions. By the late 1870s, four large downtown hotels were hosting twenty-five thousand visitors every summer.[24] Denver's function as a traveler's gateway to the delights of the central Rockies increasingly supported a broad array of services and commerce in the city. Attractions like Elitch's Zoological and Pleasure Gardens, the Manhattan Beach Amusement Park, and the Lakeside Amusement Park opened between 1890 and 1910.[25] After 1920 cabin camps, cottages, and motor courts also lined such major boulevards as Santa Fe and Colfax.

Economic growth and land development did not proceed without interruptions. The Silver Panic of 1893 devastated the Colorado economy.[26] A dozen Denver banks failed that July and many followed. The landscape unambiguously reflected the downturn: whereas more than 2,000 new homes were built in 1890, only 124 were constructed in 1894. The population fell from 106,000 in 1890 to about 90,000 five years later. The expansion of the late 1890s, boosted by the state's remarkable new gold strikes at Cripple Creek, reinvigorated the economy and reaccelerated the pace of landscape change along the Denver skyline. Thereafter, although periodic slowdowns were inevitable, Denver's economic health remained buoyant until the Great Depression swept the nation in the early 1930s.

Processes of Landscape Intensification

Downtown Denver and nearby residential neighborhoods underwent great changes between 1870 and 1920. These transformations reflected what might be called a process of landscape intensification in which the infrastructure of roads and utilities improved dramatically, the density and height of buildings increased markedly, and the architectural ornamentation and interior decoration of structures became notably and more self-consciously symbolic of the city's growth and power. It was a cultural landscape in the making that is still on the scene today in the form of surviving buildings and in the structure of land uses in and near the city's Central Business District. Indeed, the late nineteenth century marked the establishment of the present downtown area: earlier commercial activities were concentrated to the northwest along Blake, Market, and Larimer Streets, and it wasn't until the 1880s and 1890s that the focus of activity shifted to its present axis nearer Capitol Hill.

Modest changes to the downtown scene came with the solid growth of the 1870s. Commercial buildings sprouted more elaborate Gothic arches, tin and iron ornamentation, and French Second Empire styling.[27] The new look was consciously "architecture," typically borrowed from other midwestern urban examples. The same pattern was evident in nearby elite residential neighborhoods that still bordered the central city. During the 1870s the city's finest homes in the Italian Villa and French Second Empire styles concentrated along Fourteenth Street, just southeast of the commercial district. Nathaniel Hill, John Evans, David Moffat, and other representatives of the city's nouveaux riches ornamented the area with their increasingly ostentatious homes.[28]

A key participant in Denver's architectural facelift was mining magnate Horace Tabor, who wanted his presence well known in the capital city. Tabor left Leadville and moved to Denver in 1878 and imported Chicago architect Frank Edbrooke to build the city's largest business block and entertainment center. Tabor noted that "Denver was not building as good buildings as it ought . . . and I thought that I would do something towards setting them a good example."[29] His five-story Tabor Block at Sixteenth and Larimer, completed in 1880, set a new standard for commercial retailing and office construction. A year later Edbrooke's Tabor Opera House opened a few blocks east at Sixteenth and Curtis and marked a new scale of extravagance and eclecticism in Denver's architecture. Although some critics poked fun at its grandiose design and lavish interior, the Opera House was immensely popular with Denver's elite and set an architectural example in the 1880s and 1890s.

Denver was an architect's dream in the heady economy of the 1880s and early 1890s. Dozens of new commercial, public, and residential structures blossomed in and around downtown (fig. 43). The local business directory tells the story: Denver supported only three architects in 1879, but it featured no fewer than forty just five years later.[30] New commercial buildings flourished on Fifteenth and Sixteenth Streets, where department stores, banks, and office buildings concentrated, gradually shifting the center of activity away from the old commercial blocks to the northwest. Nearby Millionaires' Row on Fourteenth Street shifted from a residential street to a commercial one as new five-story office buildings crowded in from the north. The completion of the Union Depot in 1881 at the northwest end of Seventeenth Street prompted the expansion of commercial activity along that downtown corridor. In addition to the Tabor contributions, other notable downtown structures of the period included the four-hundred-room Windsor Hotel, the Boston-financed Boston (1889) and Equitable (1892) Office Buildings, the Edbrooke-designed Brown Palace Hotel (1892) and Denver Dry Goods Building (1894), and a plethora of new public edifices, including schools, fine churches, and the City Hall, Courthouse, and State Capitol.

Commercial expansion continued in the early twentieth century.[31] Seventeenth Street increased its dominance as a focus of downtown activity and a municipally funded Welcome Arch across from Union Station beckoned visitors into the bustle and excitement of the city (fig. 44). Banks, law firms, and real estate offices lined the prestigious avenue, and by the 1920s no fewer than thirteen major hotels were located along its length. The impressive Daniels and Fisher Tower dominated the land-

FIGURE 43. Downtown Denver, 1880s (Courtesy Colorado State Historical Society)

scape after 1911. Modeled after the Campanile of Saint Mark's in Venice, the department store tower became a much-touted symbol of Denver's metropolitan status. Including elegant clock tower and flagpole, the structure reached over 370 feet into the Colorado sky, and local boosters cited it as one of the three tallest towers in the country.

Increasingly elaborate residential architecture also reshaped the look of the central city, especially near Capitol Hill. Beginning in the middle 1880s Denver's upper crust built their largest and gaudiest homes on the Hill, and the trend accelerated through the decade. Local banker Charles Kountze built a forty-room residence just north of the Capitol site, and long-time Denverite Henry Brown located his mansion nearby at Seventeenth and Broadway. By the early 1890s a host of Denver notables competed on the Hill in designing a house and grounds befitting their acquired stations in life. The neighborhood was a classic example of a visible scene created explicitly for the conspicuous display of new wealth. The district's Gilded Age cacophony of turrets, towers, cupolas, Queen Anne additions, and Romanesque facades, to say nothing of peacock-endowed grounds, servants' quarters, and flagstone sidewalks, inevitably attracted the attention of travelers and commentators who marveled at the rapid appearance of the plutocratic landscape on the Hill.[32]

Landscape intensification was also apparent in the more mundane geography of the city's improving late nineteenth-century infrastructure.[33]

Tree-planting efforts of the late 1860s and 1870s bore visual fruit for the city as streets greened up in later decades. The streets themselves, however, remained either dusty or miry challenges until 1890. Even boosters remarked on the "uncomfortably muddy" unpaved streets, including those downtown. At last an aggressive street-paving program in the early 1890s improved all of the principal business thoroughfares between Fourteenth and Nineteenth and Larimer and Broadway Streets. A rudimentary sewer system was also completed, but untreated waste still poured into the South Platte, filling the bottomlands with a stench that often wafted through the city. Although the Denver Artesian Water Company was incorporated in 1870, periodic financial and engineering problems delayed a ready supply of cheap water to much of the city until the late 1880s.

   Lighting, communications, and electrical innovations added new layers of technology to the urban landscape.[34] By 1873 the Denver Gas Company illumined much of downtown, giving the nocturnal scene a new glow with hundreds of glass-enclosed gas jets mounted on posts. One of the most visible alterations in infrastructure came in 1879, when the city's first telephone exchange was established, along with the poles and wires that connected the budding metropolis. Electrical lines followed: in the summer of 1881, the Colorado Electric Company strung wires around much of the central city, often using the recently installed telephone poles to sup-

FIGURE 44. The Welcome Arch and the view up Seventeenth Street (Courtesy Colorado Historical Society)

port the electrical lines. By the middle 1890s, a flood of company takeovers, bankruptcies, and consolidations brought the local electrical network under the unified control of the Denver Consolidated Electric Company.

The public sector became more invigorated and visually dominant in the early twentieth century. Downtown Denver bore the imprint of government officials, planners, and civic architects who put their imaginative stamp upon the cityscape of Colorado's leading center.[35] Much of the genesis of that creative impulse in urban design came from the "City Beautiful" movement that swept the country following the 1893 Chicago Exposition. There the nation's leading architects constructed the archetypal "White City" of the future, which they believed would be a suitable replacement for America's increasingly ugly and congested downtowns. Prominent in this urban revamping was a commitment to new public open space and buildings, often Neoclassical in design.

Gaining popularity in the architecture and planning literature around 1900, the City Beautiful movement made an impact on the Mile High City. Mayor Robert Speer institutionalized the notion of urban beautification with the city's new charter of 1904 and with the creation of an art commission charged with planning civic improvements. Funds poured into street cleaning and sewer projects. Trees were planted by the tens of thousands, with the mayor even creating a City Forester's Office to oversee the arboreal advance. The crowning achievements of Speer's vision, however, were the grand Municipal Auditorium, opened in 1908, and the Civic Center complex, proposed in 1904 and completed in scaled-down form in later years. The Civic Center took shape just west of the State Capitol: Frederick Law Olmstead designed the extensive open spaces of the Civic Center's sunken gardens and some of the nation's finest architects contributed to the new City and County Building, Voorhies Memorial, Greek Theater, and Denver Public Library. Although the complex was not completed until the early 1930s, its growing presence added a civic dimension to the busy downtown landscape, and its gardens, pools, and esplanades formed a pleasing counterpoint to the commercial clamor on nearby Seventeenth Street (fig. 45).

Denver Extended: Processes of Expansion, 1870–1920

Homer Thayer's 1872 map of Denver reveals the beginnings of other key changes in the city's human geography (fig. 46).[36] By the early 1870s the congressional grant lands denoting the original city were surrounded by a cluster of urban additions. Some gridded blocks, such as Case and Ebert's Addition on the city's northeast side, merely extended the street grid from downtown. Other surveys, such as Brown's Addition near the future Capi-

FIGURE 45. Creating new public landscapes: Denver's Civic Center (Courtesy Denver Public Library, Western History Collection)

tol Hill, reoriented the street pattern to cardinal directions, creating a legacy of awkward intersections that plague Denver to this day. Most of these early expansions were not yet independently incorporated suburbs but newly surveyed parcels annexed to the city and controlled by local real estate interests.

Several ingredients promoted Denver's explosive physical growth between 1870 and 1920. Most obviously the city's expanding population combined with an accommodating site to promote sprawl in all directions. City residents saw advantages in moving toward the urban fringe. Many older residential neighborhoods, such as Auraria, became industrial. In other areas, homeowners faced expanding commercial businesses and increasing urban congestion, encouraging them to seek more suburban settings with their larger lot sizes and quieter streets. As politically autonomous suburbs became more popular during the 1880s, there were additional incentives to leave the moral turbulence of Denver in favor of more temperate and closely regulated communities beyond.[37]

Perhaps most important, rapid suburban expansion was aided by the close and profitable working relationship between the city's real estate de-

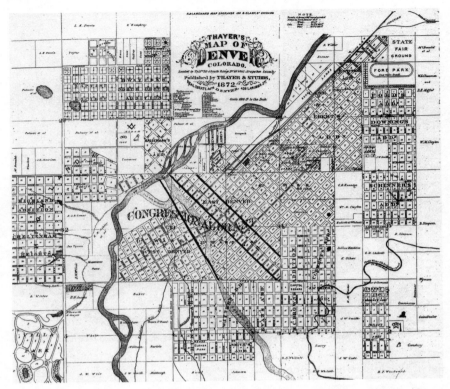

FIGURE 46. Patterns of urban expansion: Homer Thayer's map of Denver, 1872 (Courtesy Denver Public Library, Western History Collection)

velopers and those who invested in and promoted the city's expanding street and cable car systems. Without effective transportation, suburban land was worth little. Connected to downtown, however, these peripheral acres became immensely more valuable, a fact not lost on many outside investors as well as city fathers who invested both in land and in the local transportation infrastructure. The impact on the landscape was often striking, too: businesses and new houses clustered linerally along the main streetcar thoroughfares, and even the hint of a new line often meant a rapid rise in adjacent land values.[38]

The Denver City Railway Company initiated the process of expanded transportation service. By 1871 this group of Chicago capitalists constructed a horsecar line between downtown and the Curtis Park addition on the city's northeast side. Additional lines soon reached west, south, and east. In many cases landowners and community leaders of the new suburban centers actively wooed streetcar companies with promises of heavy traffic and cash payments. At other times interests combined in transparent examples of entrepreneurial collusion. In 1885 George Crofutt delighted in pointing out how owners of a suburban railway line controlled much of the adjoining real estate and used their political influence to locate a local exposition near their holdings.[39]

Expansion accelerated in the late 1880s and early 1890s. Technological changes in transportation and explosive economic growth contributed to the continued pressures for suburbanization.[40] Whereas in 1884 there were fewer than 16 miles of streetcar lines, by the early 1890s Denver's streets were "gridironed with iron tracks" and over 150 miles of the network were in operation (fig. 47). One booster publication well summed up the significance of rapid transit lines, noting that "their facility for bringing suburban residents into the heart of the city rapidly enables people to build houses where they can live cheaply and comfortably." For much of the period between 1886 and 1899, spirited rivalries between street railway companies hastened the spread of the competing networks. Finally, at the turn of the century, the Denver City Tramway Company consolidated the business across much of the city, buying out some of the financially weaker lines.

The scale of Denver's metropolitan expansion was impressive as its hinterlands were carved into a series of distinctive, politically incorporated suburbs.[41] Immediately east and southeast of downtown, the fashionable suburbs of Park Hill and Montclair were platted between 1885 and 1887. Promoters of Park Hill were quick to state that they were offering Denver's "Largest Restricted Residence District." Large lot sizes, good streetcar connections, and strict limitations on morally questionable activities were other selling points for these east side high-status suburbs. Denver's largest streetcar suburbs by far were located just west and south of the central city. Highlands, just across the Platte River to the west, was "a saucy little city" that boasted a growing mid-1890s population of more than eight thousand. A similar-sized collection of middle-class residents concentrated in South Denver, where mills and a new university campus provided suburban employment opportunities. Denver's northern metropolitan fringe was defined by the industrial suburbs of Swansea, Globeville, and Argo. Here working-class populations clustered around several smelters in what were essentially company towns. Politically, many late nineteenth-century suburbs were absorbed into the expanding city of Denver. Both Highlands and South Denver ultimately saw fiscal advantages in joining the central city. Other suburbs, including Montclair, Argo, and Globeville, were annexed in 1902 with the creation of Denver County. With these ad-

FIGURE 47. Landscapes of urban expansion: Denver's tramway network (Courtesy Colorado State Historical Society)

ditions, the city of Denver grew to almost sixty square miles, nearly ten times its size in 1874.

Lakewood and Aurora were examples of yet more distant and politically separate suburbs that continued the pattern of metropolitan expansion into the twentieth century.[42] Lakewood, on the west side, was platted in 1889, and its connections to downtown Denver via the streetcar network gradually transformed the rural center into part of the suburban fringe. East of Denver, Aurora was incorporated in 1903 as settlement increased along expanding streetcar lines. Although suburb-based automobile commuting eventually replaced the familiar streetcar grid and further extended the metropolitan fringe, much of Denver's present array of suburban clusters originated in the formative decades between 1870 and 1920, when the city grew to envelop the surrounding territory in a rush of economic growth, land speculation, and an increasingly well-integrated transportation infrastructure.

Denver's Communities: Creating a New Social Geography

As Denver grew in population and size, it became more socially complex; diverse communities were everywhere apparent on the cultural landscape. The new social reality moved from a simplified pioneer society toward an ever more culturally complex urban geography. This trend is explained in part by the city's origins: rather than being created with a common purpose or with group goals in mind, Denver was the quintessential example of what urban historian Gunther Barth has called the "instant city," in which eclectic individuals pursued diverse economic ends. In such a setting, it is hardly surprising that individual freedom and economic liberalism reigned supreme, often at the expense of cultivating social order or a common sense of community.[43] The city's social geography strikingly reflected the city's economic and cultural diversity, and the urban scene was divided into dozens of distinctive neighborhoods. These communities, though near one another, often stood at great social distances. Their most obvious expression on the landscape was the phenomenon of residential segregation by wealth, occupation, and ethnic background.

Certain Denver neighborhoods and institutions celebrated the power and accomplishments of the local elite.[44] By 1890 there were more than thirty millionaires in the city as well as a host of lesser luminaries aspiring to the same status. Some of Denver's power elite were new arrivals, either from the mines or from the East, whereas a core of longer-term residents such as William Byers and David Moffat added history and stability to the mix. Increasingly, this highly visible minority chose to separate itself spatially and socially from Denver's more ordinary folk. This bent toward exclusivity revealed itself in several settings. The move to the larger lots and elevated social prestige of Capitol Hill was all but obligatory for Denver's upper crust in the 1880s and 1890s. As Denver expanded, the nearby suburbs of Montclair and Park Hill provided additional insulation from the masses of Denver proper.

Downtown, the 1880 construction of the ostentatious Denver Club offered a congenial and confidential ambiance for elite palavering. The nearby Tabor Opera House was another paean to the plutocrats. Finally, a flurry of impressive cathedral-building projects occurred during the 1880s with the Saint John's Episcopal, First Congregational, Trinity Methodist, and First Baptist Churches all vying for visual and ecumenical dominance of the city. In 1888 *Harper's Monthly* writer Edwards Roberts marveled not only at the churches and the opera house but at all "many luxuries of city life" that had made Denver "a metropolis, a centre of refinement, a place rich in itself, influential, and the admiration of all beholders."

Unfortunately Roberts's published portrait was a highly selective view that depicted only the most gilded of Denver's many social worlds: more ordinary residents never paid an architect to design their homes nor did they frequent the elegant parlors of the Denver Club or Tabor Opera House. Denver abounded in more modest cultural landscapes that reflected the limits and values of its common working people. Even those fortunate enough to own their homes in Denver or the nearby suburbs were often crowded onto tiny 25-by-125-foot lots, and they counted themselves fortunate by late in the century to have the luxuries of rudimentary water, sewer, and telephone service. Denver's truly impoverished, though invisible in many published descriptions, were also part of the city's everyday landscape.[45] The urban poor converged on the low-lying lands along Cherry Creek and the South Platte, where their tents, tarpaper shacks, and overflowing boardinghouses mingled with the sounds, smells, and smoke of factories, railyards, and warehouses.

Wealth was not alone in imposing order upon the city's social geography. Ethnicity also left its mark and defined the character of many urban neighborhoods.[46] Not surprisingly, employment opportunities attracted sizable foreign-born populations. Complex processes were clearly at work to encourage ethnic clustering by residence in the city. Many foreign-born arrivals gravitated to neighborhoods where familiar languages were spoken and friends and relatives were present. Once a cluster of families was established, it attracted additional kith and kin. Also operating in the housing and job markets were dominant notions of "appropriate" behavior that invariably discriminated against poor and non-Anglo ethnic groups, thereby reducing their locational choices for work and residence. As ethnic clusters evolved, saloons, voluntary associations, meeting halls, and churches further defined the neighborhood boundaries. The result was an urban mosaic of well-defined ethnic communities, paralleling patterns in larger eastern and midwestern cities.

Western railroad construction swept Chinese laborers into the Rocky Mountain interior after 1870. In Denver they congregated in distinctive communities on either side of Cherry Creek just northwest of downtown. Almost a thousand Chinese lived in Denver by 1890, and although many were hard-working launderers, dishwashers, janitors, and servants, they unfailingly were the least-tolerated of Denver's ethnic groups, suffering from periodic lynchings, arson, and constant discrimination that ultimately contributed to their dwindling numbers by the turn of the century.

Just a few blocks away, the beginnings of a black ghetto were apparent on Blake and Larimer Streets by the late 1880s. Black in-migration soon increased, bringing the city's turn-of-the-century total to almost four thousand. The well-established community had its own newspapers and churches, and as the beginning of a black middle class took shape after 1900, there was a gradual migration toward more outlying neighborhoods to the northeast of the original inner city cluster.

Denver's Italian community became well-defined between 1880 and 1895. Early arrivals clustered along the South Platte bottomlands or in garden tracts in North Denver and Highlands. The completion of Mount Carmel Church in 1893, however, attracted Denver's Italians to that northside neighborhood, and within a decade there were numerous Italian-run saloons, clubs, a parochial school, and an orphanage within a few blocks of the church. Italian males frequently worked seasonal jobs on the railroads or gained temporary employment in local factories. As with Asian and black populations, Denver's early Italians contended with the prejudices of the Anglo-dominant population when it came to housing or jobs.

Germans and Slavs made distinctive contributions to Denver's turn-of-the-century ethnic diversity. Turner Hall, a German social and athletic club, became an established institution in the city by 1865. By the time a new hall was completed in 1891 just northeast of downtown, the Germans had become the city's largest immigrant group. Numerous German-owned saloons kept the beer flowing not only for their compatriots but for non-Germans as well. Unlike the Chinese, blacks, and Italians, Germans were often well off economically; men like Louis Bartels and Charles Kountze rose into the ranks of the elite. Eastern Europeans, by contrast, were poor, powerless, and strongly concentrated in the industrial suburbs of Argo and Globeville. By the late 1880s several Slavic groups, including Poles, Serbs, and Slovenes, increasingly populated the working-class neighborhoods surrounding the northside smelters. In addition to their increasingly dominant role in the industrial workforce, the Slavs established a large collection of beer parlors, ethnic meeting halls and lodges, and the predictable assortment of Catholic and Orthodox churches in the community. After 1900 arrivals of German Russians in the smelter districts added to the ethnic variety of the area.

By the early twentieth century, there could be no doubt of Denver's economic and social dominance in the state. Stroll down busy Sixteenth Street and everywhere the landscape proclaimed the city's substance and success (fig. 48). A bustling assortment of pedestrians, carriages, carts, and streetcars made their way along the city's paved streets and sidewalks. Businessmen pondered the latest trends, shoppers glanced through store windows at an abundance of goods, and the voices of downtown strollers suggested their German, Italian, and Slavic backgrounds. An impressive corridor of three- to six-story brick and stone business blocks lined the avenue, offering retailing opportunities at the street level and a variety of office space above. Streetlights brightened the nocturnal landscape and a

FIGURE 48. Denver's Sixteenth Street, early twentieth century (Courtesy Denver
Public Library, Western History Collection)

weblike network of electric and telephone lines crisscrossed the skyline
overhead. Smoke and haze occasionally drifted above the scene, remind-
ing downtown workers of nearby manufacturing plants. It was a landscape
that in the course of a generation had been created to serve the needs and
express the values of an increasingly complex urban population. The scene
was an apt visual epigram for a city that had arisen from no particular gifts
of physical geography to become the unchallenged urban place, not only
of the Piedmont, but of the entire state. Most of all, the scene articulated
the interconnections that bound Denver with the rest of the country. The
national flag, the Chicago-style commercial architecture, the eastern
dress, and the latest urban technologies all proclaimed Denver's intimate
links with a larger world, a relation that continued to shape the city's landscape and Colorado in enduring ways.

The Northern Agricultural Zone

A second zone of distinctive Piedmont settlement thrived north of the Urban Core. The Northern Agricultural Zone took shape as a subregion dur-

ing the 1860s, but population densities and the acreage under cultivation remained low until the establishment of agricultural colonies and railroad lines in the 1870s. Thereafter, the area became widely known for its extensive irrigation works, productive farmlands, and thriving agricultural towns. One of the best ways to define the spatial extent of the subregion is to examine a state irrigation map for 1900 and to observe the large zone of artificially watered lands on the northern Piedmont near the convergence of Larimer, Weld, and Boulder Counties (fig. 49).

The well-watered lands of the South Platte River east of the Front Range caught many a traveler's eye even before the Pikes Peak Gold Rush or the digging of the first irrigation ditch. Here converged the cool, clean waters of the Cache La Poudre, Big Thompson, and St. Vrain Rivers as they flowed into the main stem of the South Platte. Prairie grasses stood higher and greener than on the plains to the east, and the somewhat moister climate hinted at the region's agricultural potential.

Settlement remained scattered across the northern Piedmont during the early 1860s.[47] A small collection of farmers and ranchers established land claims in the fall of 1859, but no great settlement occurred immediately thereafter. In the Cache La Poudre Valley to the north, there was a similar trickle of early settlement, and Camp Collins was erected in 1864 to offer protection to the small rural population. The region soon became known for its cattle ranching operations and its grandiose garden vegetables, which wowed crowds at the territory's first agricultural fair in 1866. Irrigation was practiced after 1860, but it was limited to the construction of short ditches that watered nearby bottomlands. In 1870, when census takers canvassed the northern Piedmont counties of Larimer and Weld,

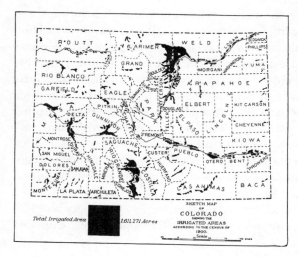

FIGURE 49. Sketch map of Colorado showing the irrigated areas according to the Census of 1900 (Source: United States Bureau of the Census, Twelfth Census of the United States, 1900)

fewer than 2,500 settlers were counted. Still, agricultural operations were on the increase, although estimates of cultivated acreage varied widely. Colorado booster William Blackmore observed that five thousand acres were being farmed in the Cache La Poudre Valley before 1870, while historian David Boyd stated that fewer than a thousand acres were actually yielding crops.

Colony Communities

Change accelerated greatly in the 1870s as the northern Piedmont acquired national fame for both its crops and its cooperative communities. Nathan Meeker, editor for the *New York Tribune,* played a key role in the saga of the northern Piedmont's development. Thirteen years in an Ohio communal farm colony convinced Meeker that a similar enterprise might thrive in the West. After traveling to Colorado and receiving encouragement for such a project from his editor, Horace Greeley, Meeker met with interested settlers in New York in December 1869. The community Meeker envisioned was no mere economic enterprise. The social vision he described to his New York audience emphasized cooperative agriculture, temperance, and development based on hard work rather than on land speculation. Meeker struck a responsive chord in his listeners; he was swamped with more than four hundred applications within the next four months. For a modest fee of $155, colony members were granted one lot of 5 to 160 acres (depending on its distance from the colony town and the quality of the land), the right to buy a town lot for a price of $25 or $50, and the further right to purchase additional rural acreage, either from government or from railroad lands.[48]

The decision to locate the Union (Greeley) Colony in the northern Piedmont was made early in 1870. After considering tracts south of Denver, Meeker was persuaded by Denver newspaperman and real estate booster William Byers to examine the more accessible and temperate South Platte Valley.[49] The location near the confluence of the South Platte and Cache La Poudre Rivers was an astute selection. Meeker identified fertile and well-watered acreage, much of which was purchased at around $5 per acre from the Denver Pacific Railroad's Denver Land Association. Not coincidentally, Byers served as a land agent for the Denver Land Association and was pleased to see the acreage transformed into needed capital. Meeker, for his part, obtained good land for the colony as well as guaranteed proximity to the new rail line.

By the time Horace Greeley arrived in October 1870 to inspect his Piedmont namesake, the town site was surveyed, initial buildings were up, and the beginnings of irrigation works had appeared. Compared to most Colorado towns, Greeley's settlement and the maturation of its village landscape had more than the usual amount of planning and foresight. It began with Meeker's New England–inspired vision of the layout and appearance of a proper town center.[50] Each settler in the colony would have the right to purchase a town lot, upon which "the highest ambition for a family should be to have a comfortable, and if possible, elegant home, surrounded by orchards and ornamental grounds." Meeker also elaborated upon the importance of "schools, refined society, and all the advantages of an old country" in creating a stable community environment. Social and economic diversity were to be encouraged in the village, and Meeker suggested that "farmers will be wanted, nurserymen, florists, and almost all kinds of mechanics, as well as capitalists, to use the coal and water power in running machinery."

These grand plans notwithstanding, Greeley's early years were painfully modest. During the first season, the primitive urban landscape was a stark reminder that Meeker's New England village would take time to materialize. Ironically, part of the town's ramshackle appearance was linked to Meeker's insistence that lot holders build upon their lands within one year, encouraging many to fulfill the requirement with a casually constructed cabin that added little to the town's image. The colony-controlled flour mill, a creature of Meeker's industrial vision for the town, also floundered. Early observers were caustic as they assessed the town's fortunes. One Illinois newspaper reporter wrote, "There is one thing we can and will say to our uneasy restless readers, don't go to Greeley, Colorado Territory. That is the last place on the face of this terrestrial ball that any human being should contemplate to remove to. . . . Greeley is located—if there be such a thing as locating a baker's dozen of slab shanties, as many tool chests, a great ditch, and twenty acres of prickly pears—on a barren, sandy plain, part and parcel of the Great American Desert, midway between a poverty stricken ranch and a prairie-dog village."[51]

Greeley soon overcame its incongruous origins, and by 1875 it was a bustling center serving the agricultural hinterlands. The relative affluence and occupational diversity of its original inhabitants no doubt contributed to its growth and subsequent stability. The town had more than its fair share of doctors, lawyers, and skilled artisans, many attracted by Meeker's special vision of western community life. In 1877 the town also wrested away the Weld County seat from nearby Evans, thus adding a political base for development. Gradually the townscape came to reflect Greeley's social maturing and economic permanence. A decade after prairie dogs and prickly pears had so dominated the scene, writers waxed eloquent on what

FIGURE 50. Prospering Greeley in 1882 (Courtesy Denver Public Library, Western History Collection)

was now often seen as "one of the prettiest towns in Colorado" (fig. 50).[52] By 1879 the town's rapidly infilling grid confirmed a promotional description offered by London's Colorado Mortgage and Investment Company:

> Where ten years ago the coyote and antelope had undisturbed possession, there is now a city of nearly two thousand inhabitants, an elegant three story brick public school building erected at a cost of $30,000, several imposing church edifices, large business blocks, attractive residences, and every street lined with shade trees, so numerous and thrifty that they almost entirely hide the buildings from view. The streets are all broad and fringed with rivulets of sparkling, running water . . . every private lot in the city is irrigated abundantly.[53]

As Greeley flourished, the Colorado State Board of Immigration extolled the virtues of group settlement: the booster literature of the early 1870s argued that collective action could (1) secure the lowest rates of transportation, (2) obtain and improve the best lands, (3) dig necessary irrigation ditches, (4) establish churches, schools, and societies, and (5) retain old ties and friendships of home.[54] Greeley's communal orientation should not be overstated, however. Aside from irrigation canals and some civic improvements in the town of Greeley, residents acted on individual initiative. They owned their land, grew or produced what they wished, and within a few years even saw the irrigation canals pass from colony control to farmer-managed irrigation districts. By 1880 the colony ceased to exist legally as a corporate body. Even so, the Greeley experience was a catalyst for other settlements in the Northern Agricultural Zone. Former Greeley settlers established farming towns at nearby Windsor and Eaton. And more generally, the Greeley story led to other "colony" ventures as well as to the in-migration of farmers impressed by accounts of the area's blossoming agricultural landscape.

Two nearby colony efforts attempted to replicate the Greeley experience.[55] Chicago promoters established another group colony southwest of Greeley along St. Vrain Creek at Longmont in the fall of 1870. The Chicago-Colorado Colony purchased more than fifty thousand acres of land, laid out the town plat, and provided initial water to the venture. As with the site at Greeley, the Chicago-Colorado Colony benefited from its location and ready access to good land and water. It also received initial counsel from Nathan Meeker himself. Another somewhat less successful group settlement took shape around the railroad town of Evans, a few miles south of Greeley. Sponsored by Illinois interests, the St. Louis–Western Company attracted several hundred settlers to the South Platte River in early 1871. James Pinkerton, a disenchanted Greeley colonist, located the lands for the company. Although settlers came and stayed, no strong group orientation emerged, nor was there the emphasis on moral virtues that stamped the Greeley settlement. In fact, the taverns and saloons of Evans proved a bother (and a lure) to the sober settlers of Greeley.

Although colony towns receive much deserved historical attention in traditional histories of the northern Piedmont, most pre-1900 settlers in the region came as individuals. One area of sustained interest outside the colony settlements was around Fort Collins. The town began as nothing more than a casually defended fort abandoned in 1872. Thereafter, a town company acquired the fort site as well as some of the surrounding rural acreage and surveyed a plat of several hundred lots just to the southwest of the Cache La Poudre River. Located twenty miles upstream from developments at Greeley, Fort Collins became an important agricultural town for the surrounding district. The town's population blossomed to thirteen hundred residents in 1880 and surpassed three thousand by 1900. The surrounding rural acreage became another area of concentrated settlement in the Northern Agricultural Zone.

Once rail lines arrived in the northern Piedmont in the middle 1870s, additional corridors of concentrated development appeared. An eastern axis of activity lined the Denver Pacific line as it passed through Platteville, Evans, Greeley, and Pierce on its way to Cheyenne. As it had with the Gree-

ley sales, the rail company became involved with land development along
this corridor in which it still held extensive acreage.[56] Just to the west, similar nodes of activity clustered along the Colorado Central line completed
across the northern Piedmont in the late 1870s. The towns of Berthoud
and Loveland were located along the Colorado Central line, as were the
older settlements of Longmont and Fort Collins. All received an economic
boost as farmers made use of the rail's proximity. Finally, some northern
Piedmont centers traced their origins to the particulars of the local resource base. The valuable coalfields of northern Boulder County attracted
special interest, and towns such as Erie, just to the south of Longmont,
owe their beginnings to the profitable extraction of coal.

The Rural Landscape, 1870–1900

Even today the rural landscape across the Northern Agricultural Zone offers an unusual display of intensive agriculture in the West. The density
and productivity of farms reveal an air of midwestern abundance not often seen in more marginal agricultural districts west of the Mississippi.
The origins of that special rural landscape are found in the nineteenth century and in the intricate manipulation and management of the area's land
and water resources. If we ascend to a point above the northern Piedmont
in 1870 and peruse the unfolding of the rural landscape for the next thirty
years, the silvery threads of rivers, irrigation canals, ditches, and storage
reservoirs guide the course of change. Also evident is the imposition of a
survey, property boundary, and road system grid reflecting the rectangular
nature of the dominant federal township and range system. Lot lines, field
boundaries, and section roads oriented the rural scene to the cardinal directions, while the region's natural streamcourses and human waterworks
varied with the topography and lay of the land.

In 1870 it was difficult to predict the future look of the northern Piedmont landscape.[57] Settlers disagreed on the area's potential, and they
avidly experimented to find appropriate adaptations to the local environment. One argument centered on irrigation. Although some boosters fore-
saw unending supplies of fresh water, others cautioned that the unpredictable flows of the South Platte and its tributaries were not capable of
supporting widespread irrigation. Even after canal-building began, engineers differed as to how best to use the ditches. Perhaps most frustrating
were basic questions regarding soil quality and crop selection. Most pioneers agreed on the potential of well-watered bottomlands, but settlers divided on the value of the uplands and the higher benches. Particularly
among the Greeley colonists, there were misconceptions about the area's
suitability for garden and orchard crops. Founder Nathan Meeker's image

of what a proper settlement should look like included flourishing apple, pear, cherry, and plum orchards, rich strawberry patches, and an arboreal canopy of walnut, chestnut, and hickory trees. Unfortunately, the local environment was less than obliging, and most of these early efforts soon withered on the vine. After a few years it became apparent that the Northern Agricultural Zone would be limited to grain and sturdier vegetable crops that could survive the uncertainties of the Piedmont climate.

The first major expansion of cultivated land through irrigation came with the Union Colony at Greeley in the 1870s. The Number Two Canal irrigated about two thousand acres by 1871, although water shortages quickly introduced colonists to the vagaries of varying stream levels and limited canal capacities. Soon, however, the number and length of irrigating canals rapidly multiplied (fig. 51). Greeley colonists enlarged the Number Two in 1872 and 1877, and the canal's users purchased it outright from the colony in 1878. Farmers at Longmont, Evans, and Fort Collins joined in with canal-building efforts. By the 1880s major canals across the region, including the Greeley Canal, the Evans Canal, the Larimer and Weld Canal, the Loveland and Greeley Canal, and the Platte Valley Canal totaled almost two hundred miles in major trunk lines.[58] Shorter laterals also crisscrossed the area. With such demands, the limits of the area's water supply surfaced quickly as rivers such as the Cache La Poudre were tapped dry by moisture-hungry farmers. In fact, an early chapter of the West's prior appropriation water doctrine was codified in the Northern Agricultural Zone as competing farmers and finally the courts decided that those residents with the *earliest* water claims in an area had priority over water use.

Of all the water management operations, none was more ambitious than that of the Colorado Mortgage and Investment Company. This venture was funded by London investors and received the enthusiastic support of a number of Colorado railroads and Denver capitalists. The key to the enterprise was the Larimer and Weld Canal, longer and larger than any of the earlier projects. Preliminary surveys in 1877 established a main canal extending from the Cache La Poudre just above Fort Collins to a point more than fifty miles east. Company engineers, realizing the limits of the river's capacity, also constructed a series of storage reservoirs to get farmers through the dry late summers of northern Colorado. Similar corporate investments financed canal and reservoir-building operations along the Big Thompson River. This marked an adaptive strategy, often quite capital intensive, that created numerous reservoirs both on the Piedmont and in nearby mountain canyons.

By 1900 the first hints of an even grander manipulation of water resources at the regional scale became the harbinger of twentieth-century

IRRIGATION IN COLORADO—LETTING WATER INTO A SIDE SLUICE-WAY.—[SEE PAGE 511.]

FIGURE 51. Refashioning the rural landscape: irrigation in Colorado, 1874 (Courtesy Colorado State Historical Society)

changes. Developers of the Larimer County Ditch diverted water from the Laramie and Colorado river systems into the Cache La Poudre drainage during the 1890s.[59] Although the volume of water introduced to the eastern slope was small, the feasibility of such interbasin projects was demonstrated, laying the groundwork for future transfers.

With the availability of irrigation water guiding the course of denser agricultural settlement, the Northern Agricultural Zone's rural landscape changed dramatically between 1870 and 1900. Early improvements were found near major streamcourses while intervening benchlands were used as open range for stock. As the network of manmade waterways threaded across the entire region, however, cultivated grain crops, particularly wheat, corn, and oats, became widespread. In some areas, potatoes and cabbages became locally dominant. Elsewhere, irrigated alfalfa and hay meadows produced more forage than the natural pasture grasses, often yielding two or three decent cuttings per season. Sugar beets, a major irrigated crop in western Colorado, also began to shift eastward to the Piedmont by the turn of the century. Overall, over 90 percent of improved farmland in the Northern Agricultural Zone was under irrigation by 1900. In addition, livestock remained an important component of this irrigated rural landscape: the 1900 Census in Weld County, for example, reported more than 65,000 cattle, 20,000 horses, and 85,000 sheep.[60]

With a few early exceptions, farmers lived in isolated farmsteads rather than concentrating in village centers. Even close-knit Union Colony residents often preferred proximity to their fields to the amenities of life in Greeley. Given the intensity and yields of irrigated operations, the relatively high price of farmland, and the ready commercial markets for crops, it is not surprising that farm sizes were small relative to the high plains further east and Colorado as a whole. The result was an agricultural landscape in which farmhouses were closer together than in many regions of the West.[61] Trees and shrubs planted near farm buildings, roads, and canals combined with the summer greenery of dependably watered fields to impart upon the northern Piedmont a verdancy unlike that of most of the Arid West. Fences were also a prominent part of the rural scene, because farmers were anxious to keep wandering stock from their fields. The Union Colony was famed for a fifty-mile-long fence that enclosed all the lands near Greeley. Another notable feature was the density of the northern Piedmont's transportation infrastructure. With its multiple rail lines and heavily used roads, the area lacked the isolation of much of the rural West. Indeed, the commercial success of the Northern Agricultural Zone was made possible by the network of transport lines that connected the region to markets in Cheyenne, Denver, and nearby mining districts.

Colorado Springs: The Crafting of an Elite Enclave

From its inception, Colorado Springs carved a unique signature at the base of towering Pikes Peak, a legacy still clearly displayed across its modern landscape. It bore the unmistakable stamp of its founder, railroad magnate General William Jackson Palmer. Although Palmer platted other Colorado communities and laid out hundreds of miles of rail lines in the state, his adopted home of Colorado Springs became his most notable legacy. In street grids, buildings, parks, and, more intangibly, the community's collective vision, Palmer's imprint distinguishes Colorado Springs and its environs from other Piedmont cities.

An array of environmental and social features also produced an unusual economic base for the region. The direct appeal to the elite tourist and health seeker, promoted so effectively by Palmer and his railroad, transformed Colorado Springs into a national and international resort of the first order. This preoccupation with recreation and rehabilitation revealed itself everywhere in a landscape of opulent hotels, tourist attractions, spas, and sanitariums. Social exclusivity was also carefully cultivated by the town's residents. Theirs was not to be the usual loose-knit community of western riffraff but rather a model society that revealed the better things in life. This, too, was displayed on the local scene in the form of exclusive clubs, elite residential neighborhoods, and private schools. Colorado Springs's elevated self-image blended the best of metropolitan and European traditions with the freshness and vitality of the Colorado environment.[62] Indeed, with these explicit links to eastern traditions, it is no accident that chroniclers of Colorado Springs termed it the "Newport of the Rockies" and labeled nearby Manitou Springs the "Saratoga of the West."

Palmer's Vision

The location of Colorado Springs represented a complex convergence of chance, physical setting, and economic enterprise.[63] The area's famous bubbling waters, actually located a few miles west of Colorado Springs at Manitou Springs, were well known to Native Americans and to such explorers as Pike, Long, and Frémont. Miners flocked to the area in the late 1850s, only to be disappointed that the Pikes Peak Gold Rush was really a misnomer and that no easy color was being taken in the vicinity of the famed mountain. By 1859, however, the bustling trading town of Colorado City flourished near the base of Pikes Peak and funneled goods into the placer camps of nearby South Park. Even though the burg harbored brief aspirations to be the territorial capital, activity faded quickly by the middle 1860s.

The area's future took a new turn in 1868, however, when William Palmer visited on a survey for the Kansas Pacific Railroad.[64] Palmer's friend and fellow Kansas Pacific employee Dr. William Bell accompanied him, and the pair delighted in the refreshing waters of Manitou Springs and the country thereabouts. Bell, a physician, saw the medicinal potential for the springs, while Palmer's vision expanded to a broader belief that "there will be a famous resort here soon after the R.Rd. reaches Denver." Over the next twelve months, Palmer convinced himself that he would be the architect of such a grand plan.

Palmer's vision for a town at the base of Pikes Peak included his own great north-south railroad, the Denver and Rio Grande. Palmer grew frustrated with the Kansas Pacific Railroad when they built to Denver because he saw greater economic potential in a line that would run south along the Rocky Mountain front, ultimately collecting traffic from Piedmont districts as well as from intersecting transcontinental routes. Palmer also surmised that the Denver and Rio Grande could be extended to Mexico, adding opportunities for international trade. Colorado Springs was to be Palmer's jewel along the route. He also quickly saw advantages in accumulating land in the area, profiting from real estate sales as the town site developed, and the added potential in owning local businesses, hotels, and tourist services.

His vision transcended purely economic motives. From its inception, Palmer's "Fountain Colony" had a utopian bent. Alcohol was banned and traditional class distinctions would be redefined. Palmer believed that "it would be quite a little family and everybody should be looked after to see that there was no distress . . . schools should be put up for them, and bathhouses, and there should be libraries and lectures, and there never would be any strikes or hard feelings among the labourers towards the capitalists, for they would all be capitalists themselves in a small way."[65] Finally, Palmer's paternalistic plans for Colorado Springs included a personal dimension: his home and, more important, that of his new wife, Queen, was to be sited there. Palmer hoped his ambitious plans lived up to Queen's expectations and that the couple would find happiness in his new town at the base of the Rockies.

More mundane tasks of land acquisition, surveying, and railroad construction came first. Palmer first contemplated the acquisition of a 320-acre town site, but in his enthusiasm he bought no fewer than nine thousand acres in the area early in 1870. He received additional financial support from several eastern and English investors. The price was right, however: his overall costs were around eighty cents per acre.[66] Within a few months Palmer profitably sold part of his real estate holdings for fifteen dollars per acre to a new corporation he formed known as the Colorado Springs Company. That entity resold the lands to members of the Fountain Colony, who each paid one hundred dollars and pledged their temperance and good moral character for the right to purchase town lots. The two-thousand-acre plat was surveyed in the summer of 1871 and included the usual gridlike pattern of streets (fig. 52).

Special touches on the landscape suggested the community's aspiring status.[67] The principal thoroughfare of Pikes Peak Avenue strategically took in a full vista of the peak itself. Lands were reserved for a park and a college. Booster George Buckman also reported that "thousands of trees were planted along the avenues of the new city and costly irrigation works constructed, making possible the umbrageous avenues and the shrubbery-

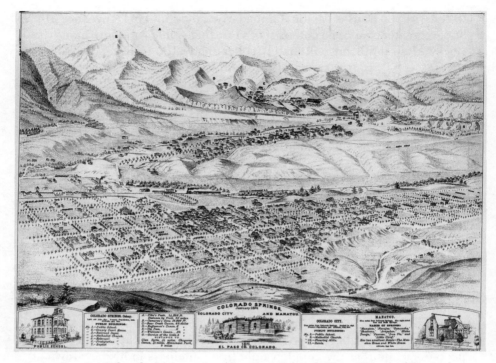

FIGURE 52. Colorado Springs, 1874 (Courtesy Colorado State Historical Society)

dotted lawns which to-day delight the eye of every visitor and form one of
the city's chief attractions." Care was given to street naming, as well, with
major east-west avenues named after western streams and with north-
south routes named for various western mountain ranges.

Even as lot surveys and irrigation canals were being completed,
Palmer's rail line worked south from Denver, arriving in the new settlement in October 1871. By then only fifty houses and a log hotel graced the
site, but the pace of change soon accelerated. In early 1872, with Palmer's
financial support, the Colorado Springs Hotel was built, and by the end of
that year fifteen hundred people relocated to the new colony town.[68]

Meanwhile, nearby Manitou Springs sprang to life.[69] By August 1872,
Palmer and William Bell had opened the fifty-eight-room Manitou House
at the springs. Additional hotel building, spring development, and walk-
way construction followed by the middle of the decade. Manitou Springs
received added legitimacy as a health resort with the arrival of Dr. Samuel
Solly in 1874. Solly promoted the medicinal and restorative charms of the
local waters and became a key booster for the region. At the close of the
1870s, the region accommodated twenty-five thousand tourists per season

and its fame as a summer retreat was augmented by a new appeal to winterbound invalids seeking a safe and healthy haven.

Between 1880 and 1920, Colorado Springs blossomed into a globally famed health resort, playground, and elite enclave.[70] The area's reputation as a "little London" became associated with some two thousand English citizens who took up seasonal and permanent residence in the area by the close of the 1880s. The city's population multiplied: by 1890 more than eleven thousand people called Colorado Springs home, and that figure almost tripled by 1920. As with Denver, the town sprawled with an expanding electric streetcar network and a series of upper-class suburbs by 1900. Of equal significance were the swelling numbers of itinerants who annually converged on the area. The dozen developed springs at Manitou attracted forty thousand visitors in 1898, and estimates for Colorado Springs itself surpassed one hundred thousand yearly visitors and health seekers by World War I.

Creating a Landscape of Urban Amenities

A closer look at the area's landscape between 1880 and 1920 reveals how the multiple charms of that physical and social environment were marketed to the larger world. Part of the area's special character was shaped by General Palmer.[71] He invested in opulent hotels and donated land for the construction of one of the region's largest sanitariums as well as for the campus of Colorado College. Palmer's nearby canyon home, a baronial English Tudor manse named Glen Eyrie, also became a prominent and much-visited part of the landscape. Built as a modest frame house in the early 1870s, Glen Eyrie underwent massive additions in 1903–4 that culminated in a sixty-seven-room palace complete with a bowling alley, a dining room that could seat three hundred, and encircling gardens and lawns that would have been the envy of British royalty.

Palmer's love of greenery extended beyond his English gardens; he donated thousands of acres to city parks to create one of the most lavishly embowered towns in the American West.[72] Palmer gave away lands in nearby North Cheyenne Canyon and on Austin Bluffs (today's Palmer Park) to serve as convenient outdoor pleasure grounds for city residents and visitors. Within the city, Acacia Park, Thorndale Park, and Dorcester Park were rooted in Palmer's beneficence. Most significant was his donation in 1907 of a 165-acre strip of in-town land along meandering Monument Creek, which transformed an ugly urban junkyard into an Anglicized retreat of winding paths, bridges, and gardens.

Beyond Palmer's personal largesse, other environmental features attracted thousands of residents and visitors.[73] The area's climate was presumed to cure the respiratory ills of the infirm and to awaken even in the healthy a new sense of strength and vigor. Elevation excited respiration, stimulated muscle growth, and relieved overworked brains, while the fresh, dry air and moderate winds were "curative of tuberculosis" and led to more rapid tissue regeneration. Promoter Edwards Roberts also recognized the toniclike qualities of the open plains east of Colorado Springs as he suggested that "a gallop across country, with neither a fence or a ditch to hinder one's progress, stirs the dormant blood, brings a flush to the pale cheek, and forces forgetfulness of the world, and its trials."

Local features became rooted in these atmospheric amenities.[74] Most prominent were sanitariums built in increasing numbers after 1880. Institutions like Saint Francis Hospital, Cragmor Sanitorium, and Glockner Sanitorium offered the virtues of the local air and settings that made the most of mountain views, pleasant walkways, and stress-free living. Numerous smaller operations similar to boardinghouses were scattered through the city. Because exposure to fresh night air was considered crucial to the treatment, sleeping rooms and appended porches became ubiquitous architectural features after 1884. Many residents also took this advice, producing a residential landscape replete with variations on the sleeping porch.

More generally, because clean air was an asset, Colorado Springs residents developed an obvious early sensitivity to air pollution and manufacturing that surely bemused residents of grimy Black Hawk or Leadville. In an environmental and aesthetic prescience motivated by preserving the pulmonary purity of the locale, city boosters advertised that "no community pays more attention to keeping the air clean and pure than does Colorado Springs. There is practically no factory smoke, as the large ore reduction mills are far from the center of the city, and . . . the burning of leaves and waste material is strictly prohibited within the city limits."[75]

Area springs offered other environmental pleasures, particularly at nearby Manitou.[76] Each bubbling orifice was accorded particular properties peculiarly appropriate for treating certain complaints. Amounts of dissolved soda, lime, iron, sodium, and magnesia were carefully measured and assessed. Synergies between chemicals in the water and the quality of the atmosphere were also postulated. Amid these aqueous amenities, Manitou Springs blossomed in the 1870s and 1880s. By the turn of the century rambling and "fashionable watering-place hotels" such as the Manitou House, Mansions, Barker, and Cliff House offered guests access to the springs and diversions from hiking to ballroom dancing. Bathhouses also became important landscape features. Spa facilities boasted Spanish-style architecture, dozens of tubs, plunges, and saunas, and standing armies of nurses, therapists, and physicians ready to massage, shock, and otherwise manipulate their patients to health. Bottling plants and drinking pavilions dotted the hills around Manitou Springs advertising that drinking ginger champagne or lemonade made from Manitou's mineral waters was "highly efficacious in the treatment of Rheumatism and all Kidney Diseases, for Bright's Disease, Diabetes, Torpid Liver, Malaria, Dyspepsia, Nervous Prostration, and Insomnia."

Opportunities for outdoor activities beckoned.[77] "America's Scenic Playground" offered the chance to hike onto a nearby peak or into a convenient canyon. Day hiking increased greatly in popularity by the late 1870s, and such later organizations as the Rocky Mountain Club and Saturday Nite Club promoted trail construction and the benefits of outdoor activity. Here one could mix the healthy act of exploring the great outdoors with a new appreciation of the eccentricities and sublimity of the natural world. Surely the most famous destination was the Garden of the Gods, where eroded sandstone bluffs and columns conjured up images of everything from the classic "Eagle with Pinions Spread" to the more fanciful "Seal Making Love to a Nun." In the Romantic traditions of the time, visitors were encouraged to envision classic ruins of the Old World amid these stony monuments, and there was no shortage of sphinxes, Greek temples, and abbeys to be seen in the "sublime awkwardness" of the place. As with the Garden of the Gods, nearby Williams Canyon also was "full of eccentricities and fanciful semblances . . . huge castles, gigantic solid cathedrals, pulpits, quaint resemblances to human faces and animals."

Pikes Peak itself became an object of increasing interest and challenge for the outdoors set.[78] The mountain Zebulon Pike had thought impossible to conquer proved remarkably accessible, given its 14,110-foot summit. By 1874 a seven-mile trail began at Colorado City and reached Jones Park at 9,000 feet. Late in the decade, a wagon road was pushed through to Seven Lakes, and from there it was only a five-mile hike to the summit. Accessibility to the stratospheric views of the peak was enhanced with the completion of a carriage road to the summit in 1889 and with the construction of a popular cog railway two years later. Finally, a remarkable auto toll road snaked its way to the summit by 1915 with entrepreneur Spencer Penrose pouring more than $250,000 into the project. The road marked the marriage of the new transportation technology with the area's reputation for astonishing scenery, and its memorable ascent awed flatlands visitors even as it overheated countless radiators (fig. 53).

For many, the region's social luxuries were as compelling as its crisp air, bubbling waters, and scenery.[79] As mentioned, Palmer's social vision included temperance and a commitment to civic planning. When easterners and Europeans increased their presence, these early notions of community were augmented to include a broad array of cultural niceties.

FIGURE 53. Pikes Peak auto highway, 1915 (Courtesy Colorado Springs Pioneer Museum, Starsmore Center for Local History)

Spurring these notions was the town's persisting Anglophilia and the pivotal role of local women who pressed from the outset for churches, schools, concerts, and other community activities. Close social links to Boston, New York, Philadelphia, and London were not sundered by distance, and these helped many residents and visitors stay in touch with the latest news, finance, and fashion.

This sense of community and social exclusivity was manifested spatially in a growing number of elite neighborhoods. As the city expanded in the 1880s, surveyors added curving streets and larger lots just southwest of Colorado College that soon became a neighborhood of upper-class homes.[80] The residential landscape itself became a symbol for one local booster, as he noted, "In speaking of the intellectual life of the community, one ought not to lose sight of the homes, which are themselves of distinct educational value. Many of these have been established by families who have brought their refinement and high conceptions of living, and the influence of these is felt in the churches and throughout the social and moral life of the community."[81]

The most dramatic expression of the exclusive residential landscape was the planned elite suburb of Broadmoor, brainchild of entrepreneur James Pourtales.[82] Dating from 1889, it was a huge 2,400-acre development focused around a lake and a lavish casino and recreation complex. Although Pourtales's initial scheme ran into terminal financial problems with the Panic of 1893, Broadmoor survived to become an "exclusive residence district" of "beautiful country residences and stately mansions" with a "quiet elegance" that appealed "to many of the prominent society people of the East." By 1918 the newly built Mediterranean-style Broadmoor Hotel offered an adjacent lake, eighteen-hole golf course, and grounds designed by the Olmstead Company of Brookline, Massachusetts (fig. 54).

Local organizations structured and defined important elite social networks, and these institutions became prominent in the urban landscape.[83] Private clubs played a crucial role in bringing like-minded people together. In 1877 the English contingent in town, led by Dr. Solly, created the El Paso Club. Club members, who included the city's leading businessmen and politicians, relaxed in the opulence of the reading or billiard room, took meals and entertained visitors in the dining hall, and struck financial deals over a casual poker game. Other men's organizations, such as the Pikes Peak Club and the Colorado Springs Club, performed similar functions in more modest surroundings, while a collection of women's organizations catered to the vision of elite females.

FIGURE 54. Playing on the Piedmont: the Broadmoor Hotel complex, 1925 (Courtesy Colorado Springs Pioneer Museum, Starsmore Center for Local History)

Country clubs gained in popularity, with Broadmoor's Cheyenne Mountain Country Club assuming a leading role after 1891.[84] Gambling, drinking, billiards, and annual ballroom fetes dominated indoor activities at the club, while golf, polo, cricket, tennis, and riding constituted proper outdoor diversions. The rambling club house had "about it an atmosphere of ease and comfort," and the sprawling grounds with their putting greens, polo fields, and stables displayed all of the classic signatures of rural luxury (fig. 55). One newspaper acknowledged the club's exclusive nature as it reported, "Membership in the club is eagerly sought and exceedingly difficult to attain. One who succeeds in obtaining admission is made socially beyond impeachment."

As with one's leisure, it was important to belong to the right churches and attend the proper schools.[85] Prominent among religious establishments was Grace Episcopal Church, housed in a proper English Gothic structure on Pikes Peak Avenue. As for education, numerous private schools offered opportunities to transcend plebeian elements, and Colorado College grew to become one of the best private colleges in the American West.

But even as Colorado Springs flowered as one of the nation's great elite enclaves between 1880 and 1920, other forces promoted the diversification

FIGURE 55. Creating an elite community: the Cheyenne Mountain Country Club House (Courtesy Penrose Library, Colorado Springs)

of the region's economy. By 1890 two new rail lines increased the area's centrality and function as a general provider of urban services. In the late 1880s, James Hagerman's amazing Colorado Midland line pierced the Rockies west of Colorado Springs, snaking its way via Leadville to the silver boomtown of Aspen.[86] During this same period the Chicago, Rock Island and Pacific Railroad also chose Colorado Springs as its western terminus. These decisions spurred the local construction economy and enlarged the manufacturing sector in nearby Colorado City.[87] There, railroad maintenance shops, a new glassworks, and mine smelters angered some of the area's promoters amid increasing factory smoke and the din of accelerating road and rail construction.

The expansion of gold mining at Cripple Creek on the southwest flanks of Pikes Peak spurred the economic diversification of the region by the middle 1890s.[88] The sedate tree-lined avenues of the Springs suddenly took on a whiff of boomtown atmosphere as dozens of mining company offices opened their doors on Tejon Street and local bank deposits increased ninefold between 1893 and 1902. The result by 1920 was a Piedmont city still defined by its unique resort and health-seeker landscapes but increasingly influenced by economic diversification.

Pueblo: "Pittsburgh of the West"

Nearby Pueblo could not have been more different from the resort setting of Colorado Springs. Ironically, Pueblo owed much of its growth to the same source of capital that spurred activity in Colorado Springs: both cities felt the guiding hand of William Jackson Palmer and benefited in different ways from the arrival of the Denver and Rio Grande Railroad in the early 1870s. In some ways, Pueblo's location in the fertile Arkansas River Valley paralleled that of Greeley, because both centers prospered from their proximity to rich agricultural hinterlands. As Pueblo grew, however, it resembled Denver more than any other Colorado city. In its size, commercial reach, and economic and cultural diversity, Pueblo assumed an importance by 1900 second only to the capital city. Indeed, given its location and rail connections, Pueblo dominated much of the regional trade in the south central and southwestern portions of the state. With the flowering of heavy industry in the city after 1880, Pueblo's sheer grittiness also distinguished it from other Colorado towns. Its late nineteenth-century landscapes and working-class communities resembled midwestern steel towns in their heady days of industrial expansion.

The town began modestly.[89] Between 1821 and 1846 a series of forts occupied the site and served as an international entrepôt in the growing trade between the Missouri Valley and the Mexican towns of Taos and Santa Fe.

With the adjacent Arkansas River serving as the border, "the Pueblos" became an important bridgehead to the Mexican Southwest. After the war with Mexico, New Mexican traders and farmers arrived in greater numbers, only to be burned out in 1854 by Ute raiding parties slow to embrace the American geopolitical vision for the region. By 1860, however, the territory's new placer-based economic geography encouraged the formal survey of Pueblo town site by a group of Denverites. Although Pueblo's development flagged in the middle 1860s, the economy turned around after 1868 as the area's reputation for fine pastures attracted increasing numbers of cattlemen. More generally, Pueblo was recognized as "the center of business and trade for Southern Colorado," and its multicultural character still revealed its strong links to New Mexico and the Hispanic Southwest.

William Jackson Palmer's arrival on the scene amplified Pueblo's prospects in the early 1870s.[90] As his Denver and Rio Grande Railroad pushed south toward Pueblo in 1872, local residents thrilled at the thought of direct rail connections to Denver and the world beyond. Sentiments soured, however, when residents found that Palmer planned to bypass their town. In fact, the entrepreneur established a new plat called South Pueblo on the opposite side of the Arkansas River and built the main depot there. In spite of Palmer's finagling, both Pueblo and South Pueblo thrived, the rail connection stimulating a building boom that led to the construction of 180 new structures in 1872. In a pattern similar to Colorado Springs, Palmer created an affiliated land company in South Pueblo that controlled the real estate at the new town site. His Central Colorado Improvement Company acquired a large acreage carved from the Nolan Mexican land grant on the south side of the river and used the site to develop his South Pueblo project. More important, Palmer extended his narrow-gauge line west to Fremont County late in 1872, to the coalfields around Walsenberg and Trinidad by 1876, to the San Luis Valley by 1878, and to the booming silver mines of Leadville by 1881. These extensions to the system focused the railroad's network on Pueblo and guaranteed its role as the major trade and transport center in the southern half of the state.

Additional rail links solidified Pueblo's urban ascendancy between 1875 and 1888.[91] The most important connection was the Atchison, Topeka, and Santa Fe line, which arrived in Pueblo in the mid-1870s and tied the center with the Midwest and New Mexico. By 1890 the Missouri Pacific, the Rock Island, and the Denver, Texas, and Fort Worth lines further connected Pueblo with both midwestern and southern cities, creating a great "spider's web" of linkages, according to the Pueblo Board of Trade in 1893. Four dozen passenger trains arrived and departed daily in Pueblo, the railyards handled three thousand freight cars a day, and the

rail industry employed more than fifteen hundred men in town. One promoter averred that the area's potential as a trade center knew no limits:

> Pueblo has all the Great West for its field. Just as all roads were said to lead to
> Rome, the transportation lines of the vast midland prairie of the Union converge
> toward it. . . . Pueblo, seated beside that gateway of the Rockies, the Grand Canon
> of the Arkansas, and equidistant from the British line and the Gulf, is an interme-
> diate port for the trans-continental argosies. As a railroad center of the far West,
> it is, in fact, in the position as to that great empery of commerce beyond the Mis-
> sissippi, that Chicago holds with regard to the region of the Great Lakes.[92]

An Economic Geography of Industry

As events unfolded in the 1880s, however, it became clear that Pueblo's
economic and cultural character would be molded more by the captains
of industry than by merchants and wholesalers. Certain macroeconomic
forces played their part: the West underwent tremendous demographic
and economic growth between 1880 and 1920, and this surge created great
new regional demands for industrial products. Accessibility was another
critical ingredient, and any city with Pueblo's railroad connections was
poised to compete in the industrial world.[93] As the Pueblo Board of Trade
boasted, "She is so located in this valley that every incoming train from
whatever direction, has a 'downhill pull' all the way from her storehouses
of wealth in the mountains," thus lowering transportation costs for potential industrialists. More specifically, Leadville's meteoric rise in the late
1870s created the need for vastly expanded smelting operations, and
Pueblo's proximity to the carbonate camp spurred the creation of a large,
centralized, and economically efficient smelting complex that served not
just Leadville but a much larger tributary region. Pueblo's industrial legacy
was assured by Palmer's decision in 1879 to establish the Colorado Coal
and Iron Company, an enterprise reorganized in 1892 as the Colorado Fuel
and Iron Company and destined to become the leading manufacturer of
steel west of the Mississippi River.

The company's direction could be gleaned in the First Annual Report
of the Denver and Rio Grande Railway in 1873. Therein Palmer informed
his shareholders that his land development operation, the Central Colorado Improvement Company, had acquired large tracts of iron and coal
lands and that soon there would be "iron manufactures established in connection with the coal."[94] Palmer assessed Pueblo's location and its proximate resource base, surmising correctly that the southern Piedmont center was ideally situated to take advantage of its surroundings (fig. 56).

Vertically integrated with company-owned coal and iron mines and affiliated with the Denver and Rio Grande Railroad, the Colorado Fuel and

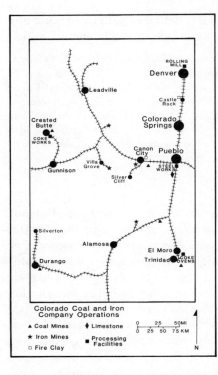

FIGURE 56. Coal and iron properties of the Colorado Coal and Iron Company, circa 1885 (Adapted from a company map reproduced in H. Lee Scamehorn, *Pioneer Steelmaker in the West: The Colorado Fuel and Iron Company, 1872–1903* [Boulder: Pruett, 1976], 21)

Iron Company was the catalyst that irreversibly thrust Pueblo into the industrial era and forged a striking industrial landscape that endures today. As Palmer's early vision presaged, the company reached far beyond Pueblo: by the mid-1880s, it owned more that one hundred thousand acres of land and leased rights to mine and develop another six hundred thousand acres in the region.[95] It operated coal mines near Canon City, Walsenberg, El Moro (near Trinidad), and Crested Butte north of Gunnison. Pueblo's setting also afforded the company ready access to "wonderfully rich" fields of raw iron: large deposits were developed in nearby Fremont, Chaffee, and Costilla Counties. Indeed, as one critic summarized early in the twentieth century, the company's purpose was to "assert ownership throughout southern Colorado, the ownership of courts, executive and legislative officials, of coroners and other juries, of the churches, of the saloons, of the schools, of the lands, of the houses upon the lands, and eventually a certain ownership over the men who toil upon the lands."[96]

Pueblo's manufacturing growth between 1880 and 1920 ranks with that of many eastern cities and was most notable in the smelting and steel-making industries.[97] Factory employment soared from less than 1,000 in the 1880s to over 6,500 in 1920. Given the timing of Leadville's boom in the late

1870s, the growth of smelting operations preceded the expansion of the local steel industry. In 1879 the firm of Mather and Geist established sizable ore refining operations in the city. By the 1890s four large smelting plants collected and processed ore from a tributary region that encompassed Colorado, Wyoming, Utah, Nevada, Arizona, New Mexico, and Mexico. The Pueblo Board of Trade proudly proclaimed that it was "the greatest smelting city on the American Continent." In particular, the mammoth Philadelphia Smelting and Refining Company, established in 1888 by Meyer Guggenheim, began a process in which large eastern investors brought Pueblo into their grasp. By the turn of the century, the Guggenheims joined forces with the Rockefellers and the Goulds to control many aspects of the Pueblo smelting industry.

The steel business underwent a similar evolution.[98] The blast furnaces of the Colorado Coal and Iron Company opened for business in the 1880s and were capable of producing 80 tons of pig iron per day that could be refined and refashioned into a variety of steel castings, forgings, and rails. The company selected land south of Pueblo for the site of their plant, naming it Bessemer after the revolutionary steel-making process. Within a few years several hundred workers were employed at the plant, and its presence created an agglomeration of related metal-working and processing factories. When it was reorganized as Colorado Fuel and Iron Company in 1892, the sprawling plant employed more than fifteen hundred workers and produced 170,000 tons of refined product annually. Although tough times forced the company into financial partnership with the Rockefellers and Goulds early in the twentieth century, the factory survived, and by World War I the expanded Minnequa works employed five thousand men and annually produced 600,000 tons of steel.

Pueblo's Cultural Landscape, 1860–1920

Pueblo's cultural landscape reflected its changing economic base. The town's polycentric expansion suggested its diverse roots.[99] A bird's-eye view of the burgeoning city from the 1880s reveals three centers of activity (fig. 57). The street grid on the north side of the Arkansas River grew from the ranching and trading plat laid out in 1860. Palmer's railroad town of South Pueblo sat directly across the river with its distinctive set of curving streets looping along low bluffs "affording the utmost latitude for landscape and building effects." Finally, hints of a third focus of activity were taking shape where the new Bessemer Steel Works were constructed by the Colorado Coal and Iron Company. Soon much of the area between the steel works and the reservoir filled in with additional industrial developments and workers' homes, making Bessemer a booming "suburb of

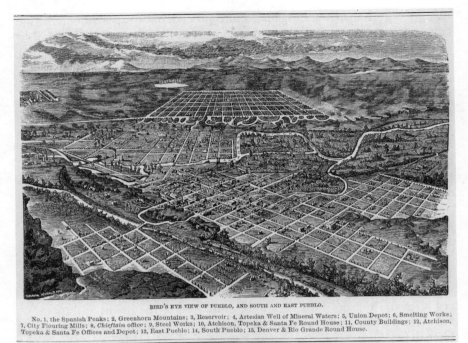

BIRD'S EYE VIEW OF PUEBLO, AND SOUTH AND EAST PUEBLO.

No. 1, the Spanish Peaks; 2, Greenhorn Mountains; 3, Reservoir; 4, Artesian Well of Mineral Waters; 5, Union Depot; 6, Smelting Works; 7, City Flouring Mills; 8, *Chieftain* office; 9, Steel Works; 10, Atchison, Topeka & Santa Fe Round House; 11, County Buildings; 12, Atchison, Topeka & Santa Fe Offices and Depot; 13, East Pueblo; 14, South Pueblo; 15, Denver & Rio Grande Round House.

FIGURE 57. Bird's-eye view of Pueblo, and South and East Pueblo, 1880s (Courtesy Denver Public Library, Western History Collection)

smelters and iron works, and of the residences of the people employed therein." These varied nuclei consolidated politically in 1886 as it became apparent that they shared a common urban destiny and that a larger municipal authority could best address issues of local governance and development.

Pueblo's visible scene changed dramatically from its cowtown days of the late 1860s to its efflorescence as a major industrial center. Given the varied topography and survey grids, the site offered many possibilities for development. Boosters may be excused for their ebullience as they pondered the local aesthetics, comparing them favorably to Denver: "There is a flatness about Denver which greatly detracts from its beauty. Pueblo, on the contrary, with her mesa and bottom lands, her bluffs and plains, her winding river and groves of cotton trees, give variety to the landscape. The time will come when the beautiful bluff will be terraced and adorned with grass, flowers, fruit and ornamental trees. . . . As the city grows in wealth and importance, she will be far more beautiful than Denver can possibly be made."[100] As it turned out, Pueblo put questions of landscaping and beauty behind the exigencies of industrial expansion, but pride in local appearances was ongoing. Part of that sensibility was cultivated by early corporate entities that controlled real estate and industry in the city. South Pueblo's Central Colorado Improvement Company, for example, constructed "an irrigating canal 20 miles in length, has made roads and bridges, graded streets, set out thousands of trees, and prepared the foundation for an attractive and busy town."[101] Nearby Bessemer also felt a corporate presence on the landscape as the Colorado Coal and Iron Company developed surrounding real estate beyond the gates of the plant and constructed much of the community's employee housing.

More broadly, the commercial scene reflected the growing presence of industrial capital in the city.[102] Between 1888 and 1892 no fewer than 3,500 brick and stone buildings were erected. A maturing urban landscape of electric streetcar lines, multistory buildings, and, most impressively, the Grand Opera House, greeted turn-of-the-century visitors to the city. Busy Main Street and Union Avenue emerged as principal commercial thoroughfares, offering early twentieth-century residents an assortment of services second in the state only to Denver (fig. 58).

FIGURE 58. A maturing urban landscape: Union Avenue, Pueblo, circa 1910 (Courtesy Denver Public Library, Western History Collection)

Ultimately the sheer size, sound, smell, and sprawl of the city's principal industrial plants most dramatically defined the landscape.[103] By the
early 1890s the steel plant at Bessemer covered 47 acres, and this ballooned
to over 580 acres by the 1920s at the expanded Minnequa Works. On site,
there were "16 furnaces, blast furnace, rail mill, bolt and spike mill, wire
mill, 40-inch mill, 25-inch mill, 14-inch merchant mill, 12-inch and 20-inch
mill, rod and 10-inch mill, pipe foundry, shops, power plant, a by-products
coke plant and a railroad system using . . . 17 locomotives and 300 cars." It
was hard to miss (fig. 59)! Dozens of smaller plants added to the din and
bustle, with many operations concentrated near the river or railroad on the
east and southeast sides of town.

Pueblo's social geography reflected its industrial roots.[104] Given the
timing of Pueblo's expansion between 1880 and 1920 and its overall level of
accessibility, it is hardly surprising that its cultural character paralleled
many industrial midwestern and northeastern cities. The "Pittsburgh of
the West" took on the ethnic complexion of steel and coal towns further
east. By 1900 more than half the city's population was foreign-born or first-
generation natives. Source regions were diverse: Irish and Germans dominated before 1880, with Germans taking an early leading role in the smelting business. Given its legacy, Pueblo supported a sizable Mexican
population whose numbers increased through labor recruitment policies
undertaken by such companies as Colorado Fuel and Iron. During the
1890s thousands of Italians arrived, many directly from southern Italy and
Sicily and others from New York City. Other southern and eastern Europeans added diversity between 1890 and 1910. A Greek community from
Chicago relocated to Pueblo, and a nucleus of Slavs, recently removed
from Joliet, Illinois, in the 1880s, set the stage for much larger arrivals from
Slovenia, Serbia, Russia, and Czechoslovakia in later decades. Pueblo's
access to an extensive rail network made the immigrant's task easier, with
many new arrivals coming from debarkation points at New York City, New
Orleans, and Galveston. Smaller populations of Japanese and Chinese
were part of the ethnic mix, along with a growing presence of American-
born blacks, who surpassed fourteen hundred residents by 1900.

Several institutions contributed to survival within the new community.
Churches provided cultural stability amid the din of diverse immigrant
communities. Catholic parishes represented those from Mexico, Italy, and
eastern Europe. Saint Michael's Greek Orthodox Church, constructed in
1903, supported growing numbers of other eastern and southern Europeans. African Methodist and Bethlehem Baptist congregations catered
to the community's black population. Fraternal and mutual aid societies
were meeting places for social activities and were often the only forms of
health and life insurance shared by ethnic groups. Pueblo examples in-

FIGURE 59. Industrial capitalism on the western landscape: Minnequa Steel Works, 1902 (Courtesy Pueblo Library District)

cluded the Ethiopian Protective and Beneficial Aid Association (1902), the Siciliana Lodge (1899), and the Croatian Fraternal Union of America (1898). Two dozen locally published foreign-language newspapers carried specialized information, and in a less formal fashion, ethnic saloons such as the Slovene-frequented Star Bar were important clearinghouses of local gossip and international news.

The city's largest twentieth-century employer, Colorado Fuel and Iron, also addressed problems of its immigrant workers. The company staffed a Sociological Department with three dozen employees "whose business it is to look after the education and amusements" of its workers as well as "teaching English and citizenship" to those in need of training.[105] The company provided employees with entertainment, preschool education, and health care benefits at its own hospital and clinic. The approach echoed the paternalistic nature of the company-worker relationship but in the end facilitated the process of cultural assimilation for thousands of Pueblo immigrant laborers.

One of the most powerful mechanisms for dealing with the challenges of immigrant life was residential clustering, a geographical process that involved the dual forces of voluntary congregation among similar migrants and the common tendency for local native white populations to segregate the newer arrivals into the less desirable and visible portions of town.[106] Actively at work in Pueblo, the process of residential clustering between 1880 and 1920 produced a striking mosaic of ethnic neighborhoods that complicated broader patterns of class-based housing within the city. Almost every steel plant or smelter was ringed by worker housing, and these areas were subdivided into zones of Mexican, Italian, or Slavic dominance.

Suburban Bessemer, just west of the Colorado Fuel and Iron Company plant, was broken into a variety of well-defined ethnically based neighborhoods. Just to the southwest, Minnequa Heights saw concentrations of Serbs, Croats, Poles, and Czechs, while Salt Creek east of the plant served as home for poorer Hispanics, including many who squatted on company-owned land. North of the Arkansas River, an originally Mexican neighborhood became Italian in the 1890s, and a nearby district along South Santa Fe Avenue became part of Goat Hill, another Italian community with strong Sicilian links. Even closer to the river, Slavs crowded into "the Grove," only a short commute to the steel works and smelters that employed them.

The eyes of a young Pueblo woman, Josephine Cardillo, only hint at the daily challenges and stresses endured by immigrant families adjusting to these new American workplaces and communities (fig. 60). According

FIGURE 60. Creating new communities: home of the Cardillo family, Josephine Cardillo on porch, Pueblo, 1908 (Courtesy Pueblo Library District)

to the Census of 1910, she and her parents lived in a modest frame home in the one-hundred-block of South Santa Fe Avenue, a neighborhood filled with dozens of other Italian-born residents.[107] Josephine's father and brother were the principal breadwinners, working at a nearby saloon to support the family of six. For many of Pueblo's immigrant arrivals, the family was the strongest institution of economic and social support. Their diverse ethnic signatures across Pueblo's early twentieth-century neighborhoods made this southern Colorado city one of the West's most culturally varied places and permanently stamped the community with a unique social identity.

5

Hinterlands
Eastern Plains, 1860–1920

Between the Rockies and the Kansas-Nebraska border are
150 miles of high plains that few Americans associate with
Colorado. Across much of this flat and gently undulating region, one cannot even see the Front Range. Its topography,
climate, and history confirm that it is a part of the Great Plains. Settlement in this region necessitated strategies of adjustment that recognized
the limits of the area's physical setting. Semiarid, treeless, and prone to
weather extremes, the high plains was subjected to a series of adaptations
between 1860 and 1920 as people experimented with living within its vast
expanse. Some argue that the tenuous tradition of experimentation continues today and that modern residents are destined to repeat the errors
of the past. Whatever the look of its future landscape, much of what is
there today springs from decisions made and actions taken in the formative period between 1860 and 1920. In those six decades Colorado's eastern
plains were radically transformed from a Native American–dominated
grassland into a largely artificial and exotic agricultural landscape reflecting varied European cultural traditions transplanted from distant and disparate environments.

The Plains as Wilderness

Traffic increased greatly across Colorado's eastern plains during the 1850s
and early 1860s. Clearly, however, the major trails crossing the Colorado
plains were paths to another place. The plains were a distance to surmount, not a destination to culminate a western journey.[1] During the Gold
Rush era, the most widely traveled routes across the plains followed the
riparian corridors of the Arkansas and Platte Rivers along which water and
timber were readily available. Adventurous argonauts also launched themselves onto the more direct but resource-poor Republican or Smoky Hill
routes, which included considerable stretches devoid of wood and water.

Published assessments of the region provide one guide to perceptions
of the plains during the early 1860s. Horace Greeley was hardly enchanted
by what he saw: western Kansas Territory equaled "any other scene on our

154

continent for desolation," and much of his narrative focuses on the "numerous and repulsive" Indians, the "devouring sands" of dry creek beds, and the sad tales of travelers on the Smoky Hill route, which proved "a sore trial for weary, gaunt, heavy-laden cattle."[2] Travel companion Albert Richardson penned a similar narrative, adding illustrations to his published account that reinforced verbal images of the region's wildness (fig. 61). Even as Pikes Peak came into view, Richardson lamented, "We are still on the desert with its soil white with alkali, its stunted shrubs, withered grass, and brackish waters often poisonous to both cattle and men."[3]

These images of aridity, reinforced a thousandfold by the experiences of ill-prepared goldseekers, confirmed earlier reports by Zebulon Pike and Stephen H. Long. Although an all-encompassing regional perception of the Great Plains as a desert is not evident in the 1860s, it was precisely the high plains of western Kansas and eastern Colorado that proved to be the persistent core of desert imagery.[4]

Clashes between Plains Indians and interloping whites between 1861 and 1869 added a further threat that confirmed for Anglos the wildness and danger inherent within the region. For Native Americans, mostly Arapaho and Cheyenne, the decade drew their occupance of the region to a climactic and devastating close through a series of actions that rapidly re-

RAILROAD TRAIN ENCOUNTERING A HERD OF BUFFALOES.

FIGURE 61. A wilderness traversed: the railroad challenges the buffalo, from Albert Richardson's *Beyond the Mississippi* (Hartford, Conn.: American, 1867, Courtesy Denver Public Library, Western History Collection)

configured the human geography of the plains and paved the way for more permanent and intrusive white settlement.

It is worth pondering Native American experiences on the high plains of eastern Colorado, for their presence proved irreconcilable with that of American settlers.[5] In the case of eastern Colorado, the long process of Indian removal began with the Treaty of Fort Laramie in 1851 and the Treaty of Fort Atkinson in 1853 in which the Cheyenne and Arapaho formally surrendered their sovereignty by acknowledging the presence of American travelers and forts. Tribal boundaries were established, starting a process of territorial circumscription that steadily eroded native control over the region and its resources.[6] As developments unfolded, conflict was perhaps inevitable: the plains became a meeting ground for two dissimilar and vigorously competitive cultural worlds. One group consisted of diverse tribes whose relatively new horse-based mobility had transformed their hunting culture and led to their expanding influence across the region after 1700. The other was an eclectic assortment of soldiers, traders, and potential settlers from a bewildering variety of mostly European backgrounds. Also interested in expansion, this group had two advantages over their native opponents: technological superiority to aid them in battle, and after the American victories of the 1840s, a single, strongly centralized political authority that ultimately triumphed over a more fragmented foe.

Seeds of conflict were planted with the divisive Treaty of Fort Wise in 1861. Several tribal leaders ceded much of the Colorado plains in exchange for a small triangular reservation just north of the Arkansas River. Along with the desolate six-hundred-square-mile Sand Creek Reserve came promised annuities and assistance to domesticate plains peoples and wean them from their wandering ways. Unfortunately, many Cheyenne and Arapaho leaders were not treaty signatories and immediately repudiated its legality. They correctly saw its incompatibility with the extensive hunting habits of their peoples. Adding to the uncertainty was the not-so-distant Civil War, which led to armed clashes with Confederate contingents in northern New Mexico as well as a fear that southerners were fomenting trouble among the natives on the plains.[7] Indeed, for whites traversing the plains in the summers of 1862 and 1863, the region never seemed more wild and unpredictable, perceptions confirmed by the increasing pace of Indian raids and attacks on what Indians saw as intrusive white wagon trains, trading posts, and ranch houses.

War broke out in 1864 and ended any hope for a Native American presence on the Colorado plains. The June massacre of the Hungate family southeast of Denver increased the call for Indian blood even as some Indian leaders wanted to end the conflict and retire peacefully to the confines of the Sand Creek Reservation. In fact, a sizable number of Cheyenne did return to the reserve in the fall of 1864, seemingly under federal protection and oversight. But Governor John Evans and the commander of the Colorado Militia, Colonel John M. Chivington, pushed their case for war, and more than two hundred Indians, many of them women and children, were slaughtered in the early morning of November 29 as they quietly camped at Sand Creek.

The Sand Creek Massacre set off a new round of conflicts: soon Julesburg and Fort Sedgwick in the South Platte Valley were destroyed, mail and telegraph links disrupted, and additional ranches raided. By October 1865, however, Indian representatives again sought peace, a process of forced negotiation that culminated two years later with the Medicine Lodge Treaty of 1867. That treaty, along with agreements made in 1869, dissolved the Sand Creek Reserve and removed Cheyenne and Arapaho peoples from Colorado's eastern plains. They were relocated to southern Kansas and finally to Indian Territory (Oklahoma). Renegade bands initially resisted, and the last battle between whites and Indians was not fought on the Colorado plains until the summer of 1869 along the South Platte Valley one hundred miles northeast of Denver.

The Plains as Pasture

Beginning in the 1860s another image of the plains as a valuable cattle-pasturing zone supplanted notions of the region as a wilderness. Clearly the removal of Native American populations was an important part of this reconfiguration. The decimation of the region's bison herds also contributed to the opening of eastern Colorado to the cattleman. Bison populations across the southern plains still averaged six or seven million in 1850 but were already in decline as drought, disease, horse competition, and the growing robe and pemmican trade pared their numbers. The railroads spelled the end of the plains bison: when the transcontinental line was completed in 1869, the southern herd still numbered over three million, but these numbers evaporated by the middle 1870s, victims of a massive new trade in buffalo hides that used the skin in the making of low-quality leather products.[8]

An important reevaluation of the plains environment came with the early trail drovers and ranchers who supplied the initial Pikes Peak miners of the early 1860s.[9] They discovered that oxen and cattle left through the plains winter thrived on the native short grasses of the region, suggesting the value of the region as a vast pasture. Even as Indian wars flared in the middle 1860s, the stage was set for a major movement of cattle and men onto the high plains of Colorado, a migration that signaled the com-modification of the plains environment and its incorporation into an ex-panding regional and national economy.

The vision of the plains grasslands as a pasture-based commodity be-came widespread after 1865. Strong demand for beef spurred the inclusion of eastern Colorado into the open range system that proved so popular in Texas. In 1859 the Dawson Trail guided herds up the Arkansas Valley to Pueblo and then north to Denver and the mines. After 1864 the Goodnight-Loving Trail took a more western course, entering the territory at Raton and Trinchera passes and paralleling the mountains north to Pueblo, Den-ver, and Cheyenne. Midwestern and eastern markets became increasingly important in the Colorado cattle trade as the Kansas Pacific, the Atchison, Topeka, and Santa Fe, and Union Pacific rail lines were completed across the region between 1870 and 1885. These links, combined with good weather and firm cattle markets, promoted the tremendous expansion of the beef business in eastern Colorado.[10] In addition, Denver's new Union Stockyards opened in 1886 and provided a more centralized regional gath-ering and processing point for Colorado cattle. As fortunes grew, promot-ers boosted legitimate investment possibilities of the beef trade in widely publicized books, pamphlets, and newspaper accounts. After 1875 more outside investors, many based in England and Scotland, joined the search for promised profits as they assembled huge herds that grazed mostly on free public grass before being shipped to packing houses in the Midwest.

Cattle numbers told the story: the 1870 Census counted approximately fifteen thousand cattle in a selection of Colorado plains counties, while ten years later the number had grown more than tenfold.[11] Much of east-ern Colorado's human geography reflected this reorientation, and the pas-toral legacy was stamped onto the regional scene in a new system of rail lines and cattle towns oriented around the needs of the rancher (fig. 62).

The South Platte and Arkansas Valleys were incorporated into the ranching economy after the Civil War.[12] In the lower South Platte Valley, John Iliff expanded his herds in the 1860s when he was contracted to sup-ply railroad construction workers on the Union Pacific line. He assembled a herd of 35,000 cattle and a collection of more than one hundred land parcels that effectively locked up much of the available water across the region. Although he claimed title to only about 15,000 acres, Iliff leased ad-ditional state lands and freely made use of federal lands so that he virtu-ally ruled a 650,000-acre block of northeastern Colorado. Smaller opera-tions in the South Platte Valley also prospered in the 1870s and early 1880s, marketing cattle in Denver or Cheyenne. Once the Union Pacific spur was completed through the lower valley in the early 1880s, centers like Brush,

FIGURE 62. Colorado pastoral: spatial patterns in the early 1880s

Sterling, and Julesburg offered convenient shipping points to distant markets.

To the south, the Arkansas Valley and the broken country near the New Mexico line evolved in parallel fashion. Such pioneer cattlemen as John Prowers and James Jones brought in Texas stock before 1880. These southern Colorado ranchers made use of shipping points along the Kansas Pacific Railroad, and Deer Trail, Hugo, Kit Carson, and Cheyenne Wells each served that purpose. Once the Atchison, Topeka, and Santa Fe line was finished in the mid-1870s, a new string of cattle towns prospered, including La Junta, Las Animas, Lamar, Granada, and Holly. There, railroad shipping agents, packing house representatives, and cattlemen met to link the far-flung pastures of southeastern Colorado with national beef markets. The largest Colorado cattle operation was found in the southeast corner of the state. The British-controlled Prairie Cattle Company bought out James Jones and his brothers in the early 1880s and controlled more than 2.2 million acres of land east and south of the Arkansas and Purgatoire Rivers.[13] As did Iliff, the Prairie Cattle Company locked up critical riverfront acreage and freely used the public domain, even adopting the brazen practice of fencing public acres for their own use.

The plains settlement landscape became organized around the production of beef and reflected cattle-raising traditions from both Texas and

the Midwest.[14] Obviously the early arrival of Texan cattle and the north-
bound trails linked eastern Colorado with the Lone Star State. The emphases on large, loosely managed herds, periodic roundups in the spring
and fall, a skilled equestrian-based cowboy workforce, and extensive use
of unimproved free land were other characteristic signatures of Texan influence on the Colorado landscape. Typically, a ranch headquarters was
on patented land near water with a series of corrals and work buildings
nearby. In a large operation, well-defined trails led from the main ranch
complex to several smaller ranch houses, each on their patented acreage
with access to a nearby stream, pond, or spring. Herds wandered exten-
sively across the ranch and the free public grass surrounding it. The near-
est neighbor might be miles away, and it could be a several-day ride to the
closest town or shipping point.

Distinct from this extensive, open-range ranching settlement pattern
was the midwestern stock-farming landscape. With its British rather than
Iberian roots, the Midwest system was more intensive, focusing on the care
and improved breeding of livestock, the use of smaller, more carefully managed and fenced pastures, and the extensive use of winter feed, often derived from irrigated hay meadows and alfalfa fields. Although less colorful
than Texas-style open-range ranching, livestock farming was widespread
across the eastern plains by the early 1880s. Ranches were smaller and dependence on free public grass diminished over time in favor of leasing lands
and use of more productive irrigated pastures. Effective land management
and improved breeding practices were keys to success and proved to be the
only sustainable adaptation to stock raising across the high plains.

The middle 1880s guaranteed the demise of the Texas open range system in eastern Colorado and pointed the way to more sedentary livestock
farming practices. The bust in the Colorado range cattle business arrived
with a vengeance between 1885 and 1887.[15] Severe winters combined with
dry and unpredictable summers, but the problems of the open range ran
much deeper than a spate of cold or dry weather. Most fundamentally, the
good years of the early 1880s led to an inevitable overuse of the range and
overproduction of cattle. When increasingly marginal pastures were used
during poor weather, productivity plunged.

The unraveling of profitable cattle markets only worsened this confluence of environmental missteps. Overproduction led to falling prices,
which prompted the forced liquidation of herds that pressured prices further. Poor management decisions before and during the downturn negated
any hope for subsequent recovery.[16] As with the mining sector, outside
forces in the cattle business combined with a limited resource base to produce markets that were unpredictable, unsustainable, and ultimately not
within westerners' control.

Still, stock raising persevered on the eastern Colorado plains after the debacle of the 1880s. What emerged between 1890 and World War I was a more successful adaptation to both environmental and economic realities. Successful ranchers shifted to sedentary stock raising, often diversifying their cattle breeding, grazing, and fattening operations with sheepherding and increasingly using irrigated hay and alfalfa pastures as well as small grain farming to broaden their agricultural base. For turn-of-the-century stockmen, the shrinking open range became less important than the quality of owned or leased property. Breeding improvements and a growing number of in-state fattening operations increased margins for those willing to invest in new techniques. In 1902, for example, Sterling rancher W. C. Harris realized that he could increase his profits by fattening large numbers of cattle locally on intensively irrigated pastures and then selling the stock for premium prices to regional and national buyers.[17]

The Denver and Rio Grande Railroad promoted the new approach to livestocking. An advertisement entitled "The Fertile Lands of Colorado" appeared in 1899. Alluding to the wild excesses of earlier years, the publication noted that "it has only been during the last decade that the live stock industry in Colorado has grown to be considered a legitimate part of the farm business."[18] Also described were the virtues of irrigated pastures and fattening operations and the expanding role Denver played in the cattle market as its primacy in the state's economy increased.

By 1906 more than a million dollars was invested into Denver packing houses and a second sizable operation thrived in Pueblo.[19] Stockmen also saw the return of better cattle markets as a huge influx of immigrants bolstered national demand and as World War I boosted beef prices. Thus, though open range days and itinerant cowboys thrived only ephemerally across the eastern plains, they led to a more sustained livestocking economy in many districts, a pastoral adaptation that survives to this day.

The Plains as Oasis

Yet another vision of the Colorado plains refashioned its settlement geography and cultural landscapes. After 1870, irrigation molded development in eastern Colorado's river valleys. Although results varied, the initial half-century of experimentation with irrigation established more essential elements of eastern Colorado's settlement geography, particularly along the well-watered corridors of the Platte and Arkansas Valleys. Just as clearly revealed by that half-century of testing and probing, however, were the stubborn limits of human dominance in a marginal land. Even so, irrigation offered one hope for a sustainable adaptation on the arid Colorado plains.

Unfortunately, climatic challenges in the eastern quarter of the state were even more daunting than in the better-watered northern Piedmont, where large-scale irrigation was pioneered in the early 1870s. To the east— along the lower reaches of the South Platte and Arkansas Rivers—annual precipitation was less than fifteen inches and rivers often ran dry after midsummer. Remarkably, these two valleys were transformed by dozens of irrigation canals between 1875 and 1920, a process that implanted into the region an increasingly productive, specialized, and commercialized agricultural system.

Eastern Colorado's love affair with irrigation was part of a larger western experience in the half-century between 1870 and 1920.[20] Millions of acres of western lands were irrigated during the period, encouraged by a combination of state and federal incentives, an evolving body of distinctive water law (much of it pioneered in Colorado), an array of speculative railroad and land development companies, and a growing regional and national economy that demanded more commercial agricultural production. Within Colorado, lands under irrigation grew to more than 1.6 million acres by 1900, accounting for over 70 percent of the improved farmland in the state. Twenty years later, after the agricultural boom times of World War I, Colorado had almost 3 million acres under irrigation.

The imposition of irrigated agriculture across the eastern plains between 1870 and 1920 says a great deal about prevailing perceptions of the region's environment. First, it recognized that in the context of the humid East, much of the West was indeed arid and would not readily submit to an easy transplantation of exotic agricultural practices. Early successes with irrigation in the Southwest, in Mormon Utah, and in the northern Colorado Piedmont suggested its greater reliability in semiarid settings. But even as investments in irrigation revealed a realistic appreciation of the West's limited rainfall, the practice of irrigation also displayed a sometimes naive confidence in the ability of people to modify, control, and manipulate the western environment.

Boosters like the Denver and Rio Grande Railroad captured the ebullience with which Coloradans pondered the potential of their irrigation projects, concluding, "The bountiful soil, aided by sunshine and irrigation seems capable of meeting every demand. Nowhere in the republic is there a truer paradise for farmers or more certain rewards for the intelligent pursuit of agriculture."[21] Confidence in the human ability to tinker with the environment extended to a belief that irrigation might alter the climate of an area, rendering it more humid and increasing its average annual rainfall. Even geologist and explorer John Wesley Powell, often cited for his sober and clear-headed views on the West's environmental limits, confidently wrote in 1888 that once irrigation was adapted across an area, "the general humidity of the atmosphere in the arid region will be increased, and hence the rains will be increased, and a smaller amount of artificial irrigation will be needed."[22]

The irrigationist's chant was clear: water was a resource, a commodity to be allocated and consumed in the chase for economic gain. Divorced from environmental context and unpredictable natural systems, western water was no different from a gold vein or a timber-covered hillside; it was another resource to be claimed and developed within the storehouse of western abundance.[23] At the core of this optimism, however, was the realization that individual effort was insufficient to develop major irrigation projects. The land could produce, but group initiative was required. In eastern Colorado this meant either private corporate investment or farmer-controlled mutual stock companies. Aside from the early utopian days at Greeley, even these agreements to cooperate in creating an irrigated landscape had for their goal the fruits of individual profit, either to corporate investors or to private farmers who used group-controlled water on their own land parcels.

Varied influences shaped the success or failure of the vast irrigation along the lower Platte and Arkansas Rivers. One critical variable was the unpredictability of the plains natural environment.[24] Most obviously, the rivers varied greatly between their seasonal high and low watermarks. Devastating floods or gripping drought often submerged or parched fields. Along with canal- and dam-building came other unpredictable environmental responses: widespread sedimentation and unwanted foliage clogged irrigation systems and increased chances for flooding. Irrigated lands were also threatened with salt buildup in the soil, a problem that grew worse downstream, particularly in the Arkansas Valley, as minerals accumulated in the flow. Initial investments in an irrigation project thus inevitably produced environmental responses that demanded additional investments simply to maintain the system.

Other environmental variables were more *local* in scale. For all its seeming uniformity, eastern Colorado offered varied ecological niches, complete with soil differences, subtle variations in slope, and microenvironmental disparities that presented diverse opportunities for success, depending on the site and the choice of crops. An orchard could thrive along one small section of a valley, while a few miles away inferior lands might offer opportunities only for a hay crop. None of this intricate local geography of varied agricultural potential was known in 1870, and it took several decades of hard-won experience to sort out more and less valuable acreages.

Although nature obviously mattered, human institutions and decisions were key determinants in the success or failure of an irrigation project. The prior appropriation water doctrine developed within Colorado dictated that early claimants and users of water had priority over later arrivals. Thus the timing of settlement and the relative seniority given to an irrigator's water claim was crucial, because river systems quickly became fully or overappropriated. A recently arrived farmer might have outstanding land, but his junior water claim meant that his fields sat high and dry while a neighbor with a senior claim could count on water when he needed it.

Access to markets and the strength of market demand for crops also shaped the success of the farmer's enterprise. Before the railroad, early irrigation operations were associated with more diversified farms that consumed much of what they grew or sold their crops locally. Once dependable national rail franchises were in place, more specialized and commercialized farms quickly found potential niches. Finally, managerial acumen in acquiring land, manipulating water resources, and experimenting with crops were keys to successful farming. For example, George Swink's willingness to experiment with cantaloupes and sugar beets in the Arkansas Valley was critical in establishing those flourishing agricultural adaptations. Swink and others who became involved with large-scale commercial investments also had to coordinate their efforts carefully with the railroads, food processing plants (particularly in the sugar beet industry), and laborers who would be willing to work in large numbers and over long hours during harvest times.

Oasis Agriculture in the South Platte Valley

Two distinctive settlement geographies dominated eastern Colorado's South Platte Valley before 1880. Upriver from Greeley the Northern Agricultural Zone was well developed: intensive commercial farming catered to regional and even national markets. East of Greeley, however, another world still held sway. Scattered ranches used a mix of private lands and open range to feed the area's livestock populations. Some river bottoms were in irrigated hay production, but without railroad connections between Julesburg and Greeley the lower South Platte Valley remained relatively isolated.[25]

The arrival of Union Pacific and Burlington rail lines in 1881 and 1882 reconfigured agricultural opportunities in the valley. One area of activity centered on Fort Morgan fifty miles downriver from Greeley. Early ditches were restricted to bottoms adjacent to the river. Once the railroads arrived the scale of irrigation expanded as entrepreneurs from Greeley, including several Union Colony members, acquired large blocks of federal and state lands in the vicinity.[26] Greeley farmers, for example, financed much of the construction of the Weldon Valley Ditch, which diverted water on the north side of the Platte just northwest of Fort Morgan (fig. 63). The Platte and Beaver and the Fort Morgan Canal projects on the south side of the river also commenced in the early 1880s. One Greeley noteworthy, Abner Baker, was a principal player in these developments. Baker and his friends and relatives filed on thousands of acres of public lands in the area, helped to finance ditch-building efforts, and struck a deal with the Burlington Railroad to plat the town of Fort Morgan.

Another locus of activity focused interest forty miles downstream near the small settlement of Sterling. During the 1870s the Sterling district supported cattle and sheep ranching along with a scattering of small-scale irrigation ditches.[27] Again the scale of investment and development accelerated during the 1880s. With remarkable speed, the twenty-five-mile Pawnee Ditch was built west of Sterling, opening bottomlands and nearby benches to settlement.

Storage reservoirs added capacity to these downriver districts between 1900 and 1920.[28] They provided critical late summer water and expanded the potential irrigable acreage to include more fertile but heretofore dry uplands. In the Fort Morgan area, farmers took advantage of the Colorado "District Irrigation" statute, which allowed them to issue bonds to raise capital for irrigation canals and reservoirs. Jackson Lake, Bijou Reservoir, Empire Lake, and Riverside Reservoir were built just after the turn of the century, and they broadened the corridor of oasis agriculture both north and south of the river (see fig. 63). Near Sterling, the Jumbo, Prewitt, and North Sterling Reservoirs, all built between 1906 and 1911, similarly expanded the irrigable acreage to the east. Local supporters in Sterling were joined by T. C. Henry, one of Colorado's leading irrigation enthusiasts.

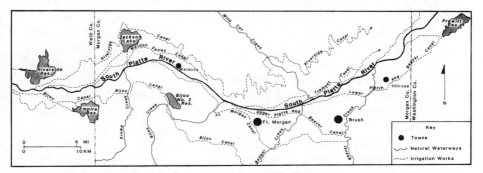

FIGURE 63. Oasis geography: irrigation in the South Platte valley near Fort Morgan (Adapted from J. M. Dille, "Irrigation in Morgan County" [Fort Morgan: Fort Morgan State Bank, 1960])

Henry was also involved in the financing and promotion of irrigation projects at Fort Morgan, in the Arkansas Valley, and along the state's western slope.

Oasis farmers focused upon a select group of crops once irrigable lands were open for development.[29] Livestock demanded irrigated feed crops. In 1890 Morgan County (in the vicinity of Fort Morgan) reported five thousand cattle and over forty thousand sheep, while Logan County (in the vicinity of Sterling) reported eleven thousand cattle and fifteen thousand sheep. Irrigated fields within these counties averaged three cuttings of hay or alfalfa every season. In fact, before 1900 production of those two crops dominated irrigation in the lower valley, with corn being used as a secondary field crop. By 1915, however, strong wheat prices globally encouraged many downriver farmers to shift out of hay, alfalfa, and corn.

Another transformation occurred after 1900 as commercial sugar beet production increased greatly throughout the South Platte Valley. Although sugar beets were first grown around Littleton as early as 1862, large-scale production in the South Platte Valley did not materialize until after 1900. By that time modest success on Colorado's western slope increased interest in the crop. Promoters from the Denver Chamber of Commerce and the State Agricultural College at Fort Collins also extolled its virtues. With encouraging results from experimental plantings in the 1890s, the sugar beet industry ignited between 1901 and 1903 with the construction of six processing factories across the northern Piedmont.[30] A symbiotic relationship developed between farmer and factory: factories were critical in providing a ready market for the specialty crop, and they in turn required a minimum threshold of beet production to guarantee their financial viability. In addition, sugar beet growers quickly established close interrelationships with valley livestock producers: the vegetable heads and beet pulp residues could be fed to cattle and sheep and their manure could then be plowed back into the beet fields to enhance yields.

Processing plants at Loveland, Greeley, Eaton, Fort Collins, Windsor, and Longmont revealed an initial concentration of beet growing in the northern Piedmont, but while this zone remained the largest producer of beets in the South Platte Valley over the next twenty years, interest in the crop quickly spread to selected downriver sites, where expanded irrigation opportunities beckoned both farmers and processors. The pace of change quickened further after 1905. Major financial consolidations put numerous valley factories under the control of the Great Western Sugar Company, an institution that long remained pivotal in Colorado's beet industry. Downriver activity picked up, too, with new acreages and factories built in Sterling in 1905 and in Brush and Fort Morgan in 1906.[31] Fort Morgan's businessmen were key players in getting nearby farmers to guarantee a minimum of 3,500 acres of sugar beet production, thus convincing the Great Western Sugar Company to add a factory in the area.

Sugar beet farming was labor intensive and contributed significantly to the population gains reported in the South Platte Valley after 1900. One estimate is that by 1909, there were over 10,000 sugar beet workers in the valley, over half of whom were ethnic German Russians, arriving either directly from Russia's Volga Valley or from other immigrant colonies in Nebraska and Kansas. That workforce grew further between 1910 and 1920 as beet acreages increased another 70 percent in Weld County and more than doubled in Morgan and Logan Counties.

Irrigation in the Arkansas Valley

A second corridor of oasis agriculture developed in southeastern Colorado along the Arkansas River between Pueblo and the Kansas line. Several small ditches were built during the territorial period, but ranching remained dominant even into the early 1880s. George Crofutt reported that "sheep, cattle and cow-boys occupy the country" east of Pueblo and that "stock-raising . . . is the chief industry" around nearby La Junta.[32]

Only two isolated zones of sizable irrigated lands were present. Near Rocky Ford, George Swink stumbled into irrigation during the 1870s when he observed that his garden crops thrived when kitchen waste water was dumped on them.[33] After informally extending a local ditch system with nearby farmers, Swink and others incorporated the Rocky Ford Ditch Company in 1882. To the east a second nucleus of canal-building took shape near Las Animas. Real estate speculation played a role in the area as Denver land developer Otis Haskell organized the Arkansas River Land Town and Canal Company in 1883. Although a fine ditch was completed on the north side of the river, irrigation lagged owing to Haskell's ongoing legal and financial problems.[34]

The golden era of oasis agriculture flowered in the valley between 1885 and 1910. During that quarter-century most of the valley's large canals were completed.[35] Near Pueblo the Bessemer Ditch watered twenty thousand acres of uplands once it was finished between 1887 and 1891. Brainchild of William Jackson Palmer, the ditch was financed through the Colorado Coal and Iron Company and irrigated lands just south of the river between Pueblo and the Huerfano River. Ownership of the ditch was gradually transferred to local farmers, who ran it as a cooperative mutual stockholding enterprise. To the east, George Swink's Rocky Ford Ditch thrived on the south side of the river near Rocky Ford and provided a fine example of local collective effort that produced "the most stable and envied irrigation enterprise in the valley." Between Rocky Ford and Lamar, the

much larger Fort Lyon Canal was built in the late 1880s and early 1890s
(fig. 64). T. C. Henry, Colorado's indefatigable irrigation enthusiast, was a
key promoter of the corporate project. With the encouragement of other
real estate and railroad interests, Henry extended the canal north of
Lamar, although these additions suffered from relatively junior water
rights and were prone to marginal appropriations in dry years. A series of
reservoirs and feeder canals also were constructed to support the Fort Lyon
system, but farmers were still vulnerable in drought periods when local
reservoirs failed to fill.

By 1900 irrigation in the valley produced an increasing scarcity of water that had divisive consequences beyond the borders of Colorado. Just
after the turn of the century, the state's extensive network of water diversion projects prompted neighboring Kansas to sue over the rapidly dwindling waters trickling eastward from the Centennial State.[36] In a decision
of 1907, the federal court largely affirmed Colorado's claims so long as the
water was put to beneficial use. Perhaps more important in the long run,
however, the decision recognized the ultimate authority of federal courts
in such contests, denying any state total control of its water.

Meanwhile, the Arkansas Valley's agricultural landscape displayed ever
more diversity. Irrigated wheat, oat, and cornfields filled some bottom and
benchland acreages. Cattle remained on the scene and increasingly depended on irrigated feed crops rather than on remaining open range. By
1920 there were over one hundred thousand cattle in Otero, Bent, and
Prowers Counties, subsisting largely on the valley's irrigated hay and alfalfa meadows.[37] Sheep were also present, particularly near and downriver
from the mouth of the Purgatoire River in the vicinity of Las Animas. As
in the case of the South Platte Valley, Arkansas Valley ranchers became increasingly sophisticated in raising, fattening, and marketing livestock in
the early twentieth century, and their techniques of concentrated fodder
production and feeding were a far cry from the romantic trail-driving days
of an earlier era. With livestock persisting in the area, irrigated alfalfa became more important in the 1880s. Introduced by Rocky Ford's George
Swink in 1878, alfalfa annually yielded between three and six tons of feed
per acre and proved immensely popular from Pueblo to the Kansas state
line.[38]

Swink's entrepreneurial knack netted him success with two other key
specialty crops by 1890.[39] Watermelons came first, and by the early 1880s
Swink shipped over two hundred thousand pounds of the crop to a variety
of local and regional markets. Additional genetic tinkering with field crops
near Rocky Ford led Swink to a type of cantaloupe that proved immensely
popular and easy to ship. With reasonable luck and dependable water,
farmers produced between 150 and 300 crates of cantaloupes per acre,

FIGURE 64. Oasis landscapes along the Fort Lyon Canal, Arkansas Valley (Courtesy Colorado State Historical Society)

adding up to tidy profits of over one hundred dollars per acre. Swink's experimental bent even led him to introduce exotic honey bees to the Rocky Ford area once he found that they thrived on alfalfa and assisted mightily in the earlier springtime pollination of the cantaloupe plants.

Orchard crops also showed promise, although early acreages remained small and focused near Pueblo.[40] After 1890, however, fruit crops were all the rage, and land salesmen and water developers had a field day with their predictions of future harvests. Calculations by the Lamar Board of Trade were representative of the fruit-raising mania of the time. The board confidently pronounced that "the Arkansas valley . . . warrants the horticulturalists in planting any kind of small fruits and deciduous tree fruits that are grown in a temperate climate. . . . The Arkansas Valley with its 1,200,000 acres of arable land will support a population of one inhabitant to each acre, if properly devoted to fruit culture. This would give the valley a population of about three times the present population of the State." Valley fruit production increased greatly by 1900, with the most notable success in Otero County near Rocky Ford. There, the 1900 Census reported 150,000 apple trees, 25,000 peach trees, and more than 17,000 cherry trees. The value of harvested fruit from the young trees remained low, how-ever, with the county reporting just $6,400 of sales in orchard crops. That result was favorable compared with Prowers County in the lower valley. There, more than 35,000 trees, mostly apple, netted less than $600 in crops.

Certainly the most obvious expression of agricultural modernity in the Arkansas Valley was the industrially organized landscape of sugar beet pro-duction in the region.[41] As with the South Platte Valley, the lower Arkansas Valley attracted the interest of beet producers, who saw the sunny climate, cheap lands, and available water as ideal for growing sugar beets. Two well-financed ventures produced major changes in the valley between 1900 and 1902. One group of investors with connections to Buffalo, New York, founded the National Sugar Beet Company in 1899 and built a large pro-cessing plant at their company town of Sugar City just north of Rocky Ford. A second group of investors, led by the Oxnard brothers, formed the Amer-ican Beet Sugar Company and in 1900 established another plant at Rocky Ford. Suddenly two boomtowns in the middle of the once-sleepy lower Arkansas Valley rivaled the excitement of earlier gold and silver mining camps in the Rockies! Within a few months, both centers boasted almost two thousand residents, with many working in the factories or as contract field laborers. Although both companies bought up their own land to guar-antee sufficient production, they needed independent farmers to shift into beets. Lucrative five-year contracts between the companies and growers, along with vigorous promotion efforts led by town businessmen, provided incentives. Potential profits on sugar beets were indeed heady: one acre could yield twelve to thirty tons of beets and produce revenues of $60 to $120 annually.

Between 1905 and 1907 the beet industry expanded east of the Sugar City–Rocky Ford nucleus. William Wiley, a disaffected American Beet Sugar Company employee, built his own processing factory at Holly in 1905, marking the birth of the Holly Sugar Company just west of the Kansas state line. Rivalry between the American and Holly interests reached a fever pitch the following year when Wiley built a second plant at Swink, only five miles from Rocky Ford. The companies fiercely com-peted for cooperating farmers and built parallel feeder railroads to lower transport costs. In addition, the American Beet Sugar Company enlarged its interests, moving into new facilities at Lamar in 1905 and at Las Animas in 1907. By the end of the decade a string of major beet-processing opera-tions lined the valley, all accessible to good irrigated lands and adjacent to rail lines connecting the plants to their regional and national markets. Consolidation followed, with the Holly, Lamar, and Las Animas facilities all closing between 1913 and 1921. Still, large beet acreages concentrated in favored valley locations, and in 1920 the original Sugar City–Rocky Ford nucleus remained the sugar heartland of southeastern Colorado with more than seventeen thousand acres of beets under cultivation.

As in the South Platte region, sugar beet cultivation reshaped the workforce and ethnic geographies within the Arkansas Valley. Sizable numbers of German Russians were invaluable in the early years. They formed distinct rural communities, preserving elements of their language, culture, and food amid a landscape dominated by native-born Americans. Many of these German Russians laborers later bought their own land, often from the beet companies themselves. By the early 1920s, however, much of the backbreaking field labor in the Colorado beet fields fell on the shoulders of Mexican workers, who found it more difficult to extricate themselves from the ranks of the agricultural underclass (fig. 65).

Oasis agriculture became firmly established along the South Platte and Arkansas Valleys between 1870 and 1920. From a grand aerial vantage point, the advancing fingers of cultivated and watered lands marked a deep and lasting penetration into the semiarid plains. Increasingly elaborate ditchworks and storage systems sustained and expanded the limits of oasis agriculture. Complementing these technological feats were legal rulings and a political environment that sanctioned and encouraged the irrigation movement. Also key were the entrepreneurs who brought together critical components of capital, land, water, and laborers to yield a diverse assortment of commercial crops and produce in the process a new oasis landscape that would be sustained until the present.

FIGURE 65. Laboring in the oasis: sugar beet workers in the early twentieth century (Courtesy Denver Public Library, Western History Collection)

The Plains as Garden

Another picture of the plains flowered in the 1880s as scientists and boosters created an image of the region as a fertile garden, capable of supporting abundant dryland crops without irrigation. Yet this perception of the plains, surely the apogee of optimism, did not stand the test of time. Within a decade, the realities of cyclical drought imposed themselves upon the region, and outmigration prevailed across the high plains during much of the 1890s. Phoenixlike, the penchant to test the odds of rain-fed agriculture returned early in the twentieth century. Emboldened by the assurances of new technologies, the later push into dry farming proved vulnerable, as well, when drought years returned in the 1920s and 1930s.

In spite of its nonsustainable and boom-and-bust nature, the dryland cropping movement enduringly shaped the settlement geography of the high plains between the major irrigated corridors of the Platte and Arkansas Valleys. But as in the mineral-rich mountains, the area's resources proved fickle and left the region's inhabitants with a reticence grounded in tough experience, an apperception of the past still visible in the faces of those who lived it and in the signatures of hope and despair still plainly left upon the land.

Things could not have been more different in the middle and late 1880s, when a boom mentality of Gold Rush proportions engulfed the region. The decade began with the peaking of the cattle trade in many areas of the plains. Ironically, the very snows that devastated the herds and the pastoral vision of the plains between 1884 and 1887 fueled a new garden imagery that became increasingly pervasive late in the decade. Many participants jumped on the booster bandwagon, including some in the scientific community, claiming that agriculture increased the region's humidity and precipitation, creating in the process a new "Rain Belt" across Colorado's high plains.[42]

Chief among the advocates of the "rain follows the plow" theory and of the associated garden imagery were the railroads, whose traffic and land sales stood to benefit greatly if anyone believed their claims. Accordingly, the railroad campaigns shifted their rhetoric concerning the region's future: before their dryland sales efforts in Colorado, for example, the Kansas Pacific line emphasized the area's ranching and irrigation potential.[43] This campaign, however, left much railroad acreage unsold and didn't maximize the traffic potential of the region if the land could be rapidly peopled and plowed into hundreds of new farmsteads. Boosters at the Burlington Railroad humbly offered their own scientific spin on the "Rain Belt" concept as they noted, "In our opinion, the change is due to the extensive irrigation of land lying along the eastern base of the Rocky

Mountains. . . . water which formerly ran wastefully into the Gulf of Mexico has been turned on to the arid plains. There it soaks into the soil. The wind sweeping over the land sucks up a large portion of it. There is then moisture in the air and it is precipitated on the high lands of Eastern Colorado."[44]

Other interests beyond the railroads trumpeted the high plains' prospects.[45] Town site and land development companies were as common as dust devils across the region between 1886 and 1888. Many participants in these ventures hailed from nearby Kansas and Nebraska, where similar schemes had been hatched in earlier years. Most had short-term gains in mind as they pedaled town lots and farm lands to gullible buyers. Local newspapers and government authorities matched the swelled language of the real estate companies. In 1890 commissioners of newly created Cheyenne County reported that local dry farmers "have plowed and seeded for three years and each autumn makes a perceptible increase in the crops, forecasting a complete transformation in time. . . . These pioneers of Eastern Colorado have opened a new kingdom to agriculture and are reaping a reward in lands. The time is near at hand when the whole of Eastern Colorado, from the line to the Rockies, will be subject to the plow."

The old claims of the Great American Desert were being stood on their head. The same dangerously dry ground that challenged the Pikes Peak goldseekers was being redefined in edenic terms. Through human-induced climate change and technological innovation, nature would surely oblige and yield a high plains garden where only bison and cattle once ranged.

Providence and good timing were in abundance during the initial wave of settlement between 1885 and 1890. In addition to being a period of relatively high rainfall, these years coincided with the arrival of agricultural adaptations that made farming easier in such settings.[46] Affordable barbed wire kept out wandering animals; the chilled metal plow provided a better way to break up tough prairie soils; and new strains of hard red winter wheat that seemed to thrive in the semiarid environment were imported from abroad. Liberalized federal land laws also made it easier for settlers on the public domain to acquire the larger acreages necessary for successful farming. Settlers could homestead a quarter section of 160 acres and take an additional 320 acres under the terms of the preemption laws and Timber Culture Act. Railroads and other settlers were additional sources of acreage. For those willing to test their luck, there was no shortage of opportunity on the eastern high plains.

The geography of high plains settlement between 1885 and 1890 followed a predictable path. The area of greatest interest lay between the Arkansas and South Platte Valleys, and over half a dozen new counties that focused on new dryland farming populations were quickly created. Not surprisingly, lands near the rail corridors attracted early attention, and towns sprinkled along the tracks, such as Yuma, Akron, Burlington, Cheyenne Wells, and Eads, became key jumping-off points for new farmers. Population gains were impressive, particularly given the earlier dearth of settlement. Phillips, Yuma, Washington, and Kit Carson Counties in northeastern Colorado experienced the largest surges, with populations averaging 2,500 residents by 1890. Even these numbers were well below peak boom totals reached two years earlier. Cultivated acreages in these northeastern high plains counties were also much higher than areas to the south.[47] But even the southeastern Colorado counties of Baca and Kiowa posted major increases in settlers and in cultivated lands in a boom that peaked in 1888 and 1889.

Farming in the "Rain Belt" focused on corn, with such small grains as wheat, oats, and rye important locally.[48] Sorghum, millets, and hay were also significant commercial crops. In spite of the hoopla, however, dryland wheat acreages were very small compared with the more productive irrigated tracts along the major river valleys. Not to be forgotten were livestock herds, which continued to be an integral part of the high plains landscape. Some early ranching operations remained and even the small farmer often kept a few head of stock for meat and dairy needs. The state's eastern strip, which included Yuma, Kit Carson, Cheyenne, and Kiowa Counties, reported over ten thousand cattle and almost as many sheep in 1890. Also critical locally were painstakingly tended and hand-irrigated small gardens. Potatoes, lettuce, peas, beans, and melons were among the precious garden crops cultivated by homesteaders.

The initial dryland boom ended as quickly as it began.[49] The swelling tide of enthusiasm reached fever pitch in 1886, 1887, and 1888 (fig. 66). Even amid this din of optimism, *The Colorado Farmer* asked soberly, "Will it last? . . . we shall wait and see and hope that there is no disappointment or disaster in store for the brave pioneers who have staked their all in opposition to the theories of the wise. Theory says that this country is a desert and that it is not possible to raise crops successfully . . . that this country is only fit for grazing." The first hints of trouble came in 1889 and 1890 as a modest drought kept precipitation below average in many eastern counties. Yet better conditions in 1891 and 1892 convinced many that dry years were aberrations and that the boom could continue indefinitely. Reality intervened more harshly for the next four years as renewed drought pressed in upon the high plains. Precipitation totals for the 1894–95 season revealed the drought cycle in full force: Akron eked out six inches of precipitation, while Burlington, near the Kansas line, did only slightly better with eight inches. As far as dryland farming was concerned, these to-

MAIN STREET OF AKRON, 1888
(Courtesy of Mr. R. B. Cooley, Publisher of the Akron News-Reporter)

FIGURE 66. Garden town on the plains: Akron in 1888 (Courtesy Colorado State Historical Society)

tals were simply too little, too late to support crops, and conditions were just as bad the following year.

The drought years yielded dramatic changes.[50] Thousands packed up and left. The dry farming belt had large population declines, with Baca, Kiowa, Kit Carson, Yuma, Washington, and Phillips Counties losing over 30 percent of settlers between 1890 and 1900 (fig. 67). The contrast between the dryland and irrigated districts was obvious: although some of the irrigated areas suffered in the low water conditions, they survived the disaster much more readily than their upland neighbors. Predictably, scientists and farm experts who embraced the "rain follows the plow" theory in the 1880s quickly discarded it, a move that surely did little to satisfy thirsty farmers leaving in droves.

Travelers in the middle 1890s described a land that had reverted to an earlier era. Anna Talhelm wrote in her diary as she crossed western Kansas and eastern Colorado in 1896, "We passed through some of the nicest-looking country this week I ever saw—so level. But one cannot live on grass as that is about all that grows here. Here home after home abandoned, many with good buildings on (except the doors and windows have been taken away) . . . we find eastern Colorado more desolate than western Kan. No settlement at all except now and then a sheep or cattle ranch. We find no water except at railroad stations." No wonder that a map of Colorado ghost towns is thick with names on the high plains, many dating from the disaster of the 1890s. Many towns disappeared entirely, while others became

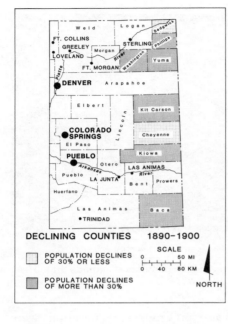

FIGURE 67. Population decline in eastern Colorado, 1890–1900 (Source: Eleventh and Twelfth Censuses of Population)

mere skeletons, their banks and stores closed to everything but the wind and perhaps a passing cattle herd.

Thanks to faded memories and a sense that new technological fixes could promise success, another round of modest settlement based on dry farming occurred in eastern Colorado between 1906 and 1910. Conditions were then set for the full-fledged boom that engulfed the region during World War I. Behind this second era of dry farming was a feeling that lessons had been learned from the heady days of the 1880s and that a more scientific approach to agriculture could mitigate the environmental incongruities of the high plains. To control rapid rates of surface evaporation, dry farming techniques emphasized deep plowing after harvests, frequent disking after rains to work moisture into the soil, packing the subsoil before covering it with a loose surface mulch, and alternating crops with summer fallow so as to accumulate moisture in one year that could contribute to the success of the following year's crop.[51]

The cast of characters who played roles in promoting the second dry farming boom of 1906–17 was familiar.[52] Governmental agencies lent their stamp of approval. A state-funded dryland experiment station at Cheyenne Wells led the call for more contour plowing and diversified farming in the region. More generally, the state's investment in the Agricultural College at Fort Collins encouraged dryland-related research in the state early in the twentieth century. Another federally sponsored experiment station opened in Akron in 1907, stimulating research on dryland farming techniques. Some of the most ambitious test plots and model farms on the Great Plains were sponsored directly by such railroads as the Northern Pacific, Chicago and Northwestern, and Burlington lines. Local chambers of commerce and business groups chimed in as they contemplated the benefits of increased retailing and agricultural implement sales. Of these groups, the Denver Chamber of Commerce was perhaps the most vocal, trumpeting the virtues of dry farming in 1906 and becoming the catalyst for the annual Dry Farming Congresses that began in Denver the following year.

Federal land laws and an abundance of accessible acreage also encouraged the dryland gamblers.[53] In 1909 the Enlarged Homestead Act doubled the allowable claim from 160 to 320 acres, provided that the secretary of the Interior Department had determined that the acreage was not "susceptible of irrigation," a precondition that certainly applied to much of eastern Colorado. In 1912 congressional modifications reduced from five to three the number of years necessary to prove up one's claim on homesteaded lands. Particularly in a region where fortunes could be made in a few bountiful years, the newly reduced qualifications were very attractive. Demand for accessible railroad lands also increased after 1905, and the rail companies gladly disposed of acreage that could not have been given away a decade earlier.

Knowledgeable local real estate entrepreneurs played a key role in assembling and peddling tracts of farmland to newcomers.[54] In Burlington, for example, A. W. Winegar formed the Kit Carson Land Company, bought up more than 32,000 acres of nearby farmland in 1906 and 1907, and subdivided the parcel into 160- and 320-acre plots. Winegar advertised his "beautiful prairie" lands in the "rain belt of eastern Colorado" in midwestern newspapers, using enticing photographs of fat cattle and productive cornfields to bring buyers west. Land values reflected the enthusiasm of the times: between 1900 and 1910, many eastern Colorado counties saw land prices increase 200 to 400 percent and the bumper crops of the war years propelled prices even higher. By 1915 public land offices in Sterling, Hugo, and Lamar reported that only three million acres (out of fifteen million) remained vacant and open to settlement and roughly half of that total lay in Colorado's remote southeastern corner.

The geography of the expansion paralleled the earlier pattern of the 1880s.[55] Many of the same counties whose populations had crashed between 1890 and 1900—Kiowa, Kit Carson, Washington, Yuma, and Cheyenne—saw their numbers grow by 300 to 600 percent between 1900 and 1910. The boom came later in more isolated Baca County, on the Oklahoma border, with notable new settlement beginning at the end of the decade and increasing by 1914. The precise year in which this new dry farming boom peaked in the area is impossible to reconstruct because many counties were already reporting outflows of people in the census year of 1920. The peak in many districts probably came in 1917, but even with the slightly ebbing numbers of 1920, eight eastern Colorado counties boasted population gains of greater than 50 percent over the previous decade.

No fundamental change in the agricultural geography of the region accompanied the renewed boom, although the relative importance of particular animals and crops shifted somewhat.[56] Grain growers became increasingly specialized and moved from corn to wheat between 1900 and 1920. Northeastern Colorado's Yuma and Phillips Counties illustrate the changes: in 1900 they jointly reported 13,400 acres in corn and 13,200 acres in wheat, whereas twenty years later the counties' 171,000 acres of corn and 225,000 acres of wheat made the district one of the breadbaskets of the state. More conservative farmers heeded the advice of extension agents and diversified their operations. J. W. Adams at the State Experiment Station at Cheyenne Wells preached this approach. Far from the wild claims of real estate agents and railroad promoters, Adams prudently observed that

> diversified farming is the most successful. A herd of milk cows with enough hogs and poultry to utilize the by-products, and a garden in a favorable place . . . insures a living. Grain farming should be on the side rather than the main business. When grain fails it will usually make feed, which could not be utilized if the farmer did not have cows. Farmers should not undertake to farm more than they can do well. The majority of people over-estimate their ability to get work done and many times make a failure for that reason.

Livestock did indeed complement cropping in many areas between 1900 and 1920, and cattle numbers increased, as did an emphasis on dairying.

Unknown then was the rarefied nature of the population boom that rushed onto the high plains between 1906 and 1917. Throughout the West, many isolated and semiarid counties from the Great Plains to the Great Basin experienced population peaks during those years that have yet to be surpassed. But the busts of the 1920s and 1930s were only dimly anticipated at the end of World War I. Optimism reigned in 1920 even as drought cycles began their inevitable return to the region and agricultural markets weakened dramatically.

Plains Settlement Geography: 1860–1920

The settlement geography of Colorado's eastern plains reflected the diverse evolutionary strands we have sketched between 1860 and 1920. Wilderness, pasture, oasis, and garden—each vision of the region con-

jured up different human responses to the plains environment—and each
has left a set of human signatures across the area.

Spatial Patterns

Any modern map of the eastern plains reveals an areal organization of
rural farmsteads, county boundaries, town sites, and transportation infrastructure created largely in the late nineteenth and early twentieth centuries. Although population densities in the high plains were low in comparison with areas farther east, the essential elements of the settlement
system within the region were transferred from the rural Midwest.[57] It
was a spatial organization that had proven its viability in that older settled
region.

Population densities varied depending on the local economic base, but
overall the pattern mirrored the American penchant for dispersed rural
settlement. The relatively large land units needed to make a living from
farming or ranching within the region put rural people at some distance
from one another. The Homestead Act in its various incarnations compelled settlers to reside on their acreage, a pattern of American occupance
typical since colonial times. The most isolated rural homes were found in
upland dry farming and ranching regions, while a somewhat denser mosaic of rural settlement and smaller and more intensely worked fields characterized the irrigated districts along the major river valleys. In the irrigated lands there were even instances of clustered settlements of farm
workers, particularly as the sugar beet industry grew and large numbers of
laborers lived in designated towns and camps.[58]

Just as rural space was divided at the microscale into dispersed farmsteads, fields, and pastures, so the region was reorganized into a new geography of political and administrative space, particularly in the late 1880s
as county boundaries proved inadequate to serve the needs of newly arrived settlers. County subdivision became a key local and state issue between 1887 and 1889. Settlers found it most inconvenient to traverse the
huge counties of eastern Colorado to conduct their business at some distant county seat. Many advocated more local representation. Some people had more direct economic arguments, too, noting that the designation
of new counties and county seats inevitably raised land values and promoted business in areas of new settlement. Indeed, the functional centrality of a county seat was immediate: clerks and surveyors recorded land
transactions, assessors and treasurers set and levied taxes, and local sher-
iffs and magistrates enforced laws and rendered justice.[59] The stimulative
effects upon the economy were considerable and much coveted by those
seeking new representation. Bitter rivalries between prospective seats also
revealed the high stakes of the new local geography that was being created.

In the case of eastern Colorado, spatial partitioning associated with county boundary changes occurred largely in two bursts of legislative activity in 1887 and 1889.[60] Not surprisingly, the greatest subdividing came in some of the more densely populated counties along the Platte and Arkansas Valleys and involved the extensive division of Weld and Bent Counties. Along the South Platte, Logan and Washington Counties were taken from Weld in 1887, and two years later new populations, in both the irrigated and dryland districts of northeastern Colorado, induced the designation of Morgan, Yuma, Phillips, and Sedgwick Counties. To the south, old Elbert and Bent Counties, amid the same hoopla of the late 1880s, were carved up to become Lincoln, Kit Carson, Cheyenne, Kiowa, Otero, and Prowers Counties. Only in the far southeast, in Las Animas County, was dissection more limited: although some town boosters advocated a four-county subdivision plan, more moderate voices intervened, creating Baca County in the very southeastern corner of the state in 1889.

As with general flows of population, towns in eastern Colorado were created in bursts of activity and were followed by periods of relative quiet or outright urban decline. The distribution of these settlements across the region followed no spatial regularity: some areas had fairly dense clusterings of towns, whereas other portions of eastern Colorado counted fifty miles or more between settlements. As John Hudson argued in his study of Dakota towns, the factors that shaped the distribution of these plains settlements can usefully be divided into two eras: a frontier era in which forts, trails, and ranching controlled placement of settlements and a subsequent era of increased commercial farming in which railroads, town companies, and large-scale demands for farm products influenced the formation of towns.[61] Such is certainly the case in eastern Colorado, where the arrival of commercial cropping proved to be a watershed period in the evolution of the region's settlement geography.

As Hudson suggests, a prerail legacy of town founding left its mark on the geography of the eastern plains. Places like Fort Lyon, Fort Morgan, and Bent's Fort represented an earlier urban order that served the region before the boom days of the 1880s. Added to this frontier fort and trading post legacy was a layer of settlements associated with the ranching economy. Some of these centers were isolated upcountry waystations that sold supplies to widely scattered ranch populations.[62] A more important class of stock-oriented towns took shape along the Kansas Pacific and Santa Fe rail corridors, both established across the region during the 1870s. Towns like Las Animas, Granada, Deer Trail, Kit Carson, and Cheyenne Wells owed their origins to their function as railhead towns for the region's cattle trade.

But it was cropping and not livestocking that truly shaped eastern Colorado's town locations and their growth and survival over time. Because

of the strongly commercial nature of both the irrigated and dryland cropping systems, farmers needed access to capital, transportation, and markets to facilitate their operations. Towns were prime providers of these
critical links to regional and national economic systems. Their distribution across the region was therefore a function of overall population densities, the intensity and productivity of nearby commercial agriculture,
the location of critical transport corridors, especially railroads, and individual decisions made by sundry boosters, promoters, and hucksters
whose vision of future wealth included a town center destined to become
a thriving plains metropolis. Although brief, the initial boom of the late
1880s sparked the largest number of actual new towns across the region.
Many of these fledgling towns did not survive the economic declines of
the 1890s, but those that did served as centers in the subsequent expansions that came with the agricultural settlements of the early twentieth
century.

Railroads played a central role in creating the urban geography of the
eastern plains. As rail lines were constructed across the region, rail companies derived immediate revenue from land sales in designated towns and
nearby farmlands. But more important, towns organized economic geographies of agricultural trade on the plains, and the control of those shipping points by a rail line meant sustained profits that far exceeded the one-
time benefits derived from the sale of real estate.[63] Thus defined, railroad
towns were strategically placed within the region to maximize the prof-
itability of shipping commercial farm products to their various markets.
Too many towns represented waste and economic redundancy in the settlement system, whereas too few towns would leave potential growers
without markets or would invite competing rail companies to invade the
territory with their own planned towns.

Regular spacing of towns along the region's rail corridors was thus no
accident.[64] Wray, Yuma, and Akron were three railroad towns established
along the Burlington line. Further south, Burlington and Flagler became
similar centers of activity along the Rock Island line, while the Missouri
Pacific established such centers as Brandon, Chivington, Eads, and
Galatea. In addition, older cow towns like Julesburg, Kit Carson, and Las
Animas took on new urban importance once crop production expanded
and railroad companies solidified their commercial hold on the region.
Each rail corridor displayed a similar spatial pattern with its linear march
of towns shaping regional patterns of settlement (fig. 68).

Independent promoters also created towns in eastern Colorado. Along
planned or existing rail lines, entrepreneurs attempted to steer the tracks
in their direction.[65] But rail executives often had their own ideas and disappointed many an erstwhile booster by bypassing planned town sites in

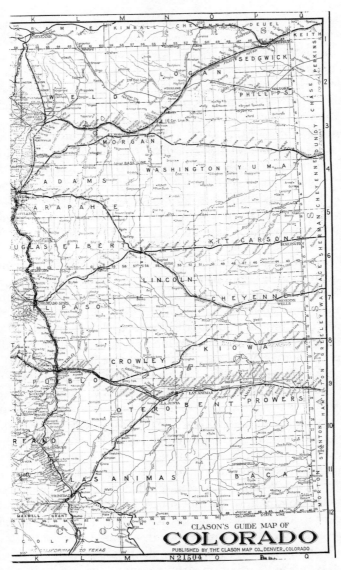

FIGURE 68. Eastern Colorado in 1917 (Source: Clason's Guide Map of Colorado, Denver, 1917)

favor of railroad-controlled centers. In southeastern Colorado, for example, many aspiring towns tried to persuade the Rock Island Railroad to build through their centers in the boom times of the 1880s. Their plans were dashed when the company decided to avoid southern Colorado altogether, opting for a more northern route via Burlington to Colorado

Springs. In other cases, town companies bribed rail officials by donating lots to get a rail station built at a locale.

The interrelationship between the region's urban and transportation geography was an intimate one: infrastructure investments provided critical links in the evolving spatial system of the eastern plains. Some prerail patterns of trails and overland roads survive across the region, particularly in the Platte and Arkansas Valleys, where early corridors of activity were sustained and reinforced in later eras. Undoubtedly, however, decisions of late nineteenth-century railroad companies were the key organizing components of the region's transportation geography.

The system began to take shape before 1880 with the construction of the Kansas (later Union) Pacific and Atchison, Topeka, and Santa Fe lines in Colorado and with the earlier completion of the transcontinental line across nearby portions of southern Wyoming and Nebraska. This wide spacing of rail corridors left huge gaps, most obviously one paralleling the South Platte River. The settlement rushes of the 1880s spurred a plethora of new lines as railroads scrambled to capture traffic in rapidly settling districts. By the early 1880s new Union Pacific and Burlington lines had carved up northeastern Colorado, including the lucrative South Platte Valley. Soon the sparsely settled country to the south was also subdivided into rail territories as the Rock Island and Missouri Pacific railroads reached across the momentarily booming dry farming districts between the Platte and Arkansas Valleys.[66] In the far southeast, only isolated Baca and eastern Las Animas Counties remained without service in the nineteenth century as rail investors wisely eschewed the sage plains and piñon-covered mesas in favor of better opportunities elsewhere.

Connecting far-flung ranches and farms to these key rail corridors were thousands of miles of unimproved roads and ruts etched across the landscape. A steady parade of wagon, horse, and foot traffic was often the only "maintenance" these roads received, though county tax dollars and an occasional state appropriation went into looking after the more heavily traveled routes and the construction of key bridges. Hints of things to come, however, were evident after 1910 as automobiles appeared on the region's infant road system.[67] Increased traffic prompted improvements, principally on roads that paralleled the major river valley and rail settlement corridors. Still, by World War I, none of the principal auto roads across eastern Colorado could boast much more than a muddy unpaved track across the prairie (see fig. 68).

Cultural Landscapes

Simplicity characterized much of the plains natural landscape, although river valleys had more variety in local topography and vegetation than the gently sloped uplands. As if to emphasize that visual economy of form, the utter rectangular monotony of the federal government's township and range survey system, imposed on the region as it was settled in the late nineteenth century, gave to the plains cultural landscape a template upon which lot lines, field boundaries, and road networks fitted with a predictable right-angled geometry (fig. 69). Each section of 640 acres was often subdivided into similarly rectangular quarter sections.[68] Within those larger boundaries appeared smaller blocks of grain and hay fields, all fitting into the rectangular mold and interrupted only occasionally by the nonlinear imposition of a stray slope or intermittent stream. As roads evolved to connect farmers with the town center, paths of least resistance also followed the surveyed section and lot lines, reinforcing the squared geometry of the plains landscape.

Once cropping began in eastern Colorado, mostly after 1875, the rural scene displayed two distinctive landscape patterns, one associated with the more continuously settled irrigated river valleys and the other found in the more ephemerally and lightly occupied upland districts. In his landmark study of life on the Great Plains, sociologist Carl Kraenzel recognized these quite different landscapes and communities. The "sutland" community was "the more densely settled, often stringlike, area of habitation" that was home to more intense agriculture, frequent towns, and key transportation infrastructure.[69] Paralleling the sutland pattern in the Piedmont's Northern Agricultural Zone, the lower South Platte and Arkansas Valleys revealed a relatively more dense and intricate landscape of smaller farms, frequent trees and farmhouses, varied crops, and concentrations of cattle and sheep. The rectangular geometry of survey lines was often interrupted by the more irregular boundaries of rivers, ditches, and reservoirs that marshaled life-giving water to the land. In the most successful irrigated districts, the landscape revealed a predictable abundance and fertility in the spring and summer as crops matured, a visual affirmation of the land's abundance.

Simplicity and a greater dispersal of landscape features marked the "yonland" beyond the valleys. Kraenzel identified yonland communities in the "in between areas . . . out yonder," where settlement densities were lower, services fewer, and families often isolated by the "social costs of space."[70] Here the rectangular settlement pattern was only rarely interrupted, houses were fewer and farther between, fields were larger and less diverse, and livestock, though found throughout the region, were likely to be more widely scattered on the visual scene. Periodically, signatures of abandonment were also more apparent. Empty shacks, stilled windmills, silent corrals, and roofless barns were constant reminders of the vagaries of yonland settlement, and their presence on the landscape must have

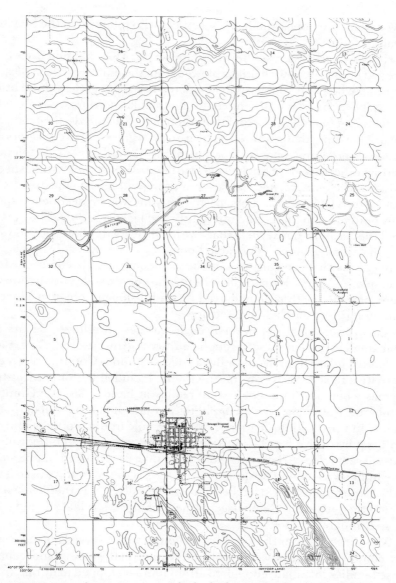

FIGURE 69. Rectangular imperative on the high plains near Otis (Source: USGS, Otis quadrangle, 1972, 1:24,000 topographic map series)

played upon the hopes and fears of settlers who followed in the footsteps of earlier failures.

Housing varied across the rural landscape. Most abundant early on were sod houses built with bricks plowed from the prairie earth.[71] Best cut in spring, when new root growth cemented the sod together, these bricks were stacked to make walls one to two feet thick. Interiors were plastered with clay and topped with a roof that often included boards, tar paper, and an earth covering that sprouted its own array of grass and cacti. Doors and windows were frame boards. Wood planking, if available, made tolerable flooring; otherwise hard-packed clay sufficed. Already well established in Kansas and Nebraska, sod houses still prompted initial adjustments for most eastern Colorado farmers, particularly for women destined to spend many hours within their dark, often dirty and leaky interiors. Boosters assured the "eastern housewife" that "with a little taste, some tact and skill the sod cabin becomes a desirable home . . . it is warm, substantial, enduring . . . as clean and airy as a brick . . . the sod cabin becomes the family temple."[72] Where local terrain offered the option, sod construction was often combined with a room carved into a hillslope to create a "dugout" cabin, but these, too, held limited appeal.

Many prairie farmers never lived in earthen dwellings. Cedars and other small trees that grew in rough country northwest of Sterling, north of Limon, and in the canyons of Baca and Las Animas Counties offered an alternative to sod. Variations on the theme included building with stone in areas where such materials were readily at hand. Clarence Grant remembered the challenges of building a stone house in isolated Baca County in 1916, noting, "Father dug a large hole in the ground about two feet deep by twelve feet by fourteen feet: this was to be the floor of our house. We hauled rocks from a self-made quarry. . . . The building rocks were built up in mud to the proper height. . . . For the roof we used a tent of the same dimensions stretched across the walls. . . . Father banked dirt around the outside of the house . . . the roof and walls leaked, and water ran in through the door."[73]

Most desirable was the wood frame house, which served both as a creature comfort and as a powerful cultural symbol on the plains landscape for those families fortunate enough to afford lumber shipped in by rail. In her study of northeast Colorado homesteading, historian Katherine Harris describes the attraction of these essentially midwestern prairie dwellings, suggesting that "frame houses reminded settlers of their former homes. They represented orderly, prosperous, and civilized living. Wood construction, moreover, was expensive and symbolized a level of comfort and respectability to which nearly all aspired. In reality, few wood houses on the plains could inspire much envy, but the occasional substantial frame house served to enhance their symbolic power."[74]

Coping with the monotony and daily challenges of the rural plains landscape varied by individual, but surely the separate and largely gender-defined roles of men and women produced distinctive responses.[75] Men were often highly mobile, augmenting farm duties with other jobs in agriculture, railroading, and construction that might take them dozens, even hundreds of miles from home. Women's work, centered on keeping house, raising children, and planting a garden, produced a very different sense of place, defined strikingly around the immediacy of the homestead and the nearby rural neighborhood.

Contrast the experiences of Calvin and Margaret Benner, who settled in Kiowa County from Kansas in the boom of 1911. Margaret's life focused around the farmstead, where she had a garden, tended the cows and pigs, and raised two small children. Her important landscapes centered on home and neighborhood. Cal, by contrast, traveled widely as he worked seasonally on cattle round-up crews and on other farms planting and harvesting wheat. Still, women's roles were changing on the plains. One study of eastern Colorado homesteading, for example, reveals that almost 18 percent of those filing for new homesteads after 1900 were women, and these statistics suggest that women and men were mutually experiencing the excitement and frustration of plowing the prairies.

Beyond the farming districts, towns added variety to the plains landscape.[76] Even a small settlement with its buildings and dapple of trees was visible for miles. Centrality was accentuated through the vertical thrusts of water towers, railroad grain elevators, sugar beet mills, and a ragtag collection of frame buildings that stood against the prairie horizon. Order was also declared in the predictable division of horizontal space. Towns were usually platted in rectangular blocks, with the overall orientation and placement of principal streets sensitive to the location of the railroad if one was present. Inevitably, the depot and grain storage facilities were key elements of the local scene, symbolizing the essential economic links that wedded the town and nearby farms with the world beyond. Town blocks were frequently square, sometimes rectangular units subdivided into small rectangular lots, with the narrow side of the lot facing the street. Buildings concentrated along the narrow lot fronts. Where a railroad was present, the tracks often formed one edge of the plat, with a main street extending in perpendicular fashion to form a so-called T-town. That pattern permitted easy access to the depot and grain storage operations but prevented the railroad from disrupting town traffic and the coherence of Main Street activities. None of these features displayed much innovation: essentially surveyors were replicating habits well developed in nearby regions. Indeed, the towns mirrored the expectations of their inhabitants because most migrated from similar settings in the eastern plains and Midwest.

A stroll down Wray's main street in 1911, for example, would have revealed a landscape indebted to the economic and cultural traditions of the agricultural and urban Midwest.[77] In Wray, just across from the rail depot, the Wray Hotel and Dad Baker's Lunch Room satisfied the needs of itinerants. The nearby City Park provided locals some open space and a splash of greenery. Another block and the post office, newspaper, and two banks all crowded into central town locations, while just to the east sat the Yuma County courthouse, the center of local political authority. Robinson Drug, Wray Music, Patton's Meat Shop, Sisson Clothing, and Wray Mercantile were found in the next block. Then came the Odd Fellow's Hall, Doc Crawford's office, and the First Christian Church.

Most town structures were modest one- or two-story frame buildings, although stone and brick gradually replaced wood on some of the larger, more successful commercial blocks. Economically, banks displayed the town's connectedness to capital and were a visual pronouncement of a center's viability. They were usually located in a prominent downtown building (fig. 70). Culturally, although schools were not typically at the commercial heart of the town, they assumed particular social importance on the landscape with communities taking pride in the erection of substantial multistory structures (fig. 71).

The built environment of the plains town and the services it provided revealed a complex set of shared beliefs and institutions.[78] Disentangling civic, economic, and cultural values in such settings is not easy, for they were closely intertwined among the countless transactions of daily life. One locus of connections intimately bound participants in local government and business. Most every eastern Colorado county seat reveals the common midwestern-style courthouse occupying a prominent central city location, surrounded not coincidentally by the heart of the business district. Politicians perennially boosted the area's agricultural and business activities, and local public officials were themselves usually drawn from the ranks of wealthier citizens who saw the civic and economic wisdom in participating in town and county governance. Churches and schools were other fixed focal points on the community landscape in both towns and rural areas. Other less formalized meeting places held additional significance for residents. Social clubs, often connected with some dimension of civic improvement, brought men and women together in their respective and usually separate activities. Perhaps most important were get-togethers that centered on dances, box suppers, or holiday merry-making. Here within a meeting hall, school, or church would assemble groups of friends and neighbors whose time together in play was often reinforced and further defined by their shared economic fortunes and activities.

All of the striving for permanence so evident in the plains townscape— from the rail depots and hotels to the business blocks and schools—

FIGURE 70. Creating capital on the plains: Seibert State Bank, 1911 (Courtesy Denver Public Library, Western History Collection)

FIGURE 71. Creating community on the plains: Cheyenne Wells School (Courtesy Denver Public Library, Western History Collection)

FIGURE 72. The modern legacy of plains settlement: quiet day in Deer Trail (Photo by the author)

assumes a particular poignancy when the geography of depopulation and abandonment plays itself out repeatedly upon the visual scene. Put simply, too many towns were built in the early twentieth century to serve the modest and often fluctuating needs of the region's agricultural base. The larger earlier centers typically fared best, as their economic and political centrality sustained some activity in good times and bad. But urban declines in the smaller, more ephemeral centers lasted for decades and continue to shape the landscape today, creating an omnipresence of emptiness that marks dozens of eastern Colorado localities. Indeed, abandoned streets and boarded-up houses remain silent but vivid testimony to the many dramas played out upon the eastern plains since their initial occupance by Americans in the late nineteenth and early twentieth centuries (fig. 72).

The Southern Periphery
1860–1920

Colorado's southern margins were shaped by persisting cultural and economic differences which produced human geographies that departed notably from patterns and landscapes elsewhere in the state. Although connections between this southern periphery and nearby mountain and Piedmont regions became increasingly intimate and complex in the twentieth century, the zone remains a recognizable entity today, born from its early isolation and the formative cultural and economic signatures stamped across its diverse landscapes between 1860 and 1920.

Child of New Mexico: The San Luis Valley, 1860–1920

The distinctive cultural roots of Colorado's southern periphery resulted from a careless bit of political geography in the early 1860s.[1] Born of the straight-line conveniences that shaped many western territories and states, the subregion was included in the new territory of Colorado upon its creation in 1861. Since the early 1850s the area had been part of New Mexico Territory's Taos or Mora Counties, and more than that, it possessed significant Hispano settlement, particularly in the San Luis Valley west of the Sangre de Cristo Mountains and along some of the favored streams east of that range. Truncated politically from their New Mexico roots in 1861, these two lobes of Hispano settlement survived, even expanding their spatial dominance during the decade while retaining cultural and economic ties to the south. Indeed, the strength and depth of that New Mexican influence guaranteed that the southern periphery became an enduring part of what Richard Nostrand has termed the Southwest's "Hispano Homeland" (fig. 73).

The San Luis Valley had been the home of Colorado's largest non–Native American population before gold was discovered in 1859. Recall the valley's healthy growth in the 1850s as new plazas were established both east and west of the Rio Grande and as an American army presence mitigated the Ute threat that periodically visited trouble upon the valley's farmers and ranchers. During the 1860s, the Utes were further and more for-

191

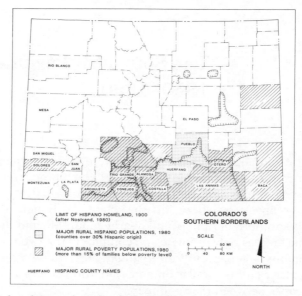

FIGURE 73. Colorado's southern borderlands (Source: Richard L. Nostrand, *The Hispano Homeland* [Norman: University of Oklahoma Press, 1992]; United States, Bureau of the Census, *Twentieth Census of the United States,* 1980)

mally removed from the scene. Treaties of 1863 and 1868 extinguished Ute claims to the San Luis Valley and relegated these people to a large reserve in the western third of the Territory.[2]

Even as the Indian threat faded, however, the persisting legacy of Mexican-era land grants shaped settlement in the valley during the 1860s (fig. 74). The Sangre de Cristo grant in the eastern valley, still controlled by the Beaubien family, was upheld by Congress in June 1860. Three years later, the remaining lands were sold to booster, land speculator, and former territorial governor William Gilpin who paid around four cents per acre for the tract.[3] Gilpin sold off huge portions to outside investors, promising them acreage that would yield mineral riches equal to those found in Gregory Gulch. He was assisted by an English attorney, William Blackmore, who largely ignored the rights of Hispano settlers residing on the tracts. Litigation commenced in the 1870s and some Hispano rights were guaranteed, though residents were compelled to "purchase" their lands from Gilpin's company.

In the western San Luis Valley, the old Conejos land grant evolved differently.[4] The grant was never upheld by Congress after the war with Mexico, and the application for its confirmation languished in the Surveyor General's office after 1861, first in New Mexico and then in Colorado. New

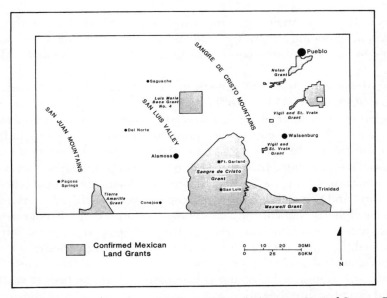

FIGURE 74. Mexican land grants in southern Colorado (Source: United States, Government Land Office, Map of the State of Colorado, 1934)

Hispano migrants merely presumed their legal status as they settled the region. As it happened, their confidence was misplaced. The grant was rejected and made part of the public domain, forcing even longtime settlers to file for their acreage with the federal government.

During the 1860s a historical oddity also occurred in the valley as a new Mexican-style land grant (the L. M. Baca Grant #4) was awarded to the heirs of Luis Maria Cabeza de Baca to settle an old land dispute that had its origins in New Mexico.[5] The unusual federal grant of some one hundred thousand acres, carved from public lands north of Fort Garland near the western slopes of the Sangre de Cristo, never experienced dense settlement but reflected Hispano traditions that continued to shape the region's cultural geography.

Even with Gilpin's speculative ventures casting a shadow over certain areas of the valley, the expansion of mostly Hispano settlement was notable in the area during the 1860s.[6] By 1870 census reports and local estimates from Conejos, Costilla, and Saguache Counties suggested that the valley's population approached five thousand, with approximately 60 percent reporting they were born in New Mexico. This figure suggests the significance of new migrations from the south, but it also included longtime valley residents acknowledging their pre-1861 status as citizens of New

Mexico Territory. Anglo observers often summarized conditions more crudely in ways similar to the Colorado Board of Immigration, which wrote simply in 1872 that the valley "has been settled for many years by Mexicans."

Settlement included the growth of such older nuclei as Conejos, a town that retained its Hispano flavor well after 1860 (fig. 75). Other new Hispano plaza-style or elongated street-style farm villages were also established, each with their Catholic churches, irrigation ditches, and mix of narrow fields and upland pastures.[7] Areas of new colonization in the western valley included irrigable lands on the Rio Grande near Del Norte and similar sites along La Garita, Carnero, and Saguache Creeks between Del Norte and Saguache. To the east, Zapata was established in 1864 near the base of Sierra Blanca, and a sprinkling of new plazas took root near the old Hispano town of San Luis. As with the pre-1860 pattern, most settlers eschewed the open drier portions of the valley in favor of better-watered bottomlands and nearby benches of selected side creeks. By the end of the decade, this traditional Hispano village pattern had reached its greatest spatial extent within the valley.

Many elements of the valley's agricultural geography in the 1860s echoed older patterns of farming and ranching, although selective changes were already under way.[8] Traditional emphases on corn, beans, and subsistence-based sheep grazing persisted in many areas. New Anglo miners and citydwellers to the north and east, however, demanded grain, fresh meat, and wool, and this proximate market for valley products prompted a more commercial agricultural orientation. Livestock imports from New Mexico increased, and the valley became well known for its emphasis on sheep grazing. Flour mills at San Luis were expanded and modernized during the early 1860s, and shipping routes out of the valley to the east and the north were made safer and improved with the presence of Fort Garland. Some valley farmers specialized in cheese and butter production, and these dairy products also found ready appetites in Denver and in the mountain mining camps. In the northern valley, lands around Saguache were homesteaded by a variety of non-Hispanos, with wheat the primary crop and cattle the principal livestock.

Even more lasting changes altered the human geography of the valley after 1870. The area's population grew from just over five thousand at the end of the territorial period to more than thirty thousand in 1920. Increasing cultural diversity accompanied these demographic changes as the old Hispano majority mixed with increasing numbers of Anglos. The "Anglos" themselves were a varied lot and included everything from ethnic Swedes and Germans to a collection of successful Mormon settle-

CONEJOS.

FIGURE 75. An enduring Hispano townscape in the San Luis Valley: Conejos in the
1870s (Courtesy Colorado State Historical Society)

ments. The area's economy became ever more commercialized, and new
technologies changed forever the fundamentals of valley farming as well
as the patterns of transportation connecting the region with the world beyond.

Three interrelated processes reveal the significance of these changes
for the area's human geography. First, such developments can be seen in
the economic context of a new and Anglo-dominated spatial system of
transportation, trade linkages, and urban centers that was being imposed
upon the older subsistence-oriented Hispano pattern. Second, the arrivals
created a new cultural geography in the valley, increasingly dominated by
the Anglo presence, but one that preserved selected elements of the earlier Hispano signature. Finally, the valley's environment was altered in lasting ways after 1870 as agricultural adaptations made greater use of large-
scale, technologically sophisticated irrigation works and as cropping
complexes became increasingly specialized, commercially oriented, and
uniquely adapted to the valley's varied environmental niches.

Transport Links and Urban Centers

Complexity characterized the valley's urban and transportation geography in the late nineteenth and early twentieth centuries. Important elements of earlier Hispano patterns persisted; many plazas survived and even thrived. The arrival of the Anglos, however, particularly in the form of the Denver and Rio Grande Railroad and in the changes it represented, introduced new elements to the valley's economic geography.[9] Railroad-sponsored towns added a layer of settlements to the valley's urban geography. Group settlements, sponsored by ethnic and religious organizations or simply by real estate boosters and land developers, created other centers in the area's settlement system.

Before the railroad arrived in the valley in the late 1870s, overland connections already improved modestly from pre–Gold Rush days. From the east, main stage and mail routes breached Sangre de Cristo and Mosca Passes. Poncha Pass provided accessibility from the north. As mining rushes took prospectors into the San Juans, additional and often hair-raising toll roads connected valley centers to the new mining camps high in the mountains. Both Del Norte and Saguache benefited greatly from these trading opportunities with the mountains, particularly before rail links to the north and south captured the San Juan trade in the 1880s and 1890s.

Within the valley, William Jackson Palmer's Denver and Rio Grande Railroad reshaped transportation geography upon its arrival in 1877. It was hardly by chance that the railroad chose La Veta Pass and lands of the Sangre de Cristo Grant for its right-of-way. Some grant owners (the U.S. Freehold Land and Emigration Company) aided Palmer in financing the rail venture, and they saw the route as an ideal opportunity to increase the value of their real estate investments.[10] Once entering the valley, the tracks passed through Fort Garland and then due west to cross the Rio Grande at the new rail-platted town of Alamosa (fig. 76). The main line then proceeded southwest through the old town of Conejos. Eschewing additional investments in the Hispano center, the company platted its own town of Antonito immediately south of Conejos, making the new center an important rail division point after 1880. From Antonito, one spur led into northern New Mexico while another more important link climbed spectacular Cumbres Pass and threaded its way into the San Juans to Durango.

Once established, this rail axis firmly connected the valley both to the southwestern mines as well as to the Piedmont heartland via Pueblo, Colorado Springs, and Denver. Additional connections and spurs cemented the railroad's dominance in later years. A lateral line followed the Rio Grande west from Alamosa to Del Norte in the 1880s and ultimately to the

FIGURE 76. An emerging Anglo townscape in the San Luis Valley: Alamosa, 1882
(Courtesy Colorado State Historical Society)

mining town of Creede a decade later. Another spur from the company's
Arkansas Valley route was built over Poncha Pass and into the northeastern edge of the San Luis Valley in the early 1880s, thus tapping into mining and agricultural markets in those areas. Finally, the Poncha Pass line
was brought south to Alamosa to link up with the rest of the valley in the
1890s, accompanied by a flurry of new town creations, including the hamlets of Moffat, Hooper, and Mosca.

Local political geography changed rapidly after 1870, but the multi-
plicity of new counties conspired against unifying the valley's interests and
identity. Instead, a mosaic of county seats and market towns grew to dominate their nearby populations.[11] In the southeast, for example, Costilla
County remained relatively rural, with the seat of government and center
of the local economy at San Luis. In neighboring Conejos County, Conejos continued as county seat, but the railroad's presence increased the importance of Antonito and La Jara.

To the north, Rio Grande County was established in 1874, carved out
of the western end of the valley with an early and vigorous focus around
the trade center of Del Norte. Monte Vista was platted during the late
1880s about a dozen miles downriver from Del Norte. It was planned as a
sober and prosperous midwestern farm town set amid an ever expanding
network of irrigation canals. The scheme was engineered by none other
than T. C. Henry, Colorado's seemingly ever-present entrepreneur and
land developer. As with his exploits on the eastern plains, however, Henry's
grand San Luis Valley visions soon fizzled for lack of financing, but not be-

fore Monte Vista was established to become a viable commercial center
amid some of the valley's better agricultural lands.

Local political and economic geography were also redefined in the
northern and central portions of the valley. Saguache County, created in
1866, was home to another cluster of communities. The county seat remained in Saguache, but subsequent railroad, mining, and farming activities added names like Bonanza, Crestone, Villa Grove, and Moffat to the
map. In the center of the valley, Alamosa County was created from northern portions of Conejos and Costilla Counties in 1913. The hard-won separation neatly divided off the prospering and more Anglo sections of the
area from the old Hispano settlements near the eastern and western
foothills and gave the valley's "principal railroad center" of Alamosa and
its residents the recognition they desired for having the largest urban nucleus in the valley.

A Changing Cultural Landscape

The valley's transportation, urban, and political geography echoed even
more fundamental changes in its cultural and social makeup as increasingly diverse immigrants, mostly non-Hispanos, arrived in the area after
1870. Many areas of the valley were opened to farming for the first time by
these migrants. Other sections of the valley saw a retreat of Hispano influences in the face of encroaching Anglos. Some districts, particularly in
the south, held onto their Hispano identities, however, guaranteeing that
certain areas became a part of a distinctive Hispano homeland that is still
much in evidence today.

The initial catalyst for change within the valley came from beyond its
borders: the 1870s mining rushes to the San Juans and to the upper
Arkansas and Gunnison drainages created tremendous demands for food
that farmers and ranchers in the San Luis Valley were well positioned to
satisfy. The railroad's arrival in the valley as well as increasingly sophisticated forms of irrigation were also powerful attractions to commercial
farmers. The fact that some of the territory's best agricultural lands were
already being snapped up elsewhere, particularly in the Piedmont, offered
incentives to look beyond the Front Range for new acreage. While Colorado's far western valleys still stood in the shadow of Ute occupance, the
treaties negotiated for the San Luis Valley in the 1860s meant that this region was fair game for new settlement. A rising number of pioneers followed the trails west and south into what was Colorado's largest intermontane basin, an area seen then as a thinly settled land ripe for the
picking. Some settlers acquired lands from the federal government

through the local land office in Del Norte, while others purchased state lands or property from Hispano owners in the valley.

Arriving Anglos selected a variety of valley settings.[12] Many early homesteaders located in the open north-central portions of the valley between Alamosa and Saguache and tried their hand at dryland wheat cultivation. In the last twenty years of the century, homesteading activity shifted south, concentrating in irrigated agricultural districts in northern Rio Grande and southern Saguache Counties. Hispano-abandoned lands within the boundaries of the discredited Conejos Grant also were homesteaded by Anglos after 1875. Another zone of encroachment was in the eastern valley as cattle-ranching operations were established in areas where cultivation was impractical. Some of these Anglo ranches were assembled from former homesteads; others were created out of Baca and Sangre de Cristo grant lands. Mining in the northern and northeastern portion of the valley also proved attractive to some Anglos. Finally, new merchants and businessmen were drawn to opportunities that developed in such towns as Alamosa, Del Norte, and Monte Vista, and their cultural presence in such places mixed with and often dominated Hispano influences still apparent on the scene.

A number of group settlements imported new cultural influences after 1870.[13] None were more distinctive than the Mormon settlements that appeared in eastern Conejos County in the late 1870s. In classic fashion, these Latter-day Saints, mostly migrants from the South and Midwest, received help from their Utah brethren in purchasing Colorado state lands in the valley, in platting several towns, including Manassas and Sanford, and then in developing nearby farmlands through a system of irrigation canals. Their efforts succeeded, and because the group belonged to the Josephite branch of the church, they did not practice polygamy and were generally well accepted by both Anglo and Hispano valley settlers. Characterized as "frugal, industrious, and prosperous" by Ernest Ingersoll in the 1880s, the Mormons were a close-knit society who lived in their farm villages and commuted daily to their nearby fields. Well respected for their deft touch in matters regarding irrigation, the Mormons developed agricultural surpluses that were marketed commercially elsewhere in the state. Other group settlements in the valley included small communities of Swedes, Germans, and French, all located in the vicinity of Del Norte by the early 1880s. Later Dutch colonists tried their luck west of Alamosa, but most left the valley within a few years.

These new cultural elements added ethnic and religious diversity to the Hispano Catholic traditions of the valley. Naturally, the Hispano community adjusted to the Anglo presence, but for most these adjustments tended to be economic shifts rather than fundamental cultural changes. Hispano farmers and ranchers selectively profited from the more commercial agricultural economy even as they held on to many of their basic ethnic and religious values. The cultural landscape reflected many of these shifting patterns: larger sheep herds, more elaborate irrigation works, some greater agricultural specialization in commercial grain crops, and modernized milling facilities indicated the more market-oriented bent of some Hispanos. Other Hispanos, drawn to the attractions of wage labor, left their land and settled in towns like Del Norte and Monte Vista, where they went to work for Anglo farmers and businessmen.

Even with these intrusions, many Hispano communities, particularly in the southern valley, retained a strong social cohesion and cultural identity increasingly rooted in place. The landscape reflected many of these ethnic and religious continuities.[14] For example, Catholic churches, often built with adobe and adorned with santos (painted or carved wooden saints) remained a ubiquitous feature of the Hispano village, suggesting the ongoing vitality of religion in the lives of residents (fig. 77). Cemeteries offered distinctive signatures with their carved sandstone markers, folk picket fences surrounding gravesites known as *cerquitas,* and the encased plaster figurines called crèches providing signposts of Hispano occu-

FIGURE 77. Persisting cultural signatures on the landscape: Catholic church at San Luis (Photo by the author)

pance. The popular Penitente movement, an offshoot of mainstream Catholicism that practiced self-flagellation and human crucifixion in its more extreme forms, also left its mark on the landscape of northern New Mexico and southern Colorado in the form of wooden crosses and adobe *moradas,* or meeting houses.

The ordinary vernacular landscape of Hispano houses, barns, schools, and stores was the most significant and omnipresent reminder of the intimate blend of people, place, and culture that continued to shape many portions of the San Luis Valley into the twentieth century.[15] The popular habit of building in adobe recognized the limits and opportunities of local geography. Color tones literally were those of the earth, the protection offered by the sun-dried bricks recognized the area's harsh climatic extremes, and the intricacies of construction, design, and floor plans mirrored generations of folk tradition developed in Iberia and modified in New Spain and later in New Mexico. Extensive log construction replaced adobe in many upland zones, and the distinctive vertically placed poles that were used in a palisade style also had roots in earlier Spanish traditions. In other locales, the easy availability of stone encouraged its use in a variety of structures. Whatever the local building material, the Hispanos' vernacular landscape remained an enduring signature of their presence in the San Luis Valley.

Still, their absolute cultural dominance of the pre-1870 era came to an end, and by 1900 the valley's landscape, though still rich in adobe barns and flat-roofed houses, also had its share of midwestern farmscapes, Victorian-style homes, and Presbyterian churches, all signatures of important and lasting cultural shifts.

Assessing and Modifying the Environment

The attractions of the San Luis Valley's resource base remained the magnet that drew residents to the region between 1870 and 1920. How did this varied Anglo population evaluate the potential of the valley's environment, and how was it transformed, often dramatically, once settlement accelerated? While inmigrating Hispanos surely saw similarities between the valley's setting and their familiar homelands to the south, Anglos were less sanguine as to the area's prospects and how to maximize the value of the local resource base. Early on, in a pattern analogous to the shifting and diverse perceptions of Colorado's eastern plains, Anglos were divided in their assessments of the valley and how to put it to good use.[16] Perhaps Albert Richardson's passing comments in 1859 were an apt summation of initial Anglo reactions. While noting that "the desert abounded in wild sage, cactus, and great herds of antelopes," he also described the fecundity of the early Hispano settlements and hinted that "irrigation makes the parched, sandy soil wonderfully productive." Less optimistic were Englishman S. Nugent Townshend's lamentations that irrigating the San Luis Valley was "the most astoundingly hopeless investment I have ever seen or heard of."

Ultimately, however, boosters and promoters won the war of image making in the San Luis Valley, and the agricultural expansion after 1870, much of it related to irrigation, was nothing short of phenomenal. In the early 1880s William Pabor summarized the valley's promise in a single line: "Without water, a desert; with water, a Garden of Eden."[17] He boldly predicted that the effective management of the valley's water resources might put no fewer than five hundred thousand acres under irrigated cultivation, a figure that was remarkably on target by 1915.

A variety of interests pushed for more irrigation.[18] The state of Colorado was a major landowner in the valley, and officials promoted the disposal and development of two hundred thousand state-controlled acres, received when the territory was admitted into the Union in 1876. T. C. Henry, along with his Colorado Loan and Trust Company, created demonstration farms and participated in the construction of the Rio Grande, San Luis, Monte Vista, and Empire Canals, all in the western portion of the valley. Although the enterprises failed for Henry and his investors, they succeeded for the farmers that ultimately controlled them in local cooperatives. In addition, a parade of other land ventures, such as the Oklahoma Land and Colonization Company, the Trinchera Land Lottery, and the Button Land Company Enterprise, continued the valley's tradition of questionable real estate dealings.

Railroads, principally the Denver and Rio Grande, also waxed eloquent on the valley's potential for irrigation. In 1899 the railroad made particular note of the "more than 600 flowing artesian wells in the San Luis Park" that represented a local technological adaptation which tapped a seemingly limitless underground water resource that dwarfed even the flow of the Rio Grande and all its tributaries.

These important changes in the scale and technology of irrigation greatly expanded the number of irrigable acres in the valley (fig. 78). Traditional Hispano-era diversions were restricted to short laterals that served nearby bottomlands. The new ditches reached higher benches, and the artesian wells watered lands wherever drilling succeeded. By 1900, as Pabor had predicted, the San Luis Valley included a block of contiguous irrigated lands that were second in the state only to the vast systems of the northern Piedmont (see fig. 49). Areas of large-scale development included Alamosa, southern Saguache, eastern Rio Grande, and central Conejos Counties.

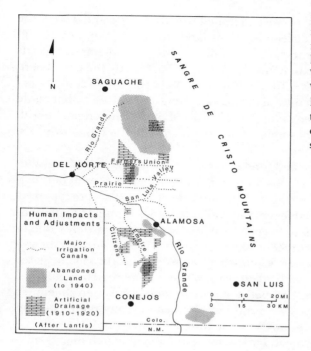

FIGURE 78. Selected human impacts and adjustments in the San Luis Valley (Adapted from David W. Lantis, "The San Luis Valley, Colorado: Sequent Rural Occupance in an Intermontane Basin" [Ph.D. diss., Ohio State University, 1950])

Modifying the valley's environment did not come without its challenges.[19] When drought struck the region in the early 1890s, the valley faced problems similar to those encountered across the eastern plains. Dryland cultivation was crippled, and even many irrigated farms shriveled in the heat as a shrunken Rio Grande failed to serve the needs of area farmers. Far-off Mexico also complained, prompting an International Boundary Commission meeting in 1896 that controlled future storage and diversion projects throughout the system. Agreements after 1906 allowed additional storage reservoirs built in the upper Rio Grande Basin while guaranteeing Mexico a dependable annual flow of water. Drilling artesian wells also had its problems, lowering local water tables and drying up several valley lakes.

In other areas, the challenge became too much water, not too little. Particularly in the north-central valley, near Mosca and Hooper, a district with no natural drainage, intense irrigation between 1880 and 1890 waterlogged thousands of acres. Alkali and salt deposits surfaced, and commercial wheat yields plummeted. The result was the widespread abandonment of more than three hundred thousand acres in the valley's center between 1890 and 1920 (see fig. 78).[20] Smaller-scale versions of the problem appeared elsewhere in the valley, an ironic hazard in an area that received some of the lowest average annual precipitation in the state.

Many valley farmers, however, lea ned from the 1890s and were more careful in locating and developing their lands in subsequent decades.[21] Extensive drainage networks, for example, mitigated problems of soil saturation and salt buildup in many districts (see fig. 78). By the early twentieth century, the valley's settlement pattern increasingly reflected selective preferences for agricultural occupance: well-drained areas that could be irrigated became ever more densely settled and commercially developed, whereas other zones more prone to environmental limits were virtually devoid of population.

Both livestock forage and food crops figured into the valley's agricultural geography between 1870 and 1920.[22] In 1880, before the era of the irrigation projects, small acreages of dryland wheat and oats were reported, with hay the dominant fodder crop for valley livestock. Animal populations included large numbers of sheep, particularly in Hispano-rich Conejos County, and a growing number of cattle, scattered widely through the valley wherever Anglo ranchers established themselves. After 1880 irrigated hay remained an important feed crop but was supplemented by field peas, sweet clover, and alfalfa. Competition also developed between sheepmen and cattlemen as livestock were routinely herded into mountain pastures only to encounter other animals on the ranges.

Among food crops, wheat, barley, and oats became much more significant after 1885. By 1900 more than sixty thousand valley acres were in wheat. That tally declined slightly between 1900 and 1920 as some wheat lands were abandoned and as the cropping mix shifted toward more specialized food crops. The biggest success story was the cultivation of potatoes, which after 1895 became focused near Monte Vista and Del Norte in the western valley. Huge increases in regional and national demand came with the strong markets of the Spanish-American War in 1898 and 1899. Another surge occurred during World War I, and by 1917 more than eleven thousand acres produced an impressive 1.7 million bushels of the crop, much of it harvested by Hispano labor. Sugar beets were briefly tried in the valley between 1911 and 1913, but local conditions proved marginal.

After 1880 mining operations provided additional environmental modifications in the northern and eastern corners of the valley.[23] Stimulated by enormous finds in the San Juans and nearby Leadville, prospectors scoured the valley's creeks for color and carbonates. Modest successes, particularly in the discovery of silver-lead ores, promoted the growth of camps at Bonanza and Sedgwick north of Saguache. Further east, good luck even visited perennial promoter William Gilpin: he purchased the Baca Grant lands in 1877, and paying quantities of gold were found in the area three years later. The largest mine operation in the valley, however, involved neither silver or gold. Canny geologists employed by the Pueblo-based Colorado Coal and Iron Company spotted iron-rich limonite deposits in the northeast corner of the valley in the 1870s and purchased a small but valuable tract southeast of Villa Grove. Soon a thriving iron mine was in operation, the metal flowing toward the company's smelting and refining operations in Pueblo and Durango. Orient City became an ethnically varied company town that provided another exotic element on the cultural landscape and persisted until 1919, when the mines were shut down, the victim of lower-cost operations elsewhere in the West.

The Creation of the Southern Coal Belt: 1860–1920

Just east of the San Luis Valley and the Sangre de Cristo Mountains, a second lobe of Hispano settlement took shape in the 1860s. Anchored around the town of Trinidad and aligned along major streamcourses including the Purgatoire, Apishapa, and Huerfano Rivers, these mostly New Mexico–rooted settlements did not take shape until after the Pikes Peak Gold Rush. Still, old, mostly never-developed land grants from the Mexican era figured significantly in the settlement story of the area (see fig. 74).[24] South of the Purgatoire River, the vast Maxwell Grant, dating from 1841, extended into Colorado Territory and was confirmed by Congress in 1860, even though its northern perimeter was only settled lightly by that date. Further north, the Nolan and the Vigil and St. Vrain Grants, both originating in 1843, were provisionally confirmed in the early 1860s but then reduced greatly in size a decade later. These legal uncertainties effectively removed from the public domain much of the area south of Pueblo along and just east of the mountains.

Northward-migrating New Mexicans eagerly filled the void, encouraged by grant owners who saw them as productive land purchasers who would enhance the value of their acreage and the legal strength of their old land claims.[25] Several dozen plazas were established in this manner along irrigable rivers and side creeks. These small settlements typically consisted of five to fifteen adobe houses, their residents linked through an extended family and often financially oriented around a male *patrón,* who managed the settlement's commercial affairs and served as local moneylender, adviser, and leader. The largest of these new settlements, Trinidad, was founded early in the decade by Felipe Baca, who liked the site along the Purgatoire River and brought family and neighbors from Mora, New Mexico, to settle the area. Nearby, smaller centers of Madrid and Tijeras also exemplified the plaza settlement pattern, as did Apodaca (later renamed Aguilar), La Plaza de los Leones (later renamed Walsenburg), and La Veta to the north. Colonists repeated the agricultural mix of the San Luis Valley: wheat and corn were important grains and sheep were more

dominant than cattle. In addition to feeding local residents, the fertile region found ready markets for its abundance in the nearby trading town of
Pueblo.

Recognizing the growing population of the area, the territory redrew
county boundaries in 1866, creating Las Animas County with its seat at
Trinidad to serve southeastern Colorado. Trinidad quickly became the
dominant urban place in the Purgatoire Valley, deriving its prominence
both from its role as a local central place serving nearby plazas and from
its transport and trade connections with Santa Fe and a number of northern New Mexico mining towns.[26] As one booster noted in 1869, "The principal roads from the States to New Mexico and from the northern part of
the Territory converge here." "Uncle Dick" Wooton made famous his toll
road through the Maxwell Grant south of Trinidad during the period as
tons of trade goods were hauled over tortuous Raton Pass into New Mexico Territory. By 1870 Trinidad claimed six hundred residents with another
twenty-eight hundred settlers living in nearby portions of the Purgatoire
Valley.

Within the dominant New Mexican population, non-Hispano influences appeared in the 1860s, drawn by Trinidad's commercial potential and
by available acreage both in the lower Purgatoire Valley and in watersheds
west and south of Pueblo. Indeed, by 1870, Hispano settlement across
southern Colorado was mixing with, modifying, and adapting to the realities of an encroaching Anglo-dominated regional economy.[27] Outsiders
filtered into the area, including miners headed for New Mexico placers, a
growing trail of inmigrating cattlemen, and an increasing number of enterprising merchants. In particular, both the lower Huerfano and Purgatoire Valleys experienced the arrival of Anglo ranching and farming populations by the late 1860s, an inmigration that increased greatly during the
following decade.

Most fundamental, however, were the sweeping geographical changes
that incorporated the region around Trinidad into the opportunities and
vicissitudes of the industrial age. An elaborate new network of mines, settlements, and railroads, dramatically imposed by a corporate nexus of mineral and transport companies and oriented around the area's enormous
coalfields, dominated this portion of the southern periphery in the last
quarter of the nineteenth century. Further twentieth-century expansion
of the coal operations, culminating in the fevered industrial activity of
World War I, fundamentally changed the economic and social geography
of this once quiet corner of Colorado. Although it retained a distinctive
Hispano flavor, the arrival of industrial capitalism reshaped the cultural
landscape and brought radically different definitions of community that
included new ethnic participants and powerful pressures to "American-

ize" local residents. In addition, a rising class consciousness in many industrial communities arose out of the common frustrations of a labor force all too intimately wed to the designs and fortunes of companies and capitalists far removed from the local scene.

A New Geography of Centers and Linkages

The distribution of coal across the brush and piñon-covered hills and canyons of southern Colorado defined a natural setting for potentially extraordinary economic development.[28] Geologically, the entire region is part of the Raton Mesa coalfield, but the surface and near-surface exposures of the black fuel are richest and most accessible in an area extending from just southeast and southwest of Trinidad toward Walsenburg. The southern end of the deposit proved especially valuable and became the focus for some of the state's largest coal mines. The sedimentary coal-bearing rocks of southern Colorado were particularly attractive for development because of their readily exposed outcrops and because they had come close to igneous intrusions that changed lower-quality lignite and sub-bituminous deposits into high-density bituminous coal ideal for coking. Such fuel could be used for gas-making, steam production, blacksmithing, and, most important, ore smelting.

The happy combination of geology and accessibility did not go unrecognized after 1870, particularly as the territory's population grew and its economy expanded. The result was the bold imposition of a new geography of settlements, one forcibly laid atop the existing infrastructure and aimed exclusively at extracting the riches of the world beneath. Its success can initially be gleaned from aggregate statistics of population change and coal production, but the longer-term implications of this new orientation, both for the land itself and for those laboring within its enormous carboniferous wealth, requires a more detailed delving into local patterns and processes. Certainly the region's population growth between 1870 and 1920 suggests some of the magnitude of the change: from a population of just over six thousand in 1870, Las Animas and Huerfano Counties multiplied ninefold to more than fifty-five thousand residents a half-century later.

The population increases paralleled the enormous growth in coal production.[29] Coal demand mushroomed nationally between 1880 and 1910 as industrial and transportation-related uses soared. In the West, coal output increased twenty-eight-fold during the period, and Colorado became the West's leading coal producer by 1893. Within Colorado, precious metals smelting and steel production combined with ever increasing rail and urban demands for the black fuel. Although Colorado had several important coal-producing districts, including mines near Boulder and Canon

City, the state's primary sources for coal after 1880 were Las Animas and
Huerfano Counties. Given the technology of the time, coal production
translated directly into large demands for labor. Shortly after 1900 between
eight thousand and nine thousand coal miners worked in the state's two
southern counties and the number of Colorado coal miners doubled once
again between 1900 and 1910 before peaking during World War I.

The economic catalysts behind this new human geography, specifically
the rail and mining companies involved in the coal extraction, processing,
and transport businesses, created a new spatial system of activities and
movements across southern Colorado after 1875 (fig. 79). Early on, the
Denver and Rio Grande Railroad dominated the region, along with its various land, mining, and ore-processing subsidiaries. General Palmer's
southward-trending rail line reached Pueblo in 1872, and tracks reached
the southern coalfields near Trinidad four years later.

In that year Palmer incorporated the Southern Colorado Coal and
Town Company.[30] He used the new entity to buy both private parcels and
available public lands that were rich in coal-mining potential. Thousands
of acres were acquired, often very cheaply. The company also identified
and platted town sites along the new tracks south of Pueblo. In a repeat of
their strategy at Pueblo, the railroad and town company avoided laying
tracks directly to Trinidad, preferring instead to stop a few miles away at
the company-created railhead of El Moro. There, hundreds of company-
financed coke ovens were constructed in the late 1870s and 1880s. Coal
markets were close at hand, including many of the company's operations
at Pueblo as well as other foundries in Leadville, Lake City, and Denver.
Not surprisingly, once large-scale production began in 1878, the Denver
and Rio Grande Railroad granted its coal subsidiary preferential shipping
rates. In addition, the company's initial coal mining town of Engle, located
on a branch line six miles south of El Moro, became a model for subsequent settlements in the area and was a reminder that corporate influence
extended directly to the provision of worker housing, stores, and even
schools.

The corporate evolution of the Southern Colorado Coal and Town
Company followed the growth and consolidation of its regional coal operations. The company merged with other arms of Palmer's industrial empire in the early 1880s to form the Colorado Coal and Iron Company.[31] It
was instrumental in greatly expanding the list of company-owned mines
and mining towns, in both Huerfano and Las Animas Counties, as its steel-
making operations in Pueblo grew and as demand for coal increased in
nearby states. Corporate muscle was added in 1892 as the company was
again merged and redefined to become the Colorado Fuel and Iron Company. This company took the coal region into its most productive and tu-

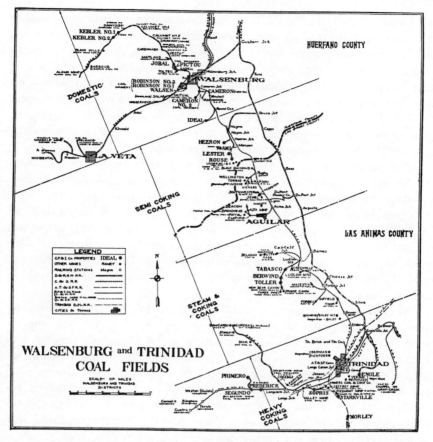

FIGURE 79. Creating a new spatial system: the Walsenburg and Trinidad coalfields
(Source: Pueblo Commerce Club, "Facts About Pueblo-Colorado," 1929)

multuous years from the middle 1890s to the early 1920s. Its industrial dominance became almost complete between 1895 and 1910 as it opened new
mines and bought out smaller competitors. The company was itself absorbed into larger corporate entities affiliated with Rockefeller interests
shortly after the turn of the century. This provided greater access to investment capital and increased the integration of the company's mining
operations, and the ever expanding network of regional and national railroads were critical to its competitive success.

Of particular importance was the consolidation of a number of local
lines to form the Colorado and Southern Railroad in the late 1890s.[32] It
became a subsidiary of the Chicago, Burlington, and Quincy line that
served many of the coal mines between Walsenburg and Trinidad and

which was closely linked to the Colorado Fuel and Iron Company. Another Colorado Fuel and Iron Company short line, the Colorado and Wyoming Railroad, was built westward from Trinidad during the same period to serve new mines in that area. Serendipity was not involved here: as one critic has noted, unlike the gamblers who made and lost fortunes in Colorado precious metals, "by contrast the coal operators were circumspect and sure-footed, intensely ambitious but planners rather than plungers, given to realistic assessment before investment, and once committed, merciless in the management and growth of their business."

All of these intricate, interconnected, and carefully structured corporate developments made sense once one looked at the increasingly integrated spatial system of mines, towns, work camps, coke ovens, rail lines, and smelters across the region (see fig. 79).[33] There on the land, more clearly displayed than in any organizational chart of holding companies and interlocking boards of directors, was the bold, innovative, and ultimately exploitative signature of late-nineteenth and early twentieth-century industrial capitalism epitomized by the dominance of the Colorado Fuel and Iron Company.

Other corporate actors also refashioned the geography of mines, urban centers, and transport links. One principal player and early competitor to Denver and Rio Grande interests was the Atchison, Topeka, and Santa Fe Railroad. In fact, the line outfoxed Palmer in the late 1870s by aggressively building into Trinidad and thus tapping into southern Colorado's largest urban center at the time. Palmer's railroad finally responded with a spur into Trinidad in the late 1880s, but by then the Santa Fe was clearly dominant and had further taken the initiative to build over Raton Pass to connect with other markets in New Mexico.

Santa Fe Railroad interests established their own coal mines and processing operations, principally to serve the railroad and nearby markets in eastern Colorado and western Kansas. Their subsidiary, the Trinidad Coal and Coking Company, developed major mining operations at Starkville, a classic company town just south of Trinidad. Finally sold to the Colorado Fuel and Iron Company in 1896, these operations added to the region's industrial geography of the late nineteenth century. Other companies, such as the Denver Fuel Company, with mines at Sopris, and the Victor Fuel Company, with its activities at nearby Hastings and Delagua, also came into the broader Colorado Fuel and Iron Company orbit by the early twentieth century, tightening the larger company's steel grip upon the local economy and society.

The coal era refashioned southern Colorado's preindustrial urban geography. Hispano plaza towns were dramatically affected by the mines, which often drew Hispano laborers, particularly males, away from the village for considerable periods.[34] Some Hispano towns also lay directly in the path of coal mine operations, with varied but always disruptive results. Aguilar, midway between Trinidad and Walsenburg, was a small Hispano village that quadrupled in size as a coal mine center. West of Trinidad, the old plaza at Tercio was disrupted early in the twentieth century when the Colorado Fuel and Iron Company simply declared the Hispano inhabitants "squatters" on corporate acreage.

Trinidad, too, experienced great change in the coal era.[35] Before the arrival of the railroad, the sleepy town of several hundred was relatively isolated, with only triweekly stage service with Pueblo in 1870. By 1890 Trinidad's bustling population of fifty-five hundred made it a sizable urban nucleus between Pueblo and Santa Fe (fig. 80). Indeed, the city's centrality within the southern coalfields, its function as a rail center, and its status as county seat and regional market town all worked in its favor after 1875.

Coal's most dramatic impact on the area's urban geography, however, came in the form of entirely new towns (fig. 81).[36] For a town to be cre-

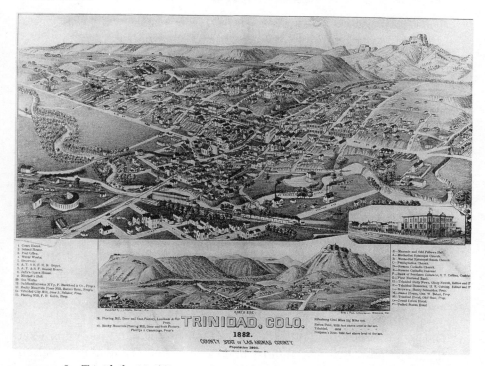

FIGURE 80. Trinidad, 1882 (Courtesy Denver Public Library, Western History Collection)

FIGURE 81. Mine operations, rail infrastructure, and worker housing in the company coal town: Starkville, 1910 (Courtesy Denver Public Library, Western History Collection)

ated, marketable coal veins were earmarked for development, a location for mining equipment and worker housing was identified, and an approach route was surveyed to allow a railroad line to access the new center. Similar to many of the metals mining settlements in the mountains, these variables produced towns in unusual locations (see fig. 79). By 1890 three of the largest towns were found within a few miles of Trinidad. Engle and Starkville each had populations of around one thousand while nearby Sopris bloomed to be the largest camp with more than fifteen hundred residents. West of Sopris, the centers of Primero, Segundo, Tercio, Cuatro, and Quinto were additional Purgatoire Valley settlements that formed a mosaic of newer coal camps amid a scattering of older plaza settlements.

About a dozen miles north of Trinidad, a second cluster of coal camps focused on Berwind Canyon. Developments commenced in the late 1880s, and by the early twentieth century Toller, Berwind, and Ludlow were major Colorado Fuel and Iron Company towns, while nearby Hastings and Delagua were controlled by the Victor Fuel Company. Other mining settlements flourished near Aguilar midway between Trinidad and Walsenburg. Finally, a sizable number of camps ringed Walsenburg and extended a short distance to the northwest to the Kebler mines.

Coal mining towns often had abbreviated lifespans, depending on their local resource base and changing market conditions. Between 1922 and 1930, for example, the Colorado Fuel and Iron Company, coping with lower postwar demand for coal, closed operations at Starkville, Engle, Sopris, Berwind, Primero, and Kebler.[37] Depression years of the 1930s brought even further cutbacks. The fledgling urban centers created in the heyday of the coal mine era proved to be just as ephemeral as many of the settlements associated with metals mining in the mountains or with dryland agriculture across the eastern plains.

The Fashioning of New Communities

Social geographies in the coal country experienced lasting shifts between 1870 and 1920 as the fabric of traditional Hispano communities frayed and as new and multiple influences imposed not only an Anglo dominance but also a many-layered ethnic mosaic across the area. Within Hispano villages, the lessened isolation that came with railroads, nearby urban growth, and the coal mining economy meant more mobility, particularly for working men and young people.[38] Many Hispanos left for the Arkansas and South Platte Valleys to labor on commercial farms, while others migrated to industrial employment in Pueblo and Denver. These workers, often seasonal or temporary, retained ties to the southern periphery and returned periodically to their home villages. Thus, even as the southern coal region became more culturally and economically heterogeneous between 1880 and 1920, the geographical extent of Hispano influence within Colorado, indeed within the West in general, actually expanded to include new rural and urban settings. In these new settings, Hispano workers selectively acculturated to obtain employment, but they retained a distinctive identity and often maintained ties to their southern Colorado homeland.

Even for Hispanos who remained in their communities, cultural change imposed itself in many ways.[39] The English language was more freely brought to the village by returning workers, and schools increasingly used English as a medium of instruction. Basic cultural artifacts like clothing and home construction also bore an increasingly Anglo stamp. Demand for food in the coal towns provided powerful incentives for Hispanos to commercialize and increase the scale of their livestock-raising operations. Many Hispano ranchers did so quite successfully, and declining sheep numbers along with rising cattle numbers between 1880 and 1920 suggest that they willingly adapted to and sometimes worked alongside their Anglo counterparts. The result was that these rural communities, while retaining many key religious and cultural institutions, actively changed with the times, embracing new opportunities and technologies as they became available, at the same time seeing, perhaps less desirably, some permanent erosion of the isolation and coherence that had so clearly bounded and defined their social experience in an earlier age.

Hispano influence also remained notable in some of the larger urban centers.[40] Trinidad in 1910, for example, still had its Spanish-language newspapers, Hispano-owned shops, vigorous Catholic institutions, and local political Hispano elite that maintained a distinctive cultural character. Trinidad's function as a market center and county seat encouraged its widespread and regular use by a large number of rural Hispano villagers. Still, the visible presence of Hispanos did not signal an economic or even cultural dominance in either Trinidad or Walsenburg after the turn of the century because coal workers in the vicinity transformed both centers into wide-open mining towns.

Change within Hispano society came most dramatically for those who left their home village for the temporary yet attractive opportunities of the coal camp.[41] Suddenly these Hispanos were outnumbered by a diverse and similarly uprooted ethnic mix, and many key economic and social institutions that traditionally defined their communities were now controlled by the coal company. Land ownership, a central, unifying, and place-defining characteristic of traditional Hispano village life, was replaced by a wage-labor system in which workers rented housing, often at high rates, from company officials. Some Hispanos kept gardens and a few livestock in the camps, but they lost a great deal of economic autonomy in their new lives. The company store controlled access to many basic goods, and even local Catholic churches were often company-subsidized, thus encouraging a religious message that stressed cooperation and Americanization over principles of traditional Hispano community cohesion. Another complicating cultural variable in many of the camps were increasing numbers of newly arrived Mexican immigrants. Friction surfaced between native Hispanos and the Mexicans, and both groups were similarly distrusted and misunderstood by the Anglo population.

Coal camp communities became ever more ethnically complex after 1890, mirroring the cultural variety of Pueblo or Denver.[42] In the early years, English-speaking miners dominated, but the growing scale of operations demanded more and more workers. Although Hispanos supplied some of the labor, operations like the Colorado Fuel and Iron Company relied increasingly on recruiting agents who traveled to Europe to round up large numbers of willing workers. Typical of the era, the main source-regions of Colorado coal miners were southern and eastern Europe. Large numbers of Italians, Greeks, and Slavs made the trek to the buttes and canyons of Huerfano and Las Animas Counties, hoping to start anew in the American West. The boisterous and ephemeral life of the coal camps disrupted their traditional lifeways, although ethnic clannishness maintained differences among national groups. Black Americans and Asian immigrants provided further cultural complexity in the camps. Longtime miners resented newcomers, whatever their background, because they were often hired by unscrupulous company managers to put downward pressure on wages or to break strikes. Particularly after an aborted strike in 1903–4, immigrants were used to divide worker interests and to keep mine operations open at the lowest costs possible.

By 1910 more than 70 percent of the area's coal miners were non-English-speaking immigrants, a polyglot population with little in common except for their common status as workers in a tough and dangerous world.[43] Initial attractions and unfulfilled promises changed the lives of arriving immigrants. Aguilar's Alex Bisulco recalled the excitement of leaving the homeland, noting, "These mines was all just getting started then. They was just opening up, and there was a lot of work. They was building the camps and railroads and mines. And so they start sending for each other and that's how they came to these mines." Once arrived, Ludlow miner Victor Bazanelle suggested that expectations were not always met amid the working conditions and xenophobia of the camps, remembering, "We come from Germany, from high civilized places. . . . I spoke already three languages—Italian, German, and Slavish. Over there, they said the 20-dollar gold pieces, coins, hanging on every post. Oh yeah. Gold all over. So I went to Tobasco Mine for 11 cents an hour. Ten hours. . . . Never the name, never the Victor Bazanelle. You was the Wop. You was the Dago. And the Slavish was Garlic Snapper and Hunk." Life was similarly difficult for immigrant women. Alex Bisulco admiringly recalled their tenacity: "I don't see how they could not go bugs. They washed clothes by hand on the board, you know, go haul the water, go haul the buckets, you see. No hydrants, no water in the house. An old two-seater can out there and all that kind of stuff. I don't see how they did it."

Fashioned from this ethnically varied, spatially isolated, and tightly clustered population was nothing less than Colorado's purest example of an industrial community, a collection of owners, managers, and workers who were brought together in a place, first and foremost, to extract coal from the earth. The epitome of turn-of-the-century industrial capitalism in the West, southern Colorado's coal mining districts, sitting as they did so apart from other major population centers, took on in unfettered form the quintessential characteristics of an imposed industrial economic and social order. Three attributes shaped the workings of the industrial community. First, it pressured its participants to Americanize, to adopt dominant economic and cultural prescriptions of Anglo society in order to survive and succeed. Second, the industrial community organized itself around technologies and institutions that rationalized and made more efficient the production of its primary output, in this case, coal and its varied byproducts. Finally, the industrial community created conditions that sowed seeds of class conflict, a set of management-worker relationships that, in this instance, produced one of the most sustained and violent clashes in American labor history.

Once the coal camps were established, powerful forces of Americanization shaped the lives of miners and their children. Most pervasively, the region's economy was built upon large investments of capital that intimately linked the area's fortunes with the nation's metropolitan and industrial heartland. But there were more local and intimate expressions of acculturating impulses, too. As the coal companies grew more powerful they took it upon themselves to encourage assimilation of immigrant workers into the mainstream of American culture. There is some irony here, because coal companies played ethnic groups off one another when it suited their needs. Clearly, however, it became company policy to educate, socialize, and entertain workers in ways that would foster American cultural values.[44]

The Colorado Fuel and Iron Company's Sociological Department, established in 1901, was responsible for developing local schools and libraries and with organizing such community events as band concerts and Fourth of July picnics.[45] Its kindergartens would "inculcate the true democratic spirit—the spirit of sympathy, of unselfishness, and of equal rights." The company newspaper, *Camp and Plant,* painted an idyllic picture with a strong social and political message as it noted the "lace curtains . . . sweet tones of a piano . . . peace, plenty, prosperity abound . . . our bright little camp full of good cheer and happiness. . . . Nature was never sunnier and the dear old flag on school and storehouse carried joy to all."

Pressures to Americanize the industrial community only increased amid the nationalistic fervor of World War I.[46] In southern Colorado "Loyalty Leaguers" and "Councils of Defense" pledged "to promote the establishment of the English language" and to swear their absolute allegiance to the American way. One cynical observer summarized the Colorado Fuel and Iron Company's commitment to nationalism, arguing that "Americanism, to this company as to others with like departments, meant the United States flag and homogeneous unity as well as respect for the authority of corporate capitalism."

Indeed, the imposition of a technologically efficient, profitable, and ultimately socially coercive system of corporate capitalism was a second attribute of southern Colorado's industrial community. Scale economies of production necessitated large investments in technology and labor. As mine output grew, so did the need for a careful rationalization of the production process: more modern extraction techniques, processing equipment, and transport facilities lowered per ton costs and raised corporate profits. Skilled technical and financial integration of these varied parts of the mining business articulated the recognized need for efficiency.

Just as important was the imposition of a similar imperative upon the mine communities themselves: an orderly workforce was a productive workforce. The key to success was controlling as many dimensions of the industrial community's life as possible. Corporate owners were keenly aware of the value in dominating many economic and social activities of the camp. As one observer noted,

> Isolated in up-canyon company towns or camps, the miners lived in shoddy company houses for which they paid an exorbitant rent, or lived in their own shacks on leased company land, from which they could be summarily evicted. They received company scrip as wages, which was discounted when converted to cash, and traded in company stores, where they paid excessively high prices. They received treatment from a company doctor . . . and their children attended company controlled schools. . . . They worshiped at company subsidized churches . . . and they submitted to surveillance by company informants, who specialized in watching for union infiltration.[47]

This penchant for control was vividly displayed on the industrial community's cultural landscape.[48] Many camp communities were isolated spatially on company land policed by private company marshals and enclosed by barbed wire fencing. Within the perimeter, an industrial landscape dominated: rail tracks and cars converged at the tipple where coal was screened and loaded, smoke curled from the local power plant, and mine cars rumbled in and out of nearby tunnel openings. Company-built stores, churches, and meeting halls structured economic and social life beyond the mine tunnels. Nearby, the camp superintendent's residence was "the most pretentious structure in any coal mining camp." After 1895 standardized worker residences often replaced earlier ramshackle collections of vernacular housing. Larger operators like Colorado Fuel and Iron Company prided themselves on the "model" communities they were providing, and the race toward efficiency and productivity was portrayed nowhere better than in the regular rows of mass-produced worker housing that increasingly characterized the camps. Periodic camp "beautification" campaigns softened the industrial harshness of the landscape in later years as companies planted trees and flower gardens amid worker and mine facilities. It was a sincere though naive attempt to produce a work environment more agreeable to employees and thus more productive for mine operators.

This ubiquitous company presence did not obfuscate the reality of their relationship to the mine workers: underground coal mining was dangerous, and working conditions were difficult, providing minimal pay and benefits. This eventually produced a powerful response among many miners. This reaction, not atypical given the social and political climate of the time, suggested that laborers became ever more aware of their common class-based status as workers. Particularly as communities expanded after 1890, many southern Colorado coal miners recognized their common plight, regardless of their diverse hometowns or cultural backgrounds. For many, ethnicity began to matter less than class, and along with some powerful agitation on the part of the mine unions, a new definition of the industrial community emerged from the workers. As southern Colorado labor history shows, this new definition stood in sharp, sometimes violent contrast from the community as it was defined from the company's perspective.[49]

In the world of Colorado coal mining, a culture of tension evolved within the industrial community of the late nineteenth century. Disputes in Fremont County near Pueblo dated to the early 1870s, and larger-scale Knights of Labor activity in the 1880s led to several unsuccessful statewide walkouts that included workers near Walsenburg and Trinidad. More union organizing on the part of the United Mineworkers Union after 1890 led to a major strike in the southern coalfields in 1903 and 1904. Even though most of the workers' demands were codified in state labor and safety laws, the coal companies resisted union actions by importing unskilled immigrant workers, evicting miners from worker housing, and appealing to the state to send in the militia to protect mine property and round up union rabble-rousers. This conflict, though it was not economically successful for the unions, unified many of the miners in their hatred and distrust of the coal companies.[50]

A decade later, labor conflicts reached their disastrous peak with the strikes of 1913 and 1914.[51] The clash received national attention and culminated in the so-called Ludlow Massacre of April 1914, in which nineteen miners died in a tent camp midway between Trinidad and Walsenburg. Thereafter, the "Rockefeller Plan," named after one of the controlling families in the Colorado Fuel and Iron Company organization, improved working conditions with a system of welfare capitalism that tried to circumvent traditional unions. Strong demand for coal also led to higher wages in the war years following the strike, lessening labor-management tensions. Even so, the character of southern Colorado's industrial community was firmly forged and with it the creation of a unique and often violent chapter in the state's evolving social geography. Without doubt, the era marked a sharp departure from an earlier cultural geography dominated by Hispano settlement. By 1920 the southern periphery's coal regions, though retaining Hispano influences, possessed a landscape and community that wed it firmly to the largesse—indeed the excesses—of early twentieth-century industrial capitalism.

The Western Slope, 1860–1920

Isolated, arid, and peopled by seminomadic Utes, Colorado's western slope was the last region in the state to be occupied by nineteenth-century Americans. Here Native Americans persisted longer than anywhere else in the state, and even as thousands rushed in to settle mountain mining towns and Piedmont farms and cities, the western slope sat quietly beyond the pale of most activity. Asher and Adams' territorial map of 1875 revealed the dramatic disparities between east and west: unsurveyed, poorly mapped, and untouched by railroads, the huge and thinly populated western counties stood in sharp contrast to the clustered mining settlements and growing Piedmont centers to the east (fig. 82). Only in the mineral-rich San Juan Mountains did a lobe of thin and mostly seasonal Anglo settlement break tentatively across the Continental Divide. Even after 1900, the western slope remained "a land apart," separated by environment, distance, and sentiment from the Piedmont heartland.

Several attributes of western slope geography contributed to its enduring exceptionalism within the state. Most obviously, physical setting precluded easy occupance during the territorial period. The region's aridity was well documented by exploring parties during the 1840s and 1850s. Few settlers wished to challenge those assertions, particularly when mineral rushes or better farmlands beckoned elsewhere. The commanding and complex spine of the Continental Divide also discouraged casual wandering across the mountains. Although a few goldseekers panned the Blue River near modern Breckenridge as early as 1859, further colonization did not follow.

Patterns of human geography also conspired against early and easy Anglo occupance. As part of the Ute Reservation through most of the 1870s, the area hardly invited stable and legal settlement by whites. Given the region's isolation and lack of transport infrastructure, most new Colorado settlers had little incentive to brave the hazards of such antipodes. Intervening opportunities were simply too compelling. These factors ensured that much of the western slope was settled ten to twenty years after many mountain, Piedmont, and eastern plains localities. Even then, no single

219

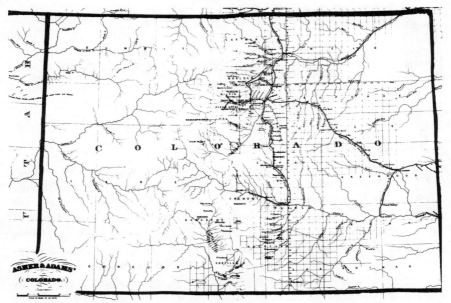

FIGURE 82. Asher and Adams' Colorado, 1875 (Courtesy Denver Public Library, Western History Collection)

wave of occupance neatly transformed the region. Settlement came in trickles and bursts and included predictable reversals and outright failures. Neither were there unifying regional attributes to lend coherence to the process: complex drainage patterns combined with a jumble of isolated plateaus and mountain ranges to segment settlement and provide considerable internal diversity.

Still, there emerged by the early twentieth century a western slope self-consciousness that persists to this day. Born of boosterism, isolation, environment, and a common ambivalence toward the state's Piedmont heartland, this regional sense of place became well articulated before World War I.[1] As early as the 1870s there were scattered calls for a separate state west of the divide. By the early 1890s, a Western Slope Congress was formed to promote the united development and settlement of the region. Similar regional-scale chambers of commerce and historical associations formed after 1900.[2] Conniving Denver politicians and businessmen as well as other unscrupulous outside corporate interests, particularly the Denver and Rio Grande Railroad, offered convenient scapegoats that brought together diverse western slope interests. Xenophobia directed east of the Continental Divide, however, was always tempered by the reality of financial dependence upon those same economic and political interests.

Large pools of investment capital for such things as infrastructure, irrigation canals, and sugar beet factories almost inevitably came from the Piedmont heartland or further east. Even the Denver and Rio Grande Railroad, often criticized for its tentacular economic grasp upon the region, was recognized as its lifeline to the outside world.

After 1870 three distinctive western slope subregions emerged as zones of settlement and development. The most extensive activity centered on the lower valleys of the Gunnison, Uncompahgre, and Colorado Rivers to the north of the San Juan Mountains. A second and smaller focus of western slope settlement concentrated south of the San Juans. This narrow strip of broken plateau country was punctuated by several southward-draining river valleys that attracted attention, particularly after Ute claims to the area were reduced in the 1880s and 1890s. Finally, a broad, diffuse, and more thinly occupied region took shape in the northwest corner of the state. There, Colorado's final frontier owed much of its initial settlement to Wyoming cattlemen, storekeepers, and town boosters who filtered south from the transcontinental railroad line to lay claim to the region's capricious though considerable resource base.

Imposing American Control

Colorado's western slope did not come under American political or economic control until the 1880s. Pre-1880 patterns of settlement and development revealed a still-isolated area populated by seminomadic Utes, a scattering of Anglo stockmen, particularly in the far northwest, and a gradually increasing influx of mainly Hispano farmers and ranchers moving north from New Mexico. As the Asher and Adams map (fig. 82) suggests, the only exception to this pattern was in the San Juan Mountains, where Anglo miners found rich caches of gold and silver. But even here, isolation in the prerail era imposed severe restrictions on sustainable and large-scale mineral developments.

Published images and impressions of the western slope before 1880 reinforced its distance from civilization. In the 1870s Ernest Ingersoll noted that the area was "a terra incognita to Coloradoans," Frank Fossett called the region an "unknown land," and the *Denver Tribune* reported that "it is apparently about as valuable as would be a representative section of the Desert of Sahara."[3] Government surveys led by Ferdinand Vandeveer Hayden between 1871 and 1876 more formally evaluated the region. Prospective settlers could hardly have been cheered by descriptions of the Colorado (Grand) River valley (near present-day Grand Junction), which reported, "With the sole exception of one little trickling stream, strongly alkaline, there is no water in the valley except the Grand River. . . . Vegetation is very scanty. . . . The soil is everywhere impregnated with alkali. It is a stiff, heavy clay, which, when dry, has a surface as hard as a board, but when wet, becomes mud of almost incalculable depth."[4] Here was an isolated, arid zone, populated by untrustworthy Indians, and, aside from its scattered mineral wealth and occasional grazing resources, offering little to potential settlers.

Visions of western Colorado's potential changed in the late 1870s, however, paralleling shifts across portions of the eastern plains. As the San Juan country opened and as population increased in the Piedmont and mountain zones, some began to look upon western Colorado in new ways. With irrigation growing in popularity east of the Rockies, some saw potential for similar projects west of the divide. In the eyes of the booster, even the most barren alkali flat could be transformed into a potential garden.

The Utes were an important ingredient in this reconfiguration of western slope potential. For those anxious to develop western Colorado, the Utes were held up as a great barrier to progress: if only the Utes would leave, a barren wilderness could be transformed into a lush and productive province. With this new interpretation, impediments to settling the western slope became human rather than environmental. Nowhere was this vision better articulated than by Governor Frederick Walker Pitkin. His late 1870s evaluation of western Colorado stands in sharp contrast to earlier assessments: "Along the western borders of the State, and on the Pacific Slope, lies a vast tract occupied by the tribe of Ute Indians. . . . It is watered by large streams and rivers, and contains many rich valleys and a large number of fertile plains . . . nearly every kind of grain and vegetables can be raised without difficulty. . . . no portion of the State is better adapted for agricultural and grazing purposes. . . . If this reservation could be extinguished, and the land thrown open to settlers, it will furnish homes to thousands of the people of the state."[5]

The governor's remarks were ominously prescient; the Utes' traditional settlement patterns across the western slope were soon dramatically disrupted and their legal claims to the region severely circumscribed by encroaching whites. After 1870 three zones of Ute settlement felt the effects of a series of increasingly unfavorable treaties.[6] White River and Uintah Utes roamed Colorado's northwest corner, focusing their hunting and pasturing activities along the Yampa, White, and Green Rivers. The Uncompahgre or Tabegauche Utes settled along the Gunnison and Uncompahgre Rivers, which drained into the Colorado. A third group, the southern Utes, including bands of Moaches, Capotes, and Weminuches, moved between northern New Mexico and the southern slopes of the San Juans in southwesternmost Colorado. In addition to these loosely defined territories, Ute seasonal hunting, raiding, and trading movements took them far to the east, including forays into the San Luis Valley, the central mountains, and the eastern plains.

Disruptions in this traditional Ute geography increased after 1860. Initially they were challenged in their more peripheral domains, including restrictions on their plains and San Luis Valley movements. Control of the valley was the main incentive behind a treaty negotiated in 1868. In that agreement, Ute claims were shifted west and south of a line that ran approximately from Pagosa Springs north to Steamboat Springs and then west to Utah Territory (fig. 83). Even though the reservation was sizable, the Utes ceded the San Luis Valley, the central mountains, and the upper reaches of the Colorado River, including Middle Park.

The Utes did not adjust to these new boundaries easily, nor did white miners and settlers respect their limits. According to the treaty the Utes were to congregate at two central agencies where annuities, supplies, livestock, and farm implements would be available. The White River agency near modern Meeker served the northern bands, while the Los Pinos agency just south of the San Juans directed activities among the southern and Uncompahgre Utes. Scant Ute enthusiasm was evident: the northern agent reported little success in domesticating a seminomadic people and the southern agency had to be located near Cochetopa Pass (actually off the reservation) along another Los Pinos Creek (so named to meet the treaty requirements) when the Uncompahgres refused to travel further south. Meanwhile, the southern Utes left and drifted south into northern New Mexico, where Indian agents loosely kept tabs on their activities. Making matters worse in the early 1870s were increasing illegal American incursions into the heart of the Ute reservation as rumors flew regarding precious metals, particularly in the San Juans.

When the floodgates opened to miners in 1874, the Brunot Treaty legalized Anglo occupance of a huge rectangle of mountain country in the San Juans, effectively acknowledging what was an accomplished fact: the Utes would not be allowed to slow the search for precious metals (see fig. 83).[7] In a story repeated endlessly across the West, this new cession took mineral land out of Native American control and further restricted the movements of the Utes. Chief Ouray represented the tribes and realized it was the best he could hope for. The White River agency was reaffirmed and a new Uncompahgre agency in the valley of the same name replaced the old Los Pinos agency. Three years later, supplemental appropriations established another agency at Ignacio south of the San Juans to better serve the southern Ute bands on either side of the Colorado and New Mexico border.[8]

Even with these territorial adjustments, more apocalyptic conflicts could not be avoided. Both Utes and whites trampled over one another's

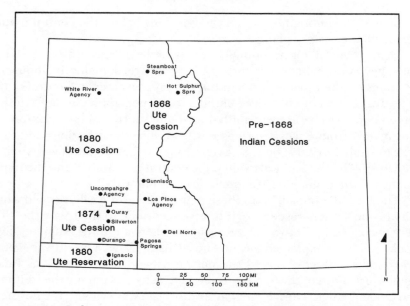

FIGURE 83. Ute Indian cessions, 1868–80 (Adapted from Kenneth A. Erickson and
Albert W. Smith, *Atlas of Colorado* [Boulder: Colorado Associated University Press,
1985], 30–31; J. Donald Hughes, *American Indians in Colorado* [Boulder: Pruett,
1977], 76–77; and Marshall Sprague, *Massacre: The Tragedy at White River* [Boston:
Little, Brown, 1957])

lands, heightening tensions in the late 1870s. Curiously, an individual from
Colorado's northern Piedmont figured prominently in the climactic clash
that all but removed the Utes from the western slope.[9] Nathan Meeker,
key figure in the successful Union Colony at Greeley, arrived on the White
River in May 1878 as the Indian agent for the White River agency. Always
the idealist, Meeker saw this as a grand opportunity to "civilize" Native
Americans and demonstrate to them the advantages of farm life. Unfortunately, Meeker significantly underestimated the cultural gap. As Meeker
and his men eagerly dug irrigation ditches in the summer of 1879, the Utes
grew restless, and most left for summer hunts in the mountains. Those
who remained busied themselves gambling at a racetrack on the agency
that Meeker blithely suggested be plowed under. As the situation deteriorated, Meeker requested troops, who were then attacked by renegade Utes
north of the agency. One day later the Indians attacked the agency itself,
Meeker and ten others were killed, and other women and children were
taken prisoner. Even though the hostages were soon freed, the national
uproar over the "Meeker Massacre" combined with local hatred of the
Utes to assure their removal from most of western Colorado.

The treaty of 1880 relocated the White River Utes to the Uintah reservation in northeastern Utah, and a similar fate met the Uncompahgre bands once it had been determined that no suitable acreage in their homeland was acceptable to all the parties involved.[10] Only the southern Utes were given any Colorado acreage whatsoever. The La Plata reservation was a narrow strip of largely indifferent lands along the state's southern border (see fig. 83). The Utes were awarded modest annuities and assistance in relocating to their new homes. The treaty required approval from three-fourths of all adult Ute males, and this seemed a dubious proposition until western Colorado road builder and entrepreneur Otto Mears offered to pay each signatory two dollars. For Mears it seemed a modest investment to open up the lucrative hinterland that he had worked so hard to develop. His efforts succeeded, and the Utes relocated to their respective reservations by the following year.[11]

Imposing effective American control over the western slope involved more than removing Native American claims to the region. A second ingredient in the process was the creation of infrastructure to link the area to the Piedmont and the rest of the nation. As elsewhere in the state, the railroad represented the key investment in creating a spatial system that connected the varied resource base of the region to appropriate regional and national markets.[12] These investments, occurring largely between 1880 and 1915, established a pattern of rail corridors and rail towns that still figure importantly in the region's urban and economic geography.

Critical rail links were forged in the early 1880s. The Continental Divide was breached in two places early in the decade by the Denver and Rio Grande Railroad (see fig. 23). In August 1881 a feeder line was completed to Gunnison over Monarch Pass and another branch line crossed the divide and reached Durango south of the San Juan Mountains.[13] The Denver and Rio Grande's hold on the western slope was strengthened in 1882 and 1883 as it quickly built down the Gunnison Valley and west to the main Colorado (Grand) River, where it soon linked up with another line to Salt Lake City.

Another burst of western slope railroad activity began in the late 1880s. Mountain mining provided the catalyst for these additions, but the entire region benefited. The silver mining town of Aspen was targeted by both the Denver and Rio Grande and Colorado Midland Railroads.[14] By late 1887 the Denver and Rio Grande Railroad reached its goal via Tennessee Pass and Glenwood Springs. Three months later the Colorado Midland's spectacular route west from Leadville via Hagerman Pass and Tunnel was also completed into Aspen. Quickly the two companies saw the folly in competing for the same traffic, and they agreed to build a joint line to connect Glenwood Springs and Grand Junction. The link, completed in 1890, became the Denver and Rio Grande's principal broad-gauge line over the Rockies, thus reducing the interregional importance of their narrow-gauge Gunnison Valley line. Still, the Denver and Rio Grande built other narrow-gauge feeders across western Colorado in the late 1880s and early 1890s to tap into new zones of mineral and agricultural production. Tracks ascended the fertile Uncompahgre Valley to the mining town of Ouray, the Lake Fork of the Gunnison to Lake City, and the North Fork of the Gunnison to the farm towns of Hotchkiss and Paonia.

Another independent western Colorado line was in the southwest corner of the state (see fig. 23). Otto Mears's Rio Grande Southern Railroad connected Durango with the mountain mining towns of Rico, Ophir, Telluride, and Ridgway near Ouray.[15] Completed in 1892, this line opened another heretofore isolated area of western Colorado. As it snaked into the Dolores River valley near Mesa Verde it proved pivotal in the settlement and economic development of such towns as Mancos and Cortez.

Reclaiming the Desert: The Colorado-Gunnison Basin

The removal of the Utes allowed for legal settlement across western Colorado, and the building of railroad lines offered a spatial infrastructure to facilitate development. Yet it would remain the job of the farmer and the canal-builder to reshape lowland landscapes of the western slope in ways that endure to the present. Nowhere was that campaign to reclaim the desert taken on with more enthusiasm and success than in the Gunnison, Uncompahgre, and Colorado (then called the Grand) River Valleys (fig. 84). The region, focused around the modern counties of Mesa, Montrose, and Delta, saw its mainly agricultural population balloon from a handful of white settlers in 1880 to almost twenty thousand in 1900 and to more than forty-five thousand by 1920. In the latter year, the district produced over 10 percent of the state's crops, accounting for more than eighteen million dollars.[16]

A New Agricultural Geography

A new agricultural geography was imposed upon the Colorado and Gunnison basins between 1880 and 1920. Oriented around irrigation, this western slope farming zone paralleled efforts in the northern Piedmont and in the oasis corridors of the eastern plains. Differences in timing, in the mix of crops, and in the complexity of the local setting, however, distinguished this agricultural region from others in the state.

A casual interloper to the valleys of western Colorado in the 1870s would not be overwhelmed by their actual or potential fecundity. Largely

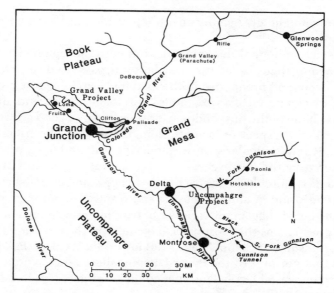

FIGURE 84. The western slope's Colorado (Grand) and Gunnison Valleys

an arid or semiarid region, the western slope's scant vegetation, sandy soils, and obvious lack of precipitation certainly dissuaded such early observers as Frémont, Gunnison, and Hayden. Even early boosters recognized that the landscape presented a desolate sight to most visitors from more humid lands.[17] Writing of the Colorado (Grand) River Valley in the 1880s, Ernest Ingersoll warned his readers to shed their traditional biases when evaluating the prospects of a region that initially appeared "uninviting and desolate looking in the extreme." Promotional brochures signaled an unusual note of caution when they stated, "We are thus explicit in speaking of the desolate appearance of the country. . . . If the reader of this lives in the east, he will almost surely be disappointed at first, if he comes out here."

Still, farmers gave the region a try once it opened to settlement in the early 1880s. Elements of the local environment created hope for good agricultural returns even in such a visually "desolate" country.[18] The region's mild "Pacific" climate and its low elevation were seen as environmental assets. Longer growing seasons were comparable to those of the Utah fruit-growing districts, suggesting similar potential for Colorado's western valleys. Boosters also averred that western Colorado's mountains acted as a buffer, protecting the region from the harsh continental air masses that regularly invaded the Piedmont and eastern plains. Overall, the region's climate was touted as possessing the "golden mean," lacking in extremes and offering an equally healthy environment for sun-loving crops or for tired lungs.

Other environmental characteristics hinted at the region's potential.[19] In the Uncompahgre Valley the river bottoms possessed "a rich alluvial soil, very deep, and productive in the extreme," while nearby mesas and uplands "are composed of an excellent sandy loam . . . and until disturbed by the busy hand of the husbandman, are covered by a good growth of nutritious grass." Prospective farmers along the nearby North Fork of the Gunnison River, particularly those pondering fruit and berry production, were cheered by the local vegetation. Pioneering horticulturalists S. A. Wade and E. T. Hotchkiss "discovered thorn apple and buffalo berry growing luxuriantly and in abundance . . . and resolved at once to make the trial" in the belief that "many varieties of fruit might be grown here." Undoubtedly, water was the most critical element in the equation for farming the Gunnison and Colorado basins. Boosters like William Pabor keenly observed that portions of the lower Uncompahgre and Colorado Valleys offered large areas of fertile land that could be irrigated given modest expenditures and sufficient water.

In addition to these ingredients of physical geography, two economic variables figured importantly in assessing agricultural prospects for the western valleys. First, farmers needed to know that they could sell what they grew. Commercial agriculture depended upon ready markets, whether the crop was grass, grain, or fruits. In the 1880s potential farmers were reminded that the fertile western Colorado valleys were "surrounded by the best mines in the world."[20] Indeed, within 150 miles sat the hungry miners of the San Juan, Gunnison, and Aspen regions, and they were willing to pay high prices for even indifferent produce. Once rail links to Denver and the East improved after 1890, national markets also beckoned, particularly for the region's specialty fruit and vegetable crops.

The effective organization and financing of large-scale real estate operations and irrigation works also sparked agricultural development within the region. In this instance, either true believers with deep pockets or gifted cons with the ability to convince others of ready rewards spurred necessary land sales and canal-building ventures. Such respected state figures as town promoter George Crawford, agricultural expert William Pabor, and irrigationist T. C. Henry threw their collective financial weight and considerable influence into various western Colorado projects. Crawford led the charge into developing Grand Junction, Pabor poured his own resources into nearby Fruita, and Henry got involved in canal-building projects in both the Colorado and Uncompahgre Valleys.

With buoyed expectations for western Colorado farming, the actual planting of crops required inevitable environmental adjustments and reassessments. Reality was more fickle than had been promised in the promotional circulars, and the years between 1890 and 1920 involved a great deal of agricultural experimentation, failure, and environmental adaptation as settlers learned about the limits and possibilities of farming the valleys of the western slope.

Early efforts involved learning what would grow well in the disparate ecological niches within the region.[21] Valley bottoms varied between narrow canyonlands and sprawling, wide-open acreage. Uplands and mesas offered other opportunities for development where water could be diverted, but these areas typically had widely differing soils, slopes, and microclimates. In the valley below Grand Junction, Ingersoll reported experiments with different varieties of corn, wheat, barley, millets, potatoes, alfalfa, and sugar beets. Pabor's efforts at nearby Fruita tested a bewildering variety of fruits and berries that were shown at a state exhibition in Denver. One valley orchard boasted 84 different crops, all an attempt to gain knowledge about the best agricultural opportunities! Upriver, the valley narrowed around Clifton and Palisade and tinkering revealed that peaches grew especially well in the sheltered lands beneath the nearby cliffs. Local winds protected against late frosts that often harmed vulnerable peach orchards elsewhere in the region. Other specialized niches for fruit were discovered in Delta County along the benches of the North Fork of the Gunnison near Hotchkiss and Paonia. Lowlands in the nearby Uncompahgre Valley proved better for grains, grass, potatoes, and sugar beets.

To add to the region's potential, farmers took an active role in modifying the local environmental shortcomings they encountered. Most obviously, the arid valleys required extensive irrigation works (fig. 85). Major networks of canals took shape above and below Grand Junction as well as in the lower Uncompahgre Valley between Montrose and Delta. Initially private projects, these efforts later received federal assistance as the national government increasingly shaped the course of western agricultural development. Smaller canal networks on the Colorado River above De Beque, on Plateau Creek northeast of Palisade, and along the Gunnison's North Fork also exemplified successful efforts to adapt to the region's aridity.

Additional environmental variables needed to be understood and controlled. By 1908, for example, thousands of smudgepots were deployed around the Colorado River Valley to battle capricious springtime frosts that nipped blossoms after spells of warm weather.[22] Other local hazards such as codling moths, woolly aphids, and red spiders were fought with an increasingly sophisticated array of sprays, introduced parasitic species, and trapping techniques. Overall, it was an ongoing and dynamic interre-

FIGURE 85. Reclaiming the desert: Orchard Mesa Canal near Grand Junction (Courtesy Denver Public Library, Western History Collection)

lationship between settlers and the ever more specialized environment they were attempting to modify.

By the turn of the century a mosaic of new and exotic agricultural zones were established within the region. The Colorado River Valley and other nearby areas of Mesa County figured most importantly into this new zone of agricultural activity.[23] Fruit farms formed the core of the valley's agricultural expansion. Beginning with Elam Blain and William Pabor in 1882 and 1883, converts planted peaches, apples, pears, and other fruits in the valley. By 1890 real estate agents were hawking ten-acre valley fruit orchards to investors in Denver and beyond. Grand Junction initiated its annual Peach Day festival that same year, bringing trainloads of visitors and prospective farmers into the area. By 1910 orchards at Fruita and Mack specialized in pears and apples, while peaches assumed particular importance around Palisade and Clifton. By then, more than twenty thousand acres of the Grand Valley were in fruit orchards, and an additional 1.4 million trees were planted in 1907 and 1908. The visual transformation was striking: although surrounding bluffs and mesas still bore the obvious earthy buff of desert land, thousands of new trees, many too young to bear fruit, brought a new look to the valley's landscape (fig. 86).

Irrigation canals were the key to the success of the valley's agriculture. Begun on a small-scale in the early 1880s, the canals quickly consolidated and coalesced into larger, more capital-intensive projects by the end of the decade.[24] Most significant was the Grand Valley Canal, itself an amalgamation of local ditches, that was extended westward along the north side of the Colorado River in the 1890s (see fig. 84). The brainchild of William Pabor and T. C. Henry, the Grand Valley Canal later fell into the hands of the Travelers Insurance Company, was privately reorganized, and was ultimately completed with federal assistance after the turn of the century.

Although the Grand Valley Canal was the catalyst for further investment into commercial farming ventures, it failed to satisfy all the demands for irrigated land. Essential to future expansion were upriver diversions at higher elevations to put more benchland acreage in reach of water. After the turn of the century, new canal construction and added catchment dams east of Palisade succeeded in putting under cultivation the Orchard

FIGURE 86. The desert transformed: a new fruit ranch near Grand Junction (Courtesy Denver Public Library, Western History Collection)

Mesa area south of the river.[25] As with the Grand Valley Canal, the Orchard Mesa project later received Bureau of Reclamation assistance. Perhaps most important, however, was the 1917 completion of the Highline Canal that stretched over fifty miles on the north side of the river from east of Palisade to west of Fruita. The canal watered higher acreage north of the Grand Valley project and significantly increased the valley's irrigable acreage in the World War I era.

In addition to orchards, cattle were important to the valley's agricultural geography. Cows were a frequent part of the rural scene as ranchers irrigated hay bottoms and alfalfa fields, usually securing three cuttings per season.[26] Running cattle into surrounding higher country in summer, valley-based ranchers used irrigated pastures for winter forage. By 1920 Mesa County agriculturalists reported over forty-four thousand acres in forage crops and more than fifty thousand cattle.

Sugar beets grown in western Colorado also were used as cattle feed, though their principal cash value was realized when the beets were processed into commercial sugar. Beet cultivation began early in the valley, the brainchild of Charles Mitchell, who brought seeds into the area from Nebraska in the 1890s.[27] Several years of experimentation proved promising, and by the turn of the century lower valley acreages were sufficient to induce the Colorado Sugar Manufacturing Company (later Holly Sugar) to build a processing plant in Grand Junction. Soon, however, interest in the crop diffused eastward to the Platte and Arkansas Valleys and by 1920 Mesa County was only a minor beet producer.

Upriver from Grand Junction smaller agricultural districts sprouted at several points in the 1880s and grew further in importance after 1890 as railroad access improved and as irrigation and reservoir construction brought new land into cultivation.[28] Settlements in the 1880s were located at Parachute and Rifle as nearby river bottoms were developed (see fig. 84). Farms also were sprinkled along Plateau Creek, although the scale of operations remained small. After 1900 some of these localities shifted to intensive fruit-growing ventures while most of the upriver acreage turned increasingly to cattle pasturing.

The Uncompahgre Valley evolved in parallel fashion to that of the Colorado River Valley, but with a different mix of crops and a separate set of irrigation-related problems.[29] After the Utes were expelled, the valley south of Montrose remained thinly settled with a sprinkling of ranches and farms that served the needs of nearby San Juan miners. Changes were afoot by the late 1880s, however, as two modest irrigation projects were initiated. South of Montrose, the Uncompahgre Canal Company constructed a series of ditches and laterals in fertile lands just west of the river. On the east side of the river the smaller Loutsenhizer Canal put additional

acreage in reach of water. But these canals and a few smaller projects below Montrose irrigated only about thirty thousand acres by the early 1890s.
Boosters saw prime agricultural lands standing dry and dormant, victim of
the Uncompahgre River's limited flow. At one extreme, the Denver and Rio
Grande Railroad asserted that Montrose County could "support a population of two million people" if only additional water could be diverted to
the area. More sober assessments reckoned that at least another fifty to
one hundred thousand acres might be developed in the valley, given sufficient water.

The answer came in the form of the Gunnison Tunnel, one of the first
federally sponsored reclamation projects as well as the longest irrigation
diversion tunnel in the world.[30] Residents speculated on the prospects of
such an engineering feat once the Uncompahgre's capacity was reached
in the early 1890s. Just northeast of the Uncompahgre Valley, the Gunnison River flowed free through the recesses of the Black Canyon and offered an ideal source of irrigation water (see fig. 84). Almost six miles of
solid rock intervened, however, and cooled the ardor of even the most optimistic developer. Yet locals convinced the state of Colorado to initiate
construction of a diversion tunnel in 1901. The magnitude of the project
quickly proved overwhelming, but serendipity intervened the following
year when the Newlands Act created the federal Bureau of Reclamation
and with it the potential for financial assistance from Washington, D.C.
The Gunnison Tunnel appealed to federal engineers and bureaucrats, and
construction began in 1905. Completed in 1909, the six-mile tunnel was an
engineering marvel, though it cost more than ten million dollars and the
lives of six workers.

Results were impressive: the valley's irrigation works, now under federal control, watered almost one hundred thousand acres by 1919, and the
project allowed the Uncompahgre Valley to become the second most important agricultural zone in western Colorado.[31] Small grains, particularly
wheat and oats, combined with hay and alfalfa as the area's major crops.
Experimenting with fruit trees led some farmers into apple production, but
the number of trees was minuscule compared with the Grand Valley operations. After 1900 others opted for potatoes and sugar beets, although
these crops never became important in the valley.

Finally, the North Fork of the Gunnison River in Delta County offered
another productive agricultural zone that underwent major development
between 1880 and 1920.[32] No broad valleys offered easy settings for extensive large-scale ditchworks. Rather, the North Fork was a long and narrow
corridor of extremely fertile alluvial soils and with a local climate well
adapted to orchard cultivation. Small ditches increased the area's irrigated
acreage fivefold between 1890 and 1920. Early experimentation with abori-

culture yielded good results in the middle 1880s, and the valley's apple and peach crops vied in importance with those of the Colorado River Valley by the turn of the century. Indeed, North Fork fruits took six first-prize ribbons at the Chicago World's Fair in 1893. Good orchard land reached three thousand dollars per acre after 1900, when the Denver and Rio Grande Railroad constructed a spur line into the valley. Lower prices after 1910 diminished the importance of fruit crops along the North Fork as farmers turned to grains and cattle to supplement their income. Still, the region's fruit-growing reputation was well established by 1920 and remained an important part of the local agricultural landscape thereafter.

The Urban Matrix

As the western slope was opened to agricultural settlement, a new geography of urban centers took shape. Gunnison dominated trade within the region in the 1870s before the removal of the Utes. It served the still-isolated hinterlands of the Colorado and Gunnison basins as well as a number of fledgling western slope mining camps.[33] Once the Utes were gone, new towns west of Gunnison were platted by the Denver and Rio Grande Railroad. Proximity to the railroad provided powerful incentives for entrepreneurs and new settlers. In addition, water was essential for town development. Also influencing settlement geography were mining ventures in nearby mountains as well as subsequent agricultural activities in the adjacent valleys.

Within twenty years a new system of small but bustling centers was in place, especially positioned to develop the region's resources and serve the needs of its new Anglo population. Urban areas sprouted in the vicinity of the three dominant agricultural districts within the Colorado and Gunnison Basins. Grand Junction, Montrose, and Delta, all railroad towns along the Denver and Rio Grande, became important agricultural service and processing centers as well as focal points of investment, real estate promotion, and trade. When Gunnison County was subdivided in 1883, the three centers also became seats for Mesa, Montrose, and Delta Counties, respectively.

Grand Junction topped the urban hierarchy. The location drew the attention of investors and real estate developers even before the region was opened for settlement. The town was situated in a wide valley at the junction of the Colorado and Gunnison Rivers and later served as a junction and maintenance center for two major branches of the Denver and Rio Grande Railroad. As the railroad's promotional literature suggested in 1899, the town was to be "the commercial capital of all Western Colorado."[34] George Crawford, James Bucklin, and Richard Mobley platted the town in 1881 and incorporated the Grand Junction Town Company. Crawford, in particular, was schooled in the business of place promotion: he developed Kansas towns in the boisterous 1850s, later speculated in real estate schemes in Oklahoma's Cherokee Strip, and generally promoted western immigration through his associate editorship of the *Kansas Farmer* newspaper.

The town's future was all but guaranteed when Crawford sold half the town company stock to the Denver and Rio Grande Railroad, securing their pledge to place a depot and later servicing shops within the town. Although the town was built "in anticipation of the agricultural productions of the valley," it was not long before surrounding irrigation canals and farms justified the early optimism.[35] Indeed, the city stimulated the farm economy: agricultural promotion and marketing organizations such as the Mesa County Board of Trade, the Mesa County Agricultural and Horticultural Society, and the Grand Junction Fruit Growers Association were headquartered there, and canning and processing plants naturally gravitated later to the new urban center positioned along the precious waters of the lower Grand Valley.

Situated between Grand Junction and Gunnison, Montrose was platted in the early 1880s and benefited from a series of locational advantages. Laid out upon the fertile bottoms of the Uncompahgre Valley in early 1882, the town became another important settlement along the Denver and Rio Grande line. The surrounding Uncompahgre Valley was readily settled once the Utes were expelled from the area. George Crofutt gushed that it was "by far the richest, best watered, and most productive agricultural valley" in western Colorado, and another advocate compared the center to thriving Greeley east of the mountains.[36] Adding further to Montrose's economic base was its role as an entrepôt and freight forwarding center for the San Juan country. As a gateway to Ouray, Lake City, Telluride, and Rico, the town captured some of the trade that might otherwise have gone to its downriver competitor at Grand Junction.

The third new urban center, appropriately named Delta, was laid out in 1881 at the confluence of the Uncompahgre and Gunnison Rivers by promoter George Crawford through his Uncompahgre Town Company.[37] Although never as large as Grand Junction, Delta became a county seat and an important agricultural center for the lower Uncompahgre Valley as well as the North Fork of the Gunnison River to the northeast.

Other settlements in the Colorado and Gunnison basins consisted mostly of small towns that sprouted in response to clusters of nearby farmers and ranchers.[38] The lower Grand Valley towns of Fruita, Clifton, and Palisade were located near rail lines and in the midst of good fruit-raising acreage. To the northeast, the fledgling centers of De Beque, Parachute, and Plateau City became gathering points for crops and cattle. Upriver from Delta, small centers performed similar functions along the North Fork of the Gunnison. In that area, Paonia and Hotchkiss served dual purposes as cattle towns and as shipping points for local fruitgrowers. Non-agricultural towns provided diversity in a few locales: New Castle in the Colorado River valley and Somerset along the North Fork of the Gunnison became coal towns of regional importance, and both centers benefited from ready railroad connections.

As cultural landscapes, these western slope communities borrowed heavily from their mostly midwestern origins. As on the eastern plains, evidence gleaned from town layouts, business types, and local commercial and residential architecture confirms that Colorado's western slope was a zone of cultural replication rather than innovation. Settlers from the Colorado Piedmont and from such states as Kansas, Nebraska, Iowa, and Missouri figure importantly into the makeup of the local townscape.

Town surveyors adopted a grid pattern, with rail and river access corridors often forming one edge of the town. Grand Junction, for example, was platted just north of the Colorado River on four quarter sections of land selected by Crawford and his associates.[39] The large survey grid clearly revealed the hopes and ambitions of its founders. Their cultural vision also contributed to the town's success: each quarter section had lands set aside for parks (Maple, Chestnut, Cottonwood, and Walnut) and schools. A procession of additional lots along White Avenue was reserved for important churches. At the city center, lots were identified as construction sites for key public buildings. Wider streets and larger lots along Seventh and Main Streets as well as Grand and Gunnison Avenues encouraged better commercial and residential developments. Local toponymy celebrated past and present fortunes: street names included references to Utes, prominent outside investors, and the predictable roll call of numbered thoroughfares.

Ambitious construction quickly created genuinely urban landscapes on the sites of the successful town plats. Initial homes and businesses offered the usual raw frontier combination of tents, log shacks, and cabins with an occasional adobe adding a southwestern flavor to the scene. Rail connections, sawmills, and brickworks, however, quickly changed such primitive townscapes in such locales as Grand Junction and Montrose. The resulting landscapes paralleled earlier growth elsewhere in Colorado. As Ernest Ingersoll described Grand Junction, the town was "an orderly jumble of brick buildings, frame buildings, log cabins, tents, and vacant spaces. . . . it is South Pueblo or Salida or Durango, or Gunnison of two years ago over again."[40] Soon, Grand Junction in particular took on metropolitan airs, with its bustling commercial avenues, crowded railyards, substantial houses, and urban horse cars connoting progress and prosperity (fig. 87). By 1920 its population topped 8,500 residents. Montrose boosters also placed a clear premium on the permanence and stability of their urban landscape. No uncivilized pioneer burg, their town had "the appearance of a homelike eastern city," with "many elegant private residences" and "handsome mercantile establishments that would be a credit to older and more pretentious communities."[41]

The Far Southwest

Colorado's southwestern corner has always been a distinct and isolated region. Encompassing the country south and west of the San Juan and La Plata Mountains—essentially Archuleta, La Plata, Montezuma, and Dolores Counties—the area bears a strong resemblance, both physically and culturally, to adjacent districts of northern New Mexico. As with the Colorado-Gunnison Basin, water resources and key transportation infrastructure guided settlement. Unlike the area to the north, however, enduring cultural diversity, particularly the presence of Native Americans and Hispanos, shaped the Far Southwest's social geography, producing a unique subregion within the western slope. As the Anglo presence increased between 1880 and 1920, formative changes to the area's economic geography came with a rush, establishing spatial patterns and cultural landscape signatures that persist today.

Before 1880, Utes retained nominal control of the Far Southwest. Portions of the region, however, were lost to the Americans in the Brunot Agreement of 1874. Still, there was no rush to develop the isolated corner of the territory south of the San Juans. Indeed, geologist Ferdinand Vandeveer Hayden's 1870s reconnaissance revealed an area still beyond the reach of American influence. Anglo settlement increased after a treaty with the southern Utes was signed in 1880. Rather than expelling the Indians, however, these agreements continued partial Ute control of the Far Southwest while offering new opportunities for both Anglo and Hispano settlement.

After 1880, southwest Colorado's distinctive drainage patterns shaped opportunities for irrigated agriculture and associated settlement. Like spokes on a wheel radiating from the mountainous knot of the San Juan and La Plata ranges, a series of south- and west-flowing watercourses alternated with steeply sloped mesas across the face of the Far Southwest. From east to west, the San Juan, Los Pinos, Animas, La Plata, Mancos, and Dolores Rivers offered niches for agricultural settlement in an otherwise broken and arid country.

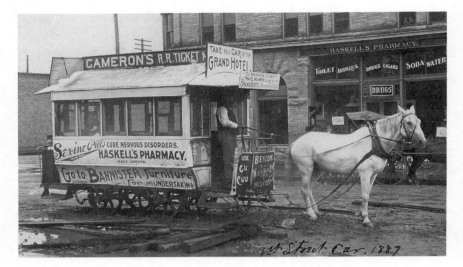

FIGURE 87. An urban landscape on the western slope: Grand Junction, 1887 (Courtesy Denver Public Library, Western History Collection)

The settlement pattern was further guided by investments in the region's railway network. The result was an incipient urban geography anchored upon Durango, the Denver and Rio Grande Railroad town that served as an entrepôt into the San Juan country to the north. The centers of Arboles and Juanita also benefited from the rail line southeast of Durango, but these small towns served only local farm and ranch populations. Once the Rio Grande Southern line was built to the west, settlement surged into Montezuma and Dolores Counties. The new centers of Mancos, Cortez, and Dolores carved up additional trade areas in these areas, but none of these towns claimed more than a few hundred residents by 1900.

A Multicultural Mosaic

Native American, Hispano, and Anglo populations contributed to the multicultural character of the Far Southwest. Several groups of southern Utes occupied the area. With the establishment of an Indian agency at Ignacio in 1877, these Utes, including members of the Mouache, Capote, and Weminuche bands, received more direct scrutiny and assistance from the federal government. The 1879 troubles on the White River agency prompted a general outcry against any Ute presence on the western slope. The 1880 treaty, while expelling the Indians from areas north of the San

Juans, created a southern Ute reservation between the mountains and the New Mexico line.[42]

Many Anglos in the Far Southwest resisted the permanent Indian presence and almost succeeded in getting the southern Utes relocated to Utah in the late 1880s. Utahans balked at the idea, however, and inertia prevailed. Pressure continued, though, to open "unused" Indian lands to white settlement, a practice that was sweeping through many other western reserves. Finally, the Hunter Act (1895) directed that the Utes be allotted lands on their Colorado reservation (160 acres per head of household) with remaining acreage opened to homesteading. The Mouache and Capote bands agreed to the proposal, but most of the Weminuche group strongly resisted the idea of breaking up the territorial integrity of their lands.

The lack of agreement among the Utes resulted in the physical and legal separation of the Indians in 1896, a process that produced increasingly disparate adaptations on the part of the two groups.[43] The Mouache and Capote bands selected more than seventy thousand acres of allotment lands in the eastern part of the reservation, showing a strong preference for the well-watered alluvial bottoms adjacent to the Piedra, Los Pinos, Las Animas, and La Plata Rivers. In these areas, families resorted to a more sedentary agricultural way of life. Activity focused around the agency town of Ignacio. Once the Utes' selections were complete, remaining lands were opened to public settlement in 1899, thus encouraging multicultural contact and mixing with both inmigrating Anglos and Hispanos.

The Weminuche bands, however, migrated westward in 1895, defying the Hunter Act. Not wanting to incite conflict, the federal government created a separate Ute Mountain reservation covering the more arid western half of the old Ute reserve. Here, several hundred Weminuche Utes held a single block of lands in common, lived off government payments, and gradually adopted a seminomadic way of life oriented around sheep and cattle grazing. The isolation of the Ute Mountain group limited their contact with outsiders and slowed processes of acculturation. In 1918 the two reserves were legally joined, forming the Consolidated Ute reservation, but the split initiated in the late 1890s continued spatially and socially to separate the two groups of southern Utes thereafter.

Complicating the cultural geography of Colorado's Far Southwest was its proximity to Hispano New Mexico.[44] Because natural drainage patterns and settler migration routes ignored artificial state boundaries, the way was open for the northward movement of Hispano farmers and ranchers into Colorado's southwest corner. Hispano migration into the San Juan Valley accelerated after 1876. Hispanos were further attracted into Colorado between 1877 and 1881 to work on the Southern Ute reservation and on the construction of the Denver and Rio Grande Railroad.

The informal northward movement of Hispano farmers and stockmen led to a number of new settlements along the upper San Juan, Piedras, and Los Pinos Rivers, and this expansion reached the southern border of Colorado by the late 1870s. Plazas such as Juanita and Trujillo marked the northern edge of this rural Hispano frontier. Fearing increased Anglo dominance in southern Colorado, most Hispanos opposed the opening of Indian lands in the area to outside settlement. Once reservation lands were made available to the public, however, Hispanos took considerable advantage of the new homesteading opportunities. The result was an intimate mixing of Native American and Hispano communities and often a shared sense of cultural solidarity defined by their separation from dominant Anglo political and economic interests. Many Ute babies had Hispano baptismal godparents, and relations between the two groups were cordial.[45] Centers like Arboles, originally strongly Indian, assumed a new character after 1900 as Hispanos acquired lands in the area, built up the sheep herds, and constructed a Catholic church.

Anglo dominance of cultural and economic affairs in southwestern Colorado was undeniable, however, and nowhere more vividly displayed than with the 1880 arrival of the Denver and Rio Grande Railroad and the creation of its company town of Durango. Durango's proximity to metals, coal, and agricultural resources made it an important service and processing center for each of these industries. By the middle 1880s, George Crofutt reported that "it has become the Commercial Center for the San Juan country, and a portion of New Mexico and Arizona."[46] Durango's twenty-seven hundred residents in 1890 made it the dominant center in the southwest corner of the state. The place had an urban and industrial air about it: smelting operations, train yards, and coal mines were visual reminders on the landscape that large-scale capital investments were rapidly transforming even this isolated corner of the state.

Although railroads and industrializing Durango provided the most dramatic examples of American dominance in the region, a more gradual infiltration of ranchers and farmers Anglicized portions of the surrounding rural scene. East and south of Durango, rugged topography and the Utes precluded Anglo inroads before 1899. One exception was the upper San Juan River in the vicinity of Pagosa Springs just north of the Ute reservation. On the site of a former military post, the springs supported bath houses and a hotel for tourists by the middle 1880s and had more than 350 residents by the turn of the century.[47]

After 1899, as the Ute reserve opened to settlement, more Anglos arrived in the region. They acquired former Indian lands, particularly well-watered tracts, at low government prices of often less than two dollars an acre. They expanded irrigation works already begun by Native Americans and Hispanos, raised cattle and sheep, and planted small grains, forage crops, and vegetable gardens in the region's fertile valleys. By 1920, seventy-five thousand acres of La Plata and Archuleta Counties were under irrigation, a total similar to Montrose County north of the San Juans.[48] Marginal lands away from water were never homesteaded or reverted to the government after Anglo efforts failed. Eventually many of these acres were returned to Southern Ute control in the Restoration Acts of 1937 and 1938.[49]

West of Durango, some Anglo inroads preceded the construction of the Rio Grande Southern Railroad in the early 1890s.[50] Cattle were herded onto lands south and west of the San Juan and La Plata Mountains by the early 1870s, a practice legalized once the Brunot Treaty was ratified in 1874. Much larger cattle operators arrived from New Mexico, Utah, and elsewhere by the 1880s, using mountain pastures in the summer and the lower valleys of the Mancos, Dolores, and San Miguel Rivers for their winter range. A further boost to the livestock business came in 1889 with the completion of a private canal funded by the Montezuma Valley Water Supply Company. It tapped into the Dolores River, running water south into the fertile but dry Montezuma Valley. The resulting irrigated hay and alfalfa fields near Cortez increased the area's ability to support livestock. Nearby Mancos also became a center of stockraising.

After the completion of the Rio Grande Southern line, livestock and farming operations west of Durango became even more commercially viable.[51] Dolores was incorporated in 1899 and Cortez in 1902. With the success of fruit growing in the Colorado-Gunnison Basin, irrigated orchard crops were tried in the Montezuma Valley. By 1920 more than ninety thousand bushels of apples were harvested in Montezuma County, with smaller productions of peaches, pears, and plums. Similar projects in Dolores and San Miguel Counties produced forage and fruit crops in those districts, too.

Preserving the Past at Mesa Verde

One chapter in the evolution of the Far Southwest's cultural landscape had truly national significance.[52] The creation of Mesa Verde National Park in 1906 marked a new level of federal participation on the western slope. The park protected a series of eight-hundred-year-old cliff dwellings constructed by the area's early Anasazi population. Although a few ranchers knew about the ruins, a team of Hayden Survey explorers first documented and publicized the dwellings in the middle 1870s. Once the ruins had been discovered, archaeologists, tourists, and looters began to visit the site (fig. 88). Calls for protection grew as artifacts were carted away. Several prominent Coloradans, including Virginia McClurg and Lucy Peabody, became key advocates for protection.

FIGURE 88. Perusing the past at Mesa Verde: Long House ruins (Source: "A Summer Among Cliff Dwellings," *Harper's Monthly* 93 [1896]: 553)

The federal government was already involved in managing Indian reservations, forest reserves, and reclamation projects, and its commitment to preserve the Anasazi artifacts and cliff dwellings southwest of Durango did not come without considerable local resistance. Utes resented any white presence in the area. Anglo homesteaders, using nearby canyons and mesas for grazing, did not want the federal government to strip them of this valuable resource for the sake of what they saw as a few Indian potsherds and crumbling kivas. Still others argued that the area's rich coal reserves should not be sacrificed for a new national park.

Compromises finally satisfied some of the suspicions concerning the new park's value, and a new constituency of park boosters insured its success. Once the park was established, existing grazing privileges were upheld. Sheep and cattle were allowed to wander park lands as long as they did not stray too close to the Anasazi sites or overgraze available pastures. Coal mining was allowed under the provision of early federal leases, but no significant deposits were developed. Meanwhile, laborers found employment constructing park buildings and roads. Merchants and hotelkeepers in the communities of Durango, Mancos, and Cortez saw opportunities as an infant tourist industry grew after 1910. The completion of a road to Spruce Tree House in 1913 and the opening of an official park museum five years later spurred regional and national interest in the park. Visitation climbed from only 250 tourists in 1910 to ten times that number a decade later. By the late 1920s, road improvements, both local and national, enabled over 16,000 tourists annually to make the trip to the once isolated stone towers and kivas tucked beneath the cliffs of Mesa Verde.

Final Frontiers: Colorado's Northwest Corner

One of the last corners of Colorado to undergo American settlement lay west of the Front Range and north of the Colorado River (fig. 89). The northwest corner of the state, wedged into a wild sage-covered, canyon-gouged, mesa-topped region between eastern Utah and southwestern Wyoming, defied early or easy occupance. Rudiments of the area's tangled geography came into focus with Frémont's traverses in the 1840s, but many of its side canyons and lonely mountain parks lay virtually undiscovered for another half-century. Metals mining provided the initial push into the area, but it was stockraising that offered limited though more sustainable adaptations across the sparsely vegetated region. Later, rumors, hopes, and even a few modest successes created a new economic base oriented around the area's abundant fossil fuel resources. Even to the present, however, the unfulfilled promises of those resources haunt the region. This land remains quiet and sparsely peopled, an enduring hinterland within the Centennial State.

An Outpost of Wyoming

Much of northwest Colorado's settlement geography was created between 1870 and 1900, and it paralleled activities in southern Wyoming. Just as eastern Colorado mirrored occupance patterns in western Kansas and as the southern edge of the state reflected the cultural geography of northern New Mexico, so the northwest corner of Colorado was an economic and cultural outpost of Wyoming. Railroad networks, stage and postal connections, and patterns of movement of cattle and capital quickly drew this lonely slice of Colorado Territory into the grasp of persons and places in southern Wyoming. The completion of the transcontinental railroad in 1869 was pivotal in this evolving spatial relation. Suddenly towns like Laramie, Rawlins, Wamsutter, and Rock Springs were direct links with the outside world (see fig. 89). Almost immediately the economic geography of the surrounding lands was redefined. Resources close to the rail line, once all but worthless because of their distance from markets, became valuable commodities.

Coincident with the creation of this new southern Wyoming axis came the discovery of gold near Hahns Peak in northwestern Colorado.[53] Although a mining district formed there in 1866, little happened until news

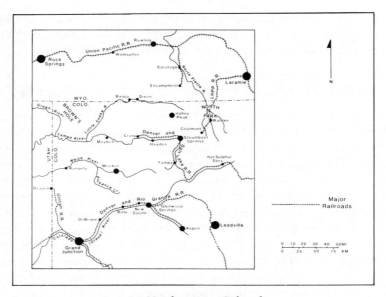

FIGURE 89. Northwestern Colorado, 1920

of a big strike reached Wyoming in 1872. Then the predictable rush was on, and miners streamed into the isolated upper reaches of the Elk River Valley. Within four years the town became the dominant center in northwestern Colorado and the seat for newly created Routt County. Stage lines linked Hahns Peak to the rail town of Rawlins. Placer mining initially dominated as the easy color was washed from area streams. By the 1880s larger-scale hydraulic mining technology was needed to free gold from nearby hillsides. As with other mining excitements, this enterprise was temporary: most efforts ceased by 1900, much of the town burned in a disastrous fire in 1910, and the center was unceremoniously stripped of its county seat status two years later.

In the seeds of Hahns Peak's ephemeral ascent were more lasting economic and cultural shifts destined to shape the region's human geography.[54] Along with miners came cattlemen, trailing their herds into the Elk River Valley and soon into the broader reaches of the Yampa. By the late 1870s the successes of early ranching operations brought a growing number of cow outfits into northwestern Colorado. Almost all these operations had links with Wyoming. The area around Brown's Hole in the far northwest corner of the territory received early attention as good winter range for Wyoming herds (fig. 90). Rancher George Baggs, based on the Little Snake River near Dixon, Wyoming, also saw advantages in using the open ranges of Colorado as winter feeding grounds. Baggs sold out to another Wyoming cattleman, William Swan, in 1883. Swan managed a vast cattle empire from the North Platte and Red Desert in Wyoming south to the Yampa River drainage of northern Colorado. Other cattlemen based in Laramie, Rawlins, and Rock Springs also ran their herds into northwest Colorado after 1875. Once the Utes were removed from the Yampa and White River Valleys, Wyoming stockmen penetrated even more deeply into northwestern Colorado's greatly expanded public domain. Postal roads, stage routes, and supply lines also linked this newly opening frontier with its Wyoming roots.

Ora Haley was a quintessential Wyoming cattleman who by 1880 had become the largest operator of range cattle in northwestern Colorado.[55] Haley, a New Englander, came west and worked as a bull-whacker, hauling freight between Denver and Central City in the 1860s. After trying his hand at butchering in Black Hawk, Haley moved to Laramie, where he opened another butcher shop. No better market for his meats appeared than the hungry construction camps of the Union Pacific Railroad, and Haley garnered the valuable contract to handle their needs. By 1871 Haley

FIGURE 90. A sustainable rural adaptation: the K Ranch, Moffat County (Courtesy Denver Public Library, Western History Collection)

had bought a small ranch of his own near Laramie, received outside capital from New York investors, and steadily enlarged his operations. Within a decade, Haley owned thousands of acres outright in southern Wyoming and northwestern Colorado and made liberal use of tens of thousands of additional acres in the public domain. Haley's Two Bar brand was renowned throughout northwestern Colorado, and his operations epitomized the close and enduring relationship between Wyoming cattlemen and their Colorado rangelands.

By the 1880s, although Wyoming links remained strong, a new chapter in northwest Colorado's ranching business began. The White and Yampa Valleys, their fertile bottoms opened to homesteading, served as headquarters to a rising number of important Colorado-based cattle companies. This marked an important shift, for although these ranches still shipped many of their cattle out of the area via Wyoming, their permanent presence in Colorado stimulated local trade and town growth. To the south, Rangely and Meeker became trade centers along the White River (see fig. 89). In the Yampa Valley, Maybell, Craig, and Steamboat Springs were established during the 1880s. Eventually, Meeker, Craig, and Steamboat Springs enhanced their centrality by becoming seats for Rio Blanco, Moffat, and Routt Counties, respectively.

These corridors of activity focused on valuable river bottoms that provided winter range.[56] In the summer, herds were "shoved up" to mountain meadows, where they were free to wander, but in winter more care and control was necessary. Particularly tough winters in the middle 1880s convinced many ranchers that they needed to increase the amount and reliability of their winter hay supply. This was less critical in the warmer lower valleys, but in areas like the upper Yampa, stockmen depended more and more upon the summer irrigation of hay lands to produce winter feed. By 1900 the White and Yampa Valleys were dotted with irrigated lands that produced the hay and alfalfa necessary for winter feeding. In fact, efforts to increase bottomland productivity were so successful that by 1910 ranchers complained that they were running out of good summer range.

Although it was east of the Continental Divide, Colorado's North Park paralleled events to the west. Drained by the North Platte River, the wide, grass-covered, and mountain-rimmed expanse opened north into Wyoming's Saratoga Valley (see fig. 89). Many of the valley's early occupants, first seasonal grazers and later resident ranchers, were from Wyoming, using the fertile grasslands as summer pasture. By the 1880s hay ranches dotted the valley, and North Park hay quickly achieved the reputation as being some of the finest in the West.[57] The discovery of coal in the southwest corner of the valley prompted railroad construction into the region after the turn of the century. In 1911 the Laramie, Hahns Peak, and

Pacific Railroad linked Laramie, Wyoming, with Walden near the valley's center. Although the coal resources never produced huge returns, the railroad and the associated increases in agricultural settlement prompted the creation in 1912 of Jackson County with its new seat at Walden.

As northwestern Colorado's rangelands were put to greater use by an expanding commercial livestock economy, one conflict assumed almost epic proportions. With horror, cattlemen witnessed a sheep invasion during the late 1880s. Utah and Wyoming sheepherders increasingly impinged upon good Colorado cattle range as the carrying capacity of the sheep land reached its limits.[58] Sheep bands arrived in the Yampa, Elk, and White River drainages from the north and west and threatened the cattlemen both ecologically and economically. Uncontrolled sheep grazing, the cattle ranchers argued, took pastures to the roots and accelerated soil erosion, thus damaging summer range and taking valuable grass from the cattle herds. Matters climaxed in the 1890s in a series of range wars that lasted for more than twenty years. Sheepmen were largely on the defensive: flocks were run off cliffs or fed strychnine and the lonely sheepherder often found himself outgunned by angry posses of cattlemen. In a latter-day drama of the "Wild West," the Battle of Yellowjacket Pass near Meeker in 1920 necessitated the intervention of the state militia. Other conflicts put federal land managers between bickering sheep and cattle interests, and the solutions proposed usually satisfied no one.[59]

A Fickle Resource Base

Some Coloradans probed the economic potential of the Northwest Corner beyond the limits of livestocking. David Moffat, one of Colorado's pioneer elite, became a key participant in this process of exploration. He arrived in Colorado in 1860, became a founding member of the First National Bank of Denver, invested heavily in a number of profitable mining ventures, and participated in building many of the state's important railroad lines. Curiously, as Moffat reached the pinnacle of his business career in 1900, the wide open spaces and economic opportunities of northwestern Colorado caught his imagination.[60] Safer investments elsewhere offered solid returns, but Moffat was struck by the untapped resource base that northwestern Colorado offered. Most obvious was the gap in transportation infrastructure: the region remained unserved by a local railroad, and it offered an ideal setting for the construction of a direct line between Denver and Salt Lake City. Moffat also was familiar with reports on the region's mineral potential, particularly the Yampa Valley's coal deposits.

Moffat formally assessed the region's economic potential in 1903. His report identified six billion tons of developable coal reserves in the middle and upper Yampa Valley. Further west, other fossil fuels such as oil, oil shale, and gilsonite (used for asphalt) were found. In addition, farming opportunities beckoned. Even the Government Land Office saw great possibilities in expanding irrigation within the Yampa Valley, especially with new reclamation projects. Elsewhere in Colorado, successes with sugar beets, fruits, and irrigated grains suggested that northwestern Colorado could greatly increase its agricultural output. Moffat realized, however, that all of these opportunities would remain unfulfilled without a railroad to connect the region's resources with their markets.

Born from these dreams of geographical dominance was the Denver, Northwestern, and Pacific Railroad, a scheme to surmount the Continental Divide west of Denver, traverse the length of northwestern Colorado and connect westward to the growing metropolis of Salt Lake City. Problems in raising money for the project suggested that Moffat's vision was not universally shared. His initial attempts to convince the Denver and Rio Grande Railroad to participate in the endeavor bore no fruit, and once he began building the line through a separate corporation, it, too, ran short of funds. Construction was costly: west of Denver, the route ascended tortuous and storm-prone Rollins Pass and reached Middle Park in 1905. There the money ran out, and it took creative fund-raising to get the line over Gore Pass and into the Yampa Valley, where it finally arrived in Steamboat Springs in 1909. The Moffat Road ended in Steamboat Springs. At a cost of over twelve million dollars, the dream had cost Moffat his fortune and perhaps his life: he died penniless in 1911.

Two years later the line was resurrected as the Denver and Salt Lake Railroad. A new group of investors, perhaps encouraged by better economic times and the logic of the direct Denver to Salt Lake connection, poured more funds into the scheme. The line's terminus, however, was the modest ranching town of Craig, Colorado, rather than Salt Lake City. Reaching Craig in 1913, the railroad benefited cattle interests in the area and stimulated coal mining in the Yampa Valley, particularly as World War I increased demand for the fuel. But perennially undercapitalized and beset by snowbound Rollins Pass, the railroad never thrived, even after the Moffat Tunnel beneath the Continental Divide was completed in the late 1920s. Moffat's dream of a new commercial empire remained just that, although the memory of his efforts survives within the region and is recognized in the name of Moffat County, created in the state's northwest corner shortly after his death.

Part of Moffat's vision was tested many years later. The region's agricultural prospects remained ill-defined. Although no large reclamation projects appeared by 1910, boosters crowed the benefits of dryland wheat farming. Captured by the same enthusiasm that had swept the eastern plains, dry farming advocates found willing listeners in the boom-time markets of World War I. Epitomizing this ebullience was the Great Divide Homestead Colony Number One.[61] Focused northwest of Craig, the well-organized venture was promoted by Volney Hoggatt. Hoggatt published promotional magazines, had good connections with the *Denver Post,* and belonged to the State Land Board, an affiliation that lent credence to the scheme. By 1916 trainloads of hopeful immigrants arrived in the region. Nearby Routt County experienced a similar inmigration of dryland culti-vators, and thousands of virgin acres were quickly plowed under and put into small grains. Dryland prospects near Steamboat Springs appeared to be particularly productive (fig. 91).

Dry farming greatly disrupted cattle operators who still made use of open range lands and stock ponds. Barbed wire fences went up every-where, and as one historian of the region suggests, "some of the best cat-tle range on earth . . . turned into some of the world's worst wheat farms."[62] Nature and grain markets refused to cooperate with the sod-busters. The area's dry climate and falling crop prices soon pressured the homesteaders, and by the late 1920s hundreds of settler shacks and gar-dens were being overrun by grazing cattle and sheep, a reminder of the fickle nature of northwest Colorado's resource base. The Moffat County assessor reported that the 130,000 acres in dryland crops in 1925 shrunk to only 35,000 acres in 1930.[63]

One dimension of Moffat's dream proved especially well founded. Ge-ology conspired to concentrate large reserves of coal, oil, and oil-bearing shales within the region.[64] It remained for the outside world to assess, ex-tract, and develop these resources, a process that began in the late nine-teenth century, boomed episodically between 1900 and 1930, and contin-ued to tease the region thereafter. Developers discovered accessible coal resources in the Yampa Valley, the Danforth Hills northwest of Meeker, and the Grand Hogback near Glenwood Springs. Other prospectors un-covered major oil and gas deposits slightly farther west in Moffat and northern Rio Blanco Counties. The best shale was found in the Piceance Creek drainage, along the edge of the Book Plateau southeast of Rangely, and northeast of Grand Junction. Rich deposits of asphalt-yielding gilsonite were also present in nearby portions of eastern Utah. As the ex-tent of this petroleum-based treasure trove became known, investors at-tempted to tap into the region's potential. The area's enduring isolation, high expenses of developing the resources, and unpredictable markets pre-cluded any extended energy-related booms within northwestern Colorado. Still, the black gold found within its boundaries contributed significantly to the making of the region's natural resource-based economy and cultural landscape.

FIGURE 91. A nonsustainable rural adaptation: dryland farming, Routt County (Courtesy Denver Public Library, Western History Collection)

Coal production soared on the southern fringes of the region beginning in the late 1880s.[65] Low sulfur coals west of Glenwood Springs were developed once railroad construction linked the area to markets. New Castle was platted, and both the Colorado Fuel and Iron Company and the Santa Fe Coal Company opened major operations there. Excellent rail connections ensured the commercial viability of the New Castle mines, in contrast to the persisting isolation that plagued the Yampa Valley. Ongoing labor troubles and large mine explosions, both in 1896 and in 1913, discouraged both mine owners and workers, however, and the area was not a lasting producer within the state. Farther north, the Moffat Road stimulated production in the upper Yampa Valley after 1900 and the nearby Danforth Hills also proved worthy of development.[66] Overall, however, the pre-1920 production of these northwestern Colorado coal mines was modest compared with the activities in the state's southern periphery near Trinidad.

Early oil and gas production centered on Rangely in western Rio Blanco County. Settlers in the 1890s were familiar with the oil-rich area in the lower White River Valley, but it was not until the Poole Well struck a gusher in 1902 that hopes for major deposits were raised. Thereafter, more concerted exploration and increasing participation by major national companies yielded significant finds. East of Rangely, geologists uncovered the Moffat and Iles fields by the 1920s, and these contributed to the state's rapidly increasing production. Natural gas production expanded more slowly, but fields sprouted in Moffat, Rio Blanco, and Garfield Counties between 1926 and 1931. A new cultural landscape was gradually being created: wildcatter oil towns like Rangely, a bewildering plethora of dirt roads and trails, and the telltale exclamation points of oil and gas derricks displayed the industry's signature upon the visual scene (fig. 92).

Although coal, oil, and natural gas became important regional products, western Colorado's early oil shale boom produced more speculative heat than anything else.[67] The first shale-related mining district formed near Parachute in 1890, but little development occurred until the early twentieth century. Rising fossil fuel consumption and still-limited supplies provoked President Theodore Roosevelt to warn of an energy shortage in 1908. Several years later, the first detailed federal oil shale surveys were completed in western Colorado. The surveys suggested that an astound-

FIGURE 92. Energy landscapes on the western slope: the Amazon Gas Well near De Beque, Colorado (Courtesy Colorado State Historical Society)

ing twenty to forty billion barrels of oil were locked within the region's rich sediments. This prompted President Woodrow Wilson to withdraw more than forty thousand acres in the area from the public domain to create the Naval Oil Shale Reserve northeast of De Beque.

Thousands of acres also opened for private shale development. By 1920 prospectors filed thirty thousand shale-related claims, and no fewer than 150 companies were incorporated within Colorado to promote shale. Events, however, confirmed that the emphasis would remain on shale promotion rather than actual development. In spite of the hoopla, total shale-related oil production stood at a paltry five hundred barrels by 1920. What flourished instead were stock schemes and real estate ventures designed to relieve the unknowing of their investment capital. Even an official government shale-processing facility, constructed on the Naval Oil Shale Reserve in 1925, failed to boost production significantly. Two persisting problems spelled the end of the Colorado boom in the 1920s: technological barriers hindered large-scale production of shale oil and oil prices fell dramatically during the decade as fields in West Texas expanded national supplies. Still, even as the local shale economy faltered, major oil companies quietly accumulated shale-rich acreage in the 1920s in the belief that such nonrenewable resources would prove valuable. Subsequent booms, particularly during the energy crisis of late 1970s, again raised hopes for the industry, but the optimism of the early twentieth century has yet to be fulfilled.

8

Geographies in Transition
Colorado, 1920–1940

Colorado's emergence into the modern world of the mid-twentieth century was a jarring and formative experience. The state's diverse human geographies reflected the era's broader economic, technological, cultural, and political shifts in dramatic, often unpredictable ways. Inextricably bound to the global and national economy from its early days, Colorado continued to be tied to the evolution of post–World War I American capitalism. The entire West felt the effects of the gyrating commodity prices, bank failures, and general economic conditions associated with the Great Depression. In addition, the New Deal, the ambitious national response to the downturn, had broad implications for Colorado and the West generally, rapidly increasing a federal role that had grown since the late nineteenth century. Colorado's cultural landscapes also revealed key changes in American capitalism as it became increasingly centered around mass consumption and the production of a broadly if loosely shared national popular culture. Technological changes in transportation and communications facilitated the shift, drawing Coloradans forever into the machinations of the modern world.

Colorado also evolved as a distinctly western American place. Within its borders, this characteristically western identity was articulated in several ways. The ongoing gyration of the economy was unpredictable as ever, with agriculture and mining experiencing severe contractions, falling prices, and declining employment between 1920 and 1940. In addition, the capricious western environment continued to surprise residents as the Great Plains were desiccated during the infamous Dust Bowl of the 1930s. Over all the West, the allocation of water resources became a pivotal regional issue. Western states and the federal government were forced to develop new and innovative solutions to water problems, a process not at all concluded by 1940. Yet key regional changes were also afoot; processes set in motion between the world wars began to assume greater importance after 1945. The American West was urbanizing, and the evolution of its cities led the nation in shaping the characteristic urban fabric of post–World War II America. Although the Pacific Coast region, particularly California, took the lead in innovative urban forms, Colorado's cities also reflected the new regional reality.

Within Colorado, major population geographies remained stable between 1920 and 1940. Established patterns of towns and connections remained intact, although some centers contracted, others grew, and the linkages binding them strengthened with the paved roads of the 1930s. Distinctive regional identities created within Colorado between 1860 and 1920 were not erased by the onrush of capitalism or by the conforming pressures of modern American culture. Still, it is hard to argue against the underlying realities of national cultural convergence across the American West after 1920. At the same time, new cultural mosaics were created as shifting patterns of migration brought people together in fresh ways. Colorado's cultural landscape echoed this tension between the homogenizing forces of modernity and the ongoing reality of disparate American cultures: even as close-knit ethnic neighborhoods in the industrial suburbs of Pueblo and Denver thrived and as Hispano communities, both rural and urban, maintained their vitality, Coloradans increasingly listened to the same radio programs, watched the same motion pictures, and consumed the same products of mass consumer culture.

Colorado and the Nation

National political and economic events greatly influenced Colorado's evolution after World War I, and the state's human geography bore the diverse signatures of these impacts.[1] Many of the state's farm regions were pressured in the 1920s as crop prices fell from wartime levels. Tenancy rates rose, particularly on the eastern plains, and farm foreclosures surged. Some specialty crop districts thrived, however. Sugar beet, cantaloupe, cauliflower, and lettuce output were robust in the 1920s, and successful operators countered soft prices with increases in production. Fewer options existed for mine operators or laborers. After the bottom fell out of metals prices at the end of World War I, production remained muted for much of the 1920s. Coal-producing districts also suffered as natural gas and oil replaced coal in many urban and industrial settings. The state's manufacturing sector remained anemic, restrained by the weakness in the agricultural and mining sectors.

In the late 1920s the state's economy finally began to emerge from its malaise. Agricultural production and profits perked up, employment rose, corporations such as Pueblo's Colorado Fuel and Iron Company reported good earnings, and national talk of prosperity and good times looked as if it might finally be rubbing off on the Intermountain West.

Unfortunately, Colorado joined the rest of the nation in being jolted by the economic events of October 1929 as the stock market crashed and as public confidence in economic institutions evaporated. The rapid sea change signaled a period of collapsing economic demand, declining wages and commodity prices, and rising levels of unemployment and homelessness. In the economic depression that unfolded after the crash, no corner of the West escaped the foreclosures, joblessness, and hopelessness that sapped the strength of Americans nationally. Overall economic activity in the West fell by over 50 percent between 1929 and 1933. Within Colorado, the statistics were similarly grim: between the late 1920s and the depths of the Depression in 1932 and 1933, per capita incomes fell 40 percent, unemployment more than quadrupled, dozens of Colorado banks and scores of major Colorado businesses failed, farm income declined by over 60 percent, and annual industrial production fell from over $300 million to less than $185 million.[2]

Geographies of Distress and Response

Although few Coloradans avoided the pain of the early 1930s, there was a widely varying geography of Depression-era impacts, depending mostly on the state's diverse economic base.[3] Suffering was high among plains farmers, a group who had enjoyed little prosperity even in the 1920s. Rural tax delinquencies in 1932, for example, concentrated in the eastern plains, where many districts reported that over half the farmland was delinquent for taxes. Such figures are hardly surprising, considering the collapse in crop and livestock prices that hit marginal eastern Colorado producers with particular ferocity. Between 1929 and 1932 corn prices shriveled from 80 to 19 cents per bushel and wheat fell from $1.04 to 32 cents. Similar declines hit cattle and sheep markets. Western slope farmers, particularly the specialized irrigated operators, fared better, but even there low fruit prices and high freight rates meant that produce rotted on the vine.

Industrial centers large and small also suffered: Durango's smelter operation closed by late 1930, the Colorado Fuel and Iron Company's steel operations collapsed in Pueblo by 1933, and the industrial suburbs of north Denver saw swelling ranks of unemployed workers as factory operations ceased or were severely curtailed. Although some Denverites managed to ride out the Depression with their jobs intact, a sizable number of residents and unemployed newcomers crowded into such urban slums as Petertown, just west of the State Capitol (fig. 93). Long-suffering mountain mining districts also failed to escape the Depression's early years. Here the immediate impacts were less dramatic because many residents had already

FIGURE 93. Denver's Depression-era landscape: the Petertown community, 1938
(Courtesy Colorado State Historical Society)

left in the doldrums of the 1920s—the severe price declines for gold, silver, copper, and lead in the early 1930s were only another replay of the price
shocks a decade earlier.

The disaster provoked an unprecedented response once President
Franklin D. Roosevelt took office in March 1933.[4] Dozens of new federal
programs had a variety of geographical consequences for Colorado. Some
initiatives affected every county of the state, while others targeted economic and regional sectors, focusing their impacts in particular areas. The
state's human geography was transformed by New Deal expenditures in
three ways: basic infrastructure—roads, mountain trails, agricultural and
municipal water works, telephone and electrical lines—was vastly improved; the state's cultural landscape displayed a new signature of federal
largesse as scores of public buildings, dams, shelterbelts, and parks were
added to the scene; and perhaps most important, many of the state's communities—both urban and rural—were stabilized, indeed saved, through
federal relief and employment programs that offered a measure of hope in
this trying economic and social environment.

Some New Deal programs had statewide significance. Between 1933
and 1935 direct federal relief payments and food distribution programs

were coordinated through the Federal Emergency Relief Administration (FERA).[5] Although Colorado politicians initially balked at such direct intervention from Washington, popular protests and federal threats to withhold support encouraged state cooperation. Eastern and southern Colorado counties were hardest hit, with Baca County reporting that 25 percent of its population had applied for relief assistance. Western Colorado's agricultural counties—Mesa, Delta, and Montrose—were in better shape, as were the mountain mining counties, where many of the unemployed had drifted away years earlier. In the state's urban areas, between 5 and 10 percent of the population applied for direct relief through FERA. Considering the fact that many individuals applying for relief were heads of household for sizable families, the overall scope of FERA assistance probably extended aid to approximately one-quarter of Colorado's population.

The federal Civilian Conservation Corps (CCC) and the Works Progress Administration (WPA) employed thousands more Coloradans in an astounding variety of public works projects. The CCC, established in March 1933, employed young men between ages seventeen and twenty-five in activities that included recreation hall and park construction in the cities, road and trail construction, tree planting, and fire fighting in the mountains, and irrigation improvements, cover crop and windbreak planting, and stock-fence construction in the rural areas (fig. 94). Between 1933 and 1942 more than thirty thousand people participated in the Colorado CCC operating from more than 150 camps around the state.

The WPA offered an even wider set of initiatives, involving 150,000 Colorado workers between 1936 and 1943. Part of Roosevelt's so-called Second New Deal, the WPA and the smaller Public Works Administration (PWA) were economic stimulus programs to put people to work while leaving welfare relief to the states themselves. Hundreds of projects large and small were funded through WPA and PWA programs in Colorado: sewage works, school and library construction, creative arts activities, and worker retraining classes were only a few of the dozens of WPA investments made in the late 1930s and early 1940s.

Other New Deal expenditures provided assistance in more focused geographical settings. The Emergency Banking Relief Act of 1933 stabilized all of the state's private financial institutions, and a provision in the bill regulating gold and silver prices offered particular aid to the state's mining communities. The act and subsequent legislation spurred price rises in gold and silver, which stimulated the mining economy. Dozens of mines reopened in the high country in the middle and late 1930s and towns like Telluride, Leadville, and Cripple Creek experienced healthy increases in population by the end of the decade.

FIGURE 94. Creating new infrastructure: road-building by the Civilian Conservation Corps (Courtesy Colorado State Historical Society)

Many federal assistance efforts concentrated upon the agricultural sector, regionally targeting the hard-hit eastern plains. The Farm Credit Administration (FCA) loaned Colorado farmers more than sixty-five million dollars between 1933 and 1939, bringing together critical capital when many individual banks were simply unable or unwilling to do so. Additional funds to farmers were provided by the Agricultural Adjustment Administration (AAA) between 1933 and 1935. Farmers were paid not to plant crops, thus reducing production, raising prices, and bringing supplies into line with demand. Such farming practices as listing (furrowing and roughening the surface to minimize erosion), contour plowing, and conservation fallowing became key initiatives of the Soil and Conservation Service (SCS) when it was created in 1935. By the early 1940s almost nine million acres of Colorado land were part of federally managed conservation districts. The Rural Electrification Administration (REA) also began its popular loan program, enabling dozens of rural cooperatives to finance the construction of electrical lines into the countryside. In addition, New Deal programs directly purchased damaged agricultural lands (both Colorado's Comanche and Pawnee National Grasslands evolved from such federal acquisitions) and resettled destitute farmers from the state's eastern counties into better-managed operations in the San Luis Valley and western slope regions.

Although better economic times came to Colorado and the nation in 1936 and 1937, another downturn late in the decade threatened a repeat of Depression days. World War II, not unlike its predecessor in the teens, provided the necessary stimulus to reinvigorate Colorado's economy. By then Colorado had benefited from almost four hundred million dollars in New Deal expenditures that provided an investment in infrastructure and people that long outlived the years of the Depression.[6] Overall the tumultuous 1920s and 1930s as well as the ambitious national response to the Great Depression altered Colorado's human geographies in lasting ways and hinted at how a new mix of capitalism and federal largesse would continue to remake the American scene in subsequent decades.

Processes of Modernization and Convergence

The common challenge of the Depression and the coordinated federal response to its ills were not the only things drawing the nation closer together in the interwar period. In addition to new economic and political realities, powerful technological and social forces combined to encourage processes of national cultural convergence between 1920 and 1940. Put simply, Americans were becoming more similar as such innovations as automobiles, airplanes, radio programs, and motion pictures bound them in loose but widely shared ways. Such cultural convergence was facilitated by and closely linked to more general processes of twentieth-century modernization. As an increasingly pervasive theme in the first half of the twentieth century, "modernization" involved a myriad of artifacts and attitudes, a habit of mind that ever more enthusiastically embraced a set of common cultural experiences.[7] Much of that experience was defined through the evolution of mass consumption capitalism and the vigorous production of a dynamic, standardized popular culture oriented around an enhanced material life as well as a set of technological innovations that made possible the almost immediate diffusion of these new shared proclivities. For the period between 1920 and 1940, these convergent and homogenizing influences of modernization appear paramount, subjecting broad areas of the United States to a common set of new technologies and experiences.

For Colorado, indeed for the entire nation, such tendencies had profound geographical consequences. Modernization's glue—both technological and cultural—redefined basic spatial relations: better roads, faster automobiles, and the miracles of air travel reduced the friction of distance and brought Coloradans closer to one another and to the outside world;

in a somewhat different fashion, communications innovations brought people the daily shared experiences of nationally syndicated radio broadcasts and Hollywood movies and worked to close the cultural distance between Americans. These fruits of the modern world were ubiquitous elements of the interwar cultural landscape, abundantly revealed in America's "automobile culture" as well as in its more general love affair with the amenities of mass consumption displayed on the everyday scene. Colorado was no different than Illinois in this regard, and although these changes were never spelled out or administered in any federal program or dictate, their pervasive nature and almost universal national adoption made them critical shaping forces to the nation's twentieth-century human geography.

New technologies wed disparate corners of the country together between 1920 and 1940. Most obviously, the invention and mass production of the automobile revolutionized both long distance and local transportation within the United States in the early twentieth century.[8] Automobiles offered Americans a more flexible and individualized mode of transportation. Although early cars were expensive hand-crafted machines that only the wealthy could afford, Henry Ford's introduction of the Model T in 1909 offered the middle class a cheap, volume-produced vehicle that became immensely popular. By 1916 more than two million vehicles were on American roads, and by 1930 that total ballooned to twenty-six million cars and trucks.

Paralleling the automobile revolution was an equally important revolution in road construction. Federal support was pivotal in the effort, and the Federal Aid Road Act (1916) and Federal Highway Act (1921) guaranteed an aggressive commitment by the national government to improve and eventually pave a truly national highway system. Combined with matching state funds, federal appropriations achieved remarkable results by the close of the 1930s. In less than twenty years a network of nationally numbered U.S. highways crisscrossed the nation, offering car and truck traffic a new scale of continental mobility. Indeed, even though most auto and truck travel remained local and regional before World War II, the concrete infrastructure that modernized American transportation was substantially in place by the early 1940s, the product of a five-billion-dollar decade-long investment effort spearheaded by the federal government.

For Colorado and the West generally, the automobile revolution brought rapid and enduring geographical change. The West embraced the automobile early on, and Colorado was no exception.[9] By 1928 Colorado ranked eighth in the nation in per capita vehicle ownership, with over 250,000 passenger cars and 20,000 trucks registered in the state. Although automobile use stagnated in the Depression years, Colorado's per capita car ownership accelerated in the late 1930s. With the formation of the Rocky Mountain Highway Association in 1908, Coloradans also pressured the state legislature to increase the funding of roads. The following year the newly created Colorado State Highway Commission did precisely that, and its annual allocation for road improvements, often matched with federal dollars, became a major state expenditure by the 1920s.

Truly remarkable changes transpired across Colorado's fledgling highway system between the late 1920s and early 1940s as thousands of miles of unimproved dirt and graveled tracks were graded and paved (fig. 95). Improvements came first in the more densely populated Piedmont, and by the early 1930s an incipient network of paved roads linked Denver with Colorado Springs, Pueblo, Boulder, and Fort Collins. By 1940 most of the major U.S.-numbered highways in the state were hard-surfaced with improvements lacking only in isolated plains and mountain locales. Federal, state, and local expenditures on Colorado highways amounted to a staggering $262 million between 1924 and 1940.

This combination of mass automobile use and greatly improved highways reverberated through Colorado's human geography in revolutionary fashion. The time distance between Colorado localities was radically reconfigured as paved linkages multiplied. In the national context, this brought Colorado nearer to the nation's economic heartland in the Midwest and East. The country was literally growing closer together, and even though high-speed trains still offered the best connections to Chicago and New York, the move toward long-distance auto and truck travel proved irresistible for both families and businesses.

Within Colorado better roads and the internal combustion engine contributed to fundamental shifts in settlement geography. In rural areas many small hamlets were made unnecessary as farm families could easily travel greater distances to larger, more diversified service centers. This accelerated the decline of many Colorado farm communities of fewer than a thousand, while larger centers benefited from their increased centrality and economic diversity. Agricultural mechanization also pressured rural populations because farms needed less labor. Larger, fewer farms were the result of mechanization as successful farmers saw the virtues of larger-scale operations.

Just as rural roads and better cars increased the farmer's access to the city, improved urban infrastructure and increased automobile adoption propelled city-dwellers into the surrounding countryside. Suburbanization accelerated after 1920, a precursor of even larger postwar migrations. By the 1930s, for example, more Denverites were using autos than streetcars in their daily work and shopping trips within the city. One result of

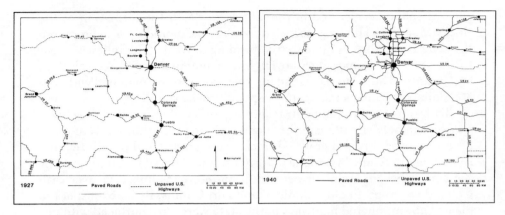

FIGURE 95. Major highways in Colorado: (A) 1927 (Source: *Auto Road Atlas of the United States* [Chicago: Rand McNally, 1927]); (B) 1940 (Source: Conoco Oil Company, "Official Road Map of Colorado" [Chicago: H. M. Gousha, 1940])

this process was the growth of satellite communities and subdivisions on the edge of Colorado's larger cities, with Denver clearly providing the most dramatic example of the automobile's impact.

Automobility's signature on the Colorado cultural landscape was ubiquitous (fig. 96). Cars, garages, trucks, new roads, bigger, more distracting billboards, and parking lots were everywhere. Commercial thoroughfares such as Denver's Broadway and Colfax Avenues were lined with gas stations, repair shops, and tire stores.[10] Colorado's tourist landscape was rapidly refashioned to cater to the car-traveling public. In urban areas, commercial auto strips were born with their array of auto camps, cottage courts, motels, cafés, and drive-ins designed to serve the traveling middle-class motorist. Denver's Overland Park, a municipally owned auto camp, became known as one the largest and best of its kind in the nation. Elsewhere, new resort clusters sprouted in scenery-rich, high-amenity mountain settings. In particular, Colorado's national forests, parks, and monuments grew increasingly popular in the 1920s and 1930s as better roads and automobile tourism made these diversions more accessible. Even the smallest hamlet needed its gas station and auto garage to meet the needs of local residents and travelers.

Less visibly, the automobile refashioned basic relationships between people and place, and the result altered the identity and character of many Colorado communities. Although it increased individual flexibility and mobility, the mass consumer-oriented car culture also had the potential to weaken the coherence of traditional community ties. Liberating isolated eastern plains farmers much as the horse liberated earlier Native Americans, the automobile, along with better roads, granted rural residents a

FIGURE 96. The automobile arrives on Main Street: Durango in the early 1930s (Courtesy Colorado State Historical Society)

much wider range of movement. The earlier pattern, however, often contributed to a cohesiveness within the rural community that disappeared with the new mobility. Historian Donald Worster's observations on the automobile in western Kansas ring true for rural Colorado, as he notes, "paradoxically, although it facilitated the gathering of rural neighbors for an ice cream social, it also loosened the bonds that had held people together in a single community and had nurtured their devotion to place. Because of the automobile . . . the individual is now the center and looks about him in all directions. His life had been broken into many segments and lay scattered over a fifty-mile radius."[11]

Urban communities were also refashioned amid the din of Buicks, Fords, and Chryslers. Well-established neighborhoods fragmented as suburban life beckoned to many who tired of urban ills and congestion. The urban landscape itself became less human in scale, catering more to the needs of the motorist than the pedestrian. Streets were widened, traffic redirected onto planned highway grids, and a new barrage of signs put in place, all for the benefit of the driving public. Indeed, epitomizing the turn toward twentieth-century modernity and the growing homogeneity of American life, the automobile transformed the lives of all Coloradans, both rural and urban, by the close of the 1930s.

More selectively, airplanes affected Colorado life during the interwar period.[12] Denver's Municipal Airport was dedicated in the fall of 1929, and by 1934 fifteen other Colorado towns completed their commercial or municipal airfields. Still, in the early years of aviation, Colorado was on the periphery of transcontinental linkages, much as it had been in the eras of overland trails and railroads. When four cross-country air mail routes were established in 1934, Denver was not on any direct transcontinental line. Only three feeder airlines served Denver and a scattering of smaller Colorado fields. Colorado travelers journeyed north to Cheyenne or south to Albuquerque to make longer-distance jumps to the East or West Coasts. That changed in 1937, when United and Continental Air Lines established trunk lines into Denver. Travelers made easy connections with Wyoming or Nebraska via United or they could travel directly to the Southwest with Continental. The following year, with the help of WPA funds, Denver's airport was enlarged, its runways were improved, and a new control tower was built. Commercial linkages improved to smaller Piedmont cities such as Colorado Springs and Pueblo by the late 1930s, but Denver clearly emerged as the region's air traffic hub (fig. 97).

Although faster cars and expanding airlines ensured closer spatial links between Colorado and the rest of the nation, two other powerful technological forces also worked toward modernization and national cultural convergence. Motion pictures and commercial radio broadcasts inundated Americans between 1920 and 1940. They provided a common set of daily cultural experiences from one coast to the other. Indeed, knowingly or not, Americans by 1940 were spending a great deal of their leisure time together.

Motion pictures, first silent and then sound, burst upon the American scene in the twentieth century.[13] By the early 1920s an astounding forty million theater tickets per week were being sold nationally, and that figure more than doubled by 1930. Americans embraced such popular films as *The Jazz Singer* (1927), *King Kong* (1933), *Snow White and the Seven Dwarfs* (1937), *Gone with the Wind* (1939), and hundreds of less epic films that portrayed "powerfully persuasive examples of modern American life . . . not the level most common in America, but one to which most Americans aspired and felt was within possible reach."[14] Movie theaters became prominent symbols on the cultural landscape: major cities boasted ever more gaudy and ornate theater architecture, while small towns had to have at least one theater to claim their legitimate place in the modern world. Theaters, typically in highly visible, downtown locations, became centers of community, both local and national.

Coloradans embraced the movie industry with enthusiasm. Not surprisingly, Denver became a focal point of activity: by the 1930s it supported more than forty movie theaters and became a major regional film distribution center for the surrounding states, funneling the celluloid images

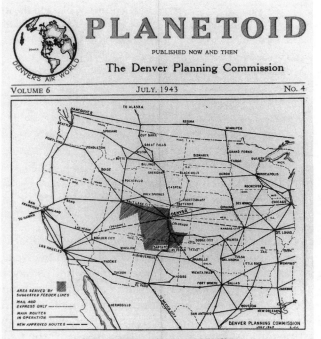

THE CENTRAL WEST AIR CENTER

THE air map of Denver reveals many new and important developments. Denver, the largest city in the Central West, with its ideal climatic flying conditions, its adequate airfields, and its strategic location, is becoming a key point in the domestic aviation picture of the Western United States.

FIGURE 97. Denver: the "Central West Air Center," *Planetoid*, July 1943 (Courtesy Colorado State Historical Society)

from Hollywood into small town locales throughout the Rockies and Plains.[15] By 1934 four Denver theaters accommodated more than two thousand moviegoers apiece. The relatively modest investment required to outfit a movie house and acquire the current outpouring of films resulted in a ready diffusion of theaters to virtually every corner of the state (fig. 98). The geography of theaters echoed larger patterns of population: the Piedmont enjoyed the greatest access to entertainment, but even such small and previously isolated towns as Cheyenne Wells, Rico, and Craig claimed a direct connection to the latest films, fads, and fashions that flickered on the screen every Saturday night.

Colorado's geography of radio stations also suggested the widespread adoption of that technology during the interwar period (fig. 99).[16] Pioneered in Pittsburgh in 1920, commercial radio broadcasting spread rapidly across the nation. Denver's KLZ went on the air in 1922, the brain-

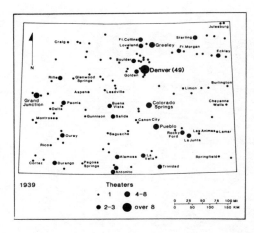

FIGURE 98. Geographies of popular culture: Colorado theaters, 1939 (Source: *Colorado State Business Directory*, 1939)

child of radio enthusiast and Colorado dentist "Doc" William Reynolds. More important, General Electric's KOA was licensed two years later, establishing a presence in the region that continues to this day. Indeed, by the middle 1930s, KOA's fifty-thousand-watt, clear-channel broadcasts became a symbol of Denver's regional dominance. Smaller Colorado towns also acquired stations, blanketing the state by 1940 with a network of local broadcasting outlets. Increasingly by the late 1930s, the Colorado stations became affiliated with such national companies as CBS and NBC, significant because listeners had local programming supplemented with and replaced by nationally produced shows and advertising that originated on the East or West Coasts. Coloradans swung in unison to the sounds of the Big Bands, chuckled at the antics of Fibber McGee and Molly, and followed the news with reports by Lowell Thomas. By 1940 over 80 percent of Colorado's families owned radios, and the technology joined motion pictures as preferred forms of daily entertainment and education.

In a different way, processes of cultural intolerance were also reinforced during the interwar era through Colorado's changing ethnic geography and political environment.[17] Immigrant populations declined in significance and xenophobia discouraged non-white and non-Protestant Coloradans from playing a role in state affairs. National tolerance of immigrants ebbed after World War I as both conservative nativists and liberal Progressives doubted whether the onrush of new migrants, many from southern and eastern Europe, could fully embrace the nation's democratic traditions. The result was an increasingly exclusionary attitude toward foreigners: Congress adopted general immigration quotas in 1921 and went much further eight years later by passing the National Origins Act, severely restricting overall immigration and limiting it mostly to

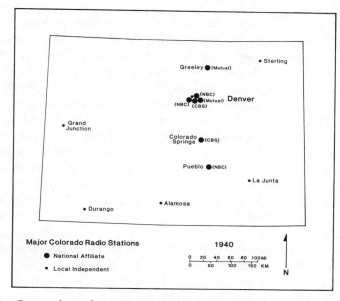

FIGURE 99. Geographies of popular culture: Colorado radio stations, 1941 (Source: Calso Gasoline Company, "Road Map of Colorado, 1941" [Chicago: H. M. Gousha, 1941])

northwestern Europeans. Colorado's foreign-born population declined from 16 percent to 8 percent between 1910 and 1930. Fewer Germans, Italians, and eastern Europeans arrived to reinforce ethnic settlements and neighborhoods established between 1880 and 1910. In addition, the state's struggling economy and anemic job markets in the 1920s and 1930s dissuaded potential in-migrants, both foreign and domestic.

Making matters worse for practically any non-white, non-Protestant Coloradan in the early 1920s was the ugly rise of the Klu Klux Klan (KKK), vividly representing the antiforeign tenor of the times.[18] Many state and local elections between 1920 and 1924 saw the KKK successfully influence the rise of sympathetic politicians in the state legislature, even in the governor's office. The anti-Jewish, antiforeign, antiblack, and anti-Catholic Klan pushed for a legislative agenda to restrict immigrant rights and even prevent the sacrament of wine drinking by "Papists." Beyond the rhetoric and the cross-burning, however, little came of the Colorado Klan, although the group was particularly popular in Denver until the movement fizzled in the late 1920s.

Even though the Klan enjoyed brief notoriety, its success suggested deeper resentments toward important segments of Colorado's population. One ethnic group that bore more than its share of personal and political abuse was the state's Hispano population.[19] Foreign-born Mexicans were particularly singled out for discrimination. Unlike most foreign-born groups, their numbers increased rapidly between 1910 and 1930, quintupling during the period to more than thirteen thousand residents. Many were recruited by the sugar beet companies to labor in the fields. In the off-season, Mexican workers migrated to Denver or smaller towns, where they picked up odd jobs. Others worked in the coal and rail industries, although both activities were severely curtailed during the Depression.

White Coloradan resentment of all Hispanos reached a fever pitch in 1936, when state officials illegally prohibited their movement into the state, setting up "border crossings" on the New Mexico line and turning back suspected "foreigners." The blockade produced a flurry of heated exchanges between Colorado and New Mexico authorities and was quickly ruled illegal by the federal government. As with the Klan in the 1920s, however, such incidents pointed out the increasingly parochial ways in which some Americans saw themselves after the political crisis of World War I. Defined in this way, the cultural convergence that was powerfully shaping Colorado between the wars also carried a message of exclusion and intolerance that contrasted with the lighter side of radio comedians or the dynamism of the new automobile culture.

Colorado and the West

Just as Colorado was shaped by national, even global forces between 1920 and 1940, other more regionally based trends molded Colorado's human geography and linked the state more closely with its neighbors. Three typically "western" characteristics of Colorado's geography are particularly noteworthy during the period: first, Denver's rising prominence reflected important regional trends toward urbanization; second, the changeable and often fragile western environment repeatedly challenged the region, and Coloradans found themselves squarely in the midst of the difficulties; and third, larger issues of regional water management produced dramatic changes, with Colorado at the center of many litigious and technological challenges.

The Urban West

By 1940 almost 60 percent of the West's population lived in cities, suggesting that the region's character was increasingly bound to its urban experience.[20] Rural residents also found their lives more intertwined with urban economic, political, and cultural forces. Many western cities grew particularly rapidly during the 1920s—the population of Los Angeles doubled during the decade—but even the tougher times of the 1930s produced gains in such cities as Phoenix and San Diego. By the eve of World War II, over 70 percent of California's 6.9 million residents were urban, and Utah, Washington, and Colorado counted well over half their residents in cities. Laggards in the urbanizing process included Idaho, New Mexico, and Montana, where strong rural communities and farming traditions held sway, but even in these states, cities like Boise, Albuquerque, and Great Falls grew considerably between 1920 and 1940.

California dominated the urban West (fig. 100). Dense constellations of central cities and blossoming suburbs clustered along the southern coast and in the Bay Area. Smaller urban agglomerations dotted western Oregon and Washington, northern Utah, and the Colorado Piedmont. Beyond these concentrations, only isolated urban oases interrupted the arid and mountainous interior. These western cities increasingly gained economic and political control over their rural hinterlands.[21] Creating regional "empires," the West's large cities tapped into the natural resource bases of their rural peripheries in a process of geographical expansion that was no less significant than the national move west during the nineteenth century had been. By the 1940s the resulting pattern created a series of large rural tributary areas surrounding the West's major metropolitan centers, marking zones of urban influence that extended far beyond city limits and even state borders.

The urban West also achieved even larger national significance. As a new variant of the urban built environment, it led the nation toward the structure and appearance of the American city that became the national norm after World War II.[22] The western city featured a distinctive, often planned spaciousness that typically blended, visually and functionally, such surrounding natural features as mountains, seashore, and open land into the urban landscape. Its relatively decentralized populations became oriented around suburban growth, multicentered nodes of commercial activity, and frequent commuting. Its architectural character emphasized the horizontality of the urban landscape with its generally low-profile downtown skylines, sprawling suburbs, and plethora of one-story bungalow- and ranch-style single family homes. The urban West became a much-advertised and frequently promoted ideal that compared favorably to the gritty and aging cities of the East.

Colorado's urban evolution in the first forty years of the twentieth century paralleled the larger regional realities of the metropolitan West. A population dot map produced by the Colorado State Planning Commission in the late 1930s (based on the 1930 Census) reveals the overwhelming urban dominance of the Piedmont, with a dense collection of towns spreading from Fort Collins to Denver and with smaller but notable centers of pop-

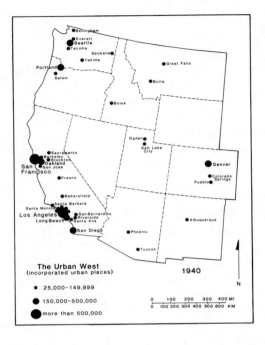

FIGURE 100. The urban West, 1940
(Source: United States, Bureau of
the Census, *Sixteenth Census of
the United States*, Census of
Population, 1940)

ulation at Colorado Springs, Pueblo, and Trinidad (fig. 101). Denver's nu-
merical and functional dominance within Colorado's urban hierarchy
were absolute: in 1940 its population of 322,000 included almost one-third
of the state's residents and was several times the size of Pueblo (52,000) or
Colorado Springs (37,000). Smaller urban centers at Greeley (15,595),
Boulder (12,958), and Fort Collins (12,251) served the densely settled
Northern Agricultural Zone, while more peripherally located towns met
the needs of hinterlands at places like Grand Junction (12,479), Alamosa
(5,613), Sterling (7,411), and La Junta (7,040). Dozens of smaller, local centers provided more limited goods and services in between these main urban nuclei. Only some mountain districts and the remote northwest corner were devoid of urban settlements.

   In terms of regional dominance, Denver's primary status in the state,
indeed across surrounding portions of the Mountain West and western
plains, remained unchallenged in 1940. Although smaller Colorado centers might have claimed limited primacy in such things as steel output
(Pueblo), bluebloods per capita (Colorado Springs), or intellectuals (Boulder), Denver became the capital of the "Rocky Mountain Empire," dominating political, financial, and cultural affairs throughout the state as well
as northward into Wyoming and eastward into the Nebraska Panhandle
and western Kansas.[23]

Denver's location placed it in the midst of a resource-rich zone that included metals, crops, livestock, and energy (oil and coal). The city's tradition as a regional trade center also expanded: by the end of the 1920s the city's wholesalers conducted over half the trade between Omaha and the Pacific Coast, involving over five hundred million dollars in goods annually. Denver banks increasingly became regional centers of industrial and finance capital for the interior West, the city remained a central nexus for rail, auto, and air transportation, and its political and cultural influence permeated the everyday experiences of almost everyone in the surrounding hinterlands.

Denver's dominance was dramatically reflected in the number and variety of federal offices in the city. The city's success in garnering federal representation was no accident: the Chamber of Commerce coordinated a "Little Capital of the United States" campaign during the 1930s, pressuring Washington through Colorado's congressional representatives to locate regional offices and federal employees in the state capital.[24] Boosters claimed that by the early 1940s Denver had more agencies of the federal government than any American city outside Washington, D.C. Some

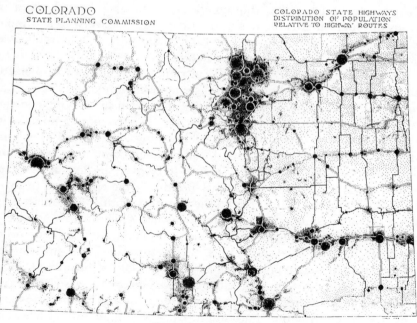

FIGURE 101. Colorado's population geography, 1936 (Source: Colorado State Planning Commission)

185 administrative offices of federal departments, bureaus, and divisions were located in Denver, and over 70 percent of those agencies claimed administrative jurisdiction beyond Colorado, suggesting Denver's truly regional importance. Major offices for the Departments of Agriculture (U.S. Forest Service), Interior (Fish and Wildlife Service, General Land Office, Geological Survey, Office of Indian Affairs, Bureau of Reclamation, National Park Service), Commerce (Bureau of the Census, and Weather Bureau), and Treasury (U.S. Mint and Internal Revenue) coordinated these federal activities in Colorado and many surrounding states. The temporary stimulus of New Deal programs increased the capital city's prominence during the 1930s, and many of the programs (such as the Soil and Conservation Service and the Social Security Administration) remained as permanent fixtures of Colorado life.

Denver's internal layout and landscape also reflected certain aspects of the new western urban geography, although its formative evolution in the first four decades of the twentieth century produced an urban scene that was an amalgam of eastern and California-style experiences. Much of Denver's built fabric in 1940 represented midwestern and eastern traditions of commercial and residential architecture. Its prominent downtown office blocks and bustling thoroughfares could have been located in dozens of other American cities of the time (fig. 102). Most of its fundamental political, economic, and cultural institutions merely replicated habits of urban life in the rest of the nation.

Still, the city possessed distinctive attributes that revealed its regional character. In the central city, Denver's emphasis on planning, civic improvement, and regulation of key utilities and urban services echoed elements of the City Beautiful movement that were becoming popular in many western American cities.[25] In such settings, open space, aesthetically pleasing public buildings, and well-planned community expansion added to the quality of life of its residents. In Denver, the downtown Civic Center with its new City and County Building were completed in 1932. Mayor Benjamin Stapleton created the Denver Planning Commission in 1926, and commissioners were anxious to fashion a high-quality urban environment devoid of the "evils of tremendous congestion and vile overcrowding" that typified eastern cities.[26] The efforts of the commissioners in concert with the supportive mayor and a variety of business leaders yielded substantial results. The city embarked on an aggressive program of park expansion, street widening, and tree plantings in the 1920s and 1930s that received national attention. Dozens of laudatory articles appeared in popular national magazines and in urban planning publications, portraying Denver as a model of urban evolution.

FIGURE 102. Cityscape: Denver's Sixteenth Street, circa 1940 (Courtesy Denver Public Library, Western History Collection)

Beyond the central city, suburban Denver mirrored common western urban patterns. Countless California-style bungalows were built between 1910 and 1930. The low roof lines, porches, numerous windows, flexible house plans, and general informality of the California bungalow agreed with westerners, and Denverites were no exception.[27] The expanding commercial landscape in Denver's urban periphery also displayed distinctive regional characteristics. Block after block of low-profile buildings, including many auto-related and tourist facilities, became ubiquitous features of the western American commercial strip, and Denver's Broadway, Santa Fe, and Colfax Avenues exemplified the phenomenon as the city spread outward between 1920 and 1940.

Much of Denver's metropolitan growth, however, did not involve the formal political annexation of outlying areas.[28] More complex processes were at work on Denver's periphery, paralleling a similar phenomenon that was unfolding in more dramatic ways across southern California. Independent suburbs such as Littleton, Englewood, Aurora, and Lakewood grew and became more closely integrated with Denver as improved roads, more automobile commuting, and a myriad of local economic linkages wove the outlying nuclei into a coherent metropolitan fabric with Denver as its spatial and functional center. In 1923 the Ingersoll-Rand Company established its headquarters in suburban Littleton, a corporate decision of considerable prescience that later became the western American norm. By 1940, the city of Englewood, located just south of Denver, became the ninth largest urban place in the state, even though in many ways it was functionally bound to the capital city, much as many of southern California's suburbs became satellites loosely orbiting about the central city of Los Angeles.

An Unpredictable Environment

Even with its growing cities, the West did not divorce itself from its unpredictable physical setting. The human consequences of the West's fickle environment increased greatly as new settlements probed into virtually every corner of the region between 1870 and 1920. New people, crops, and animals modified the setting, making it more vulnerable to the cyclical vagaries destined to revisit the region. The magnitude of these changes across the Arid West, propelled by the power and imprimatur of commodity- and industry-based capitalism, set the stage for an agricultural disaster by the early twentieth century.[29] Regional droughts in the 1890s and late 1910s, as well as long-documented instances of severe overgrazing dating back to the 1880s and 1890s, merely hinted at what was in store for large portions of the West in the 1930s. When dry years returned, destructive forces, both environmental and human, converged upon the region and produced a legacy of dust bowls, grasshopper invasions, and severe overgrazing that assumed legendary proportions.

Many variables shaped the evolution of the Dust Bowl, which gripped eastern Colorado during much of the 1930s.[30] The region's soils, particularly when disturbed, were subject to rapid wind erosion. Deposited from the Rocky Mountains, the brown and sandy soils of eastern Colorado were better adapted to modest grazing or well-maintained row crops than they were to the extensive wheat cultivation that became the norm in the region by the early twentieth century. Cyclical elements of the Plains climate provided another ingredient in the creation of the Dust Bowl. Record heat and drought ravaged eastern Colorado for most of the years between 1931 and 1939. Moisture deficits grew so large that there seemed little hope of "normal" patterns of rain and snowfall ever returning. Obviously, the stretch of dry and warm weather, not convincingly broken until the early 1940s, played a triggering role in the crop failures and dust storms of the period.

Most critical, however, were the human-induced changes across the region. Speculative pressures encouraged the plowing of the native plains landscape in the first third of the twentieth century. Farmers, many of them nonlocal, acquired large acreages and reaped quick gains, mostly through wheat cultivation of ever more marginal lands. Increasing agricultural mechanization also enabled farmers to plow and harvest larger acreages during the 1910s and 1920s. Once broken, the prairie soil's ability to resist wind erosion declined greatly. Wheat farming techniques did little to ameliorate the potential for erosion, although a straggling grain crop was better than naked topsoil. Ironically, as the drought intensified, conditions worsened because it was too dry even to plant wheat. The very understandable strategy of land abandonment actually enhanced the expansion of the Dust Bowl, and failure built upon failure as increasing drought, heat, and omnipresent dust prompted still more abandonment.

Beginning with isolated reports across the Texas Panhandle in 1932, the gritty regional extent of the phenomenon was not in evidence before the summer of 1934. By then huge dust storms blackened skies over large portions of the plains, with one early May blast moving an estimated three hundred million tons of prairie earth in a single day.[31] In succeeding years, the location of the worst-hit counties included the Oklahoma Panhandle, west Texas, western Kansas, eastern Colorado, and northeastern New Mexico. Impacts were made all the more capricious by the chimerical rains that might douse, even flood a county in May, then vanish in mid-June amid 105° temperatures and newly born dust clouds.

Within eastern Colorado, many farmers, though stung by the dry conditions of 1931–33, vowed to remain on their land, hoping for better spring planting conditions in 1934. But the spring rains never came. By the end of the year, farmers abandoned 46 percent of their cropland and concentrated instead on keeping their livestock alive. Total farm production plummeted. By the spring of 1935, regional-scale dusters obliterated the sky in Pueblo, Denver, and Fort Collins. The state's southeastern corner emerged as the worst-hit zone as residents were repeatedly thrown into virtual darkness at midday, cars and homes were all but buried in the accumulating dunes of former topsoil, and mysterious respiratory illnesses such as "dust pneumonia" took an increasing toll on the region's animal and human populations. Farmers who still had livestock searched in vain for surviving yucca stalks or thistles to feed their animals. Grasshoppers often stripped even these plants of their value, with the years 1934 and 1937 particularly notorious for insect invasions across much of eastern Colorado.[32]

The middle 1930s revealed a desolate and forlorn plains landscape, particularly in areas of eastern Colorado south of the Arkansas River. The parched visible scene must have scorched devastated residents even more

FIGURE 103. The new great American desert: Dust Bowl landscape in Baca County, Colorado (Courtesy Denver Public Library, Western History Collection)

than those lucky enough to be only briefly passing through (fig. 103). Writer Dorothy Hogner summarized the landscape around her as she traveled into the heart of the Dust Bowl:

> As we went south away from the valley of the Arkansas, the plains seemed to get increasingly drier. . . . There was literally nothing growing, but a few of the indomitable Russian thistles, and the desert yucca fruiting here and there. Aside from this, the plains were burned as if fire had swept them clean. . . . Here and there, ranch homes stood out above the flatness. . . . And they were in many cases deserted, the windows broken, the doors barred, the windmills still . . . the whole countryside looked as if a terrible plague had struck it.[33]

More dry years in 1936 and 1937 led to increased outmigration as farmers, despite their perennial optimism and a spate of New Deal relief programs, finally threw in the towel. Baca County, for example, severely affected by the drought, saw its population dwindle from twelve thousand residents in 1931 to half that number by the end of the decade.

Although land abandonment and outmigration were rational responses to the Dust Bowl disaster, some residents remained and were aided by federal agricultural programs directed at western drought relief as well as by innovations designed to mitigate the impact of aridity and wind.[34] As conditions worsened, President Roosevelt appointed a federal drought committee that coordinated activities of the FERA, AAA, FCA, CCC, and other New Deal agencies. Millions were spent in eastern Colorado in direct relief, in crop, livestock, and land purchases, and in public works projects. By the early 1940s the combination of federal programs and better growing conditions palpably improved eastern Colorado's farmlands, and the recovery of the visible scene was matched by at least the temporary stabilization of regional populations and communities.

The Great Plains was not the only area of the West plagued by human-environmental maladaptations in the early twentieth century. The region's publicly owned grazing lands, mostly national forest acreage in the mountains and unappropriated public domain in the deserts, were also subject to overuse. The fragile environments of these regions—their steep slopes, delicate vegetation, and extreme climates—hindered the recovery of damaged areas. Decades of human abuse took their toll: the West's 130 million acres of national forests and more than 140 million acres of other public grazing lands were worked hard between 1900 and 1920, with wartime demands for sheep and cattle putting particular pressure on range resources. The West's devastated livestock ranges finally prompted adjustments during the 1920s and 1930s, and the changes again demonstrated an increased level of federal involvement in shaping the region's cultural landscape.

Approximately 10 percent of the West's national forest lands were located in Colorado. Although a fee permit and grazing allotment system was imposed across the West and within Colorado in 1906, heavy use continued on national forests thereafter, particularly during World War I, when demands for meat prompted the Forest Service to allow over one million more head of livestock onto national forest ranges.[35] By the 1920s, however, federal officials saw the need for a comprehensive survey of range conditions across the West's overused forest lands. The survey suggested the wisdom of reducing livestock numbers on overused ranges, creating longer-term permits to stabilize range use on allotments, and preparing range management plans that established the actual carrying capacity of western lands. The policy shift helped the Forest Service reduce livestock grazing in the West by more than 50 percent between the late 1910s and the early 1940s. Colorado national forests participated in these adjustments, with the dry 1930s prompting further reductions in sheep and cattle on the state's distressed forest lands.

Adjustments to overuse came more slowly to the more than 140 million acres of western public grazing lands beyond the bounds of the regulated national forests. Unappropriated federal lands, typically in dry and isolated corners of the West, remained essentially open range. In Colorado, 6 million acres of unappropriated public domain were scattered across the state, particularly west of the Continental Divide, and they offered sheepmen and cattlemen a ready source of cheap forage. Colorado's longtime western slope congressman Edward Taylor was familiar with the wretched condition of his district's public grazing lands. He also knew dozens of ranchers who, despite their general mistrust of the federal government, recognized that regulations were needed to save these acres from destruction.

The catalyst for action came in the early 1930s, when climatic conditions deteriorated across the Intermountain West much as they did on the Great Plains. Grazing lands were decimated by poor forage growth and continued overuse. The Colorado congressman successfully passed the Taylor Grazing Act of 1934, legislation designed "to stop injury to the public grazing lands by preventing overgrazing and soil deterioration, to provide for orderly use, improvement and development . . . upon the public range."[36] It permanently closed all unreserved federal lands to homesteading, set up a new geography of federal grazing management districts in the West, and created a Division of Grazing within the Interior Department to administer the program.

Colorado's 6.5 million acres of public domain were divided into six districts with the largest blocks of newly regulated acreage in the state's remote northwest corner.[37] The same region of the state produced the first national director of the Interior Department's Grazing Division. With Taylor's urging, Farrington Carpenter, a lawyer and cattle rancher from Hayden, Colorado, was hired to oversee the program. Carpenter and his staff mapped and assessed range lands and developed a program of management that included a permit system, reasonable fees, and an emphasis on local participation by area ranchers in regulating rangelands in a particular district. Carpenter also garnered CCC, SCS, and WPA appropriations to erect fences, trails, and stock ponds and to assist in the general rehabilitation of the western range. By the early 1940s more than eleven million livestock grazed on public lands throughout the West, and the improving quality of the western range revealed the fortuitous combination of more careful federal regulation and better climatic conditions.

Managing Water in the West

Colorado and the West also shared the challenge of manipulating and managing the region's scarce water resources. That task grew more complex during the twentieth century, and decisions allocating water between western states and within Colorado exerted an increasing influence on the region's human geography. The water itself was a finite resource, subject to wide annual variations in supply and to never-ending increases in demand. For much of the West, the unpredictability inherent in that relationship came into sharp focus between 1900 and 1940. Put simply, the key western water problem was getting enough water to the right place at the right time, a classic spatial dilemma that was characterized by excesses of the precious resource in some locations with large deficits elsewhere.

Attempting to redress these perceived imbalances, the federal government, through its Bureau of Reclamation, the U.S. Army Corps of Engineers, and various New Deal–era agencies, made large public investments in the West's water infrastructure during the 1930s, adding hundreds of dams, irrigation canals, diversion tunnels, and municipal waterworks to the western landscape.[38] The results were wide-ranging: in addition to massive new federal signatures on the landscape, such as the Boulder, Fort Peck, and Bonneville Dams, the region's settlement pattern was altered as agricultural acreage increased and per-acre output of irrigated farmlands rose. Urban geographies were also reconstituted through the altered hydrologic calculus of federal largesse: many western cities were able to grow beyond the limits of their arid environmental settings. Particularly in the dry Southwest, accelerating patterns of urban growth after 1930 would not have been sustainable without the promised arrival of exotic moisture supplies from better-watered lands.

Because of Colorado's central and mountainous location in the heart of the West, it was in the thick of many of the region's major water management issues. As journalist John Gunther wrote in the 1940s, "Touch water, and you touch everything; about water the state is as sensitive as a carbuncle. Water—as is true all over the West—is everybody's chief preoccupation."[39] Indeed, Colorado's headwaters location was pivotal within the West: it was an important catchment zone for the Platte, Arkansas, Rio Grande, and Colorado River systems. Downriver states in every direction were keenly interested in how much water flowed out of Colorado. Their residents argued that it hardly seemed fair that Colorado had no limits placed on its use of water simply because seasonal snowpacks were deepest there.

Tensions between Colorado and its neighbors led to dozens of lawsuits, courtroom debates, appeals, multistate compacts and agreements, and an evolving federal presence. The story forms an important if litigious chapter in the changing geography of the twentieth-century West and is a reminder of how water both linked and divided the region. The general trend of such interstate water arrangements is clear: western states were unable to work out many of their differences and the federal government increasingly found itself mediating, arbitrating, and simply imposing itself into western water management issues.[40]

Colorado's turgid relationships with neighboring states over questions of water allocation began in the late nineteenth century. By 1890 Kansas farmers grumbled that the Arkansas River was monopolized by Colorado industrialists and irrigators. As public haggling between the two states grew, Congress argued that such interstate water matters should be arbitrated directly by the federal government. Others, such as John Wesley Powell, advocated a river basin approach, suggesting that interested states could work out their own regional-scale solutions to water allocation problems. Kansans, seeing no solutions on the horizon, sued Colorado in 1901, arguing that Coloradans were stealing their water.[41] Colorado lawyers retorted that their state had a sovereign right to resources within its bounds. Federal attorneys argued that the national government had an implied constitutional right to regulate the flow of any unnavigable river in the arid states.

The Supreme Court's decision in 1907 satisfied no one: it suggested that Kansas water users were not materially damaged by upstream users in Colorado, but it also denied Colorado's claims to absolute control of the Arkansas, suggesting that both states were entitled to a portion of the flow, based on an equitable sharing of the river's benefits. Another solution of sorts was hit upon with the crucial aid of federal funding: simply build a large dam on the river in eastern Colorado and increase the overall output of water to basin users in both states. With the muscle of the Army Corps of Engineers behind it, the federal government completed construction of the John Martin Dam west of Lamar in the late 1930s. A decade later Colorado and Kansas signed the Arkansas River Compact, further codifying water allocation policies between the two states.

To the north and east, Colorado's watery connections to Wyoming produced other conflicts during the same era.[42] The Platte River and a number of its tributaries such as the Laramie River originated in Colorado but then flowed through sections of southeastern Wyoming and central Nebraska on the way to join the Missouri River. Colorado farmers gazed longingly at the northward-flowing Laramie River, which began west of Fort Collins before joining the North Platte in Wyoming. Why not divert its flow eastward and into the South Platte's drainage in northern Colorado? Naturally, Wyoming interests protested the scheme. Wyoming filed suit in 1911, but it took eleven years for the Supreme Court to render a decision. Federal attorneys also participated, claiming again that unappropriated waters in the West were never ceded to the states and that Washington had the power to allocate such resources as it saw fit. As with *Kansas v. Col-*

orado (1907), the Court's decision on *Wyoming v. Colorado* (1922) frustrated all parties involved: the Court acknowledged Colorado's right to divert water from the North to the South Platte, but it recognized Wyoming's claim that seniority rights crossed state lines, thus guaranteeing senior Wyoming users a share of the Laramie's flow. Sidestepping issues of federal control, the Court did not rule explicitly on federal claims to the unappropriated waters of the West.

On the south, drainage patterns linked Colorado with other western neighbors, including New Mexico, Texas, and Mexico.[43] Water shortages in the 1890s and pressures from New Mexico and Texas prompted an 1896 embargo against the construction of new Colorado water storage facilities in the mountains above the San Luis Valley. In addition, a 1906 agreement guaranteed sixty thousand acre-feet of Rio Grande water to Mexico, prompting the construction of the Elephant Butte Dam along the river south of Albuquerque. A regional commission created a Rio Grande Compact in the 1920s to divide the Rio Grande's flow between interested states. More than a decade of exhaustive surveys and debates produced a permanent agreement in 1939 that acknowledged the rights of all states involved as well as those of Mexico, Native Americans in the region, and the federal government. A simpler agreement between New Mexico and Colorado was also worked out during the period (1923), adjudicating the flows of the nearby La Plata River southwest of Durango.

By far the most complex setting for managing the West's interstate water problems was the Colorado Basin, and once again Colorado was a central player.[44] The state's western slope was an essential watershed for the entire Colorado Basin, and snow that fell along Colorado's Continental Divide was increasingly seen as an invaluable regional resource after 1900. Fortunately for all the states involved, the dilemma of allocating the Colorado's annual flow was not thrown initially into the maw of Supreme Court litigation, where it might have remained for decades. Instead, events took a different course. One key participant in developing a western consensus over the Colorado River was a regional booster organization known as the League of the Southwest. Formed in 1917 by business and professional leaders in the region, the group worked cooperatively toward a basin development plan that appealed to a broad spectrum of growth-oriented interests across the Southwest. Conferences between interested state governors and federal representatives followed, and a meeting in Salt Lake City in early 1919 produced glimmerings of an emerging consensus on a regional allocation and development plan. Within two years and under intense federal arm-twisting, western governors presented President Warren Harding an interstate agreement that has henceforth shaped water policy along the entire course of the Colorado River.

Signed into law in 1922 (and fully in force by 1929), the Colorado Compact represented the successful negotiating prowess of parties that shared an honest desire to arrive at an agreeable solution. Unfortunately, their zeal for resolving the water management issues at hand was not matched by appropriate fact-finding when it came to the behavior of the river. Federal reclamation officials erroneously estimated the river's annual flow at more than seventeen million acre-feet of water, several million acre-feet above the actual average for most of the twentieth century. Upper basin states like Colorado were particularly at risk over these miscalculations because they promised to deliver 7.5 million acre-feet annually to the lower basin states. Ultimately, an international treaty with Mexico apportioned that country its own 1.5 million acre-feet of Colorado River water, further pressuring upper basin claims. The initial compact also left out Arizona, paving the way for additional conflicts and litigation in later years. Importantly for Colorado, however, it received more than half of the upper basin's allocation in the agreement and was guaranteed the right to divert Colorado River water to other basins. Colorado was effectively given a long-term incentive to encourage diversions so that it could argue that it was putting all of its allocation to beneficial use and so thwart lower basin claims to additional upper basin flows.

Within Colorado, intrastate transmountain water transfers reached a new level of activity between 1920 and 1940 as eastern slope users, both urban and rural, successfully tapped into western slope water surpluses. An increasingly elaborate infrastructure of ditches, tunnels, and reservoirs resulted from such initiatives, substantially redefining Colorado's geography of water allocation.

The pace of transmountain transfers accelerated greatly between 1920 and 1935.[45] The Busk-Ivanhoe Tunnel, an abandoned Colorado Midland Railroad right-of-way, began carrying water from the western slope's Roaring Fork River to the Arkansas River after 1922. By the end of the 1920s another railroad passage through the Rockies caught the eye of thirsty eastern-slope residents. West of Denver, the Moffat Tunnel was completed for the Denver and Salt Lake Railroad in 1929, and the Denver Water Board leased the rights to the pioneer bore hole for water diversions in later years. The dry 1930s and New Deal–era federal financing spurred Denver's city fathers into action, and residents were benefiting from Fraser River (a tributary of the Colorado) water by 1936. Several years later, a similar project over Jones Pass brought Williams Fork (of the Colorado) water to Denver, mostly to update and expand the city's municipal sewage treatment system. Meanwhile, a larger diversion tapped the Roaring Fork River, ran the water under the Rockies through the Twin Lakes Tunnel, and stored it in the Twin Lakes Reservoir near Leadville for use in the lower Arkansas River basin. Dating from 1935, the Twin Lakes project, pushed hard by beet and melon farmers east of Pueblo, also benefited from substantial federal assistance.

As impressive as these alterations of natural hydrography were, they paled in complexity and significance when compared to the labyrinthine infrastructure of the Colorado–Big Thompson Project, which, though begun in the 1930s and opened for initial use in 1947, was not finished until 1954.[46] Once completed, the ambitious federally funded diversion ranked as one of the most dramatic human signatures upon Colorado's twentieth-century landscape. Hatched in the imaginative minds and watering mouths of eastern slope agriculturalists, the project took Colorado Basin water from near Grand Lake and passed it under the Continental Divide, debouching it into the Big Thompson River near Estes Park. In addition to the water diversion, hydroelectricity was generated in the process, helping the project to pay for itself.

The project profoundly affected the Colorado mountain landscape as well as that of the South Platte Valley. Eventually it included ten reservoirs, fifteen dams, twenty-five tunnels totaling thirty-five miles, eleven canals, three pump plants, six power plants, and forty-three power substations. On the west side of the divide, water was stored at Granby Reservoir and Shadow Mountain Lake and then taken to Grand Lake just to the west of the mountain crest. A thirteen-mile tunnel bored through the Rockies took the water beneath Rocky Mountain National Park, with the water emerging near Estes Park. Power plants along the Big Thompson River generated electricity as water tumbled east toward a series of reservoirs that eventually released it onto the fields of South Platte Valley farmers. When finished in the 1950s, this great west-to-east siphon became an enduring regional symbol: to many it suggested an elegant and ambitious correction of nature's shortcomings, while to others it more poignantly and provocatively revealed the lengths westerners were willing to go to defeat the region's natural limitations in the name of unquestioned economic expansion. Whatever its ultimate legacy, the project remains one of the region's most visible monuments to the westerners' dynamic encounter with their environment and to the undeniable role played by the federal purse in refashioning the region's cultural landscapes and economy.

Colorado and Its Regions

By the eve of World War II, the inevitability of the modern world permeated even the isolated corners of the state. Even so, Colorado's major regions experienced different transitions during the interwar period. Each segment of the state, representative of the West's larger diversity, traveled distinctive paths to modernization, and these varied trajectories were reflected in patterns of settlement, rates of population change, and in the evolution of the visible scene. Thus landscape and life in the mountains differed from that of the plains; Denver's increasingly affluent suburbs contrasted sharply with the dying coal towns of southern Colorado; and eastern and western slope interests eyed each other as suspiciously as ever when it came to questions of resource development or state budget expenditures.

Human geographies in mountainous Colorado were shaped by several formative processes between 1920 and 1940. Populations changed little overall, although that general pattern fails to reveal the significant internal transformations that were taking place within the region. In the 1920s most mountain communities experienced sustained population declines as mining remained mired in recession. The 1930s, however, for a variety of reasons, brought relatively better times.[47] Teller County (Cripple Creek), for example, lost 38 percent of its population in the earlier decade but gained back 56 percent during the 1930s. A gradual end to alpine isolation helps explain the mountain renaissance. The twin impacts of the automobile and paved highways brought mountain centers much closer to the rest of the world. As the middle class grew more mobile and tempted by the pleasures of camping, fishing, and hiking, Colorado's national parks and forests were a natural destination for westbound vacationers. Even during the Depression, annual visits to Rocky Mountain National Park more than doubled. Skiing gained in popularity, too, especially as facilities were upgraded at Winter Park (near Denver), Berthoud Pass, Aspen, and Gunnison.

Colorado's mountain counties received a large federal stimulus during the New Deal years. Although the counties were not densely populated, their recreational, forest, and water resources prompted large investments by the CCC, WPA, and other federal aid programs. The modest turnaround in mountain mining, also a function of federal policy, reversed the economic and demographic decline that accompanied that sector's long downward spiral. The Climax operation near Leadville was the region's quintessential reborn mining venture as rising demand for molybdenum, particularly in the auto industry, spurred tremendous activity during the 1930s, an upsurge further stimulated during the war years.

The Piedmont followed a somewhat different regional course during the period, although it, too, was experiencing a pivotal economic and cultural shift that set the stage for lasting geographical changes. The northern Piedmont, already the most densely populated part of the state, increased its relative demographic, political, and economic dominance:

Denver County grew by more than sixty thousand, and even more rural Weld County saw its numbers jump almost 20 percent between 1920 and 1940. The northern Piedmont remained the most accessible of Colorado's regions: paved roads came early, and by 1940 the area was blanketed with a density of good highways that was comparable to many areas of the Midwest and East. Colorado Springs and Pueblo also grew modestly, although Pueblo in particular was hit hard economically by the Depression's downturn in manufacturing.

Elsewhere the Piedmont fared relatively well during the troubled 1930s. The Northern Agricultural Zone escaped the worst of the Dust Bowl. Denver's economic diversity and its regional role as a center of federal largesse also cushioned the Depression's impact. Most fundamentally, the era marked the transition when this most metropolitan and modern of Colorado's regions became fully integrated with the American economy and society. An abundance of landscape signatures told the story—automobiles, mechanizing agriculture, chain store businesses, new suburban settlement patterns, movie theaters and radio towers—all suggested an evolving western setting increasingly shaped by the nationally converging leanings of its residents.

Colorado's eastern plains displayed largely stricken landscapes and communities at the end of the 1930s. Most eastern plains counties experienced significant absolute population losses through the period. Even without the Depression and the withering reality of the Dust Bowl, Colorado's plains region was in for some challenging geographical transitions after 1920. Although many eastern Colorado counties saw modest population gains during the 1920s, the arrival of the automobile, the quickening mechanization of agriculture, and the move toward larger, fewer farms encouraged a growing number of young people to leave the land and search for new lives in other, often more urban settings.[48] Farm towns struggled to hold their own in such an environment. With the crash in farm prices and the arrival of the "Dirty Thirties," these demographic trends were painfully accelerated, producing the ubiquitous signatures of abandonment so commonly seen on the plains landscape. Also apparent, however, were visible signatures of massive federal response: by the late 1930s, just about every plains county could point to better roads, new power lines, assortments of New Deal–era public buildings, added windbreaks, and examples of contour plowing and strip farming.

In the state's southern periphery, sustained declines in coal production after World War I contributed to employment shrinkage and population outmigration in Huerfano and Las Animas Counties. These trends worsened in the late 1920s and early 1930s as labor troubles, corporate mine closures, increased discrimination against Hispano workers, and a deteriorating agricultural economy added to the area's regional difficulties. Here, landscapes of industrial abandonment vied with those of nearby rural decline to reveal some of the state's hardest-hit localities during the Depression.

Remarkably, the nearby San Luis Valley fared much better.[49] All five valley counties gained population between 1920 and 1940, with Alamosa County more than doubling its count during the period. Most important, the area's agricultural sector performed relatively well: although everyone was hurt in the low prices of the early 1930s, the increasingly specialized production of potatoes, lettuce, cauliflower, and peas found continuing commercial markets. Irrigation also protected valley farmers from the worst vicissitudes of dry farming so common on the eastern plains. In fact, a number of failed plains farmers were relocated to the San Luis Valley by the federal government's Resettlement Administration in the late 1930s. At the same time, the San Luis Valley received all of the New Deal stimuli seen elsewhere in the state, and the elevated government payrolls contributed significantly to the growth of such valley towns as Alamosa. The cultural mix also evolved: Japanese farmers from California brought new agricultural techniques, and more Hispano laborers, many direct from Mexico, filtered into the valley's employment pool.

A complex interwar picture emerged across the state's western slope, producing a variety of demographic, economic, and cultural responses. Mesa County and its principal town of Grand Junction were relative bright spots. The county grew 16 percent in the 1920s and an even more impressive 30 percent in the 1930s. Although fruit growers were hurt by the same price declines as every farming region, the buoyancy of national markets and the timely injection of federal aid prompted a quick recovery by the early 1940s. Modest population gains in Delta, Montrose, La Plata, and Montezuma Counties also attested to the relative vitality of these crop-growing areas in comparison to the disaster unfolding on the eastern plains. Better highways as well as proximity to numerous national forests, Mesa Verde National Park, and Black Canyon of the Gunnison and Colorado National Monuments buoyed the tourism economies of several western slope towns, including Durango, Cortez, and Grand Junction. Colorado's northwest corner, however, remained one of the state's quietest and least accessible localities: earlier dreams of a major rail link never materialized and later highway improvements threaded only a single paved road, U.S. 40, through the area. Both Moffat and Rio Blanco Counties lost population between 1920 and 1940. Isolated activities in the oil and gas business could not counterbalance an agricultural bust, mostly related to failed dry farming ventures and weakening livestock markets, which gripped the area by the late 1920s.

Envoi: Location, Place, and Landscape

As we complete our reconnaissance of the Centennial State, it is appropriate to revisit the fundamental elements of the historical geographer's view. Initially we saw that location, place, and landscape were essential concepts in producing a coherent geographical synthesis. Colorado's evolution suggests that these geographical themes are played out somewhat differently in each of the state's varied regions but that a larger set of ideas can also help us understand common processes at work across the state, indeed across much of the West. Thus, throughout these geographical explorations we considered the changing chronological and spatial applicability of (1) the *doctrine of first effective settlement*—that is, the argument that initial occupants exerted an especially formative influence on localities; (2) the setting of Colorado and the West as a unique *cultural meeting ground;* (3) the predominance of *capitalism and liberal individualism* as guiding regional leitmotivs; (4) the formative, often fickle role played by a *dynamic western environment;* and (5) the *close relation between human geographies and political institutions* in shaping land and life in Colorado and the American West.

Location

Colorado's basic pattern of settlements and the networks of circulation that linked them were forged between 1860 and 1920. Native American and European imprints, as well as the pre-1860 Anglo-American presence proved ephemeral, except to establish a base of geographical knowledge across the region. Characteristically, the first large-scale, post-1860 capital investments into transportation infrastructure and commercially oriented economic enterprises gave formative shape and structure to the state's fundamental spatial organization. Once initial patterns and linkages were established, subsequent flows of people, capital, and products usually reinforced existing networks of activity (fig. 104).

The region's environment, including its climate, soils, water, and mineral base, contributed to Colorado's settlement geography, but it was the decisions of key individuals and investors, both local and nonlocal, that gave structure and order to the state's overall areal organization and its emergent capitalist economy. It also must be emphasized that the resulting spatial patterns represented neither a coherent regional plan of development nor the spontaneous and providential expression of a frontier populace; rather, they resulted from thousands of decisions by ordinary Coloradans whose lives were oriented around broadly shared, mostly unchallenged, and individually realized goals of capital accumulation and re-

FIGURE 104. Geography and location: building links between Denver and Colorado Springs in the early twentieth century (Courtesy Denver Public Library, Western History Collection)

gional economic growth that, with almost breathless rapidity, reconfigured Colorado's fundamental areal organization within a few decades. In addition, once enduring American political control was asserted by the mid-nineteenth century, the phalanx of essentially private entrepreneurial capital was complemented and assisted by sympathetic territorial, state, and national governments. For example, both railroad and automobile inroads into the state were supported by public institutions that actively encouraged and sometimes directly financed such critical infrastructural initiatives.

Place

Colorado places produced in this onrush of settlement were the collective expressions of the people who inhabited them. Colorado's varied regional societies created diverse social geographies and many different examples of how people invested meaning in place (fig. 105). As the doctrine of first effective settlement asserts, early arrivals exerted a disproportionately large influence upon subsequent community evolution and institutions. But the incredible mobility and dynamism of Colorado's diverse populations suggest that the formative power of such initial influences was weaker here than on more slowly evolving frontiers. Thus social geographies in place in 1870 were not necessarily there in 1900: rural areas experienced rapid population turnover with varied boom and bust periods, and cities such as Denver and Pueblo possessed enormous social plasticity that changed neighborhoods readily over time as new mixtures of class-, occupation-, and ethnic-based communities formed and dissolved upon the urban scene.

For most Coloradans, whatever their location, community was most intensely grounded in the integrity of the nuclear family. Beyond the home, ethnic and church affiliations as well as local neighborhoods—both rural and urban—held social meaning for many. Most broadly and with increasing significance after 1920 was a widely shared collection of popular cultural beliefs anchored in a common national political experience and in the virtues of liberal individualism, typically expressed in material terms

FIGURE 105. Geography and place: creating community at Red Rocks Amphitheater near Denver, constructed by the Civilian Conservation Corps, 1936–41 (Courtesy Denver Public Library, Western History Collection)

and through the transformative technologies of mass consumer-based capitalism.

That said, the sheer vitality of the West's cultural diversity and the new ways in which groups mingled and clashed within the region is also abundantly illustrated through the Colorado experience. Native American communities, themselves dynamic over time, were permanently disrupted and all but removed by European and Anglo-American invasions after 1700. Hispano settlements, the relict articulation of Spain's presence in the Southwest, possessed more staying power, particularly across Colorado's southern periphery, where changing political and economic conditions produced a variety of adaptive responses allowing the survival and even the spatial expansion of Hispanic influences after 1860. Native-born Anglo Americans, who made up the majority of the state's new residents between 1860 and 1940, reflected a strong midwestern bent, both in terms of their origins and in their ongoing political and cultural predispositions. But Colorado, as much as any western state, also felt the varied imprint of foreign-born European populations, with Germans, Italians, and a variety of eastern Europeans shaping communities in many settings, both agricultural and industrial. Often redefining and ultimately weakening such traditional ethnic ties were relentless pressures of Americanization as well as new definitions of community based on one's class and occupation rather than on one's homeland. Ultimately, however, Colorado places were utterly personal creations, localities invested with meaning by varied peoples who tied their life's hopes to a miner's cabin and nearby claim, to a new farmhouse and its surrounding fields, or to a rented tenement and the factory down the street.

Landscape

While the thousands of places created through those juxtapositions of intermingled everyday lives came and went with the people they sustained, the legacy of human occupance was also etched upon the Colorado scene in more enduring and visible ways. The cultural landscape, a material artifact of human presence, is dense with meaning and full of insights into how people interacted with the natural environment, reshaped it, and apprehended it. The Colorado landscape demonstrates that fundamental changes, often with enduring environmental consequences, were ubiquitous across the Centennial State between 1860 and 1940 (fig. 106). Illustrating the doctrine of first effective settlement, some elements of the landscape, such as place names and initial land survey patterns, became lasting legacies of an area's earliest European and American inhabitants. Most landscape modifications, however, came much later. Unlike the ba-

FIGURE 106. Geography and landscape: transforming the nineteenth-century environment, mining in Leadville, Colorado (Courtesy Denver Public Library, Western History Collection)

sic organizing structure of the settlement system, largely in place by 1920, the pace and significance of post-1920 human landscape modifications increased as rising twentieth-century populations and ever more transmogrifying technologies reshaped the visual scene in ways impossible to anticipate a generation earlier. Thus although Colorado's basic geography of settlements and linkages was well established early in the twentieth century, the precise look and texture of those settings evolved with increasing rapidity thereafter.

Once fundamental patterns of settlement were established, the cultural landscape changes that followed reflected the importance of several of our guiding regional themes. Multicultural signatures were abundantly present: Hispano place names and Catholic churches, Mormon street plans and irrigation works, Italian social clubs and corner stores, working-class labor unions and fraternal meeting halls all symbolized the ongoing integrity of cultural inheritances brought to Colorado by its varied populations. The typically close spatial juxtaposition of these diverse signatures as well as the daily spatial mixing of their creators were also signs, often unappreciated at the time, that propinquity would bring with it forces of assimilation and cultural mingling. These processes, though never fulfilling the stereotype of the "melting pot," nevertheless produced, often within a generation, a new cultural amalgam unique to the region. As we have seen, the landscape particularly reflected that inclination toward cultural convergence after 1920 as homogenizing national forces diminished the power of local cultural identities.

Colorado's cultural landscape, no matter the city or subregion, also exuded the dominance and vitality of capitalism. Early on, imprints included the lightly etched signatures of pioneer-era resource extraction. After gold was found in sizable quantities, more dramatic and lasting impacts of commodity-based and industrial-era capitalism quickly revealed themselves by 1880. This phase centered on the large-scale production and processing of the state's considerable resource base, much of it for export to the East. Finally, in still fragmentary ways between 1920 and 1940, we also traced the selective decline of commodity-based and industrial-era capitalism in the state, particularly in some of its agricultural and mining regions. Abandoned plains farms, depopulated silver mining towns, and struggling coal and steel industries offered visual testimony to the human and structural adjustments precipitated by such a shift. This transition, however, also involved the rise of postindustrial consumer-oriented capitalism across the Colorado scene that paralleled its appearance elsewhere in America during the interwar period.

Through these evolutionary phases within Colorado and the West, capitalism was not just a series of economic arrangements and institutions that bound together centers of production and consumption; rather, it was a way of life, an encounter with the world that brought with it a series of widely understood attitudes and expectations. The landscape itself became an expression as well as an instrument of that way of life: the everyday world of frontier trading posts, mining camps, company coal towns, grain elevators, railroad stations, suburban homes, and commercial strips reflected the mostly unquestioned dominance of capitalism in its varied forms. In such a way, the landscape acted as a pervasive cultural symbol that vividly articulated geographies of economic and cultural power as they were played out in particular places, and it reinforced, shaped, and confirmed the shared ways in which Coloradans lived their lives.[50]

The creation of a landscape of capitalism, though surely structured by national, even global economic imperatives, remained grounded in the character of particular localities. In other words, setting mattered. Colorado's human geographic evolution was intimately molded by the interplay of human intent and natural environment. Native Americans had a close relationship with Colorado's varied natural resource base, and later Spanish, French, and American explorers were drawn to the region by its rumored natural abundance. Indeed, as rapid inflows of population occurred after 1860, Colorado's metal, soil, and energy resources acted as powerful magnets that shaped initial destinations and subsequent fortunes of new immigrants. As this volume's regional structure suggests, natural settings played pivotal roles as new occupants invested their time, money, and lives in the state's varied localities.

Over time, the character and very definition of the state's natural resources also changed with the needs and technological adaptations of its inhabitants: worthless oil became valuable in an age of automobiles; dry farming opened the high plains to new forms of cropping; and alpine settings became valued more for their scenery than for their silver. However, just as surely as humans had the power to modify and to reevaluate their physical setting, nature also proved unpredictable, prompting constant human adjustments, often at quite a price. Polluted mountain rivers, silted irrigation canals, dry wells, tapped-out gold mines, devastated rangelands, and dust-blown plains were only some of the reminders on the Colorado landscape that the state's environment, though rich and spacious, was also fragile, vulnerable to precisely the kind of rapid development that characterized the Colorado scene between 1860 and 1940.

The unfolding geography of political control across Colorado and the West also suggests that these institutions contributed important elements to the cultural landscape. The defining of political space began with the loosely bounded territories of varied Native American peoples followed by the broadly asserted but little-pursued claims of the Spanish and French. Of much more enduring import were American declarations of control, which were accompanied by accelerating patterns of exploration and permanent settlement between 1840 and 1860. Thereafter, a complex web of local, territorial, state, and federal institutions structured the course of settlement and the conduct of society through a political process that included the survey and disposal of land, frameworks for legally incorporating places and businesses, initiatives for developing infrastructure and industry, and thousands of laws designed to promote a civil society. For the most part, the political process at all levels remained closely intertwined with the state's dominant private economic institutions, although the rising power of federal authority after 1890 created friction, well illustrated by the turn-of-the century clamor over managing the state's national forest lands. The federal role became even more evident during the New Deal, when no corner of the state's landscape remained untouched by federal relief, stimulus, and development programs.

Coloradans produced a mosaic of localities that varied in their texture and character. Many threads contributed to these new geographies: a dense, multilayered, and spatially variable physical framework established their broad contours; a set of political and economic imperatives structured their form and function; a layering of diverse cultural elements gave personality and feel to the fabric; and, perhaps most important, the experiences of individuals shaped the everyday reality of Colorado landscapes, imputing each place with their evanescent but palpable presence. The product of these interweavings was nothing simpler or more complex than the Colorado scene itself. Recalling L. C. McClure's photograph of South Park, our Colorado explorations remind us that by studying past geographies we can learn to look more intently at the ordinary world around us and see in the process both a clearer vision of who we once were as well as who we are in the process of becoming. For Colorado and all the American West, that is an exhilarating and sobering task.

Notes

Chapter 1: Colorado

1. W. C. Jones and E. B. Jones, *Photo by McClure: The Railroad, Cityscape and Landscape Photographs of L. C. McClure* (Boulder: Pruett, 1983).

2. Geographers address the West's internal diversity in D. W. Meinig, "American Wests: Preface to a Geographical Interpretation," *Annals of the Association of American Geographers* 62 (1972): 159–84, and in William Wyckoff and Lary M. Dilsaver, eds., *The Mountainous West: Explorations in Historical Geography* (Lincoln: University of Nebraska Press, 1995). Rising interest in such questions among western American historians is suggested in Dan Flores, "The Rocky Mountain West: Fragile Space, Diverse Place," *Montana: The Magazine of Western History* 45, 1 (1995): 46–56, and by Susan Neel, "A Place of Extremes: Nature, History, and the American West," *Western Historical Quarterly* 25 (1994): 488–505.

3. D. W. Meinig illustrates the approach at the national scale in his *The Shaping of America* (New Haven and London: Yale University Press): vol. 1: *Atlantic America, 1492–1800* (1986), vol. 2: *Continental America, 1800–1867* (1993), and vol. 3: *Transcontinental America, 1850–1915* (1998). Attention to a settlement systems approach is also illustrated in such regional studies as Carville V. Earle, *The Evolution of a Tidewater Settlement System: All Hallow's Parish, Maryland, 1650–1783*, University of Chicago, Department of Geography, Research Paper no. 170 (Chicago, 1975); James Lemon, *The Best Poor Man's Country: A Geographical Study of Early Southeastern Pennsylvania* (Baltimore: Johns Hopkins University Press, 1972); and Robert Mitchell, *Commercialism and Frontier: Perspectives on the Early Shenandoah Valley* (Charlottesville: University Press of Virginia, 1977). Geographers pose useful conceptual frameworks detailing the evolution of urban systems in Michael Conzen, "The Maturing Urban System in the United States, 1840–1910," *Annals of the Association of American Geographers* 67 (1977): 88–108; David Ralph Meyer, "A Dynamic Model of the Integration of Frontier Urban Places into the United States System of Cities," *Economic Geography* 56 (1980): 120–40; Allen Pred, *Urban Growth and City-Systems in the United States, 1840–1860* (Cambridge: Harvard University Press, 1980); and James Vance, *The Merchant's World: The Geography of Wholesaling* (Englewood Cliffs, N.J.: Prentice Hall, 1970). Two empirical examples of such an approach from Colorado are William Wyckoff, "Incorporation as a Factor in Formation of an Urban System," *Geographical Review* 77 (1987): 279–92, and Wyckoff, "Revising the Meyer Model: Denver and the National Urban System, 1859–1879," *Urban Geography* 9 (1988): 1–18.

4. The world-systems approach illustrating the expanding global reach of capitalism is explored in Immanuel Wallerstein, *The Capitalist World-Economy* (New York: Cambridge University Press, 1979), and Wallerstein, *The Politics of the World-Economy: The States, the Movements, and the Civilizations* (Cambridge: Cambridge University Press, 1984). Nationally, the perspective is employed by Meinig in *Atlantic America, Continental America,* and *Transcontinental America* to trace America's imperial and economic expansion. Regionally, western American historians assess the impacts of capitalism in Patricia Nelson Limerick, *The Legacy of Conquest: The Unbroken Past of the American West* (New York: W. W. Norton, 1987); William G. Robbins, *Colony and Empire: The Capitalist Transformation of the American West* (Lawrence: University Press of Kansas, 1994); Richard White, *"It's Your Misfortune and None of My Own": A New History of the American West* (Norman: University of Oklahoma Press, 1991); and Donald Worster, *Rivers of Empire: Water, Aridity, and the Growth of the American West* (New York: Oxford University Press, 1985).

5. The geographer's concern with culture and community is discussed in Meinig, "American Wests"; Meinig, "The Continuous Shaping of America: A Prospectus for Geographers and Historians," *American Historical Review* 83 (1978): 1186–1205; and Wilbur Zelinsky, *The Cultural Geography of the United States: A Revised Edition* (Englewood Cliffs, N.J.: Prentice Hall, 1992). A similar emphasis is urged in Limerick, *Legacy of Conquest,* 27, 179–292, and in White, *New History,* 298–327. Examples of studies in social geography, social history, and community evolution in the Transmississippi West include Alvar Carlson, *The Spanish-American Homeland: Four Centuries in New Mexico's Río Arriba* (Baltimore: Johns Hopkins University Press, 1990); David M. Emmons, *The Butte Irish: Class and Ethnicity in an American Mining Town, 1875–1925* (Urbana: University of Illinois Press, 1989); Katherine Harris, *Long Vistas: Women and Families on Colorado Homesteads* (Niwot: University Press of Colorado, 1993); Jeanne Kay, "Landscapes of Women and Men: Rethinking the Regional Historical Geography of the United States and Canada," *Journal of Historical Geography* 17 (1991): 435–52; Richard L. Nostrand, *The Hispano Homeland* (Norman: University of Oklahoma Press, 1992); John G. Rice, "The Role of Culture and Community in Frontier Prairie Farming," *Journal of Historical Geography* 3 (1977): 155–75; and Kathleen Underwood, *Town Building on the Colorado Frontier* (Albuquerque: University of New Mexico Press, 1987).

6. The cultural landscape theme in American cultural and historical geography is emphasized in Michael P. Conzen, ed., *The Making of the American Landscape* (Boston: Unwin Hyman, 1990); D. W. Meinig, *The Interpretation of Ordinary Landscapes: Geographical Essays* (New York: Oxford University Press, 1979); Thomas R. Vale and Geraldine R. Vale, *Western Images, Western Landscapes: Travels Along U.S. 89* (Tucson: University of Arizona Press, 1989); William Wyckoff, *The Developer's Frontier: The Making of the Western New York Landscape* (New Haven and London: Yale University Press, 1988); and Zelinsky, *Cultural Geography.*

7. Among environmental historians, important studies suggesting major themes are William Cronon, *Nature's Metropolis: Chicago and the Great West*

(New York: W. W. Norton, 1991); Cronon, *Changes in the Land: Indians, Colonists, and the Ecology of New England* (New York: Hill and Wang, 1992); William deBuys, *Enchantment and Exploitation: The Life and Hard Times of a New Mexico Mountain Range* (Albuquerque: University of New Mexico Press, 1985); Richard White, "American Environmental History: The Development of a New Historical Field," *Pacific Historical Review* 54 (1985): 297–335; and Donald Worster, ed., *The Ends of the Earth* (Cambridge: Cambridge University Press, 1988), 289–307.

Among geographers, studies in human-environment interactions in the West include Conrad J. Bahre, *A Legacy of Change: Historical Human Impact on Vegetation in the Arizona Borderlands* (Tucson: University of Arizona Press, 1991); Craig Colten and Lary Dilsaver, "Historical Geography of the Environment: A Preliminary Literature Review," in Dilsaver and Colten, eds., *The American Environment: Interpretations of Past Geographies* (Savage, Md.: Rowman and Littlefield, 1992), 1–18; Richard Francaviglia, *Hard Places: Reading the Landscape of America's Historic Mining Districts* (Iowa City: University of Iowa Press, 1991); Randall Rohe, "Man and the Land: Mining's Impact in the Far West," *Arizona and the West* 28 (1986): 299–338; Robert A. Sauder, *The Lost Frontier: Water Diversion in the Growth and Destruction of Owens Valley Agriculture* (Tucson: University of Arizona Press, 1994); Thomas T. Veblen and Diane C. Lorenz, *The Colorado Front Range: A Century of Ecological Change* (Salt Lake City: University of Utah Press, 1991); and William Wyckoff and Katherine Hansen, "Settlement, Livestock Grazing, and Environmental Change in Southwest Montana, 1860–1990," *Environmental History Review* 15 (1991): 45–71.

8. Within the field of American history, important examples of this perspective include Anne Farrar Hyde, *An American Vision: Far Western Landscape and National Culture, 1820–1920* (New York: New York University Press, 1990); Roderick Nash, *Wilderness and the American Mind* (New Haven and London: Yale University Press, 1982); and Alfred Runte, *National Parks: The American Experience* (Lincoln: University of Nebraska Press, 1984). Scholarship that examines western images in art and literature includes Henry Nash Smith, *Virgin Land: The American West as Symbol and Myth* (New York: Vintage Books, 1950); Patricia Trenton and Peter H. Hassrick, *The Rocky Mountains: A Vision for Artists in the Nineteenth Century* (Norman: University of Oklahoma Press, 1983); and William H. Truettner, ed., *The West as America: Reinterpreting Images of the Frontier, 1820–1920* (Washington, D.C.: Smithsonian Institution Press, 1991). Cultural and historical geographers have also contributed to the literature on perception and images of the American West. For example, see John L. Allen, *Passage Through the Garden: Lewis and Clark and the Image of the American Northwest* (Urbana: University of Illinois Press, 1975); Allen, "Horizons of the Sublime: The Invention of the Romantic West," *Journal of Historical Geography* 18 (1992): 27–40; and Brian W. Blouet and Merlin Lawson, eds., *Images of the Plains: The Role of Human Nature in Settlement* (Lincoln: University of Nebraska Press, 1975).

9. Zelinsky, *Cultural Geography*, 13.

10. The importance of this factor is discussed in Edward K. Muller, "Regional Urbanization and the Selective Growth of Towns in North American Regions," *Journal of Historical Geography* 3 (1977): 21–39.

11. The American West as a region of multiple cultures and as a zone of cultural mixing and conflict are themes discussed in Terry G. Jordan, *North American Cattle-Ranching Frontiers: Origins, Diffusion, and Differentiation* (Albuquerque: University of New Mexico Press, 1993); Limerick, *Legacy of Conquest*; Meinig, "American Wests"; White, *New History*; and Zelinsky, *Cultural Geography*.

12. This ideological and economic milieu is explored in Gunther Barth, *Instant Cities: Urbanization and the Rise of San Francisco and Denver* (New York: Oxford University Press, 1975); Lemon, *Best Poor Man's Country*; Mitchell, *Commercialism and Frontier*; and Robbins, *Colony and Empire*. The vagaries of the economic cycle receive particular attention in two recent general western American histories. See Limerick, *Legacy of Conquest*, and White, *New History*. The classic statement asserting the West's colonial status is Bernard De Voto, "The West: A Plundered Province," *Atlantic* 169 (August 1934): 255–64. De Voto is revisited in William Robbins, "The 'Plundered Province' Thesis and Recent Historiography of the American West," *Pacific Historical Review* 55 (1986): 577–97. Center-periphery relations within the West are assessed from various perspectives in Meinig, "American Wests"; Peter Wiley and Robert Gottlieb, *Empires in the Sun: The Rise of the New American West* (New York: G. P. Putnam's Sons, 1982); and Donald Worster, "Beyond the Agrarian Myth," in Patricia Limerick, Clyde Milner, and Charles Rankin, eds., *Trails: Toward a New Western History* (Lawrence: University Press of Kansas, 1991), 21.

13. The limits and unpredictability of the western environment are discussed in Neel, "Place of Extremes"; John Wesley Powell, *Report on the Lands of the Arid Region of the United States* (Washington, D.C.: Government Printing Office, 1879); Wallace Stegner, *The American West as Living Space* (Ann Arbor: University of Michigan Press, 1987); Walter Prescott Webb, *The Great Plains* (New York: Grosset and Dunlap, 1931); White, *New History*, 212–35; and Donald Worster, *An Unsettled Country: Changing Landscapes of the American West* (Albuquerque: University of New Mexico Press, 1994), ix–xii, 91–120.

14. The important role of government in shaping the West is discussed from a variety of perspectives in William H. Goetzmann, *Exploration and Empire: The Explorer and the Scientist in the Winning of the American West* (New York: Vintage Books, 1966); Limerick, *Legacy of Conquest*, 78–96, 293–321; Michael P. Malone, "Beyond the Last Frontier: Toward a New Approach to Western American History," *Western Historical Quarterly* 20 (1989): 409–27; Meinig, "American Wests," Meinig, *Continental America*, 170–218; White, *New History*; and Wilbur Zelinsky, "The Imprint of Central Authority," in Conzen, *Making of the American Landscape*, 311–34.

15. This humanistic dimension within geography can be explored through John Fraser Hart, "The Highest Form of the Geographer's Art," *Annals of the Association of American Geographers* 72 (1982): 1–29; D. W. Meinig, "Geography as an Art," *Transactions of the Institute of British Geographers*, n.s., 8 (1983): 314–28; and Meinig, "The Historical Geography Imperative," *Annals of the Association of American Geographers* 79 (1989): 79–87.

16. The multidimensional nature of space and place is a major theme within

John Agnew and James Duncan, eds., *The Power of Place* (London: Unwin Hyman, 1989).

17. Wallerstein, *Capitalist World-Economy;* Wallerstein, *Politics of the World-Economy;* and Robbins, *Colony and Empire.*

Chapter 2: Pre-1860 Geographies

1. John Chronic and Halka Chronic, *Prairie, Peak, and Plateau: A Guide to the Geology of Colorado,* Colorado Geological Survey Bulletin 32 (Denver: Colorado Geological Survey, 1972); Kenneth A. Erickson and Albert W. Smith, *Atlas of Colorado* (Boulder: Colorado Associated University Press, 1985), 4–7; Mel Griffiths and Lynnell Rubright, *Colorado: A Geography* (Boulder: Westview, 1983), 11–33.

2. Erickson and Smith, *Atlas of Colorado,* 10–11; Griffiths and Rubright, *Colorado,* 61–74.

3. Griffiths and Rubright, *Colorado,* 18–25; William D. Thornbury, *Regional Geomorphology of the United States* (New York: John Wiley, 1965), 322–51.

4. J. Donald Hughes, *American Indian Ecology* (El Paso: Texas Western Press, 1983); Christopher Vecsey and Robert W. Venables, eds., *American Indian Environments: Ecological Issues in Native American History* (Syracuse, N.Y.: Syracuse University Press, 1980), 4–25; Richard White, "American Indians and the Environment," *Environmental Review* 9 (1985): 101–3.

5. J. Donald Hughes, *American Indians in Colorado* (Boulder: Pruett, 1977), 9–13; Bruce Estes Rippeteau, *A Colorado Book of the Dead: The Prehistoric Era* (Denver: Colorado State Historical Society, 1978), 1–23; Walter Ebeling, *Handbook of Indian Foods and Fibers of Arid America* (Berkeley: University of California Press, 1986), 22–25.

6. Ebeling, *Handbook,* 540; Hughes, *American Indians in Colorado,* 16–18.

7. Ebeling, *Handbook,* 547–58; Hughes, *American Indians of Colorado,* 13–19; Kenneth Lee Petersen and Meredith H. Matthews, "Man's Impact on the Landscape: A Prehistoric Example from the Dolores River Anasazi, Southwestern Colorado," *Journal of the West* 26, 3 (1987): 4–16; and Rippeteau, *Colorado Book of the Dead,* 33–39, 54–55.

8. Hughes, *American Indians of Colorado,* 20; Rippeteau, *Colorado Book of the Dead,* 38; Omer C. Stewart, "Ute Indians: Before and After White Contact," *Utah Historical Quarterly* 34 (1966): 45.

9. Rippeteau, *Colorado Book of the Dead,* 34–38.

10. Jack Forbes, *Apache, Navajo, and Spaniard* (Norman: University of Oklahoma Press, 1960), xv–xx; Hughes, *American Indians of Colorado,* 29–31; Richard J. Perry, *Western Apache Heritage: People of the Mountain Corridor* (Austin: University of Texas Press, 1991).

11. Carl Abbott, Stephen J. Leonard, and David McComb, *Colorado: A History of the Centennial State* (Niwot: University Press of Colorado, 1994), 22–32; Frank Gilbert Roe, *The Indian and the Horse* (Norman: University of Oklahoma Press, 1955); George Hyde, *Indians of the High Plains: From the Prehistoric Period to the Coming of Europeans* (Norman: University of Oklahoma Press, 1959), 63–116; Ernest Wallace and E. Adamson Hoebel, *The Comanches: Lords of the South Plains*

(Norman: University of Oklahoma Press, 1952); Donald Berthrong, *The Southern Cheyennes* (Norman: University of Oklahoma Press, 1963), 3–49; John H. Moore, *The Cheyenne Nation: A Social and Demographic History* (Lincoln: University of Nebraska Press, 1987).

12. James Jefferson, Robert Delaney, and Gregory Thompson, *The Southern Utes: A Tribal History* (Ignacio, Colo.: Southern Ute Tribe, 1972); Stewart, "Ute Indians"; Richard K. Young, *The Ute Indians of Colorado in the Twentieth Century* (Norman: University of Oklahoma Press, 1997).

13. Richard L. Nostrand, "The Spanish Borderlands," in Robert D. Mitchell and Paul A. Groves, eds., *North America: The Historical Geography of a Changing Continent* (Totowa, N.J.: Rowman and Littlefield, 1987), 48–64; Alfred Barnaby Thomas, ed., *After Coronado: Spanish Exploration of Northeast New Mexico, 1696–1727* (Norman: University of Oklahoma Press, 1935), 11–12, 16–22, 59–72; David J. Weber, *The Spanish Frontier in North America* (New Haven and London: Yale University Press, 1992).

14. A. P. Nasatir, ed., *Before Lewis and Clark* (Saint Louis: Saint Louis Historical Documents Foundation, 1952), 3–27; Ralph Ehrenberg, "Exploratory Mapping of the Great Plains Before 1800," in F. C. Luebke, F. W. Kaye, and G. E. Moulton, eds., *Mapping the North American Plains* (Norman: University of Oklahoma Press, 1987), 4–7; John Francis Bannon, *The Spanish Borderlands Frontier: 1513–1821* (New York: Holt, Rinehart, and Winston, 1970), 124–42; Henri Folmer, "Etienne Veniard de Bourgmond in the Missouri Country," *Missouri Historical Review* 36 (1942): 279–98; Carl I. Wheat, *Mapping the Transmississippi West*, 6 vols. (San Francisco: Institute of Historical Cartography, 1957–63), 1:63–64; W. Raymond Wood, "Mapping the Missouri River Through the Great Plains, 1673–1895," in Luebke, Kaye, and Moulton, eds., *Mapping*, 27–30.

15. Wallace and Hoebel, *Comanches*, 4–9.

16. Thomas, *After Coronado*, 33–39, 133–37; Abbot, Leonard, and McComb, *Colorado*, 24–32; Wallace and Hoebel, *Comanches*, 288–89; Ehrenberg, "Exploratory Mapping," 11; Henri Folmer, "The Mallet Expedition of 1739 Through Nebraska, Kansas and Colorado to Santa Fe," *Colorado Magazine* 16 (1939): 163–73; G. Malcolm Lewis, "Three Centuries of Desert Concepts in the Cis-Rocky Mountain West," *Journal of the West* 4, 4 (1965): 461; and Nasatir, *Before Lewis and Clark*, 28.

17. Joseph J. Hill, "Spanish and Mexican Exploration and Trade Northwest from New Mexico into the Great Basin, 1765–1853," *Utah Historical Quarterly* 3 (1930): 2–7; Fray Angelico Chavez and Ted Warner, eds., *The Dominguez-Escalante Journal* (Provo, Utah: Brigham Young University Press, 1976); Wheat, *Mapping*, 1:94–116.

18. Charles O. Paullin and John K. Wright, *Atlas of the Historical Geography of the United States* (Baltimore: Carnegie Institute of Washington, 1932), 63; Ray Allen Billington and Martin Ridge, *Westward Expansion: A History of the American Frontier* (New York: Macmillan, 1982), 386–87; William H. Goetzmann, *Exploration and Empire* (New York: Vintage Books, 1966), 13–17, 41–43; Nasatir, *Before Lewis and Clark*, 58–115; A. P. Nasatir, *Borderland in Retreat* (Albuquerque: University of New Mexico, 1976), 21–85.

19. Elliott Coues, ed., *The Expeditions of Zebulon Montgomery Pike,* vol. 2 (New York: F. P. Harper, 1895).

20. Ibid., 525.

21. John Allen, "Maps and the Mountain Men: The Cartography of the Rocky Mountain Fur Trade," in William Wyckoff and Lary M. Dilsaver, eds., *The Mountainous West: Explorations in Historical Geography* (Lincoln: University of Nebraska Press, 1995), 63–91; Bannon, *Spanish Borderlands,* 217–18; Goetzmann, *Exploration and Empire,* 27–28, 40–41; Carl Ubbelohde, Maxine Benson, and Duane A. Smith, eds., *A Colorado History* (Boulder: Pruett, 1982), 31–35; Ezekiel Williams, "Ezekiel Williams' Adventures in Colorado," *Missouri Historical Society Collections* 4 (1913): 194–208.

22. Goetzmann, *Exploration and Empire,* 64–70; LeRoy Hafen and Ann Hafen, eds., *Central Route to the Pacific* (Glendale, Calif.: A. H. Clark, 1957), 39; David Lavender, *Bent's Fort* (New York: Doubleday, 1954), 58; John L. Allen, "Division of the Waters: Changing Concepts of the Continental Divide, 1804–1844," *Journal of Historical Geography* 4 (1978): 361–65; Hill, "Spanish and Mexican Exploration," 7; Wheat, *Mapping,* 2:124–35.

23. Maxine Benson, ed. *From Pittsburgh to the Rocky Mountains: Major Stephen Long's Expedition, 1819–1820* (Golden: Fulcrum, 1988); Goetzmann, *Exploration and Empire,* 57–64; Lavender, *Bent's Fort,* 159–62; Wheat, *Mapping,* 2:149–50.

24. Donald Jackson and Mary Spence, eds. *The Expeditions of John Charles Frémont,* 3 vols. (Urbana: University of Illinois Press, 1970); Goetzmann, *Exploration and Empire,* 240–50.

25. Goetzmann, *Exploration and Empire,* 265–305; E. G. Beckwith, Report of Exploration for a Route for the Pacific Railroad, by Capt. J. W. Gunnison, Topographical Engineers, *Pacific Railroad Reports,* vol. 2 (Washington, D.C., 1855).

26. F. T. Cheetham, "The Early Settlements of Southern Colorado," *Colorado Magazine* 5 (1928): 3–4.

27. Ubbelohde, Benson, and Smith, *Colorado,* 56; Billington and Ridge, *Westward Expansion,* 593.

28. Lavender, *Bent's Fort,* 106–7; Ubbelohde, Benson, and Smith, *Colorado,* 40.

29. Lavender, *Bent's Fort,* 132–35, 168; Ubbelohde, Benson, and Smith, *Colorado,* 46–47.

30. Abbott, Leonard, and McComb, *Colorado,* 39; Beckwith, "Report of Exploration," 34; Lavender, *Bent's Fort,* 212–13; Nolie Mumey, *John Williams Gunnison* (Denver: Artcraft, 1955), 47, 70; Ubbelohde, Benson, and Smith, *Colorado,* 47; Marianne L. Stoller, "Grants of Desperation, Lands of Speculation: Mexican Period Land Grants in Colorado," *Journal of the West* 19, 3 (1980): 22–39.

31. Lavender, *Bent's Fort,* 173, 184–85; Ubbelohde, Benson, and Smith, *Colorado,* 40–41.

32. Abbot, Leonard, and McComb, *Colorado,* 37; Hafen and Hafen, *Central Route,* 158; Jackson and Spence, *Frémont,* 1:707–9; Lavender, *Bent's Fort,* 139–40; Ubbelohde, Benson, and Smith, *Colorado,* 37.

33. D. W. Meinig, *Southwest: Three Peoples in Geographical Change,*

1600–1970 (New York: Oxford University Press, 1971), 25; Richard Nostrand, *The Hispano Homeland* (Norman: University of Oklahoma Press, 1992); Hafen and Hafen, *Central Route*, 30–31; Stoller, "Grants of Desperation."

34. Hafen and Hafen, *Central Route*, 120–21; Meinig, *Southwest*, 32; Mumey, *Gunnison*, 75.

35. Alvar Ward Carlson, "Rural Settlement Patterns in the San Luis Valley: A Comparative Study," *Colorado Magazine* 44 (1967): 111–28; Cheetham, "Early Settlements."

Chapter 3: Mountain Geographies

1. Patricia Limerick, *The Legacy of Conquest* (New York: W. W. Norton, 1987), 100.

2. J. G. Pangborn, *The New Rocky Mountain Tourist* (Chicago: Knight and Leonard, 1878), 56.

3. Stanley Dempsey and James E. Fell, Jr., *Mining the Summit: Colorado's Ten Mile District, 1860–1960* (Norman: University of Oklahoma Press, 1986), 23–24; Sandra Pritchard, "Landscape Changes in Summit County, Colorado, 1859 to the Present" (Ph.D. diss., University of Oregon, 1982), 16; Duane A. Smith, *Rocky Mountain Mining Camps* (Lincoln: University of Nebraska Press, 1974), 10.

4. Limerick, *Conquest*, 29; Carl Ubbelohde, Maxine Benson, and Duane A. Smith, eds., *A Colorado History* (Boulder: Pruett, 1982), 118; Dempsey and Fell, *Mining the Summit*, 24; Pritchard, "Landscape Changes," 16; Caroline Bancroft, *Gulch of Gold: A History of Central City, Colorado* (Denver: Sage Books, 1958), 69; George A. Crofutt, *Crofutt's Grip-Sack Guide of Colorado* (Omaha: Overland, 1885), 142.

5. Crofutt, *Grip-Sack Guide*, 112.

6. Bayard Taylor, *Colorado: A Summer Trip* (Niwot: University Press of Colorado, 1989), 62.

7. Bancroft, *Gulch of Gold*; Terry Cox, *Inside the Mountains: A History of Mining Around Central City, Colorado* (Boulder: Pruett, 1989).

8. Horace Greeley, *An Overland Journey* (New York: Alfred A. Knopf, 1969), 104–5.

9. Dempsey and Fell, *Mining the Summit*; Charles W. Henderson, *Mining in Colorado* (Washington, D.C.: Government Printing Office, 1926); Pritchard, "Landscape Changes"; Stephen M. Voynick, *Leadville: A Miner's Epic* (Missoula, Mont.: Mountain Press, 1984).

10. L. P. Brockett, *Our Western Empire* (Philadelphia: Bradley, Garretson, 1881), 660; Dempsey and Fell, *Mining the Summit*, 24–25.

11. Voynick, *Leadville*; William S. Greever, *The Bonanza West: The Story of the Western Mining Rushes, 1848–1900* (Norman: University of Oklahoma Press, 1963), 185; Henderson, *Mining*, 40–43.

12. William Wyckoff, "Incorporation as a Factor in Formation of an Urban System," *Geographical Review* 77 (1987): 279–92.

13. Duane A. Smith, *Song of the Hammer and Drill: The Colorado San Juans, 1860–1914* (Golden: Colorado School of Mines, 1982), 34–35.

14. Malcolm Rohrbough, *Aspen: The History of a Silver Mining Town, 1879–1893* (New York: Oxford University Press, 1986), 208–21; Ubbelohde, Benson, and Smith, *Colorado History,* 227–36; Henderson, *Mining,* 45–46.

15. Clifford C. Hill, "Wagon Roads in Colorado, 1858–1876" (M.A. thesis, University of Colorado, 1949), 45–46; Michael Kaplan, *Otto Mears: Paradoxical Pathfinder* (Silverton: San Juan County Book Company, 1982), 53–82; Cathy E. Kindquist, *Stony Pass: The Tumbling and Impetuous Trail* (Silverton: San Juan County Book Company, 1987).

16. Smith, *Rocky Mountain Mining Camps,* 53; Rohrbough, *Aspen,* 37–38.

17. Hill, "Wagon Roads"; Kaplan, *Otto Mears.*

18. Kaplan, *Otto Mears.*

19. J. L. Frazier, "Early Stage Lines in Colorado, 1859–1865" (M.A. thesis, University of Denver, 1959); Hill, "Wagon Roads," 21; W. Turrentine Jackson, *Wells Fargo in Colorado Territory* (Denver: Colorado Historical Society, 1982).

20. Crofutt, *Grip-Sack Guide,* 112; James E. Fell, Jr., *Ores to Metals: The Rocky Mountain Smelting Industry* (Lincoln: University of Nebraska Press, 1979), 40–41; Smith, *Rocky Mountain Mining Camps,* 134–35.

21. Richard White, *"It's Your Misfortune and None of My Own": A New History of the American West* (Norman: University of Oklahoma Press, 1991), 246–58.

22. Henry Williams, *Williams' Tourist's Guide to the San Juan Mines* (New York, 1877), 3.

23. O. L. Baskin, *History of Clear Creek and Boulder Valleys, Colorado* (Chicago: O. L. Baskin, 1880), 179–203.

24. Henderson, *Mining;* John J. Lipsey, *The Lives of James John Hagerman: Builder of the Colorado Midland Railway* (Denver: Golden Bell, 1968); Rohrbough, *Aspen,* 143–57; Ubbelohde, Benson, and Smith, *Colorado History,* 183–94.

25. Richard L. Fetter and Suzanne Fetter, *Telluride: From Pick to Powder* (Caldwell: Caxton Printers, 1982); Kaplan, *Otto Mears;* Smith, *San Juans.*

26. Richard McCloud, *Durango, As It Is* (Durango: Board of Trade, 1892).

27. Ovando J. Hollister, *The Mines of Colorado* (Springfield: Samuel Bowles, 1867), 98–99; Kindquist, *Stony Pass;* Williams, *Tourist's Colorado,* 10; Smith, *Rocky Mountain Mining Camps,* 65–66.

28. Rohrbough, *Aspen,* 39; Robert L. Thompson, *Wiring a Continent: The History of the Telegraph Industry in the United States, 1832–1866* (Princeton: Princeton University Press, 1947); Smith, *Rocky Mountain Mining Camps,* 65–66.

29. William Wyckoff, "Mapping the New El Dorado: Pikes Peak Promotional Cartography, 1859–1861," *Imago Mundi* 40 (1988): 32–45; Ubbelohde, Benson, and Smith, *Colorado History,* 68–69.

30. William Blackmore, *Colorado: Its Resources, Parks, and Prospects* (London: Sampson Low, Son, and Marston, 1869); Hollister, *Mines of Colorado;* Joel Whitney, *Silver Mining Regions of Colorado* (New York: D. Van Nostrand, 1865); Thomas Corbett, *The Colorado Directory of Mines* (Denver: Rocky Mountain News Printing, 1879); Crofutt, *Grip-Sack Guide;* Frank Fossett, *Colorado: Its Gold and Silver Mines* (New York: C. G. Crawford, 1879); Colorado Territory, Board of Immigration, "Official Information, Colorado, A Statement of Facts" (Denver: Rocky Mountain News, 1872); Samuel Cushman, *The Mines of Clear Creek*

County (Denver: Times Steam Printing House, 1876); Samuel Cushman and J. P. Waterman, *The Gold Mines of Gilpin County* (Central City: Register Steam Printing House, 1876); Kansas Pacific Railroad, "Colorado Tourist and Illustrated Guide to the Rocky Mountain Resorts" (Kansas City: Ramsey, Millett, and Hudson, 1880); McCloud, *Durango;* Williams, *Tourist Guide;* Joseph King, *A Mine to Make a Mine: Financing the Colorado Mining Industry, 1859–1902* (College Station: Texas A&M University Press, 1972).

31. E. L. Berthoud and S. W. Burt, *Rocky Mountain Gold Regions* (Denver: Rocky Mountain News Printing, 1861).

32. William Wyckoff, "Revising the Meyer Model: Denver and the National Urban System, 1859–1979," *Urban Geography* 9 (1988): 1–18.

33. Wyckoff, "Incorporation as a Factor"; Wyckoff, "Revising the Meyer Model"; King, *Mine to Make a Mine;* Pangborn, *Rocky Mountain Tourist,* 52.

34. King, *Mine to Make a Mine,* 165, 169; Wyckoff, "Incorporation as a Factor."

35. Albert Richardson, *Beyond the Mississippi* (Hartford, Conn.: American, 1867), ii.

36. John Reps, *The Forgotten Frontier: Urban Planning in the American West Before 1890* (Columbia: University of Missouri Press, 1981); C. E. Stoehr, *Bonanza Victorian Architecture and Society in Colorado Mining Towns* (Albuquerque: University of New Mexico Press, 1975).

37. Pangborn, *Rocky Mountain Tourist,* 34.

38. Fetter and Fetter, *Telluride;* Pritchard, "Landscape Changes"; Randall Rohe, "Environment and Mining in the Mountainous West," in *The Mountainous West: Explorations in Historical Geography,* ed. William Wyckoff and Lary Dilsaver (Lincoln: University of Nebraska Press, 1995), 169–93.

39. Kansas Pacific Railroad, "Colorado Tourist," 30.

40. Baskin, *History,* 287.

41. Smith, *Rocky Mountain Mining Camps,* 148, 191; Stoehr, *Bonanza Victorian Architecture,* 17.

42. Benjamin Draper, "Cultural Life in Georgetown, Colorado, 1859–1900" (M.A. thesis, University of Denver, 1936), 27; Stoehr, *Bonanza Victorian Architecture,* 13.

43. Greeley, *Overland Journey,* 104–5; Henderson, *Mining,* 29; Hollister, *Mines of Colorado,* 114–15; King, *Mine to Make a Mine,* 150–51; Rohrbough, *Aspen,* 25, 122.

44. Richard V. Francaviglia, *Hard Places: Reading the Landscape of America's Historic Mining Districts* (Iowa City: University of Iowa Press, 1991), 152–53; Kingston Heath, "False Front Architecture on Montana's Urban Frontier" (paper presented at the VAF Annual Meeting, Salt Lake City, May 1987); Terry Jordan, "The North American West: Continuity or Innovation?" *Brandon Geographical Studies* 1 (1991): 1–17; Terry Jordan, Jon Kilpinen, and Charles Gritzner, *The Mountain West: Interpreting the Folk Landscape* (Baltimore: Johns Hopkins University Press, 1997); Stoehr, *Bonanza Victorian Architecture.*

45. Baskin, *History,* 288.

46. Fetter and Fetter, *Telluride,* 34–36; Stoehr, *Bonanza Victorian Architecture,* 128–30.

47. Fetter and Fetter, *Telluride*, 36; Smith, *San Juans*, 37–38; Smith, *Rocky Mountain Mining Camps*, 111; Rohrbough, *Aspen*, 136; Ubbelohde, Benson, and Smith, *Colorado History*, 86–87; Stoehr, *Bonanza Victorian Architecture*, 130–36.

48. Dempsey and Fell, *Mining the Summit*, 84; Draper, "Cultural Life," 182; Fetter and Fetter, *Telluride*, 75.

49. John W. Horner, *Silver Town* (Caldwell, Idaho: Caxton Printers, 1950), 40–41; Stoehr, *Bonanza Victorian Architecture*, 103–8; Smith, *Rocky Mountain Mining Camps*, 222–24.

50. Smith, *Rocky Mountain Mining Camps*, 171–72.

51. Rohrbough, *Aspen*; Smith, *Rocky Mountain Mining Camps*.

52. Francaviglia, *Hard Places*, 156–57.

53. Horner, *Silver Town*, 38–40; Stoehr, *Bonanza Victorian Architecture*, 13; Fetter and Fetter, *Telluride*, 81; Pritchard, "Landscape Changes," 19.

54. Rohrbough, *Aspen*, 129–33; Smith, *Rocky Mountain Mining Camps*, 24, 29, 35.

55. Francaviglia, *Hard Places*, 43; Rohrbough, *Aspen*, 118, 130–32.

56. Carl Abbott, Stephen J. Leonard, and David McComb, *Colorado: A History of the Centennial State* (Niwot: University Press of Colorado, 1994), 107–8; Ronald C. Brown, *Hard-Rock Miners: The Intermountain West, 1860–1920* (College Station: Texas A&M University Press, 1979); Richard E. Lingenfelter, *The Hardrock Miners: A History of the Mining Labor Movement in the American West, 1863–1893* (Berkeley: University of California Press, 1974); Smith, *San Juans*, 59; George G. Suggs, Jr., *Colorado's War on Militant Unionism* (Detroit: Wayne State University Press, 1972); Voynick, *Leadville*, 65–66; Mark Wyman, *Hard Rock Epic: Western Miners and the Industrial Revolution, 1860–1910* (Berkeley: University of California Press, 1979).

57. Dempsey and Fell, *Mining the Summit*, 16, 29–34, 108–10; Fetter and Fetter, *Telluride*, 16; Henderson, *Mining*, 29; Hollister, *Mines*, 77–82.

58. Pritchard, "Landscape Changes"; Randall Rohe, "Man and the Land: Mining's Impact in the Far West," *Arizona and the West* 28 (1986): 299–338; Duane A. Smith, "My Profit, Your Land: Colorado Mining and the Environment, 1858–1900," in Duane A. Smith, ed., *A Taste of the West: Essays in Honor of Robert G. Athearn* (Boulder: Pruett, 1983), 87–108.

59. Quoted in Rohe, "Man and the Land," 315–16.

60. Cox, *Inside the Mountains*; Henderson, *Mining*, 28–30, 33; Crofutt, *Grip-Sack Guide*, 75.

61. Kansas Pacific Railroad, *Colorado Tourist*, 30; Francaviglia, *Hard Places*, 50; Stoehr, *Bonanza Victorian Architecture*, 140–42.

62. Bancroft, *Gulch of Gold*, 53; Greeley, *Overland Journey*, 103–6.

63. Taylor, *Colorado*, 56.

64. Duane A. Smith, *Mining America: The Industry and the Environment, 1800–1980* (Lawrence: University Press of Kansas, 1987), 54–66; Michael Williams, *Americans and Their Forests: A Historical Geography* (Cambridge: Cambridge University Press, 1989); Cox, *Inside the Mountains*, 25; Fell, *Ores to Metals*, 31; Pritchard, "Landscape Changes," 15, 19; Rohe, "Man and the Land," 308–14;

Thomas T. Veblen and Diane C. Lorenz, *The Colorado Front Range: A Century of Ecological Change* (Salt Lake City: University of Utah Press, 1990).

65. Voynick, *Leadville*, 34.

66. Fell, *Ores to Metals*, 49–51; McCloud, *Durango*, 11; Rohrbough, *Aspen*, 192; Smith, *Mining America*, 11–12; Cox, *Inside the Mountains*, 26–27.

67. Abbott, Leonard, and McComb, *Colorado*, 276–77; Dempsey and Fell, *Mining the Summit*, 251–60; Henderson, *Mining in Colorado*; Ubbelohde, Benson, and Smith, *Colorado History*, 255, 299.

68. Henderson, *Mining in Colorado*.

69. Cox, *Inside the Mountains*, 43; Harold A. Hoffmeister, "Central City Mining Area," *Economic Geography* 16 (1940): 96–104.

70. Dempsey and Fell, *Mining the Summit*, 253–55; Francaviglia, *Hard Places*; Pritchard, "Landscape Changes."

71. Rohe, "Man and the Land"; Veblen and Lorenz, *Colorado Front Range*.

72. Valerie Fifer, *American Progress: The Growth of the Transport, Tourist, and Information Industries in the Nineteenth-Century West* (Chester, Conn.: Globe Pequot, 1988), 7–9; John F. Sears, *Sacred Places: American Tourist Attractions in the Nineteenth Century* (New York: Oxford University Press, 1989), 212–13; Marguerite Sands Shaffer, "See America First: Tourism and National Identity, 1905–1930" (Ph.D. diss., Harvard University, 1994), 2–3.

73. Anne Farrar Hyde, *An American Vision: Far Western Landscape and National Culture, 1820–1920* (New York: New York University Press, 1990); Sears, *Sacred Places*.

74. Patricia Trenton and Peter Hassrick, *The Rocky Mountains: A Vision for Artists in the Nineteenth Century* (Norman: University of Oklahoma Press, 1983), 141.

75. Hyde, *An American Vision*, 1–106; Taylor, *Colorado*, 35; Samuel Bowles, *The Switzerland of America: A Summer Vacation in the Parks and Mountains of Colorado* (Springfield, Mass.: Samuel Bowles, 1869).

76. Fifer, *American Progress*, 303–4.

77. Ibid.

78. Ibid., 267–68, 334.

79. Ibid., 366–67; Crofutt, *Grip-Sack Guide*, 41; Kansas Pacific Railroad, *Colorado Tourist*, 28.

80. Hyde, *American Vision*, 148–61; Ernest Ingersoll, *The Crest of the Continent* (Chicago: R. R. Donnelley and Sons, 1888), 33–35; Fifer, *American Progress*, 317–20, 368.

81. Robert G. Athearn, *The Mythic West in Twentieth-Century America* (Lawrence: University Press of Kansas, 1986), 149; Lawrence R. Borne, *Dude Ranching: A Complete History* (Albuquerque: University of New Mexico Press, 1983), 11–12; C. W. Buchholtz, *Rocky Mountain National Park: A History* (Boulder: Colorado Associated University Press, 1983), 60–86; Robert C. Black III, *Island in the Rockies: The History of Grand County, Colorado, to 1930* (Boulder: Pruett, 1969), 91–92, 157–99; Stanley Wood, *Over the Range to the Golden Gate: A Complete Tourists' Guide* (Chicago: R. R. Donnelley and Sons, 1912), 67; Hyde, *American Vision*, 187–90.

82. Crofutt, *Grip-Sack Guide,* 53.

83. Ingersoll, *Crest of the Continent,* 116–17.

84. Fifer, *American Progress,* 324–34; Earl Pomeroy, *In Search of the Golden West: The Tourist in Western America* (Lincoln: University of Nebraska Press, 1990), 112–83; Sears, *Sacred Places,* 209–16; Shaffer, "See America First."

85. Pomeroy, *In Search of the Golden West,* 73–111, 139–83; Fifer, *American Progress,* 327–34.

86. Fifer, *American Progress,* 364–68; U.S. Department of the Interior, *Report of the Director of the National Park Service,* 1917, 1918, and 1919 (Washington, D.C.: Government Printing Office, 1917, 1918, 1919). The quotation on Denver parks is found in Thomas J. Noel and Barbara S. Norgren, *Denver: The City Beautiful and Its Architects, 1893–1941* (Denver: Historical Denver, 1987), 26.

87. Stephen J. Leonard and Thomas J. Noel, *Denver: Mining Camp to Metropolis* (Niwot: University Press of Colorado, 1990), 255–76; "Enjoy Your Vacation Denver Way" (Denver: City and County of Denver, 1916).

88. Buchholtz, *Rocky Mountain National Park,* 117–19; Borne, *Dude Ranching.*

89. Buchholtz, *Rocky Mountain National Park,* 135; Frederick H. Chapin, *Mountaineering in Colorado: The Peaks About Estes Park* (Boston: Appalachian Mountain Club, 1890); William M. Bueler, *Roof of the Rockies: A History of Mountaineering in Colorado* (Boulder: Pruett, 1974), 30–46; Jack Benson, "Before Aspen and Vail: The Story of Recreational Skiing in Frontier Colorado," *Journal of the West* 22, 1 (1983): 52–61; Abbott Fay, *Ski Tracks in the Rockies: A Century of Colorado Skiing* (Evergreen, Colo.: Cordillera, 1984).

90. Cultural geographer Wilbur Zelinsky has assessed the impact of the federal government on the American landscape generally in "The Imprint of Central Authority," in Michael P. Conzen, ed., *The Making of the American Landscape* (Boston: Unwin Hyman, 1990), 311–34.

91. William H. Goetzmann, *Exploration and Empire* (New York: Vintage Books, 1966).

92. Ibid., 467–529.

93. F. V. Hayden, *Ninth Annual Report of the United States Geological and Geographical Survey of the Territories* (Washington, D.C.: Government Printing Office, 1877), 371.

94. "The Wheeler Expedition in Southern Colorado," *Harper's New Monthly Magazine* 102 (1876): 807.

95. Goetzmann, *Exploration and Empire,* 512–13.

96. Peter B. Hales, *William Henry Jackson and the Transformation of the American Landscape* (Philadelphia: Temple University Press, 1988).

97. Goetzmann, *Exploration and Empire,* 577–601; Samuel F. Emmons, *Geology and Mining Industry of Leadville, Colorado,* U.S. Geological Survey Monograph no. 12 (Washington, D.C.: Government Printing Office, 1886); Waldemar Lindgren and Frederick Leslie Ransome, *Geology and Gold Deposits of the Cripple Creek District, Colorado,* U.S. Geological Survey Professional Paper no. 54 (Washington, D.C.: Government Printing Office, 1906).

98. Duane Vandenbusche, *The Gunnison Country* (Gunnison: B and B Print-

ers, 1980), 303–22; Duane A. Smith and Duane Vandenbusche, *A Land Alone: Colorado's Western Slope* (Boulder: Pruett, 1981), 155–57.

99. Ubbelohde, Benson, and Smith, *Colorado History*, 286–89; Michael McCarthy, *Hour of Trial: The Conservation Conflict in Colorado and the West, 1891–1907* (Norman: University of Oklahoma Press, 1977), 18–19. Ebert's quotation is taken from Ubbelohde, Benson, and Smith, *Colorado History*, 286.

100. McCarthy, *Hour of Trial*, 29–43.

101. A brief, useful overview of the early years of the national forest reserves is found in Joseph M. Petulla, *American Environmental History* (Columbus, Ohio: Merrill, 1988), 229–34, 308–12.

102. McCarthy, *Hour of Trial*, 50–51.

103. Ora Brooks Peake, *The Colorado Range Cattle Industry* (Glendale, Calif.: Arthur Clark, 1937), 87–88.

104. For the preservationist perspective, see John Muir, "The Wild Parks and Forest Reservations of the West," *Atlantic Monthly* 81 (1898): 15–28.

105. McCarthy, *Hour of Trial*, 56–59, 64–67.

106. Ibid., 131.

107. Ibid., 132–54; Abbott, Leonard, and McComb, *Colorado*, 128–29; Paul M. O'Rourke, *Frontier in Transition: A History of Southwestern Colorado* (Denver: Bureau of Land Management, 1980), 126–38.

108. McCarthy, *Hour of Trial*, 155–275.

109. Peake, *Colorado Range Cattle*, 92; McCarthy, *Hour of Trial*, 68.

110. Peake, *Colorado Range Cattle*, 92–95.

111. An excellent overview of the overall history of Rocky Mountain National Park is Buchholtz, *Rocky Mountain National Park*.

112. U.S. Department of the Interior, National Park Service, "General Information Regarding Rocky Mountain National Park" (Washington, D.C.: Government Printing Office, 1917).

113. Buchholtz, *Rocky Mountain National Park*, 173–78; U.S. Department of the Interior, National Park Service, "Rocky Mountain National Park, Colorado" (Washington, D.C.: Government Printing Office, 1936), 12–14.

114. Buchholtz, *Rocky Mountain National Park*, 154–57.

Chapter 4: Piedmont Heartland

1. Thomas Tonge, *All About Colorado* (Denver: Thomas Tonge, 1913), 73.

2. Stephen J. Leonard and Thomas J. Noel, *Denver: Mining Camp to Metropolis* (Niwot: University Press of Colorado, 1990), 6–8; John Reps, *Cities of the American West: A History of Frontier Town Planning* (Princeton: Princeton University Press, 1979), 457–59; Carl Ubbelohde, Maxine Benson, and Duane A. Smith, *A Colorado History* (Boulder: Pruett, 1982), 64.

3. Gunther Barth, *Instant Cities: Urbanization and the Rise of San Francisco and Denver* (New York: Oxford University Press, 1975), 113–17; Thomas C. Jepsen, "The Telegraph Comes to Colorado: A New Technology and Its Consequences," *Essays and Monographs in Colorado History* 7 (1987): 1–26; Leonard and Noel, *Den-*

ver, 16–17; Albert D. Richardson, *Beyond the Mississippi* (Hartford, Conn.: American, 1867), 186–87.

4. Lyle W. Dorsett, *The Queen City: A History of Denver* (Boulder: Pruett, 1977), 5–6; Leonard and Noel, *Denver*, 9, 33; Thomas J. Noel, *The City and the Saloon: Denver, 1858–1916* (Lincoln: University of Nebraska Press, 1985), 7–8; Reps, *Cities of the American West*, 463.

5. Dorsett, *Queen City*, 4, 22–23; Richard Hogan, *Class and Community in Frontier Colorado* (Lawrence: University Press of Kansas, 1990), 39–40, 121–50; Leonard and Noel, *Denver*, 34–39; Reps, *Cities of the American West*, 477; Ubbelohde, Benson, and Smith, *Colorado*, 122–23, 147.

6. Stanley Wood, *Over the Range to the Golden Gate: A Complete Tourists' Guide* (Chicago: R. R. Donnelley and Sons, 1912), 11.

7. George A. Crofutt, *Crofutt's Grip-Sack Guide of Colorado* (Omaha: Overland, 1885), 36, 96–97; Ned Farrell, *Colorado, The Rocky Mountain Gem* (Chicago: Western News, 1869), 32; Hogan, *Class and Community*, 121–50.

8. Carl Abbott, Stephen J. Leonard, and David McComb, *Colorado: A History of the Centennial State* (Niwot: University Press of Colorado, 1994), 130–31; Crofutt, *Grip-Sack Guide*, 73; Maurice Frink, *The Boulder Story: Historical Portrait of a Colorado Town* (Boulder: Pruett, 1965).

9. Frink, *Boulder*, 34.

10. Reps, *Cities of the American West*, 458–62.

11. Richardson, *Beyond the Mississippi*, 177.

12. Leonard and Noel, *Denver*, 22–31.

13. Ibid., 13–21.

14. Bayard Taylor, *Colorado: A Summer Trip* (Niwot: University Press of Colorado, 1989; orig. publ. 1867), 37.

15. Richard R. Brettell, *Historic Denver: The Architects and the Architecture, 1858–1893* (Denver: Historic Denver, 1979), 1–7.

16. Leonard and Noel, *Denver*, 49–50.

17. Harry W. B. Kantner, *Information of Denver, Colorado* (Denver: Fleet Engraving, 1892), 47.

18. Edwards Roberts, "The City of Denver," *Harper's Monthly* 76 (1888): 950–52.

19. Barth, *Instant Cities*, 216; Leonard and Noel, *Denver*, 39; Roberts, "City of Denver," 950–52.

20. Barth, *Instant Cities*, 216; Wood, *Over the Range*, 15.

21. *Historical and Descriptive Review of Denver* (Denver: G. M. Collier, 1894), 16; Kantner, *Information of Denver*, 95–97; Roberts, "City of Denver," 950–52.

22. Leonard and Noel, *Denver*, 116–27.

23. Roberts, "City of Denver," 952.

24. Ubbelohde, Benson, and Smith, *Colorado*, 156.

25. Valerie Fifer, *American Progress: The Growth of the Transport, Tourist, and Information Industries in the Nineteenth-Century West* (Chester, Conn.: Globe Pequot, 1988), 364–67; Leonard and Noel, *Denver*, 150–66.

26. Leonard and Noel, *Denver*, 57.

27. Brettell, *Historic Denver*, 9–13.

28. Ibid., 18; Leonard and Noel, *Denver*, 47—48.

29. Leonard and Noel, *Denver*, 45—46.

30. Brettell, *Historic Denver*, 20.

31. Thomas J. Noel and Barbara S. Norgren, *Denver: The City Beautiful* (Denver: Historic Denver, 1987), 95—99, 106—7, 111—13.

32. *Historical and Descriptive Review of Denver*, 32; Roberts, "City of Denver," 956.

33. Roberts, "City of Denver," 956; *Historical and Descriptive Review of Denver*, 12—13; Dorsett, *Queen City*, 79—80, 92; Leonard and Noel, *Denver*, 49—52.

34. Ellen Kingman Fisher, *One Hundred Years of Energy: Public Service Company of Colorado and Its Predecessors, 1869—1969* (New York: Garland, 1989), 2—33, 55; Barth, *Instant Cities*, 225.

35. Noel and Norgren, *Denver*, 1—27; Leonard and Noel, *Denver*, 140—49; William H. Wilson, "A Diadem for the City Beautiful: The Development of Denver's Civic Center," *Journal of the West* 22, 2 (1983): 73—83.

36. *Thayer's Map of Denver, Colorado* (Denver: Thayer and Stubbs, 1872); Reps, *Cities of the American West*, 485—87.

37. Leonard and Noel, *Denver*, 53—64.

38. William C. Jones, Gene C. McKeever, F. H. Wagner, Jr., and Kenton Forrest, *Mile-High Trolleys* (Boulder: Pruett, 1975); Leonard and Noel, *Denver*, 70.

39. Crofutt, *Grip-Sack Guide*, 32.

40. Kantner, *Denver*, 97; Jones, McKeever, Wagner, and Forrest, *Mile-High Trolleys*, 59. The quotation is from *Historical and Descriptive Review of Denver*, 35.

41. Leonard and Noel, *Denver*, 53—64; *Historical and Descriptive Review of Denver*, 44—47; Dorsett, *Queen City*, 80; Noel and Norgren, *Denver*, 9.

42. Leonard and Noel, *Denver*, 302—7, 350—58.

43. Barth, *Instant Cities*.

44. Dorsett, *Queen City*, 68—71, 87—90; *Historical and Descriptive Review of Denver*, 35—36; Leonard and Noel, *Denver*, 29—30; Norgren and Noel, *Denver*, 81; The Roberts quotation is from Roberts, "City of Denver," 944—45.

45. Dorsett, *Queen City*, 90—94; Leonard and Noel, *Denver*, 86; Norgren, *Denver*, 8—9.

46. Dorsett, *Queen City*, 87—117; Leonard and Noel, *Denver*, 180—89; Noel, *City and the Saloon*, 53—66; Giovanni Perilli, *Colorado and the Italians in Colorado* (1922); Kenneth W. Rock, *German Footprints in Colorado* (Denver: German Heritage Festival, 1983).

47. Hogan, *Class and Community*, 79—81; Ubbelohde, Benson, and Smith, *Colorado*, 156—57; Colorado Water Conservation Board, *A Hundred Years of Irrigation in Colorado* (Fort Collins: Colorado Agricultural and Mechanical College, 1952), 32; William Blackmore, *Colorado: Its Resources, Parks, and Prospects* (London: Sampson Low, Son, and Marston, 1869), 148—49; David Boyd, *A History: Greeley and the Union Colony of Colorado* (Greeley: Greeley Tribune Press, 1890), 88.

48. Hogan, *Class and Community*, 79—91; Ubbelohde, Benson, and Smith, *Colorado*, 134—38.

49. Boyd, *Union Colony*, 39—40.

50. The quotation regarding town lots is from Kenneth I. Helphand, *Colorado: Visions of an American Landscape* (Niwot: Roberts Rinehart, 1991), 233. The quotations describing community stability and composition are from Boyd, *Union Colony,* 33–34.

51. Boyd, *Union Colony,* 52–53.

52. William E. Pabor, *Farmers' Guide to Northern Colorado: A Manual for Intending Settlers* (Denver: Colorado Farmer, 1882), 6.

53. Colorado Mortgage and Investment Company of London, "Farm Lands in Colorado" (Denver: Rocky Mountain News, 1879), 13.

54. Boyd, *Union Colony,* 29, 197–201; Frederick Joseph Doyle, "Zion in the Wilderness: The Movement of Colonies into Colorado, 1869–1872" (M.A. thesis, Denver University, 1974).

55. Abbott, Leonard, and McComb, *Colorado,* 163–64; Dean F. Krakel, *South Platte Country* (Laramie: Powder River, 1954), 217–19; J. A. Blake, *Handbook of Colorado* (Denver: J. A. Blake, 1871), 44.

56. Abbott, Leonard, and McComb, *Colorado,* 163–64.

57. Boyd, *Union Colony,* 80–81, 88–118, 142.

58. Crofutt, *Grip-Sack Guide,* 28–29.

59. Colorado Water Conservation Board, *Irrigation,* 38.

60. United States, Bureau of the Census, *Twelfth Census of the United States,* 1900.

61. Ibid.; Pabor, *Farmers' Guide,* 6; Colorado Mortgage and Investment Company, "Farm Lands"; William E. Pabor, *Colorado as an Agricultural State* (New York: Orange Judd, 1883), 87; Boyd, *Union Colony,* 68–70.

62. Reps, *Cities of the American West,* 682; Edwards Roberts, *Colorado Springs and Manitou* (Chicago: R. R. Donnelley and Sons, 1883), 8; *Facts* (Colorado Springs), January 1, 1902; Jane Furey, "Tourism in the Pikes Peak Area, 1870–1880" (M.A. thesis, University of Colorado, 1958), 81–82; Marshall Sprague, *Newport in the Rockies* (Chicago: Swallow, 1980).

63. Sharon A. Cunningham, *Manitou: Saratoga of the West* (Colorado Springs: El Paso County Medical Society Auxiliary, 1980), 1–11; Sprague, *Newport,* 15.

64. Sprague, *Newport,* 15–21; Cunningham, *Manitou,* 1–11; Robert Athearn, *Rebel of the Rockies: A History of the Denver and Rio Grande Railroad* (New Haven: Yale University Press, 1962), 8, 13–14. The Palmer quotation is from Athearn, *Rebel of the Rockies,* 8.

65. Athearn, *Rebel of the Rockies,* 9.

66. Reps, *Cities of the American West,* 583–91; Sprague, *Newport,* 23–32.

67. George Rex Buckman, "Colorado Springs, Colorado and Its Famous Scenic Environs" (New York: Alley-Allen, 1892), 9; Sprague, *Newport,* 33–34.

68. Furey, "Tourism," 21–24.

69. Cunningham, "Manitou"; Sprague, *Newport,* 34–35, 67; Abbott, Leonard, and McComb, *Colorado,* 229–32; J. G. Pangborn, *The New Rocky Mountain Tourist, Arkansas Valley and San Juan Guide* (Chicago: Knight and Leonard, 1878), 38–39.

70. Sprague, *Newport,* 80–89; Manly Dayton Ormes, *The Book of Colorado*

Springs (Colorado Springs: Dentan, 1933), 83–90; "Colorado Springs: City of Sunshine" (Colorado Springs: Prompt Printery, 1915), 73; Cunningham, *Manitou*, 112–13.

71. "City of Sunshine," 76–77; Reps, *Cities of the American West*, 591; Sprague, *Newport*, 36–37, 63, 151–53, 274–81.

72. Ormes, *Colorado Springs*, 103–4; Park Commission of Colorado Springs, "Report of the Park Commission of Colorado Springs, Colorado" (1908).

73. Abbott, Leonard, and McComb, *Colorado*, 229–32; Roberts, "Colorado Springs," 11–12, 15; Sprague, *Newport*, 71–72. The Roberts quotation is from Roberts, "Colorado Springs," 15.

74. "City of Sunshine," 35–38, 50–55.

75. Ibid., 37.

76. Cunningham, *Manitou*, 12–19, 22–28, 45–51, 57; S. K. Hooper, "Story of Manitou" (Chicago: Town of Manitou, n.d.), 19–23, 55. The quotation regarding the mineral waters is from Cunningham, *Manitou*, 57.

77. "City of Sunshine," 73; Sprague, *Newport*, 47–48, 91–98. The quotation describing Williams Canyon is from Kansas Pacific Railroad, *Colorado Tourist and Illustrated Guide to the Rocky Mountain Resorts via the Golden Belt* (Kansas City: Ramsey, Millett, and Hudson, 1880), 62.

78. Sprague, *Newport*, 94–96, 108–11, 223–24, 255–58.

79. Ibid., 38–46; Furey, "Tourism," 72–83.

80. Reps, *Cities of the American West*, 589–91.

81. "City of Sunshine," 78.

82. Sprague, *Newport*, 115–27, 259–61. The quotations regarding Broadmoor are from "City of Sunshine," 72.

83. *Facts* (Colorado Springs), January 1, 1902; Sprague, *Newport*, 226–28; Buckman, "Colorado Springs," 32; Ormes, *Colorado Springs*.

84. Ormes, *Colorado Springs*, 265–75; Buckman, "Colorado Springs," 33; Sprague, *Newport*, 227–31; the newspaper quotation is taken from *Facts* (Colorado Springs), January 1, 1902.

85. Sprague, *Newport*, 88, 274–81; "City of Sunshine," 76–77; Roberts, "Colorado Springs," 20.

86. Athearn, *Rebel of the Rockies*, 154–88; Sprague, *Newport*, 103–8.

87. Sprague, *Newport*, 113–14.

88. Ibid., 166–75.

89. Ubbelohde, Benson, and Smith, *Colorado*, 21; Abbott, Leonard, and McComb, *Colorado*, 39; Hogan, *Class and Community*, 151–52; Janet Lecompte, *Pueblo, Hardscrabble, and Greenhorn* (Norman: University of Oklahoma Press, 1978); Anne Wainstein Bond, "Pueblo on the Arkansas River: Crossroads of Southern Colorado," *Colorado Heritage* (Autumn 1992): 22, 27; Hogan, *Class and Community*, 151–61, 177; Ned E. Farrell, *Colorado: The Rocky Mountain Gem* (Chicago: Western News, 1869), 44.

90. Hogan, *Class and Community*, 170–71; Athearn, *Rebel of the Rockies*, 25; Denver and Rio Grande Railway, "First Annual Report of the Board of Directors of the Denver and Rio Grande Railway" (Philadelphia: J. B. Lippincott, 1873); H.

Lee Scamehorn, *Pioneer Steelmaker in the West: The Colorado Fuel and Iron Company, 1872–1903* (Boulder: Pruett, 1976), 7–19.

91. Pueblo Board of Trade, *Fifth Annual Report of the Pueblo Board of Trade Association* (Pueblo: Central Printing, 1893), 36, 135–36; Bond, "Pueblo," 30.

92. Andrew Morrison, ed., *The City of Pueblo and the State of Colorado* (Saint Louis: G. W. Engelhardt, 1890), 96.

93. Pueblo Board of Trade, *Fifth Annual Report,* 50; Hogan, *Class and Community,* 174.

94. Denver and Rio Grande Railway, "First Annual Report," 26.

95. Crofutt, *Grip-Sack Guide,* 70–71; Pueblo Board of Trade, *Sketch of the Pueblos and Pueblo County, Colorado* (Pueblo: Chieftain Steam Print, 1883), 46; Scamehorn, *Pioneer Steelmaker,* 21; Pueblo Board of Trade, *Fifth Annual Report,* 43.

96. Costigan is quoted in Abbott, Leonard, and McComb, *Colorado,* 152.

97. Ibid., 90; Pueblo Commerce Club, "Facts About Pueblo-Colorado" (Pueblo: Pueblo Commerce Club, 1929), 1–3; Hogan, *Class and Community,* 174, 177; Pueblo Board of Trade, *Fifth Annual Report,* 53–55, 136. The quotation is taken from Pueblo Board of Trade, *Fifth Annual Report,* 53–55.

98. Pueblo Board of Trade, *Sketch of the Pueblos,* 45; Scamehorn, *Pioneer Steelmaker,* 45–71, 166–67; Pueblo Board of Trade, *Fifth Annual Report,* 36, 51–52; Pueblo Commerce Club, "Facts," 1, 3.

99. Morrison, *City of Pueblo,* 36.

100. Pueblo Board of Trade, *Sketch of the Pueblos,* 20.

101. Denver and Rio Grande Railway, *First Annual Report,* 27.

102. Pueblo Board of Trade, *Fifth Annual Report,* 136; Pueblo Commerce Club, "Facts," 1–3.

103. Pueblo Board of Trade, *Fifth Annual Report,* 51. The description of Pueblo's industrial might is from Pueblo Commerce Club, "Facts," 3.

104. Abbott, Leonard, and McComb, *Colorado,* 203–4, 324–25; Hazel M. Cross, "Federal Writers' Project, Pueblo, Colorado: Social and Ethnic Survey" (typescript, Pueblo Regional Library, Pueblo); Joanne West Dodds, *Pueblo: A Pictorial History* (Norfolk, Va.: Donning, 1982), 28, 103–19; *Pueblo Star-Journal and Sunday Chieftain,* "The Pueblo Mosaic," July 30, August 6, 13, 20, 1978 (hereafter cited as "Pueblo Mosaic"); Norma J. Stephenson, "Pueblo: The People, An Oral History" (Pueblo, 1978); M. James Kedro, "Czechs and Slovaks in Colorado, 1860–1920," *Colorado Magazine* 54 (1977): 93–125; George H. Wayne, "Negro Migration and Colonization in Colorado, 1870–1930," *Journal of the West* 15, 1 (1976): 102–20.

105. Cross, "Social and Ethnic Survey," 14, 51; Scamehorn, *Pioneer Steelmaker,* 139–55.

106. Abbott, Leonard, and McComb, *Colorado,* 203–4, 324–25; Pueblo Mosaic; Stephanson, "Pueblo"; Wayne, "Negro Migration."

107. United States, Bureau of the Census, Manuscript of the Thirteenth Census of the United States, 1910. Population schedules, Pueblo County, Colorado.

Chapter 5: Eastern Plains

1. William Wyckoff, "Mapping El Dorado: Pikes Peak Promotional Cartography, 1859–1861," *Imago Mundi* 40 (1988): 32–45.

2. Horace Greeley, *An Overland Journey* (New York: Alfred A. Knopf, 1969), 80–97.

3. Albert D. Richardson, *Beyond the Mississippi* (Hartford, Conn.: American, 1867), 176.

4. John L. Allen, "The Garden-Desert Continuum: Competing Views of the Great Plains in the Nineteenth Century," *Great Plains Quarterly* 5 (1985): 207–20.

5. Virginia Cole Trenholm, *The Arapahoes: Our People* (Norman: University of Oklahoma Press, 1970), 133–230; Carl Ubbelohde, Maxine Benson, and Duane A. Smith, eds., *A Colorado History* (Boulder: Pruett, 1982), 103–16; Robert Utley, *The Indian Frontier of the American West, 1846–1900* (Albuquerque: University of New Mexico Press, 1984), 86–98.

6. Richard White, *"It's Your Misfortune and None of My Own": A New History of the American West* (Norman: University of Oklahoma Press, 1991), 89–91.

7. J. Donald Hughes, *American Indians of Colorado* (Boulder: Pruett, 1977), 56–58; Ubbelohde, Benson, and Smith, *Colorado,* 103–16.

8. Utley, *Indian Frontier,* 227–30; White, *New History,* 216–27.

9. Carl Abbott, Stephen J. Leonard, and David McComb, *Colorado: A History of the Centennial State* (Niwot: University Press of Colorado, 1994), 168–72; Allen, "Garden-Desert Continuum," 214–18; Gene M. Gressley, *Bankers and Cattlemen* (New York: Alfred A. Knopf, 1966).

10. Ora Brooks Peake, *The Colorado Range Cattle Industry* (Glendale: A. H. Clark, 1937); Lewis Atherton, *The Cattle Kings* (Bloomington: Indiana University Press, 1961); Gressley, *Bankers and Cattlemen,* 42–58; Abbott, Leonard, and McComb, *Colorado,* 168–72.

11. United States, Bureau of the Census, *Ninth Census of the United States,* 1870; *Tenth Census of the United States,* 1880.

12. Alvin T. Steinel, *History of Agriculture in Colorado* (Fort Collins: State Board of Agriculture, 1926), 108–65; Abbott, Leonard, and McComb, *Colorado,* 168–72.

13. Peake, *Colorado Range Cattle,* 58–61, 72–75.

14. Terry G. Jordan, *North American Cattle-Ranching Frontiers* (Albuquerque: University of New Mexico Press, 1993), 208–40, 267–307; Rufus Phillips, "Early Cowboy Life in the Arkansas Valley," *Colorado Magazine* 7 (1930): 165–79; East Yuma County Historical Society, *A History of East Yuma County* (East Yuma County Historical Society, 1978), 6; Atherton, *Cattle Kings,* 159; Kenneth I. Helphand, *Colorado: Visions of an American Landscape* (Niwot: Roberts Rinehart, 1991), 167; O. L. Baskin, *History of the Arkansas Valley, Colorado* (Chicago: O. L. Baskin, 1881), 65, 848–49; William E. Pabor, *Colorado as an Agricultural State* (New York: Orange Judd, 1883), 118, 189.

15. Jordan, *North American Cattle-Ranching,* 236–40; Peake, *Colorado Range Cattle,* 273–76; White, *New History,* 222–27.

16. Gressley, *Bankers and Cattlemen*, 243–72.

17. Bud Wells, ed., *Logan County: Better by One Hundred Years* (Dallas: Curtis Media, 1987), 32.

18. Denver and Rio Grande Railroad, "The Fertile Lands of Colorado" (Denver: Denver and Rio Grande Railroad, 1899), 67.

19. Peake, *Colorado Range Cattle*, 279–81.

20. Helphand, *Colorado*, 113–41; Donald J. Pisani, *To Reclaim a Divided West: Water, Law, and Public Policy, 1848–1902* (Albuquerque: University of New Mexico Press, 1992).

21. Denver and Rio Grande Railroad, "Fertile Lands," 9.

22. Powell is quoted in Walter and Johanna Kollmorgen, "Landscape Meteorology in the Plains Area," *Annals of the Association of American Geographers* 63 (1973): 439.

23. James E. Sherow, *Watering the Valley: Development Along the High Plains Arkansas River, 1870–1950* (Lawrence: University Press of Kansas, 1990); Donald Worster, *Rivers of Empire: Water, Aridity, and the Growth of the American West* (New York: Oxford University Press, 1985).

24. Sherow, *Watering the Valley*, 3–11.

25. William E. Pabor, *Farmers' Guide to Northern Colorado* (Denver: Colorado Farmer Print, 1882), 10.

26. J. M. Dille, "Irrigation in Morgan County" (Fort Morgan: Farmer's State Bank, 1960), 7–8; Don English, "The Early History of Ft. Morgan, Colorado" (Fort Morgan: Fort Morgan Heritage Foundation Museum, 1975), 16–18.

27. Katherine Harris, "Women and Families on Northeastern Colorado Homesteads, 1873–1920" (Ph.D. diss., University of Colorado, 1983), 48; Wells, *Logan County*, 10.

28. Dille, "Irrigation"; English, "Early History," 32; "A Story of the Attractions and Wonderful Resources of Morgan County" (Fort Morgan, Colo.: Herald Art Printing, 1909); Harris, "Women and Families," 91; Wells, *Logan County*, 10; James E. Sherow, "Marketplace Agricultural Reform: T. C. Henry and the Irrigation Crusade in Colorado, 1883–1914," *Journal of the West* 31, 4 (1992): 51–58.

29. Thomas J. Noel, Paul F. Mahoney, and Richard E. Stevens, *Historical Atlas of Colorado* (Norman: University of Oklahoma Press, 1994), 20–21; English, "Early History," 27; Katherine Harris, *Long Vistas: Women and Families on Colorado Homesteads* (Niwot: University Press of Colorado, 1993), 103–4; United States, Bureau of the Census, *Eleventh Census of the United States*, 1890; United States, Bureau of the Census, *Fourteenth Census of the United States*, 1920.

30. Ubbelohde, Benson, and Smith, *Colorado*, 269–72; Kenneth W. Rock, " 'Unsere Leute': The Germans from Russia in Colorado," *Colorado Magazine* 54 (1977): 162–64.

31. Rock, " 'Unsere Leute' "; Harris, "Women and Families," 90–91; English, "Early History," 32–37.

32. George A. Crofutt, *Crofutt's Grip-Sack Guide of Colorado* (Omaha: Overland, 1885), 111, 135.

33. Sherow, *Watering the Valley*, 12–13.

34. James E. Sherow, "Utopia, Reality, and Irrigation: The Plight of the Fort Lyon Canal Company in the Arkansas River Valley," *Western Historical Quarterly* 20 (1989): 162–84.

35. *Irrigation Era*, August 1899; Sherow, *Watering the Valley*, 17; Sherow, "Utopia, Reality, and Irrigation."

36. Sherow, *Watering the Valley*, 103–19; Ubbelohde, Benson, and Smith, *Colorado*, 264–67.

37. United States, Bureau of the Census, *Fourteenth Census of the United States*, 1920.

38. Lamar Centennial History Committee, *Lamar, Colorado—Its First Hundred Years, 1886–1986* (Shawnee Mission, Kans.: Kes-Print, 1986), 57–61; Andrew Morrison, ed., *The City of Pueblo and the State of Colorado* (Saint Louis: G. W. Engelhardt, 1890), 17–18.

39. Colorado, Bureau of Immigration and Statistics, *The Natural Resources and Industrial Development and Condition of Colorado* (Denver: Bureau of Immigration, 1889), 102; Baskin, *Arkansas Valley*, 887; Sherow, *Watering the Valley*, 14; *Irrigation Era*, January 1901, 13–17.

40. Lamar Board of Trade, "Prowers County, Colorado. Its Advantages and Attractions" (Lamar: Lamar Board of Trade, 1892), 9–10; United States, Bureau of the Census, *Twelfth Census of the United States*, 1900.

41. Crowley County Heritage Society, *The History of Crowley County* (Dallas: Taylor, 1980); *Irrigation Era*, August 1900, January 1901; Dena Markoff, "The Sugar Industry in the Arkansas River Valley: National Sugar Beet Company," *Colorado Magazine* 55 (1978): 69–92; Markoff, "A Bittersweet Saga: The Arkansas Valley Beet Sugar Industry, 1900–1979," *Colorado Magazine* 56 (1979): 161–78; Rock, "Germans from Russia"; Sugar City Book Committee, *Attached to Sweetness: Chronicle of Sugar City* (Riverside Printing, 1982).

42. David Emmons, *Garden in the Grasslands: Boomer Literature of the Central Great Plains* (Lincoln: University of Nebraska Press, 1971), 128–61; Kollmorgen and Kollmorgen, "Landscape Meteorology."

43. Emmons, *Garden in the Grasslands*, 31–39.

44. Quoted in Ubbelohde, Benson, and Smith, *Colorado*, 202.

45. Morris F. Taylor, "The Town Boom in Las Animas and Baca Counties," *Colorado Magazine* 55 (1978): 111–32; N. E. Woodard, "Brief History of Baca County, Colorado" (typescript, 1934), 4–5; Colorado Bureau of Immigration and Statistics, *Natural Resources and Industrial Development*, 57–58; Emmons, *Garden in the Grasslands*, 47–77; Steinel, *History of Agriculture*, 252–53. The quotation is taken from Cheyenne Board of County Commissioners, *Cheyenne County, Colorado: Its Resources and Advantages* (Cheyenne Wells: Republican, 1890), 4.

46. Ubbelohde, Benson, and Smith, *Colorado*, 202–3; Helphand, *Colorado*, 153.

47. United States, Bureau of the Census, *Eleventh Census of the United States*, 1890.

48. Ibid.; Colorado Bureau of Immigration, *Natural Resources and Industrial Development*; C. V. Dedman, "The History of Yuma County, Colorado" (M.A. thesis, Colorado State Teachers College, 1932); Harris, *Long Vistas*, 103–4.

49. Abbott, Leonard, and McComb, *History*, 175; Harris, *Long Vistas*, 39–40; Taylor, "Town Boom," 131–32. The quotation is taken from Steinel, *History of Agriculture*, 254–55.

50. Emmons, *Garden in the Grasslands*, 167–68; Noel, Mahoney, and Stevens, *Atlas*, 23; The quotation from Talhelm is taken from Diary of Anna Stanley Talhelm, 1896, Manuscript, Denver Public Library, Western History Collection.

51. Mary W. M. Hargreaves, *Dry Farming in the Northern Great Plains, 1900–1925* (Cambridge: Harvard University Press, 1957), 85–95; Fred R. Marsh, "Souvenir of Wray and of Vernon, Colorado" (Wray: Wray Gazette, n.d.); Ubbelohde, Benson, and Smith, *Colorado*, 261–63.

52. Steinel, *History of Agriculture*, 262–70, 276–80; Hargreaves, *Dry Farming*, 85–119; 223–34, 246–54.

53. Hargreaves, *Dry Farming*, 347; Thomas A. Harper, "The Development of a High Plains Community: A History of Baca County, Colorado" (M.A. thesis, University of Denver, 1967), 47–51.

54. Henry Y. Hoskin, "Burlington, Colorado" (typescript, Burlington Public Library, Burlington, Colorado); A. W. Winegar, "Farming in Eastern Colorado" (1906); Hargreaves, *Dry Farming*, 429–30; George S. Clason, *Free Homestead Lands in Colorado Described: A Handbook for Settlers* (Denver: Clason Map, 1915).

55. Ubbelohde, Benson, and Smith, *Colorado*, 263–64; Harper, "Baca County," 36–38; 47–51; Taylor, "Town Boom," 132.

56. Harris, *Long Vistas*, 103; United States, Bureau of the Census, *Twelfth Census of the United States*, 1900; United States, Bureau of the Census, *Fourteenth Census of the United States*, 1920; Clason, *Free Homestead Lands*, 51; Eastern Colorado Historical Society, *Cheyenne County*, 73–76. The Adams quotation is taken from Steinel, *History of Agriculture*, 279.

57. John C. Hudson, *Plains Country Towns* (Minneapolis: University of Minnesota Press, 1985), 10.

58. Wells, *Logan County*, 38; Sugar City Book Committee, *Attached to Sweetness*.

59. Wells, *Logan County*, 2; Taylor, "Town Boom," 126–30.

60. Noel, Mahoney, and Stevens, *Atlas*, 16.

61. Hudson, *Plains Country Towns*.

62. Woodard, "Brief History," 7.

63. Hudson, *Plains Country Towns*, 54.

64. Sugar City Book Committee, *Attached to Sweetness*, 1–11; Ubbelohde, Benson, and Smith, *Colorado*, 203.

65. Eberhart, *Ghosts*, 125–29; English, "Early History," 19.

66. Hudson, *Plains Country Towns*, 66–69.

67. Harris, "Women and Families," 113.

68. For an excellent overview of the impact of the township and range system on the American landscape, see Hildegard Binder Johnson, *Order upon the Land* (New York: Oxford University Press, 1976).

69. Carl F. Kraenzel, *The Great Plains in Transition* (Norman: University of Oklahoma Press, 1955), 196.

70. Ibid., 196–204.

71. Harper, "Baca County," 19–20; Harris, *Long Vistas*, 89–97; Steinel, *History of Agriculture*, 257–59.

72. Cheyenne Board of County Commissioners, *Cheyenne County*, 24.

73. Harper, "Baca County," 54–55.

74. Harris, *Long Vistas*, 95.

75. Ibid., 115–75; Jeanne Kay, "Landscapes of Women and Men: Rethinking the Regional Historical Geography of the United States and Canada," *Journal of Historical Geography* 17 (1991): 435–52; Kiowa County Public Library, *A Kiowa County Album: Biographies of Pioneer Women, 1887–1920* (Eads: Kiowa County Public Library, 1984), 15.

76. H. Roger Grant, "The Country Railroad Station in the West," *Journal of the West* 17, 4 (1978): 28–40; John R. Stilgoe, *Metropolitan Corridor: Railroads and the American Scene* (New Haven: Yale University Press, 1983), 193–221; Hudson, *Plains Country Towns*, 86–103; Colorado Bureau of Immigration and Statistics, *Natural Resources and Industrial Development*, 119; Harris, *Long Vistas*, 58–59.

77. East Yuma County Historical Society, *History of Wray, Colorado, 1886–1986* (Dallas: Curtis Media, 1986).

78. Hudson, *Plains Country Towns*, 86–120.

Chapter 6: Southern Periphery

1. Judith L. Gamble, "Colorado's Hispanic Heritage: An Overview," *Colorado Heritage* (Winter 1988): 4; D. W. Meinig, *Southwest: Three Peoples in Geographical Change, 1600–1970* (New York: Oxford University Press, 1971), 25–29; Richard Nostrand, *The Hispano Homeland* (Norman: University of Oklahoma Press, 1992), 7–19.

2. Virginia Simmons, *The San Luis Valley: Land of the Six-Armed Cross* (Boulder: Pruett, 1979), 64–67.

3. Ibid., 8–83; Marianne L. Stoller, "Grants of Desperation, Lands of Speculation: Mexican Period Land Grants in Colorado," *Journal of the West* 19, 3 (1980): 34–35.

4. Purnee A. McCourt, "The Conejos Land Grant of Southern Colorado," *Colorado Magazine* 52 (1975): 34–51; Stoller, "Grants of Desperation."

5. Alvar W. Carlson, "Rural Settlement Patterns in the San Luis Valley," *Colorado Magazine* 44 (1967): 111–28.

6. Pueblo Board of Trade, "The Geography, Description and Resources of Central and Southern Colorado" (Pueblo: Board of Trade of Southern Colorado, 1869), 9; United States, Bureau of the Census, *Ninth Census of the United States*, 1870; Elizabeth H. Jackson, "An Analysis of Certain Colorado Atlas Field Records with Regard to Settlement History and Other Factors" (Ph.D. diss., University of Colorado, 1956), 5–7; Board of Immigration of Colorado Territory, *Official Information: Colorado, A Statement of Facts* (Denver: Rocky Mountain News, 1872), 10.

7. David W. Lantis, "The San Luis Valley, Colorado: Sequent Rural Occupance in an Intermontane Basin" (Ph.D. diss., Ohio State University, 1950), 142–51; Frederic J. Athearn, *Land of Contrast: A History of Southeast Colorado* (Denver: Bureau of Land Management, 1985), 53–55; McCourt, "Conejos Land

Grant," 40; Nostrand, *Hispano Homeland*, 85; Frances L. Swadesh, *Los Primeros Pobladores: Hispanic Americans of the Ute Frontier* (Notre Dame, Ind.: University of Notre Dame Press, 1974), 133.

8. Athearn, *Land of Contrast*, 52, 88; Ned E. Farrell, *Colorado: The Rocky Mountain Gem* (Chicago: Western News, 1868), 42; Pueblo Board of Trade, "Geography"; Alvin T. Steinel, *History of Agriculture in Colorado* (Fort Collins: State Board of Agriculture, 1926), 146; Carl Ubbelohde, Maxine Benson, and Duane A. Smith, eds., *A Colorado History* (Boulder: Pruett, 1982), 181; United States, Bureau of the Census, *Ninth Census of the United States*, 1870; Simmons, *San Luis Valley*, 59.

9. Meinig, *Southwest*, 38–52; Nostrand, *Hispano Homeland*, 98–130.

10. Simmons, *San Luis Valley*, 85–100.

11. Mieir and West, *Souvenir of the San Luis Valley* (Monte Vista: Monte Vista Journal, 1906); Thomas J. Noel, Paul F. Mahoney and Richard E. Stevens, *Historical Atlas of Colorado* (Norman: University of Oklahoma Press, 1994), 16; George A. Crofutt, *Crofutt's Grip-Sack Guide of Colorado* (Omaha: Overland, 1885), 67, 83, 111; Ernest Ingersoll, *The Crest of the Continent* (Chicago: R. R. Donnelley and Sons, 1888), 166–67; Ralph H. Brown, "Monte Vista: Sixty Years of a Colorado Community," *Geographical Review* 18 (1928): 567–78; Simmons, *San Luis Valley*, 94–95, 122–24, 134–36; James E. Sherow, "Marketplace Agricultural Reform: T. C. Henry and the Irrigation Crusade in Colorado, 1883–1914," *Journal of the West* 31, 4 (1992): 56; Denver and Rio Grande Railroad, "The Fertile Lands of Colorado" (Denver: Denver and Rio Grande Railroad, 1899), 16–21.

12. Carlson, "Rural Settlement Patterns," 115–25.

13. Lantis, "San Luis Valley," 199–227; Crofutt, *Grip-Sack Guide*, 117; Nostrand, *Hispano Homeland*, 114–16; Carlson, "Rural Settlement Patterns," 119–24; William E. Pabor, *Colorado as an Agricultural State* (New York: Orange Judd, 1883), 123–24; Simmons, *San Luis Valley*, 128. The Ingersoll quotation on the Mormons is from Ingersoll, *Crest of the Continent*, 80.

14. Robert Adams, *The Architecture and Art of Early Hispanic Colorado* (Denver: Colorado Historical Society, 1974), 46–48, 64–65, 78–79; Simmons, *San Luis Valley*, 54–58.

15. Adams, *Architecture and Art*; Alvar Carlson, *The Spanish-American Homeland: Four Centuries in New Mexico's Río Arriba* (Baltimore: Johns Hopkins University Press, 1990), 129–58; Nostrand, *Hispano Homeland*, 213–32; Charles F. Gritzner, "Log Housing in New Mexico," *Pioneer America* 3, 2 (1971): 54–62.

16. Albert Richardson, *Beyond the Mississippi* (Hartford, Conn.: American, 1867), 270–71; S. Nugent Townshend, Jr., *Colorado: Its Agriculture, Stockfeeding, Scenery, and Shooting* (London: Field Office, 1879), 15.

17. W. H. Olin, "The Fertile Lands of Colorado and Northern New Mexico" (Denver: Denver and Rio Grande Railroad, 1915); Pabor, *Colorado as an Agricultural State*, 121–35.

18. Pabor, *Colorado as an Agricultural State*, 132–33; Lantis, "San Luis Valley," 238–54, 399–420; Sherow, "Marketplace Agricultural Reform." The quotation pertaining to artesian wells in the valley is from Denver and Rio Grande Railroad, "Fertile Lands of Colorado," 18.

19. Lantis, "San Luis Valley," 295–300, 340–55; Simmons, *San Luis Valley*, 140; Athearn, *Land of Contrast*, 141.

20. Carlson, "Rural Settlement Patterns," 120; Lantis, "San Luis Valley," 300–307; Simmons, *San Luis Valley*, 137–40.

21. Lantis, "San Luis Valley," 388–96.

22. Carlson, "Rural Settlement Patterns"; Simmons, *San Luis Valley*; United States, Bureau of the Census, *Ninth–Fourteenth Censuses of the United States, Census of Agriculture*, 1870–1920; Lantis, "San Luis Valley," 317–18, 360–61, 430–33; Alvar W. Carlson, "Seasonal Farm Labor in the San Luis Valley," *Annals of the Association of American Geographers* 63 (1973): 73, 97–100; Irwin Tomle, "Rise of the Vegetable Industry in the San Luis Valley," *Colorado Magazine* 26 (1949): 112–25; Pabor, *Colorado as an Agricultural State*, 124–26.

23. Athearn, *Land of Contrast*, 107–9, 119–20; Simmons, *San Luis Valley*, 101–10.

24. Noel, Mahoney, and Stevens, *Historical Atlas*, 10; Stoller, "Grants of Desperation."

25. Robert A. Murray, *Las Animas, Huerfano, and Custer: Three Colorado Counties on a Cultural Frontier* (Denver: Bureau of Land Management, 1979), 42–46; Nostrand, *Hispano Homeland*, 82–88; Honora Smith, "Early Life in Trinidad and the Purgatory Valley" (M.A. thesis, University of Colorado, 1930), 58; Adams, *Architecture and Art*, 16–17.

26. Murray, *Las Animas, Huerfano, and Custer*, 47; Farrell, *Colorado*, 45; Smith, "Early Life," 58; Morris F. Taylor, *Trinidad, Colorado Territory* (Trinidad: Trinidad State College, 1966); Henry Williams, *Williams' Tourist's Guide to the San Juan Mines* (New York, 1877), 15–16; Athearn, *Land of Contrast*, 66. The quotation on Trinidad's centrality is from Pueblo Board of Trade, "Geography," 14.

27. Farrell, *Colorado*, 41–42; Pabor, *Colorado as an Agricultural State*, 115–17; Pueblo Board of Trade, "Geography," 13.

28. Noel, Mahoney, and Stevens, *Historical Atlas*, 40; Ingersoll, *Crest of the Continent*, 177–80; George S. McGovern and Leonard F. Guttridge, *The Great Coalfield War* (Boston: Houghton Mifflin, 1972), 2–3; Murray, *Las Animas, Huerfano, and Custer*, 60–61.

29. Eric Margolis, "Western Coal Mining as a Way of Life: An Oral History of the Colorado Coal Mines to 1914," *Journal of the West* 24, 3 (1985): 11; H. Lee Scamehorn, "Coal Mining in the Rocky Mountains: Boom, Bust and Boom," in T. G. Alexander and J. F. Bluth, eds., *The Twentieth Century American West* (Midvale, Utah: Signature Books, 1983), 30; Sarah Deutsch, *No Separate Refuge: Culture, Class, and Gender on an Anglo-Hispanic Frontier in the American Southwest, 1880–1940* (New York: Oxford University Press, 1987), 88; George G. Suggs, Jr., "The Colorado Coal Miners' Strike, 1903–1904: A Prelude to Ludlow?" *Journal of the West* 12, 1 (1973): 38.

30. H. Lee Scamehorn, *Pioneer Steelmaker in the West: The Colorado Fuel and Iron Company, 1872–1903* (Boulder: Pruett, 1976), 27–38, 46; Morris F. Taylor, "El Moro: Failure of a Company Town," *Colorado Magazine* 48 (1971): 129–45.

31. Scamehorn, *Pioneer Steelmaker*, 50–51, 61–71, 169; Athearn, *Land of Contrast*; Murray, *Las Animas, Huerfano, and Custer*, 60–61.

32. McGovern and Guttridge, *Great Coalfield War,* 6–8; Scamehorn, "Coal Mining," 32–34. The quotation describing coal mining investors is from McGovern and Guttridge, *Great Coalfield War,* 6.

33. Scamehorn, *Pioneer Steelmaker,* 29–30, 70; Taylor, "El Moro"; Crofutt, *Grip-Sack Guide,* 145; Murray, *Las Animas, Huerfano, and Custer,* 62; Suggs, "Colorado Coal Miners' Strike," 39.

34. Deutsch, *No Separate Refuge,* 87–106; Nostrand, *Hispano Homeland,* 98–155.

35. Murray, *Las Animas, Huerfano, and Custer,* 58; Margolis, "Western Coal Mining," 46.

36. Margolis, "Western Coal Mining," 56; McGovern and Guttridge, *Great Coalfield War,* 25–26; Murray, *Las Animas, Huerfano, and Custer,* 61–62; Scamehorn, *Pioneer Steelmaker,* 30, 69, 169–70; Taylor, "El Moro," 144.

37. Scamehorn, *Pioneer Steelmaker,* 170.

38. Murray, *Las Animas, Huerfano, and Custer,* 62–71; Nostrand, *Hispano Homeland,* 131–55, 189–91; Deutsch, *No Separate Refuge,* 34–40.

39. Nostrand, *Hispano Homeland,* 122–27; Murray, *Las Animas, Huerfano, and Custer,* 62–71.

40. Deutsch, *No Separate Refuge,* 99–100; Murray, *Las Animas, Huerfano, and Custer,* 62–71; Margolis, "Western Coal Mining," 50.

41. Margolis, "Western Coal Mining," 34–36; Deutsch, *No Separate Refuge,* 87–126; Nostrand, *Hispano Homeland,* 156–68; Ingersoll, *Crest of the Continent,* 177–78.

42. Deutsch, *No Separate Refuge,* 88–89, 104–5; Murray, *Las Animas, Huerfano, and Custer,* 70–71; Margolis, "Western Coal Mining," 44–45; Suggs, "Colorado Coal Miners' Strike."

43. McGovern and Guttridge, *Great Coalfield War,* 51–52; Margolis, "Western Coal Mining," 43–45, 53–54. All quotations from Margolis, "Western Coal Mining": Bisulco quotations, 43–44, 53–54, Bazenelle quotation, 44–45.

44. Deutsch, *No Separate Refuge,* 95–96.

45. The quotation concerning company kindergartens is taken from Deutsch, *No Separate Refuge,* 95. The quotation from the *Camp and Plant* is taken from McGovern and Guttridge, *Great Coalfield War,* 11.

46. Deutsch, *No Separate Refuge,* 95, 111–12.

47. Suggs, "Colorado Coal Miners' Strike," 37.

48. McGovern and Guttridge, *Great Coalfield War,* 23; Scamehorn, *Pioneer Steelmaker,* 36; Margolis, "Western Coal Mining," 46–69; H. Lee Scamehorn, *Mill and Mine: The C F and I in the Twentieth Century* (Lincoln: University of Nebraska Press, 1992).

49. Carl Abbott, Stephen J. Leonard, and David McComb, *Colorado: A History of the Centennial State* (Niwot: University Press of Colorado, 1994), 141–42; Murray, *Las Animas, Huerfano, and Custer,* 92–93; Noel, Mahoney, and Stevens, *Historical Atlas,* 55.

50. Murray, *Las Animas, Huerfano, and Custer,* 92; Suggs, "Colorado Coal Miners' Strike."

51. McGovern and Guttridge, *Great Coalfield War;* Margolis, "Western Coal

Mining," 69–106; Murray, *Las Animas, Huerfano, and Custer*, 93–94; Scamehorn, *Mill and Mine*, 56–81; Scamehorn, *Pioneer Steelmaker*, 172–73.

Chapter 7: Western Slope

1. Duane A. Smith, "A Land unto Itself: The Western Slope," *Colorado Magazine* 55 (1978): 181–204.

2. Duane Vandenbusche and Duane A. Smith, *A Land Alone: Colorado's Western Slope* (Boulder: Pruett, 1981), 206.

3. Fossett is quoted in Smith, "Land unto Itself," 187. The Ingersoll quotation is from Ernest Ingersoll, *The Crest of the Continent* (Chicago: R. R. Donnelley and Sons, 1888), 243. The quotation from the *Denver Tribune* is taken from Alvin T. Steinel, *History of Agriculture in Colorado* (Fort Collins: State Board of Agriculture, 1926), 504–5.

4. F. V. Hayden, *Ninth Annual Report of the United States: Geological and Geographical Survey of the Territories . . . 1875* (Washington, D.C.: Government Printing Office, 1877), 345.

5. Quoted in Robert Emmitt, *The Last War Trail: The Utes and the Settlement of Colorado* (Norman: University of Oklahoma Press, 1954), 21–22.

6. Robert Delaney, "The Southern Utes a Century Ago," *Utah Historical Quarterly* 39 (1971): 114–28.

7. Frederic J. Athearn, *An Isolated Empire: A History of Northwest Colorado* (Denver: Bureau of Land Management, 1982), 48–49.

8. Wilson Rockwell, *The Utes: A Forgotten People* (Denver: Sage Books, 1956), 81.

9. Ibid., 111–65; Athearn, *Isolated Empire*, 49–50; Marshall Sprague, *Massacre: The Tragedy at White River* (Boston: Little, Brown, 1957).

10. Rockwell, *Utes*, 166–73.

11. Ibid., 168–70.

12. Vandenbusche and Smith, *Land Alone*, 82–103.

13. Duane Vandenbusche, *The Gunnison Country* (Gunnison: B and B Printers, 1980); Duane A. Smith, *Rocky Mountain Boom Town: A History of Durango* (Albuquerque: University of New Mexico Press, 1980).

14. Malcolm Rohrbough, *Aspen: The History of a Silver Mining Town, 1879–1893* (New York: Oxford University Press, 1986), 143–57.

15. Vandenbusche and Smith, *Land Alone*, 95–98.

16. United States, Bureau of the Census, *Fourteenth Census of the United States*, Census of Agriculture, 1920.

17. Michael Eastin, "The Little Empire of the Western Slope: Boosterism in the Early Grand Valley," *Journal of the Western Slope* 3 (Spring 1988): 30; for both quotations regarding the area's visual bleakness, see Ingersoll, *Crest of the Continent*, 296.

18. Ingersoll, *Crest of the Continent*, 301; George A. Crofutt, *Crofutt's Grip-Sack Guide of Colorado* (Omaha: Overland, 1885), 98; William E. Pabor, *Colorado as an Agricultural State* (New York: Orange Judd, 1883), 143–47; Colorado Loan and Trust Company, *Agriculture by Irrigation* (Denver: Colorado Loan and Trust,

1885), 16–19; Evelyn J. Brown, "Early History of Montrose County, Colorado and Its Settlement Years, 1880–1910" (M.A. thesis, Western State College, 1987), 98–103.

19. The quotation concerning the Uncompahgre Valley is from the Montrose Chamber of Commerce, *Montrose County* (Denver: Republican, 1887), 6. The quotation concerning the horticultural potential of the North Fork of the Gunnison River is taken from Steinel, *History of Agriculture*, 507. Pabor, *Colorado*, 143–47.

20. Pabor, *Colorado*, 145.

21. Eastin, "Little Empire," 39–40; Ingersoll, *Crest of the Continent*, 300–301; Steinel, *History of Agriculture*, 506; Emma McCreanor, *Mesa County, Colorado: A One-Hundred-Year History (1883–1983)* (Grand Junction: Museum of Western Colorado Press, 1986), 5.

22. Mary Rait, "Development of Grand Junction and the Colorado River Valley to Palisade from 1881 to 1931," *Journal of the Western Slope* 3 (Summer–Autumn 1988): 47–48.

23. McCreanor, *Mesa County;* Mary Rait, "Development of the Peach Industry in the Colorado River Valley," *Colorado Magazine* 22 (1945): 247–58; Vandenbusche and Smith, *Land Alone*, 150–51; Rait, "Grand Junction," 23–24; Eastin, "Little Empire," 27–49.

24. Ingersoll, *Crest of the Continent*, 296–302; McCreanor, *Mesa County*, 18–20; Rait, "Grand Junction," 18–19; James E. Sherow, "Marketplace Agriculture Reform: T. C. Henry and the Irrigation Crusade in Colorado, 1883–1914," *Journal of the West* 31, 4 (1992): 51–58.

25. McCreanor, *Mesa County*, 18–20; Vandenbusche and Smith, *Land Alone*, 189–90.

26. Denver and Rio Grande Railroad, "The Fertile Lands of Colorado" (Denver: Denver and Rio Grande Railroad, 1899), 40–45; McCreanor, *Mesa County*, 16–18; United States, Bureau of the Census, *Fourteenth Census of the United States*, Census of Agriculture, 1920.

27. McCreanor, *Mesa County*, 2–4; Steinel, *History of Agriculture*, 299–303; Vandenbusche and Smith, *Land Alone*, 151.

28. Andrew Gulliford, *Boomtown Blues: Colorado Oil Shale, 1885–1985* (Boulder: University Press of Colorado, 1990), 24–28, 41–43; McCreanor, *Mesa County*, 9–11.

29. Ingersoll, *Crest of the Continent*, 273–77; Colorado Loan and Trust Company, *Agriculture*, 18–19; Montrose Chamber of Commerce, *Montrose County*, 8; Sherow, "Marketplace Agriculture"; Richard G. Beidleman, "The Gunnison River Diversion Project," *Colorado Magazine* 36 (1959): 187–201, 266–85. The promotional quotation from the railroad is found in Denver and Rio Grande Railroad, "Fertile Lands," 24.

30. Beidleman, "Gunnison River," 187–201; Kenneth I. Helphand, *Colorado: Visions of an American Landscape* (Niwot: Roberts Rinehart, 1991), 129; Donald A. McKendrick, "Before the Newlands Act: State-Sponsored Reclamation Projects in Colorado, 1888–1903," *Colorado Magazine* 52 (1975): 1–22; Paul M. O'Rourke, *Frontier in Transition: A History of Southwestern Colorado* (Denver: Bureau of Land Management, 1980), 144; Vandenbusche and Smith, *Land Alone*, 185–87.

31. O'Rourke, *Frontier in Transition*, 136; United States, Bureau of the Census, *Fourteenth Census of the United States*, Census of Agriculture, 1920.

32. O'Rourke, *Frontier in Transition*, 123–24, 130–31, 136; Steinel, *History of Agriculture*, 507–8; Vandenbusche and Smith, *Land Alone*, 148–49.

33. Ingersoll, *Crest of the Continent*, 250; Kathleen Underwood, *Town Building on the Colorado Frontier* (Albuquerque: University of New Mexico Press, 1987), 7.

34. Denver and Rio Grande Railroad, "Fertile Lands," 45; Underwood, *Town Building*, 8–9.

35. Ingersoll, *Crest of the Continent*, 298.

36. Colorado Loan and Trust Company, *Agriculture*, 16; Crofutt, *Grip-Sack Guide*, 57.

37. Carl Ubbelohde, Maxine Benson, and Duane A. Smith, eds., *A Colorado History* (Boulder: Pruett, 1982), 193.

38. McCreanor, *Mesa County*, 8–10; Gulliford, *Boomtown Blues*, 24–31; O'Rourke, *Frontier in Transition*, 123–24, 130–31; Vandenbusche and Smith, *Land Alone*, 149.

39. Rait, "Grand Junction," 14–17; Underwood, *Town Building*, 11–12, 41.

40. Ingersoll, *Crest of the Continent*, 298.

41. Montrose Chamber of Commerce, *Montrose County*, 14.

42. Robert Delaney, *The Southern Ute People* (Phoenix: Indian Tribal Series, 1974), 52–75.

43. Ibid.; Harold Hoffmeister, "The Consolidated Ute Reservation," *Geographical Review* 35 (1945): 601–23; Rockwell, *Utes*, 246–48.

44. Richard Nostrand, *The Hispano Homeland* (Norman: University of Oklahoma Press, 1992), 82–88; Frances L. Swadesh, *Los Primeros Pobladores: Hispanic Americans of the Ute Frontier* (Notre Dame, Ind.: University of Notre Dame Press, 1974).

45. Swadesh, *Hispanic Americans*, 122.

46. Crofutt, *Grip-Sack Guide*, 88–89.

47. Ibid., 127; O'Rourke, *Frontier in Transition*, 85–86.

48. O'Rourke, *Frontier in Transition*, 136.

49. Hoffmeister, "Consolidated Ute Reservation," 602–3.

50. O'Rourke, *Frontier in Transition*, 84–86, 122–23, 131–36.

51. Ibid., 130–31; Duane Mercer, "The Colorado Cooperative Company, 1894–1904," *Colorado Magazine* 44 (1967): 293–306.

52. Duane A. Smith, *Mesa Verde National Park: Shadows of the Centuries* (Lawrence: University Press of Kansas, 1988).

53. Athearn, *Isolated Empire*, 39–41; Crofutt, *Grip-Sack Guide*, 102.

54. John Rolfe Burroughs, *Where the Old West Stayed Young* (New York: William Morrow, 1962), 31–57, 78–100.

55. Ibid., 69–77.

56. S. F. Mehls, "An Area the Size of Pennsylvania: David H. Moffat and the Opening of Northwest Colorado," *Midwest Review* 7 (Spring 1985): 15–26; Charles M. Davis, "Changes in Land Utilization on the Plateau of Northwestern Col-

orado," *Economic Geography* 18 (1942): 382–83; Vandenbusche and Smith, *Land Alone,* 156.

57. Athearn, *Isolated Empire,* 5–6, 73.

58. Ibid., 71–72; Burroughs, *Old West,* 136–45, 338–50; Vandenbusche and Smith, *Land Alone,* 156–60.

59. Michael McCarthy, *Hour of Trial: The Conservation Conflict in Colorado and the West, 1891–1907* (Norman: University of Oklahoma Press, 1977).

60. Athearn, *Isolated Empire,* 91–98; Mehls, "David H. Moffat."

61. Athearn, *Isolated Empire,* 105–7; Burroughs, *Old West,* 318–37; Davis, "Changes in Land Utilization," 384–85.

62. Burroughs, *Old West,* 322.

63. Davis, "Changes in Land Utilization," 386.

64. Kenneth A. Erickson and Albert W. Smith, *Atlas of Colorado* (Boulder: Colorado Associated University Press, 1985), 24–29; Thomas J. Noel, Paul F. Mahoney, and Richard E. Stevens, *Historical Atlas of Colorado* (Norman: University of Oklahoma Press, 1994), 39–40; Mehls, "David H. Moffat," 15.

65. Gulliford, *Boomtown Blues,* 26–35.

66. Athearn, *Isolated Empire,* 84–85, 95–96; Mehls, "David H. Moffat."

67. Gulliford, *Boomtown Blues,* 45–83.

Chapter 8: Geographies in Transition

1. Carl Abbott, Stephan J. Leonard, and David McComb, *Colorado: A History of the Centennial State* (Niwot: University Press of Colorado, 1994): 275–78; Stephan J. Leonard, *Trials and Triumphs: A Colorado Portrait of the Great Depression, with FSA Photographs* (Niwot: University Press of Colorado, 1993), 7–9; John T. Schlebecker, "The Federal Government and the Cattlemen on the Plains, 1900–1945," in K. Ross Toole et al., eds., *Probing the American West* (Santa Fe: Museum of New Mexico Press, 1964), 117–19; Richard White, *"It's Your Misfortune and None of My Own": A New History of the American West* (Norman: University of Oklahoma Press, 1991), 463–95.

2. Leonard, *Trials and Triumphs,* 17–33; White, *New History,* 463–95; James F. Wickens, *Colorado in the Great Depression* (New York: Garland, 1979).

3. Leonard, *Trials and Triumphs;* Michael P. Malone and Richard W. Etulain, *The American West: A Twentieth-Century History* (Lincoln: University of Nebraska Press, 1989), 12–23; Carl Ubbelohde, Maxine Benson, and Duane A. Smith, eds., *A Colorado History* (Boulder: Pruett, 1982), 289–97, 309–10; *Yearbook of the State of Colorado, 1933–1934* (Denver: Bradford-Robinson Printing, 1934), 99–101, 276–77.

4. The impact of New Deal programs can be followed in Leonard, *Trials and Triumphs;* Richard Lowitt, *The New Deal and the West* (Bloomington: Indiana University Press, 1984); Malone and Etulain, *American West,* 94–107; Robert B. Parham, "The Civilian Conservation Corps in Colorado, 1933–1942" (M.A. thesis, University of Colorado, 1982); and Wickens, *Colorado in the Great Depression.*

5. Works Progress Administration, Division of Social Research, *Workers on*

Relief in the United States in March 1935, vol. 1: *A Census of Usual Occupations* (Washington, D.C.: Government Printing Office, 1938), 217–32; *Yearbook of the State of Colorado, 1935–1936* (Denver: Bradford-Robinson Printing, 1936), 288–89; Wickens, *Colorado in the Great Depression*, 119.

6. Leonard, *Trials and Triumphs*, 261.

7. Useful discussions on the geographical and cultural impacts of modernization can be found in Peter J. Hugill, *World Trade Since 1431: Geography, Technology, and Capitalism* (Baltimore: Johns Hopkins University Press, 1993); D. W. Meinig, "American Wests: Preface to a Geographical Interpretation," *Annals of the Association of American Geographers* 62 (1972): 178–82; Donald Worster, *Dust Bowl: The Southern Plains in the 1930s* (New York: Oxford University Press, 1979), 164–80; and Wilbur Zelinsky, *The Cultural Geography of the United States*, rev. ed. (Englewood Cliffs, N.J.: Prentice-Hall, 1992), 85–88.

8. The impact of the automobile on the American cultural landscape is summarized in Hugill, *World Trade*, 207–48; John A. Jakle, "Landscapes Redesigned for the Automobile," in M. P. Conzen, ed., *The Making of the American Landscape* (Boston: Unwin Hyman, 1990), 293–310; and Peirce Lewis, "America Between the Wars: The Engineering of a New Geography," in Robert D. Mitchell and Paul A. Groves, eds., *North America: The Historical Geography of a Changing Continent* (Totowa, N.J.: Rowman and Littlefield, 1987), 411–17.

9. The impact of the automobile on Colorado and the West is explored in Kenneth I. Helphand, *Colorado: Visions of an American Landscape* (Niwot: Roberts Rinehart, 1991), 187–95; Stephan J. Leonard and Thomas J. Noel, *Denver: Mining Camp to Metropolis* (Niwot: University Press of Colorado, 1990), 255–76; Malone and Etulain, *American West*, 40–45; and *Yearbook of the State of Colorado, 1941–1942* (Denver: Bradford-Robinson Printing, 1942), 363.

10. Automobile tourism is addressed in William Wyckoff, "Denver's Aging Commercial Strip," *Geographical Review* 82 (1992): 282–94; Warren J. Belasco, *Americans on the Road: From Autocamp to Motel, 1910–1945* (Cambridge: MIT Press, 1979); John Jakle, *The Tourist: Travel in Twentieth-Century North America* (Lincoln: University of Nebraska Press, 1985); John Jakle, Keith A. Sculle, and Jefferson S. Rogers, *The Motel in America* (Baltimore: Johns Hopkins University Press, 1996); and Leonard and Noel, *Denver*, 263–64.

11. Worster, *Dust Bowl*, 168.

12. Hugill, *World Trade*, 279–81; Leonard, *Trials and Triumphs*, 14–17, 226–29; Jeff Miller, *Stapleton International Airport: The First Fifty Years* (Boulder: Pruett, 1983), 8–60; *Yearbook of the State of Colorado, 1933–1934*, 450–52; *Yearbook of the State of Colorado, 1941–1942*, 211–12.

13. Leonard, *Trials and Triumphs*, 219–21; Lewis, "America Between the Wars," 418–19; Worster, *Dust Bowl*, 168–69.

14. Meinig, "American Wests," 179.

15. *Yearbook of the State of Colorado, 1933–1934*, 407; *Yearbook of the State of Colorado, 1941–1942*, 388.

16. Leonard, *Trials and Triumphs*, 219; Leonard and Noel, *Denver*, 160–61; Clark Secrest, "With a Song in the Air," *Colorado Heritage* (Winter 1993): 13; Ubbe-

lohde, Benson, and Smith, *Colorado,* 327; *Yearbook of the State of Colorado, 1933–1934,* 447–50; *Yearbook of the State of Colorado, 1941–1942,* 209–10.

17. Lewis, "America Between the Wars," 420–21; Ubbelohde, Benson, and Smith, *Colorado History,* 321–22; *Yearbook of the State of Colorado, 1941–1942,* 20.

18. Ubbelohde, Benson, and Smith, *Colorado History,* 296–99.

19. Sarah Deutsch, *No Separate Refuge: Culture, Class, and Gender on an Anglo-Hispanic Frontier in the American Southwest, 1880–1940* (New York: Oxford University Press, 1987), 127–61; Lyle W. Dorsett, *The Queen City: A History of Denver* (Boulder: Pruett, 1977), 226; Leonard, *Trials and Triumphs,* 70–80.

20. United States, Bureau of the Census, *Sixteenth Census of the United States, Census of Population,* 1940.

21. White, *New History,* 415; Carl Abbott, *The Metropolitan Frontier: Cities in the Modern American West* (Tucson: University of Arizona Press, 1993), 149–72.

22. Abbott, *Metropolitan Frontier,* 123–48; John M. Findlay, *Magic Lands: Western Cityscapes and American Culture after 1940* (Berkeley: University of California Press, 1992), 1–51; Lewis, "America Between the Wars," 431–33.

23. Abbott, *Metropolitan Frontier,* 152; Meinig, "American Wests"; William G. Robbins, "The 'Plundered Province' Thesis and Recent Historiography of the American West," *Pacific Historical Review* 55 (1986): 589–90; Wickens, *Colorado in the Great Depression,* 4.

24. Dorsett, *Queen City,* 220–21; *Yearbook of the State of Colorado, 1941–1942,* 443–50.

25. White, *New History,* 416–23.

26. Dorsett, *Queen City,* 228–31.

27. Abbott, *Metropolitan West,* 132–35; Larry R. Ford, *Cities and Buildings* (Baltimore: Johns Hopkins University Press, 1994), 146–53; Barbara S. Norgren and Thomas J. Noel, *Denver: The City Beautiful* (Denver: Historic Denver, 1987), 67–72.

28. Dorsett, *Queen City,* 200; Leonard and Noel, *Denver,* 280, 285–86, 302–12, 350–58.

29. Worster, *Dust Bowl,* 3–8.

30. R. Douglas Hurt, *The Dust Bowl: An Agricultural and Social History* (Chicago: Nelson-Hall, 1981), 17–31.

31. Lowitt, *New Deal,* 64–80.

32. Helphand, *Colorado,* 150; Parham, "Civilian Conservation Corps," 97–99; Wickens, *Colorado in the Great Depression,* 232; Frederic J. Athearn, *Land of Contrast: A History of Southeast Colorado* (Denver: Bureau of Land Management, 1985), 159; Thomas A. Harper, "The Development of a High Plains Community: A History of Baca County, Colorado" (M.A. thesis, University of Denver, 1967), 129–30.

33. Hogner is quoted in Wickens, *Colorado in the Great Depression,* 253.

34. Hurt, *Dust Bowl,* 67–86, 121–37; Leonard, *Trials and Triumphs,* 112–28; Wickens, *Colorado in the Great Depression,* 217–79.

35. Charles F. Wilkinson and H. Michael Anderson, *Land and Resource Planning in the National Forests* (Washington, D.C.: Island, 1987), 104–6; Harold K.

Steen, *The U. S. Forest Service: A History* (Seattle: University of Washington Press, 1976), 162–67.

36. The Taylor Grazing Act is quoted in Lowitt, *New Deal*, 65.

37. Ubbelohde, Benson, and Smith, *Colorado History*, 315; John R. Burroughs, *Where the Old West Stayed Young* (New York: William Morrow, 1962), 354–59; Lowitt, *New Deal*, 64–80.

38. Lowitt, *New Deal*, 81–99, 157–71; White, *New History*, 401–6, 483–87; Donald Worster, *Rivers of Empire: Water, Aridity, and the Growth of the American West* (New York: Oxford University Press, 1985).

39. John Gunther, *Inside U.S.A.* (New York: Harper and Brothers, 1947), 214.

40. Worster, *Rivers of Empire*, 211.

41. Norris Hundley, Jr., *Water and the West: The Colorado River Compact and the Politics of Water in the American West* (Berkeley: University of California Press, 1975), 74–76; James E. Sherow, *Watering the Valley: Development Along the High Plains Arkansas River, 1870–1950* (Lawrence: University Press of Kansas, 1990), 103–65.

42. Donald B. Cole, "Transmountain Water Diversion in Colorado," *Colorado Magazine* 25 (1948): 129–30; Hundley, *Water and the West*, 76–78, 177–81; Ubbelohde, Benson, and Smith, *Colorado History*, 300–303.

43. Hundley, *Water and the West*, 98–99; David W. Lantis, "The San Luis Valley, Colorado: Sequent Rural Occupance in an Intermontane Basin" (Ph.D. diss., Ohio State University, 1950), 501–8.

44. Cole, "Transmountain Water Diversion," 61, 130; Hundley, *Water and the West*; Worster, *Rivers of Empire*; Duane Vandenbusche and Duane A. Smith, *A Land Alone: Colorado's Western Slope* (Boulder: Pruett, 1981), 191.

45. Cole, "Transmountain Water Diversion," 49–60; Dorsett, *Queen City*, 206–7; Ubbelohde, Benson, and Smith, *Colorado History*, 316–20.

46. Cole, "Transmountain Water Diversion"; Oliver Knight, "Correcting Nature's Error: The Colorado Big-Thompson Project," *Agricultural History* 30 (1956): 157–69; Daniel Tyler, *The Last Water Hole in the West: The Colorado–Big Thompson Project and the Northern Colorado Water Conservancy District* (Niwot: University Press of Colorado, 1992).

47. Abbott Fay, "Pioneer Slopes: Early Colorado Ski Resort Development, 1920–1950," *Colorado Heritage* (Winter 1985): 2–12; Ronald L. Ives, "Population Changes in a Mountain County," *Economic Geography* 18 (1942): 298–306; Duane A. Smith, "Boom to Bust and Back Again: Mining in the Central Rockies, 1920–1981," *Journal of the West* 21, 4 (1982): 4–6.

48. Bradley H. Baltensperger, "Larger and Fewer Farms: Patterns and Causes of Farm Enlargement on the Central Great Plains, 1930–1978," *Journal of Historical Geography* 19 (1993): 301; R. Douglas Hurt, "Agricultural Technology in the Twentieth Century," *Journal of the West* 30, 2 (1991): 16–28, 45–49.

49. Lantis, "San Luis Valley," 446–532.

50. Such a notion of landscape is explored in Peter J. Hugill, *Upstate Arcadia: Landscape, Aesthetics, and the Triumph of Social Differentiation in America* (Lanham, Md.: Rowman and Littlefield, 1995).

Index